BAPTISTS AND THE BIBLE

The Baptist doctrines of biblical inspiration and religious authority in historical perspective

L. RUSS BUSH

and

TOM J. NETTLES

MOODY PRESS

CHICAGO

© 1980 by
THE MOODY BIBLE INSTITUTE
OF CHICAGO

Third Printing, 1981

In an effort to provide full documentation in a readable form, we have used a special system for the documentation in this book. At the end of each chapter, full bibliographical information for that chapter is provided. Within the chapters, shortened references with page numbers are provided for direct quotations. Subsequent quotations from the same source within the immediate context are documented by page number only.

Library of Congress Cataloging in Publication Data

Bush, L. Russ, 1944-
   Baptists and the Bible
   Includes index.
   1. Bible—Inspiration—History of doctrines. 2. Bible—Evidences, authority, etc.—History of doctrines. 3. Authority (Religion)—History of doctrines. 4. Baptists—Catechisms and creeds—History and criticism. 5. Baptists—History. I. Nettles, Tom J., joint author. II. Title.
BS480.B83   220.1'3   80-11694
ISBN 0-8024-0466-9

Printed in the United States of America

Contents

Part Three

"WHOM SAY YE THAT I AM"

To L. R. Bush, Sr.,
    Russell Bush, Jr.,
    Parks R. Warnock, Sr.,
        who are chief among the faithful
                L. Russ Bush

To Carey E. Cox,
        who taught me to believe the Bible
                Tom J. Nettles

Acknowledgments

Many fingers have stabbed at typewriter keys in the long process of producing rough drafts and final drafts and then final-final drafts ad infinitum. The people most often dedicating their fingers to this task were Kathy Patterson, Shirley Williams, Tileta Burkhead, and Mary Anne Barroz. We give them our sincere thanks, even though thanks is not enough to give for their help.

Rosalie Beck and Terry Condren, student assistants, provided helpful insights from their personal research and bibliographical work. They also provided flattery, praise, and adulation at critical moments in the process. For all those things, we thank them.

Writing a book like this one is not easy. Both authors were involved in the research, writing, and revising of each chapter. Each author produced the first drafts of several chapters, which were then read and frequently rewritten by the other author. Only after the reevaluation by the first writer was the manuscript typed in "final" form. Then a series of rereadings and reevaluations were made. Final-final drafts were typed and then corrections were made. The frightening thing is that so much had to be left out.

Several people have read portions of the manuscript and have frequently enlightened the authors by their comments. We are grateful for that enlightenment, but we take all the responsibility for any remaining errors or weaknesses in this book.

Foreword

Baptists and the Bible naturally go together. It would be unthinkable to find Baptists apart from the Bible. As in our day, so in our past, there has been a strong trust and acceptance on the part of Baptist people for God's Book. Baptists are a diverse people, but they are bound together by their common faith in Christ as He is revealed to us in Scripture.

In 1 Corinthians 4:15, Paul reminds the early Christians of their apostolic heritage. Apparently, some had been suggesting that it was time to move forward, to give up the old moral standards, the old doctrines, and the old faith. But it was the old faith by which they had come to know the gospel. We are not wise to forget our heritage.

Baptist people have a rich heritage. Some of the greatest theological minds the world has ever known have been Baptists. We can all learn from them. Baptists have no popes, we have no college of cardinals, we have no ecclesiastical hierarchy. We do not read our forefathers uncritically, nor do we forfeit our own responsibility to be led by God's Spirit. But we do need to hear our Baptist forefathers and learn what they can teach. These men have not only formulated verbal expressions of our doctrines, but they have also obeyed the God who spoke to them in the words of Holy Scripture.

This book is the first major objective study of Baptist views on biblical inspiration and religious authority that has found its way into print. It is wide-ranging and fair. No presupposed theories are imposed on these theologians. Each speaks for himself, and that is as it should be. The selection of theologians is not limited to those who expound only one viewpoint. But theological unity does not come from ignoring issues; it comes by facing them, discussing them, looking at their historical context, and seeking to know through them the mind of Christ.

Upon the truth of God's Word we proclaim that Christ died for our sins and was raised for our justification. His Great Commission and mandate is that we take this message to all the world and make disciples of every nation. That involves baptizing those disciples and helping them learn the teachings of Christ. May those who read this book be so filled with confidence that God's Word is true that they will eagerly seek to be filled with the Holy Spirit and thus boldly go where none has yet dared to go, to preach the precious gospel of God's grace to a lost and dying world. Maranatha!

W. A. CRISWELL
First Baptist Church
Dallas, Texas

11

Fig. 1. BALTHASAR HUBMAIER

From *Balthasar Hubmaier: Anabaptist Theologian and Martyr* by Torsten Bergsten. Translated by W. R. Estep. Valley Forge, Pa.: Judson, 1978, p. 4.

Preface

In 1524 Balthasar Hubmaier, a powerful preacher who later became a leader in the Anabaptist movement, produced *Eighteen Dissertations Concerning the Entire Christian Life and of What It Consists.* On October 26-28 of the previous year, Hubmaier had supported Zwingli at the second religious disputation at Zurich in his opposition to the Roman Catholic mass and in his rejection of the worship of holy images. With these *Eighteen Dissertations* Hubmaier challenged the clergy in his own area of Waldshut to a debate. He began:

> Beloved men and brethren: it is an old custom that comes to us from the times of the apostles, that when evil things befall concerning the faith, all the men who wish to speak the word of God, and are of a Christian way of thinking, should assemble to search the Scriptures. This is done so that in nourishing the Christian flock, according to the word of God, the utmost care might be taken.

In a sense this book is in keeping with that old custom. However, the assembly here gathered spans nearly four hundred years. All the men assembled come from the same denominational tradition. As Baptists, they and we should be able to respond to Hubmaier's call:

> For we should nourish, not our bodies alone but also our souls, with food and drink, and thus be more useful to our flocks, and feed them the Word of God in peace and unity. To this end, all contentious and abusive words should be laid aside.

We do not find unity by producing polemics. We do not grow in grace through personal attacks. Baptists have had their share of battles over the Word of God; not all of them have ended yet. But when such "evil befalls the faith" it seems appropriate to call our Baptist leaders together to hear their wise counsel. Our forefathers "being dead yet speak," and we shall do well to hear them.

Among Hubmaier's *Eighteen Dissertations* are several that call for an investigation of the scriptural foundation of our faith:

> 8. Since every Christian believes for himself and is baptized for himself, everyone must see and judge by the Scriptures whether he is being properly nourished by his pastor. . . .

11. All teachings that are not of God are in vain and shall be rooted up. Here perish the disciples of Aristotle, as well as the Thomists, the Scotists, Bonaventure and Occam, and all teaching that does not proceed from God's Word. . . .

12. The time will come—and now is—when no one will be deemed a true priest save the man who preaches the Word of God. . . .

17. He who misrepresents the Word of God for temporal gain, or conceals it, sells the grace of God, like red Esau for a mess of pottage and Christ will deny him.

Not being a creedal people, Baptists need to find their unity in the Bible. We could wish that all evangelical Christians would search the Scriptures and thus prove what is true faith and practice. But Baptists must not let themselves fall from their place of unique service in God's kingdom either because of a loose understanding of the Word of God or because of a lax commitment to it.

Baptists are a great people. They love God and they believe the Bible. Jesus is the center of their interest. Discipleship is their goal in life. Evangelism and missions tie them together in voluntary organizations. Economic strength is their achievement. Faith and hope shape their theology. Love is their unity.

May the dear Lord bless those who read these pages, and may He always keep us all close to Him.

Introduction

Why a book on Baptists and the Bible? Perhaps because the controversial issues surrounding the various ideas about biblical authority have recently been thrust into the forefront of theological discussions in many Christian denominations. Baptists, no less than other denominational groups, need to reach some kind of a consensus on what they believe doctrinally if they are to face the future with an effective, bold mission thrust.

However, the roots of this study are primarily theological, not pragmatic. Robert G. Torbet, in his *History of the Baptists* (rev. ed.; Valley Forge, Pa.: Judson, 1963), entitles his final chapter "Baptist Contributions to Protestantism." His first section in this chapter deals with doctrinal contributions, and the first of those is the Baptist view of Scripture. Torbet writes:

> Baptists, to a greater degree than any other group, have strengthened the protest of evangelical Protestantism against traditionalism. This they have done by their constant witness to the supremacy of the Scriptures as the all-sufficient and sole norm for faith and practice in the Christian life. . . .
>
> It was Balthasar Hubmaier, that stalwart Anabaptist, who dared to challenge Zwingli on this very point. He insisted, in a conference with the Swiss reformer, that "in all disputes concerning faith and religion, the Scripture alone, proceeding from the mouth of God, ought to be our level and rule." Baptists have maintained this consistent stand through all the centuries that have followed Hubmaier's day, even at the expense of their personal safety [p. 483].

Torbet then traces several of the Baptist confessional statements about Scripture. For example, he mentions the articles of faith proposed by John Smyth, the *Declaration of Faith* drawn up by Thomas Helwys in 1611, the *London Confession of 1660,* and the *London Confession of 1644.* Torbet also mentions the 1742 *Declaration of Faith* of the Philadelphia Association and the *New Hampshire Confession* of 1830. He concludes:

> It may be said without hesitancy that Baptists generally have quite universally placed their uncompromising faith in the authenticity of the Sacred writings through divine inspiration of the writers by the Holy Spirit, and have stressed the necessity of Bible reading by every Christian for himself [p. 485].

This is only one of many Baptist contributions to Protestantism, but it is one that has a special importance for the whole evangelical theological community. However, many evangelicals have questioned the Baptists' commitment to a strict doctrine of biblical inspiration. That these questions have been raised should not be totally surprising to Baptists. It is precisely the question of biblical authority that has been at the root of many recent controversies within Baptist life. For example, Southern Baptist life was interrupted by controversy when Ralph H. Elliott published *The Message of Genesis*. In January, 1962, Broadman Press defended its publication of the book "in light of the historic Baptist principle" that each individual has the freedom to hold any particular theory of the inspiration of the Bible "which seems most reasonable to him." At the 1962 annual meeting of the Southern Baptist Convention, the messengers, in response to Elliott's book, passed a resolution. They specifically opposed the teaching of any theory of biblical criticism which undermines the "historical accuracy and doctrinal integrity" of Scripture. They also requested that the Sunday School Board remedy situations that threaten "our historic Baptist position." The careful observer will notice that the historical stance of Baptists has here been summoned to support two opposing positions. One could wonder, what is this "historic Baptist position"?

Lack of historical awareness will lead a denomination to walk down some of the same roads they have walked before. A strong historical identity, on the other hand, should give them the ability to correct their directions where necessary and to move forward with strength and unity. The Baptist contribution to the Protestant community in the area of biblical authority can only benefit the people of God if it is clearly defined and expressed.

Edwin Scott Gaustad wrote an article entitled "Themes for Research in American Baptist History" in *Foundations* (April 1963). Among other things "topical treatments, dealing with single doctrines and the changes they undergo, are highly appropriate," he said (p. 162). This book is an attempt to investigate the Baptist doctrine of Scripture in a systematic, historical fashion. Such a study should prove to be of interest to a large segment of the Christian community. According to the *Yearbook of American and Canadian Churches 1979*, the Baptist World Alliance, a voluntary organization of 111 Baptist bodies around the world, include over 29 million baptized believers in the membership of the cooperating groups. In the U.S.A. and Canada there are approximately 100,000 Baptist churches. The Southern Baptist Convention alone includes well over 35,000 churches and has a total membership of more than 13 million. The two National Baptist Conventions count something over 8 million members. The American Baptist Association has 1,350,000 members in 4,500 churches, while the American Baptist Churches in the U.S.A. count 1,304,088 members in 5,888 churches. Other prominent Baptist groups include the Baptist General Conference (120,222); Baptist Missionary Association of America (218,361); Conservative Baptist Association of America (300,000); Free-Will Baptists (216,831); General Association of Regular Baptist Churches (235,918); National Primitive Baptist Convention (250,000); Progressive National Baptist Convention (521,692); Baptist Federation of Canada (129,762); and fourteen other groups with 100,000 or fewer members (one of the smallest being the Primitive Baptist Convention of New Brunswick having 15 churches and 1,050 members). Hopefully some non-Baptists will be interested in this study as well.

Few areas of theology have the inherent importance of the doctrine of Scripture. The attitude toward Scripture can and does set the whole tone of doctrinal study.

Baptists have been characterized throughout their modern history by a particular doctrine of the nature of the church. Baptists believe that two ordinances (not sacraments) were instituted by Christ. Baptism by immersion is the initial act of obedience to Christ's command. It symbolizes the reality of the believer's baptism (complete immersion) into the body of Christ by the Holy Spirit. The act itself symbolizes the death and resurrection of Christ (the substitutionary atonement), the believer's spiritual death to the old life and his resurrection to walk in spiritual newness (his regeneration by grace upon the occasion of personal, individual repentance and faith), and the believer's future resurrection (the Christian's assurance based upon God's faithfulness in keeping His promises). The memorial supper is to be practiced by the church as a remembrance of the Lord's atoning death until He returns. The New Testament Church functions with only two types of officers (pastor and deacon). Several different functional terms describe the leader of the church ("overseer," "elder," and "pastor"), and it seems likely that some New Testament churches may have had a multiple ministerial "staff," though the exact structure seems to depend upon the needs of the local situation. Historically there have been both Calvinistic and free-will Baptists. This diversity has been tolerated because Baptists have consistently celebrated the liberty of conscience, which created their fervor for religious freedom and the free church in a free state.

What then have Baptists contributed specifically to the doctrine of Scripture? No comprehensive study of this has been widely available prior to this present attempt. Thus Baptists have sometimes been thought of by the scholarly world as primarily a people of practical interests. Baptists are known for men like Roger Williams, who established freedom of religion in Rhode Island. But Williams is less well known for his doctrinal contributions.

One factor leading to this state of affairs is the very emphasis on liberty of conscience mentioned earlier. Baptist confessions of faith, though numerous, are not considered to be binding over the individual's conscience. Baptists are not creedal in the traditional sense. Those outside Baptist life tend to interpret this emphasis as a strength and a weakness. The strength is obvious: religious liberty. But the weakness is just as obvious to those from strong confessional backgrounds. They tend to see Baptists as lacking strong doctrine. The very fact that both Calvinists and Arminians can be Baptists is enough to make it obvious for many that Baptists must be rather loose in their doctrinal thinking.

Like many "obvious" conclusions, however, this one needs further analysis. That there is difference of opinion among Baptists is not to be denied, but that this is due to loose thinking or lack of doctrinal concern is demonstrably false. The present study will show that Baptists do have a heritage of strong doctrine. The diversity of theological ideas within the Baptist framework has, on the other hand, kept Baptists from becoming theologically stagnant. Differences between fellow Baptists call forth persuasive and logical arguments based on careful exegesis, while at the same time the fact that one's opponent is also a Baptist serves to support if not demand Christian attitudes and Christian brotherhood.

This is not to suggest that all has been perfect in exegesis, logic, or attitude within Baptist life. Yet a common theme of concern for truth and an equal concern for people characterize Baptist theology from the inside out. In the pages that follow, the doctrine of Scripture will be studied as it has been elaborated by Baptist theologians and Baptist people. Perhaps non-Baptists who even now are struggling with doctrinal matters in their own denominations can learn from Baptist patterns, and Baptists themselves can surely profit from a careful review of their doctrinal heritage.

Historically, Baptists have built their theology from a solid foundation. Holy Scripture was taken to be God's infallible revelation in words. What God said, Baptists believed. No creed held them together, though Baptists never hesitated to write and affirm their doctrinal confessions. No church covenant was mandatory for all Baptist churches; yet hardly a church has not adopted strongly worded covenants. Scripture has been the cornerstone, the common ground, the point of unity.

With assurance that God's blessing will fall on the one who not only reads the Bible but also believes it, and with a prayer that this volume may contribute to that end, the authors send it forth to lift up that preacher who stands to proclaim the Word of God, to encourage that theologian who humbly bows before the Word of God, and to challenge that critic who scoffs at the Word of God.

The chapter titles for this particular study have been chosen with care. By no means are they intended as examples of Baptist exegetical theory, but neither are they simplistic plays on words. Each title is from the King James Version of the Bible, and they do follow canonical sequence. Nevertheless, no allegory is intended.

Part One, "In the Beginning God" (Genesis 1:1), is an affirmation of God's leadership in the establishment of modern Baptist church life. The first seven chapters, then, trace the Baptist heritage up through the middle of the nineteenth century. Each chapter title in this section is taken from Genesis, the book of beginnings. Because Baptists are so obviously characterized by their emphasis upon full immersion in water as the biblical, and thus the only, proper mode of baptism, it did not seem inappropriate to use the creation account by way of analogy. Chapter one, "The Spirit of God Moved upon the Face of the Waters" (Genesis 1:2), traces the rise of General Baptists in seventeenth-century England. Here and throughout all of the following chapters the emphasis is on the view of Scripture held by these early Baptist leaders. Chapter two, "And God . . . Divided the Waters" (Genesis 1:7), investigates the rise of the Particular Baptists. Special emphasis is given to the doctrine of Scripture upon which the *1644 Confession of Faith* was based. Chapter three, "And God Saw That It Was Good" (Genesis 1:10), includes a careful analysis of the 1689 *Second London Confession,* one of the most influential of all Baptist confessions. The doctrine of Scripture is quite clear in this confession.

Baptists have a rich heritage of leaders who made contributions to society as well as to the Christian world. Benjamin Keach, John Bunyan, and Roger Williams are studied in chapter four, "The Waters Brought Forth Abundantly" (Genesis 1:21). John Gill, one of the Baptists' most productive theologians, and Andrew Fuller, a founder of the modern mission movement, are the subjects of chapter five, "Be Fruitful, and Multiply" (Genesis 1:22). From the story of Abraham comes the title for chapter six, "Unto a Land That I Will Shew Thee" (Genesis 12:1). This chapter recalls the importance of Scripture in the beginnings of the foreign-mission movement under William Carey and Adoniram Judson. Chapter seven, "They Separated Themselves the One from the Other" (Genesis 13:11), recalls the separation of Abraham and Lot for practical not theological reasons and applies that separation by way of analogy to the division of Baptists in America into a Northern and a Southern Convention. Baptists were not divided over their view of Scripture, as a study of the writings of Francis Wayland and J. L. Dagg makes clear.

Part Two, "A New King . . . Which Knew Not Joseph" (Exodus 1:8), recognizes the philosophical changes that swept through the world during the nineteenth century. New issues and new controversies arose. Baptists have struggled as have other denominational groups with this changing world. Chapter eight, "Their Gods Shall Be a Snare" (Judges 2:3), recalls the warning from the angel of the Lord to the children of Israel that they would be led astray by false ideas. The chapter is a brief cultural analysis, a history of ideas showing some of the factors that have led to the theological tensions of the modern day.

After Saul defeated the Ammonites, Samuel said to the people, "Come, and let us go to Gilgal, and renew the kingdom there" (1 Samuel 11:14). J. P. Boyce and Basil Manly, Jr., must have had a similar spirit of rejoicing as they went to Greenville, South Carolina, to found the Southern Baptist Theological Seminary in 1859. Thus chapter nine is titled "Come, and Let Us Go to Gilgal." The first theological crisis among Southern Baptists came over the view of Scripture held by one of the faculty members at this new seminary. The issues involved had nothing of the spirit of personal invective in them. John A. Broadus deeply loved Crawford H. Toy. The story of this crisis as it relates to the matter of biblical authority is found in chapter ten, "O My Son Absalom" (2 Samuel 18:33).

Just before David died, he ordered his son Solomon to "keep the charge of the LORD thy God, to walk in his ways, to keep his statutes, and his commandments, and his judgments, and his testimonies, as it is written in the law of Moses" (1 Kings 2:3), so that he would prosper in all that he was to do. From that passage chapter eleven takes the phrase "That the LORD May Continue His Word" (1 Kings 2:4), as a title for a study of the crisis over biblical authority in England at the end of the nineteenth century. The two principals of the "Downgrade Controversy" were John Clifford and Charles Spurgeon.

Theological tensions also began to grow in America. In the North, A. H. Strong, though increasingly influenced by evolutionary thought, nevertheless held the line in basic doctrinal matters as long as he lived. Alvah Hovey was perhaps the greatest biblical theologian in the North at this time. Taking an analogy from the biblical account of the reign of King Josiah, we called chapter twelve "All His Days They Departed Not" (2 Chronicles 34:33), meaning, of course, that they "departed not from following the LORD." In the South, several outstanding theologians appeared. The nature of biblical authority was increasingly a subject of debate. Chapter thirteen, "Then Rose up the Chief of the Fathers" (Ezra 1:5), recalls those Jews who centered their lives in the teaching of the sacred Book, rose up to build the house of the Lord, and thus maintained the faith through difficult days. E. Y. Mullins and A. T. Robertson were such "chiefs." In the southwest a new Baptist seminary (destined to become the world's largest) was founded in 1908 by B. H. Carroll. Next to Carroll, Southwestern Baptist Theological Seminary's most famous theologian was W. T. Conner. These men are treated in chapter fourteen, "Now These Are Thy Servants" (Nehemiah 1:10).

In His Sermon on the Mount, Jesus warned of false prophets in sheep's clothing. Good trees bring forth good fruit. By their fruits they could be known, the Lord said. The Modernist-Fundamentalist controversy was especially important in early-twentieth-century Baptist development. Chapter fifteen, "Do Men Gather Grapes of Thorns?" (Matthew 7:16), collects from a few of the Baptist leaders not studied in other chapters an extensive series of their quotations concerning the issues of religious authority and biblical criticism. According to the eschatological warnings of Jesus, rumblings and battles were to characterize the Christian era. Baptists have experienced spiritual rumblings and battles throughout the twentieth century. A brief survey of the struggles that relate to Scripture is found in chapter sixteen, "The Beginning of Sorrows" (Matthew 24:8). This is by no means an exhaustive chapter. The issues debated are not new. Yet this chapter does give the overall study a sense of chronological completeness, and it serves as a hint of the relevance of this study to people living in today's world.

Part Three, "Whom Say Ye That I Am?" (Mark 8:29), calls for something more than a simple, descriptive analysis of historical views. Conclusions must be drawn and suggestions must be offered. Baptists have never hesitated to express their views; thus an obvious area to investigate in this concluding section is the doctrine of Scripture as it is expressed in written confessions of faith. These confessions contain far more than statements about Scripture; they usually express Baptist views of the gospel in its fullness. Chapter seventeen, "Things Which Are Most Surely Believed Among Us" (Luke 1:1), looks at most of the Baptist confessions of faith written in America. However, this chapter concentrates attention on confessional statements about Scripture. Finally, chapter eighteen, "Of Them Which Keep the Sayings of This Book" (Revelation 22:9), recalls the beautiful scene that closes the last book in the Bible. John hears the angel proclaim, "These sayings are faithful and true: and the Lord God of the holy prophets sent his angel to shew unto his servants the things which must shortly be done" (Revelation 22:6). John fell down to worship the angel who showed him these things, but the angel replied, "See thou do it not: for I am thy fellowservant, and of thy brethren the prophets, and of them which keep the sayings of this book: worship God" (v. 9).

Truly the authors of this book have those sentiments exactly. God is the sovereign authority over all. He is the one from whom truth flows. We are fellow servants with our Baptist brethren. However, Baptist unity is threatened by controversy over God's Word itself, the one standard by which all religious opinions ought to be tried. How can two walk together unless they be agreed (Amos 3:3)? Even more, how can we pray "Even so, come, Lord Jesus" (Revelation 22:20) if we doubt the truth of his Word? May the grace of our Lord Jesus Christ be with us all. Amen.

Part One

"IN THE BEGINNING GOD"

CHAPTER ONE

"The Spirit of God Moved Upon the Face of the Waters"

Baptists seek to conform local expressions of the Christian church to the New Testament. A church must not confuse ancient social customs with normative principles, but it should seek to duplicate the polity and the normative practice of the churches in the New Testament era. Therefore, Baptists believe that the church should have only two ordinances: baptism by full immersion in water upon the public profession of obedient trust in Jesus Christ as Lord, and the memorial observance of the Lord's Supper. Baptists seek to maintain a regenerate church membership; espouse separation of church and state; have only two officers, pastor and deacon; and consider the Great Commission binding on today's church.

However, one quickly discovers in the study of church history that these principles that Baptists believe should govern the local church have not always been held in their biblical purity. In fact, finding a church that manifested all these principles in late patristic and medieval times becomes exceedingly difficult. Many groups continued to hold one or more of these New Testament principles after the second century, but to find them all concentrated in one group is next to impossible with the records that are presently available.

The Reformation of the sixteenth century revitalized the basic principle of *sola scriptura*. This principle eventually led to efforts at establishing churches based upon the New Testament witness. The formal principle of *sola scriptura*, Scripture only, captured the minds of men like Martin Luther, Ulrich Zwingli, and John Calvin, but somehow escaped full expression in their respective efforts to establish a true church.

The Anabaptists, considered radical for their conviction that only believers should be baptized, broke with these Reformers and sought to implement churches consistent with the testimony of the New Testament. The radical changes in society called forth by these New Testament ideas made the Anabaptists extremely unpopular. They were persecuted and hounded from one place to another, but many eventually found some de-

gree of refuge in the Netherlands. Menno Simons organized some of them
into churches that continue to the present. They are known as Mennonites.

Anabaptists should not be simplistically identified with modern Baptists.
Some significant points of difference exist. However, Anabaptists set forth
many ideas that influenced the eventual development of Baptist life and
gave living proof that the principle of *sola scriptura* could lead to determined efforts to reestablish the New Testament pattern for the church.

Baptists as we know them today can be traced directly to forces at work
within seventeenth-century English church life. The desire for a pure
expression of New Testament Christianity was so strong in England that
many Christians who desired complete purification from any vestige of
Roman Catholicism were called "Puritans." They remained within the
Church of England, considering it the true church, but worked for its
radical cleansing. Many Puritans became disillusioned with the possibilities of ever salvaging purity from a daughter of Rome, whom they considered to be the harlot of the book of Revelation. Therefore, they drew
the conclusion that the Church of England was not a true church but was,
just like her Roman Catholic mother, a harlot and therefore antichrist.
These people renounced the Church of England and became Separatists,
because they separated themselves from the established Church of England.

What eventually became the first modern Baptist church was established
in Amsterdam in 1609 as a result of the meeting of a group of English
Separatists with the Dutch Anabaptists, the Mennonites. The leader of
this group of pioneering individuals was John Smyth.

JOHN SMYTH

Although the early years of Smyth stand under a cloak of mystery, his
journeys as a mature adult are quite well documented. He received both
the B.A. and M.A. degrees from Christ's College, Cambridge University.
The latter degree was earned in 1593. One contemporary, John Hethering-
ton, testifies that "Master Smiths bringing up hath not beene so Swine-
heard and Shepherd like: He is a scholler of no small reading, and well
seene and experienced in Arts." While at Cambridge, Smyth was a loyal
member of the Church of England—of Puritan persuasion—and probably
a Calvinist in theology. However, he was exposed to the Presbyterian
tendencies of a preacher named Francis Johnson (who later became a
Separatist) and the anti-Calvinistic stances of a student named Barrett
and a professor named Baro.

Prominent Puritan businessmen desired more Bible teaching and spiritual preaching than they received in the parish churches. Therefore,
communities in which Puritanism was a dominant persuasion of the peo-

ple would often hire Puritan preachers to lecture to the townspeople. Because these preachers were hired by the private sector, the bishop had little authority over them. In September of 1600 Smyth was elected lecturer to the corporation of the city of Lincoln, an exceedingly enviable position. He performed so admirably that he was elected to a lifetime position as city preacher in August of 1602. This lifetime position lasted for only three months. It seems that he was too personal in his preaching (at least some of the people thought so). Smyth claimed that he wounded "him whom he never aimed at."

After leaving Lincoln, Smyth became somewhat of an itinerant preacher and was apprehended at least three times for illegal preaching. During this time he was trying to find a satisfactory reason to stay within the Church of England. The failure of the Puritans to gain the sympathy and aid of James I at the Hampton Court conference in 1604 served only to disillusion Smyth of the possibility of further reform within the Church of England.

Joining with several others seeking the true church, Smyth became part of a Separatist church in 1607. The members vowed to shake "off this yoke of antichristian bondage" and unite with each other "into a church estate." The model of this church was the Old Testament covenant, not baptism according to the New Testament plan; but an admirable open-endedness characterized their pledge "to walk in all his wayes, made known, or to be made known unto them, according to their best endeavors, whatsoever it should cost them, the Lord assisting them" (Bradford, p. 31).

Smyth and his Separatist church moved to Amsterdam in 1608 with the full intention of joining Francis Johnson's "Ancient" church when they arrived there. Johnson's congregation had been in the Netherlands since 1593 and in Amsterdam since 1597. However, there were unforeseen differences between the two congregations, and Smyth refused the merger. He enumerated the differences in a writing entitled *The Differences of the Churches of the Separation.* One of the differences related to worship practice sheds light upon Smyth's view of Scripture at this stage of his pilgrimage.

This specific difference Smyth called the "matter" of worship. Separatists characteristically refused to use the *Book of Common Prayer* for help in worship. Smyth, however, called for an exclusion of all written aids to worship. He refused to use any books to help in the singing or books to aid in the preaching parts of worship. So radical did Smyth become that he even called for the suspension of the use of the Bible itself. True spiritual worship must depend only on the immediacy of the Spirit, not on any books or helps whatsoever.

Smyth was not led into this position because of any low view of the

Scripture, however. Quite to the contrary, an extremely elevated view of the original manuscripts led him to reject the reading of Scripture in worship. Translations, though necessary, are man's invention, he said, not the original inspired Scriptures. Therefore, reading a translation in worship focuses attention on a product of human labor. To that extent, even the reading of the Bible perverts the worship of God. Nor may one legitimately, in public worship, read the Scripture in the original languages. Few if any of the worshipers would understand what was read, for it would be in Hebrew or Greek, and to speak in an unknown tongue without an interpretation is expressly forbidden by Scripture. Therefore, Smyth concluded that Scripture-reading is not to be a part of worship.

In his argument for excluding all books from worship, Smyth affirmed the inerrancy of the autographs of Scripture.

> Men are of two sortes: Inspired, or ordinary men. Men Inspired by the Holy Ghost are the Holy Prophets & Apostles who wrote the holy scriptures by inspiration. 2. Pet. 1.21. 2. Tim. 3.16. Rom. 1.2. namely the Hebrue of the ould testament & the greeke of the new Testament.
> The holy Scriptures viz. the Originalls Hebrew & Greek are given by Divine Inspiration & in their first donation were without error most perfect & therefore Canonicall [Smyth, 1:279].

Ordinary men write various types of theological literature, and the highest of them is a translation of Scripture. However, none of the writings of ordinary men is given by inspiration. Their writings are therefore subject to error and are thus to be excluded from spiritual worship. Books given by inspiration are not subject to error.

Smyth goes on to explain the difference between the tongue of Scripture and the matter (by which he meant the logic, history, chronology, cosmography, philosophy, and theology) of Scripture. A translation may accurately express much of the matter signified by the original tongue. However, "no translation can possibly express all the matter of the holy originalls, nor a thousand things in the Grammar, Rhetorick, & character of the tong" (Smyth, 1:280).

If Scripture is not to be used in worship, how is it to be used? The Holy Scriptures are the fountain of all truth (John 17:17; 2 Timothy 3:16-17) and are the ground and foundation of our faith, says Smyth. All doctrine and every spirit is to be judged by them. They are to be read and interpreted in the church but not during spiritual worship (Smyth, 1:282).

In 1609 Smyth allowed the logic of his convictions concerning the purity of the church and the purity of worship to reach their full conclusion. The members of the church came together to dissolve their union of 1607 that had been effected by a covenant, or vow, and they reconstituted themselves as a church on the basis of believer's baptism. John Robinson, pastor of the church that eventually became the Pilgrim Church, recorded the events of that meeting:

> Mr. Smyth, Mr. Helwys & the rest haveing utterly dissolved, & disclaymed their former Ch: state, & ministery, came together to erect a New Ch: by baptism: unto which they also ascribed so great virtue, as that they would not so much pray together, before they had it. And after some streyning of courtesy, who should begin, . . . Mr. Smith baptized himself, & next Mr. Helwis, & so the rest, making their particular confessions [Burrage, 1:237].

This famous baptism is known to historians as Smyth's "se-baptism" (baptism of one's self). The mode of baptism used in this case was the pouring of water on the head. After constituting this new church, Smyth wrote a book in defense of believer's baptism. The title of the book is *Character of the Beast.* Smyth set forth two propositions for defense: (1) That infants are not to be baptized; (2) That anti-Christians converted are to be admitted into the true church by baptism. The basic argument Smyth proposed against infant baptism was that it lacked specific scriptural authority.

> There is neyther precept nor example in the new Testament of any infants that were baptized, by John or Christ's disciples: Only they that did confesse their sinnes, & confesse their fayth were baptized [Smyth, 2:574].

Lack of a proof text was not as significant as his positive, fully biblical theology, however, in moving Smyth to reject infant baptism. The first forty-three pages of *Character of the Beast* consist of a very thorough interpretation of seven critical passages of Scripture. These interpretations were set in the context of a debate between Smyth and Richard Clifton, a Separatist. Smyth, well aware of the covenant view of baptism (which relates baptism to the Old Testament ceremony of circumcision), displays a comprehensive understanding of both the Old and New Testaments. He indicates no reticence in accepting their full authority. However, the Old Testament, though absolutely true, must be related primarily to physical Israel. In Smyth's view only the moral teaching of the Old Testament is incumbent on the church, for this teaching is eternal and relates to all people of every age. The ceremonial requirements of the Old Testament (for example, circumcision) relate to the church only typologically and spiritually. Therefore, circumcision of infants does not require baptism of infants but merely typifies or symbolizes spiritual circumcision of the heart for Christians. Baptism is the outward sign of the spiritual Israel (the church) and must not be practiced on any except those who have been circumcised of heart: true volitional believers, not infants of believers. His argument was not an attempt to discredit the Old Testament but an attempt to relate it properly to the New Testament. The church must submit to the authority of biblical truth or become antichrist, said Smyth.

Smyth's last confession of faith, entitled *Propositions and Conclusions,* was written in an attempt to unite his church with the Mennonite church of Amsterdam. It contains one hundred articles, ninety-seven of which contain at least one Scripture reference. However, he endorses a subjectivity that later was harmful to General Baptists in England. His optimism concerning the spiritual possibilities of the "new creature" led him to assert that "the new creature needeth not the outward scriptures . . . seeing he hath three witnesses in himself . . . which are better than all scriptures" (article 61).

The new creature, though above laws and Scripture, will do nothing against law and Scripture but will conform to it. In fact, faith, according to Smyth, is "a knowledge in the mind of the doctrine of the law and gospel contained in the prophetical and apostolical scriptures of the Old and New Testament" (article 68). The true Christian is both above Scripture and bound to Scripture. He is above Scripture, Smyth claims, because of the personal presence and leadership of the triune God. He is under Scripture because it is unerringly true and cannot be contradicted by the Christian's conduct or thought. His practice must conform to law; his faith must be identical with the content of the Scriptures.

THOMAS HELWYS

When John Smyth began in 1609 to seek union with the Mennonites, a group of about ten people from within Smyth's church recoiled and refused to move further. Thomas Helwys led these people to reaffirm their belief in the validity of their baptism. Smyth had come to the conclusion that it had been disorderly and therefore regrettable because God was a God of order, not confusion. To defend and clarify his position, Helwys wrote a confession of faith in 1611 entitled *A Declaration of Faith of English People Remaining at Amsterdam in Holland.* This confession deserves to be called the first English Baptist confession of faith. Several points of disagreement with Smyth emerge as the confession unfolds. Helwys believed that man is justified solely by the righteousness of Christ. Smyth, on the other hand, believed justification before God came partly by Christ's righteousness and partly by inherent righteousness in the believers themselves. Helwys affirmed the reality of original sin and stated that we are by nature children of wrath. Smyth claimed that there is no original sin; it is but an idle term. Helwys also said that the magistrate could be a Christian. Smyth, however, denied even the possibility of Christian magistrates, because the very function of a magistrate, "vengeance," requires him to disobey the commands of Christ.

Helwys' confession also reveals several doctrines that represent theological shifts away from Calvinism. One major shift concerning the extent of the atonement earned the name General Baptists for Helwys and his group. They claimed that Christ died for all men rather than for the elect only. This view is spoken of as the doctrine of general atonement. They also rejected the doctrine of the perseverance of the saints and said that men may fall away from the grace of God and thus be lost even though they once had been saved.

The doctrine of Scripture in Helwys' confession is very simple. Each article lists at least one Scripture reference. In fact, in the full twenty-seven articles, 104 Scripture texts are listed as supporting the positions set forth. Article twenty-three is the specific statement concerning Scripture:

> That the scriptures off the Old and New Testament are written for our instruction, 2. Tim. 3.16 & that wee ought to search them for they testifie off CHRIST, Jo. 5:39. And therefore to bee used withall reverence, as conteyning the Holie Word off GOD, which onelie is our direction in al things whatsoever [Lumpkin, p. 122].

Helwys makes several brief points: One, the Scriptures instruct us. Two, the focus of their instruction is Christ. Three, one should handle them with reverence, for they contain the Holy Word of God. Four, this word of God serves as our ultimate and exclusive direction in all things whatsoever.

We should not view Helwys' third point as the parallel of modern claims that the Scripture "contains" the word of God as opposed to "being" the word of God. He is not saying that the Scripture contains, among other things, the word of God; rather, he is saying that it contains exclusively the word of God. Therefore, it is to be handled with reverence. It is as though one were saying, "See that this letter gets to the general, for it contains a word from the President." In reality it contains nothing else but a word from the President. "It contains" is a common figure of speech meaning "all of its contents are." Thus, "it contains the Holy Word of God" means "all of its contents are the Holy Word of God."

Point four does not mean that Scripture is, for Helwys, a storehouse of knowledge on all academic pursuits (for example, astronomy, navigation, chemistry, and so forth). It does affirm, however, that Scripture cannot be controverted in any area where it intends to speak. In Scripture, "our onelie direction in al things whatsoever," we find certain affirmations concerning what we are to believe and certain limitations concerning what we are not to believe about God, man, the world (including its origin and its demise), sin and evil, salvation, and the church.

After Helwys and his group moved back to England in 1612, they established the first Baptist church on English soil. Immediately they began
to fight for liberty of conscience, for they were in a country hostile to
their dissenting religious position. Helwys produced the first volume in
English on the right of universal religious liberty, *A Short Declaration of
the Mistery of Iniquity*. His belief that Scripture was true and binding
on the actions of men prompted him to write this volume. As he expresses it:

> But that the Word of God compells us, which commands us strickly to
> shewe ourselves faithful in a little: Matt. 25:19-30. From which ground
> (by the grace off God:) we have been drawn to doe that little we have
> formerly done, and undertake . . . now to doe that wee shall doe [*Mistery
> of Iniquity*, p. 2].

His commitment to the truth of Scripture also served as the basis for
bringing judgment upon the various ideas he discusses. According to
Helwys, Scripture, the word of truth, stands as an unerring guide against
which all error may be exposed:

> Now if it can bee shewed by the word of truth, that deep error of darkness
> doth possesse the two last . . . then the first that cannot mourne must needs
> fall under the sharpe censure of great harnes of hart, and incensible dead-
> ness of all affections [*Mistery of Iniquity*, p. 2].

Helwys was imprisoned very soon after the appearance of this work and
died by 1616. Perhaps his boldness to King James earned for him his mar-
tyrdom. He wrote a personal preface to the King in one copy of *Mistery
of Iniquity*:

> Hear, O King, and despise not the counsel of the poor, and let their com-
> plaints come before thee. The king is a mortal man and not God: therefore
> hath no power over the immortal souls of his subjects, to make laws and
> ordinances for them, and to set spiritual Lords over them. If the king have
> authority to make spiritual Lords and laws, then he is an immortal God,
> and not a mortal man. O King, be not seduced by deceivers to sin against
> God whom thou oughtest to obey, nor against thy poor subjects who
> ought and will obey thee in all things with body, life and goods, or else
> let their lives be taken from the earth. God save the King. Spittlefield,
> near London. Tho. Helwys.

James was probably not eager to be instructed by so mean a subject as
Thomas Helwys. Nevertheless, Helwys felt bound even unto death by the
"word of truth" and did not fear to brave James to the face if he felt that
Scripture required it.

JOHN MURTON

The leadership of the church fell into the hands of John Murton after the death of Helwys. He continued the protest against religious persecution by producing two books. *Objections Answered* was published in 1615 and *A Most Humble Supplication of Many of the King's Majesty's Loyal Subjects, Ready to Testify All Civil Obedience . . . who are Persecuted (Only for Differing in Religion), Contrary to Divine and Human Testimonies* in 1620.

Murton's first writing breathes the breath of submission to Scripture throughout. True worship can only be defined by Scripture, "for the word of God is the only ground of faith" (Underhill, p. 104). We are free to submit to earthly ordinances of the king that are "not against the manifest word of God" (Underhill, p. 107). Murton (through the mouth of a character, Christian) pleads that "the words of God, might be accepted of his majesty, set down by the Holy Spirit." Indifferent, another character in the book, desires to know the truth, things evidently manifested by the Scripture, and is appalled when he learns that "we have been besotted in these things [errors] for want of true knowledge and understanding from the scriptures. . . . we judged ourselves by our own persuasions, and not by God's word" (Underhill, p. 153). According to Murton, we have confidence that God communicates His truth to us as clearly as He did to John the Baptist, for "the same God spake to us in his Scriptures the same word he spake to John; and therefore seeing the Lord hath spoken, who shall not preach and practice according to his word?" (Underhill, p. 167).

Murton's second writing, *An Humble Supplication,* is much more direct in its approach. Chapter one is based on this thesis:

> The rule of faith is the doctrine of the Holy Ghost contained in the sacred scriptures, and not any church, council, prince, or potentate, nor any mortal man whatsoever [Underhill, p. 193].

The phrase "contained in the sacred scriptures" is explained by what follows it immediately. It could be stated "limited to the Holy Scriptures" as opposed to any church, council, or so forth.

Three reasons support Murton's thesis. First, the Scriptures are inspired of God. Second, they are written for the purpose of providing certainty, increasing joy, engendering belief, and imparting life. Third, we are commanded not to presume or be wise above what is written in Scripture. Christ Himself employed Scripture as a weapon in His battle with Satan. We are commanded to search the Scriptures. Whoever will not believe these writings "will not believe Christ's words, nor one that should come from the dead" (Underhill, p. 193).

Murton then offers twelve evidences that the Scriptures are inspired of God. Their majesty, the excellence of their teachings, and the fulfillment of their prophecies testify to their inspiration. The agreement of all parts of the Scripture, their preservation through the ages, and the vicious opposition of the forces of evil to their teaching prove their divine origin. Other evidences of their inspiration include: the conversion of thousands by the power of their doctrines; the miracles confirming them from heaven; their provision of a sight of a Savior to man; the simplicity of the writers and the plainness of the writings. Murton claims that his position is not unique; rather, he says, it represents what all Protestants "affirm and prove."

In chapter two Murton seeks to demonstrate the thesis that "the interpreter of this rule is the scriptures, and Spirit of God in whomsoever." This principle (called the analogy of faith) that Scripture interprets Scripture is based on the assumption of the entire truthfulness and consistency of Scripture. It will never deceive the earnest reader or contradict itself. Therefore, even though "many dark places . . . hard to be understood" are in it, these same doctrines are "plain and manifest" in other places of Scripture, "for all the words of the Lord are plain to him that will understand" (Underhill, pp. 197-98).

The second help in interpreting the Scripture is the Spirit of God in the believer.

> The truth of this is as plain as may be, that the scriptures being the rule of faith, perfect and absolute, and that the plainness of them is such, as by the spirit of God they may be easily understood of those that fear and obey God [Underhill, p. 201].

Murton was convinced that the poor and despised of the world made up the greatest part of those who had the Spirit. Murton severely censured Protestants who by their principle of *sola scriptura* encouraged each man to study the Scriptures and thereby know the will of the heavenly Master but then would not "suffer us to practice that we learn and know" (Underhill, p. 209).

In summary, Murton's view of Scripture is simple. The words of the Bible are the words of God set down by the Spirit. They are perfect and absolute in truth because they are thus inspired. Scripture is our sole authority in all matters of faith, conduct, worship, and doctrine because Scripture is incontrovertibly true. A sufficient number of external factors serve to verify the inspiration of Scripture. Finally, Scripture serves as its own interpreter because of its consistency. Scripture may be understood by believers because the Spirit opens their minds to its clarity.

LATER GENERAL BAPTISTS

During the period of the Commonwealth and Protectorate in England (1649-58), General Baptists confronted the threat of Quakerism. William C. Braithwaite, in *The Beginnings of Quakerism,* credits the General Baptists in 1648 with providing encouragement and a haven of fellowship for George Fox, the founder of the Quaker movement. A shattered Baptist group in Mansfield, England, proved to be the first congregation to become Quakers. Baptists expected little problem with Quakers until they began to schedule great public meetings to "conquer London" (Emmott, *Short History of Quakerism,* p. 137).

By 1654 many General Baptists had become converts to Quakerism, perhaps because of the similarity between Smyth's earlier concept of spiritual worship and the Quaker's view of the inner light. This fact upset several of the more perceptive General Baptists who recognized the devastating results of the Quaker's subjectivity. In practice the "inner light" served to exclude the external, objective work and Word of Christ from their theology. John Griffith, an influential General Baptist pastor, identified the problem in *A Voice from the Word of the Lord to those Grand Imposters called Quakers.* Among the errors Griffith identified was a "rejection and despising of the Word." Griffith urged Baptists to be loyal to the Word of Christ.

Following quickly upon Griffith's salvo, a confession of faith entitled *The True Gospel Faith* was adopted. This confession was not original: it had been prepared earlier by Thomas Lover. Griffith's group did prepare a letter to the reader in which was bemoaned the recent developments that threatened to extinguish the gospel light by subjecting the Scriptures to the whims of subjectivity, the Quaker inner light.

> We therefore do desire that whosoever read it [the confession] may weigh the Scriptures produced; and if it be according to the Scriptures, there is light in it; for its the Scriptures of the Prophets and Apostles that we square our faith and practice by, accounting that light within (not witnessed by the Scriptures without) which some so much talk of to be deep darkness. . . . Let the Scripture therefore be the rule of thy faith and practice [Lumpkin, p. 191].

Doctrinal problems within General Baptist ranks prompted a group of churches in the Midlands to produce a major confession of faith known as the *Orthodox Creed.* An eminent Sussex pastor, Matthew Caffyn, was accused of propagating erroneous views concerning the humanity of Christ. These accusations embroiled the General Baptists in controversy for several years. Eventually, Caffyn, all the while defending his orthodoxy, became essentially Unitarian in theology. By 1750 a majority of the General Baptists followed his precedent.

The *Orthodox Creed* reflects the controversy of the time in a dramatic way. The first eight articles are limited to the doctrines of the Trinity and the person of Jesus Christ. The title, *Orthodox Creed,* is entirely appropriate for this document. It purposefully duplicates the language of the orthodox creeds of the early church. The articles on the deity and humanity of Christ provide striking examples of this:

> The Son of God . . . is very and true God, having his personal subsistance of the father alone. . . . There was never any time when he was not. . . . He is of one nature and substance with the father neither made, nor created, nor adopted, but begotten before all time.
> We believe that the only begotten son of God, . . . took to himself a true, real, and fleshly body, and reasonable soul . . . and became very and true man like unto us in all things [Lumpkin, pp. 299-300].

This reflection of orthodox language continues in an article on the union of the two natures in Christ. The "inseparable and indissolvable" union of the divine and human in one person was accomplished "without change of either nature, or mixture of both" and has produced one Christ, God-man, or Immanuel, God with us.

Further evidence of the conflict is seen in article thirty-eight. The Apostles' Creed, the Nicene Creed, and the Athanasian Creed are all recommended as worthy "thoroughly to be received," for they may be proved by "most undoubted authority of Holy Scriptures." All Christians should understand those creeds, and ministers should be careful to instruct the people in them "according to the analogy of faith, recorded in sacred scriptures, upon which these creeds are grounded." Thus, the appeal to the early creeds represents an oblique appeal to the authority of Scripture.

Though the article on Scripture does not appear until article thirty-seven, an assumption of its authority is evident throughout, as is shown by the appeal to Scripture described immediately above. The first eight articles are paralleled by 111 Scripture passages. There is reference to every book of the New Testament except Philemon and 2 and 3 John. The only books in the Old Testament not directly referred to are Judges, Ruth, Esther, Song of Solomon, Lamentations, Obadiah, Nahum, and Haggai.

XXXVII. ARTICLE.

Of the sacred Scripture.

> The authority of the holy scripture dependeth not upon the authority of any man, but only upon the authority of God, who hath delivered and revealed his mind therein unto us, and containeth all things necessary for

salvation; so that whatsoever is not read therein, nor may be proved thereby, is not to be required of any man, that it should be believed as an article of the christian faith, or be thought requisite to salvation. Neither ought we, since we have the scriptures delivered to us now, to depend upon, hearken to, or regard the pretended immediate inspirations, dreams, or prophetical predictions, by or from any person whatsoever, lest we be deluded by them. Nor yet do we believe, that the works of creation, nor the law written in the heart, viz. natural religion, as some call it, or the light within man, as such, is sufficient to inform man of Christ the mediator, or of the way to salvation, or eternal life by him; but the holy scriptures are necessary to instruct all men into the way of salvation, and eternal life. And we do believe, that all people ought to have them in their mother tongue, and diligently, and constantly to read them in their particular places and families, for their edification, and comfort; and endeavour to frame their lives, according to the direction of God's word, both in faith and practice, the holy scriptures being of no private interpretation, but ought to be interpreted according to the analogy of faith, and is the best interpreter of itself, and is sole judge in controversy. And no decrees of popes, or councils, or writings of any person whatsoever, are of equal authority with the sacred scriptures. And by the holy scriptures we understand, the canonical books of the old and new testament, as they are now translated into our English mother-tongue, of which there hath never been any doubt of their verity, and authority, in the protestant churches of Christ to this day.

[Then follows the names of the books of the Old and New Testament.]

All which are given by the inspiration of God, to be the Rule of faith and life.

Article thirty-seven, "Of the sacred Scripture," (Lumpkin, pp. 324-25), contains a thorough summary of the General Baptists' understanding of scriptural authority. However, the detail one might wish is absent because they saw nothing unique in their expression. *The Westminster Confession of Faith (Presbyterian), The Savoy Declaration* (Congregational), the 1644 *London Confession* (Baptist), and the 1677 edition of the *Second London Confession* (Baptist) had already appeared, and these Baptists felt that their view of scriptural authority was perfectly consonant with what had already been said. The last line of this article says of Scripture: "there hath never been any doubt of their verity, and authority, in the protestant churches of Christ to this day."

Therefore, the General Baptists align themselves with the details of the view of Scripture expressed by Protestants before them. One should also bear in mind the views expressed by Smyth ("without error in the originalls"), Helwys ("our only direction in all things"), and Murton ("words of God set down by the Spirit"). The *Orthodox Creed* assumes the truth of those statements and has no desire to dissociate itself from this historical stream of orthodox theology.

In addition to all that the article assumes, it nevertheless does make very specific and strong affirmations regarding the Bible. First, the *Orthodox Creed* makes it very clear that the authority of Scripture is dependent on God alone and not on the decision of any council or man. It depends on God because He "hath delivered and revealed his mind therein unto us." Therefore, no creature can add to the authority of Scripture any more than one could add to the mind of God; nor can one change or correct Scripture any more than one could change or correct the mind of God.

Second, Scripture is considered exclusively authoritative. Nothing can be required of a man for salvation or doctrine that is not in the Scripture or "proved thereby." Specifically, immediate inspiration, dreams, or prophetical predictions by or from any person whatsoever are excluded as sources of authority.

Third, the Scriptures are necessary "to instruct all men into the way of salvation and eternal life." The law within the heart, the works of creation, and the light within man are all insufficient sources of revelation and will never lead a person to knowledge of Christ as Mediator, the way of salvation, or eternal life.

Fourth, translations of the Scriptures are necessary, for all people "ought to have them in their mother tongue" to study privately and in their families. Only by personal knowledge can believers frame their lives according to God's Word "both in faith and practice."

Fifth, because no Scripture is of private interpretation, the principle governing our interpretation must be the analogy of faith. The Scripture is the best interpreter of itself, and it is to be the sole judge in controversy. "No decrees of popes, or councils, or writings of any person whatsoever, are of equal authority."

Sixth, the sixty-six books of the Old and New Testaments are declared to be holy Scripture. They are listed as they appear in the King James Version. The final statement of the article reads: "All which are given by the inspiration of God, to be the Rule of faith and life."

Thomas Grantham

Thomas Grantham (1634-92), a Lincolnshire man, was for many years the principal minister among the General Baptists. In 1653 he was baptized in Boston, Lincolnshire, and immediately began laboring for the increase of the group's numbers and procuring preachers for the small congregations. His gifts were so evident to the small group of Baptists that they pressed him into service as their pastor in 1656. Grantham's own testimony reveals his reticence to undertake what he considered so high and responsible a calling:

> The greatness of the work, and my poor and low capacity, and great un-fitness for so sacred a work, did cause me to strive much against many pressures in my spirit, which yet I hope were from the Lord. . . . I had rather have been sent to any drudgery in the world, than to preach. . . . I was chosen, though God knows unwillingly, to the office of presbyter, to take the oversight of a small congregation; and solemnly ordained by fasting and prayer, and laying on of hands, of such as were ordained before me [Taylor, pp. 129-30].

In 1660, Grantham wrote and presented a petition to the restored monarch, Charles II, asking for clemency and toleration for the harassed dissenters of Lincolnshire. The petition was signed by thirty-five men and "approved by more than 20,000." Though Charles' word to them was positive, an attempted insurrection led by Thomas Venner and the circulation of un-favorable literature about the Baptists brought renewed repression and resulted in several periods of imprisonment for Grantham.

So highly esteemed by his Baptist brethren was Grantham that in 1666 he was appointed as a General Baptist Messenger, a position similar to that of an itinerant evangelist. His zeal in that position led to the found-ing of several churches in Lincolnshire, Norfolk, Warwickshire, and other counties.

As well as proving himself an effective evangelist and church founder, Grantham was quite proficient in his exposition of Baptist doctrine and his defense of Baptist practice. He wrote one of the most successful and scholarly works produced by a General Baptist during this period. In 1678, the same year in which the *Orthodox Creed* was produced, Grantham published *Christianismus Primitivus*, a defense of the nature, certainty, excellency, and beauty of the ancient Christian religion. A unique first edition of this publication has been preserved in the Treasure Room of Southwestern Seminary's Fleming Library, Fort Worth, Texas. It contains a handwritten copy of Grantham's dying words, spoken by him on Janu-ary 17, 1692, "within two minutes of his death." The words were recorded by a witness and signed by eight people who were with him when he died, including Ann Grantham. Among other things Grantham said:

> I have not defrauded or polluted any person in the world, as now I am go-ing to answer before God the Father. I came not amongst you for riches or honour, but to preach the gospel of Jesus Christ, to spend and to be spent for your good, both by preaching and printing; which words and works I recommend unto you, to strengthen you. . . . In which faith I live and die.

Though this volume is divided into four books, much of it is a simple presentation of basic Christian doctrines. However, Grantham clearly intended the study to include the extensive exposition of such Baptist principles as believer's baptism by immersion. Three portions are devoted specifically to the authority of Scripture. In his general introduction to the work, Grantham devotes five sections to "shewing the truth and Divine Authority of the Scripture, as being the undoubted oracles of God" (Introduction, p. 1).

As early as 1624 Herbert of Cherbury had written *De Veritate (On Truth)* in which he argued that special supernatural revelation is unnecessary. He believed that Christianity could be supported by innate truths that could be known by mental reflection apart from special revelation. This persuasion continued to spread throughout England, resulting in the Deist movement of the next century. Grantham does not specifically mention Herbert of Cherbury, but in light of Grantham's wide reading, he was surely aware of Lord Herbert's growing influence. Roman Catholics and Quakers, however, are targeted for special attention in Grantham's writing.

In his introduction, Grantham approaches several basic issues relating to the accuracy of the revealed knowledge of God through Scripture. In his confrontations with "papists," "Quakers," and perhaps other more liberal theologians, his submission to the sole authority of Scripture had apparently been ridiculed. The original manuscripts no longer exist, some had contended, and no copy can be demonstrated to be perfect. Thus, it is impossible to submit oneself totally to Scripture, for no one knows exactly what the authentic text said. Moreover, the copies clearly contain errors. How could one possibly argue that the originals did not contain the same (or similar) errors? Since the originals had been lost, one could never know for sure that the Scripture was true or even what the Scripture taught unless church tradition or an inner light or human reason were used to discover truth. This oblique attack upon the sacred Oracles would have devastating results, as far as Grantham was concerned, because the Christian faith is so absolutely dependent on the truth of the Scriptures that "if they prove false, Christianity cannot be true" (Introduction, p. 2).

Grantham's first line of rebuttal to this attack consisted of a defense of God's providence in allowing the original manuscripts to perish. If they had endured, in Grantham's opinion, they could have become objects of abuse. Those who possessed them might be tempted to alter the text, and those who did not possess them would be hard pressed to discover the cheat. By what means could anyone correct the (altered) original? It must be remembered, wrote Grantham, that many copies of the original were made immediately and that several translations were made soon after the production of these first copies. Therefore, because only a few churches ever had the originals of any New Testament books, even in the first century, the possibility of arrogant abuse is gone, and men "are all forced to be more peaceable than perhaps they are willing to be, since they have only copies of the Sacred Oracles." One should not construe Grantham to mean that he approves of "altering the Holy Writings, no not in the least iota." He is only asserting that "God's wisdom disposed better for the church than she could have thought or desired" by placing all men on equal ground through the available texts, while the "Holy doctrine therein was not violated" (Introduction, p. 2).

Grantham enlarges upon that last thought in his second argument. "I conceive it abundantly satisfactory, that the Copies of the Sacred Oracles . . . have no corrupt Doctrine in them." The sheer number of copies produced virtually eliminates the possibility of a major fraud being inserted undetected. The reader of the Bible has abundant notice that some supposed believers misinterpret Scripture and "wrest . . . [it] unto their own destruction" (2 Peter 3:16). If the apostles inform us of that phenomenon, how much more would they point out that the sacred Oracles themselves were changed by evil men. Yet they do not report that; so we may assume that the copies made in the days of the apostles (and there were many, for each church would have begun to gather a collection of the apostolic writings very early) were without purposeful and flagrant departure from the original words.

> We therefore conclude, that such hath been the Providence of God, that Men could not corrupt those Holy Writings which he had ordained for the Generations to come; neither can all the Art of Evil Men rase out, or foist into the Greek copies, so much as one Sentence, but either Friend or Foe would soon detect them [Introduction, p. 3].

The accuracy of Protestant English translations and the integrity of the translators were maligned by "the Papists," according to Grantham. He countered their accusations by demonstrating that the Protestant translations were far superior to the Rhemist, or Roman Catholic, translation; for the Protestants used Greek and Hebrew as the source, while the Roman Catholics used the Latin Vulgate. Grantham emphatically asserted the superiority of the original languages to any secondary language for authority in translation. Combining the use of the Greek and Hebrew manuscripts with reverent and trustworthy scholarship produces a translation that may effect a man's "growth in Christian Vertue and Knowledg" and will "stand [as] a witness against those that Contemn it, and scorn to Read it" (Introduction, p. 4).

An additional and more important question remains to be resolved.

Given the integrity of the text and the accuracy of the translation, may one go so far as to assert that these writings are "the true Word of God, . . . God's Holy Oracle?" Grantham's answer, though lengthy, is actually simple. The Bible is either the Oracle of God, or the oracle of Satan, or Man's devices. It cannot be the oracle of Satan, for it warns against him and leads its readers toward virtue and holy living. Nor would man have produced such a volume of his own initiative. The doctrines are such that man would never have conceived them, and the fearful warnings and condemnations against wicked men are so strong and antithetical to man's conceit that the impartial reader must conclude that man is not the author of such a book. Therefore, because it is neither of Satan nor of man, and by virtue of its claims to be the Word of God, the conclusion is inescapable—the Scriptures are the true Word of God (Introduction, pp. 5-7).

In book four, Grantham speaks more directly to the Roman Catholics and the Quakers. Out of forty-two pages in his section on Roman Catholicism, twenty-five are devoted to recording a literary debate between Grantham and an anonymous Papist over the query "Whether we are to resolve all Difference in Point of Religion, only out of the written Word of God?" (book 4, p. 3). The position Grantham was set to defend is stated in two ways at the beginning of the discussion:

> That amongst all such Parties of the Sons of Men, the only Infallible and Authoritative Judg of their Controversies about Religion, is the Lord Himself, as he speaketh by his Spirit in the Holy Scriptures; together with right Reason: Or thus, which is all one, the Apostles and Prophets, as they speak in their Holy Writings, are the only Infallible Authoritative Judg in these Controversies [book 4, pp. 1-2].

Grantham refused to concede that Christ's doctrine could be discerned from any authority other than the written Word. He rejected the Roman Catholic acquiescence to unwritten tradition and the elevation of the church above Scripture. He would maintain his position, he claimed, until his opponent could show that the apostles "may be heard as infallible by some other means, as by the holy Scripture" (book 4, p. 21).

Grantham exhibited little patience with the "pernicious queries" of the Quakers. One such query implied that Moses was not the writer of the five books attributed to him. Grantham answers by listing several references to the writings of Moses in the speeches of Jesus and the writings of the apostles. He concludes:

> Yea, it appears that places have been alledged out of all the Five Books of Moses by Christ and his Apostles, more than Fifty times in the New Testament. . . . Having therefore the Authority of Christ, and his holy Writers of the New Testament, avouching Moses as the Penman of the

first Books of the sacred Scripture, we explode R. [obert] R. [uckhill] his Query, as rude and unlearned, and formed on purpose to engender strife; abhorring to think that our Saviour was either Unskillful, or Unfaithful, in recommending to us any supposititious Writings, instead of the sacred Oracles [book 4, pp. 44-45].

The Quakers also sought to cloud the issue of the inspiration of Scripture by asking if there were not some words in Scripture spoken by "the grand Imposter," by wicked men, by wise men but ill expressed, by false prophets, and so on. Grantham calls this sort of inquiry "mischievous," for it tends to "prejudice the weak Reader against the Authority of the Sacred Scripture." Grantham affirms his belief in the inspiration of all the Scripture and vindicates God's wisdom in recording even the most scurrilous lies of Satan:

And this I shall make appear by a due consideration of one of the worst attempts, and mischievous discourses of the Devil himself, recounted in the holy Scripture, as Gen. 3. &c. where he falsly gives Posterity to misery and death. And yet behold how gracious God was in causing this to be written, that the riches of his Grace might appear in providing a Salve for this dreadful Wound; and to cause us to hate that Enemy for ever, and to shun his Temptations. Yea, this very passage I do affirm to be written by the Inspiration of God's Spirit, or the Motion thereof; and consequently all such-like passages also. Otherwise this passage would be doubtful, and all the Historical part of the Scripture also, which declares matter of Fact: For either these things were written in the Book of God, by the Motion and Direction of his Spirit, or else they only rest on Humane Authority, and Conjecture: For it is not likely, that Moses wrote the Account he gives of the Creation, the fall of Man and Angels, the means of his Recovery, &c. upon the bare report of Men; which we know by the Fragments which Ovid and others have left, are contradictory, and incredible; and why Moses his Relation should be received, unless revealed to him by God, rather than the rest, it will be hard to render a satisfactory Reason; but when God speaketh, we must submit our Reason; by Faith receive, what by Science we cannot understand [book 4, p. 46].

Grantham closes his discussion of the Quaker's view of Scripture by soundly rejecting their pretentions to direct revelation from the Spirit. The authority of the Spirit cannot be separated from the authority of Scripture. The Spirit will never speak in any manner opposed to what He has already spoken in Scripture. New revelation is unnecessary, for the depth of spiritual mysteries contained in Scripture goes beyond the ability of any Christian to comprehend fully in this life. The Spirit speaking in the Scriptures ought to be heard rather than any person speaking without or against the authority and truth of them.

Grantham's commitment to Scripture led him to a thorough and staunch defense of Baptist theology in a generation that ridiculed the Baptists. In addition to his various imprisonments, Grantham suffered many other annoyances during his long ministry. Opponents called him a Jesuit in disguise and accused him of drunkenness, thievery, and immorality.

He defended and cleared himself of all these charges, and when his accusers confessed their slanders, he readily forgave them and on one occasion paid the enemy's fine. Scripture was authoritative for Grantham not only in matters of fact but also in matters of practice. He admonished his friends to hold the same point of view:

> As for my part, since I have been amongst you, I have been made a scoff and a gazing stock of many people, which I freely forgive them all: and heartily pray that God would forgive them, and shew them the error of their ways: I desire that you would pray for them, and not seek any revenge. . . . And now I commit you to the grace of our Lord Jesus Christ; and the love of God, and the communion of the Holy Ghost, be with you all. Amen [from a handwritten note in *Christianismus Primitivus*].

Conforming to the Letter

The founder of the General Baptists, John Smyth, believed that the "first donation" of Scripture was without error. Though he came to believe that the "new creature" by virtue of its relation with the triune God had a special place of blessing over those who possessed the Scripture only, he continued to teach that even the new creature could do or think nothing contrary to Scripture. Helwys, while approving of Smyth's view of the truth of Scripture, did not adopt his subjectivity. He maintained that Scripture "onlie is our direction in al thinges whatsoever," and thus employed it as if it were without error. Murton affirmed the verbal inspiration of the whole Scripture by calling the Bible "the words of God set down by the Spirit" and based his main principle of interpretation, the analogy of faith, upon the assumption of the Bible's internal consistency, clarity, and truthfulness. Later General Baptists rejected Quaker claims of immediate inspiration in favor of biblical authority. In the *Orthodox Creed* they aligned themselves with mainstream Protestant thought, which expressed its view of biblical authority in terms of the infallibility of Scripture. Thomas Grantham reinforced this view of scriptural authority in his book *Christianismus Primitivus*.

In 1818 Adam Taylor wrote *A History of the English General Baptists*. Chapter four of that work is entitled "An inquiry into the Doctrine and Discipline of the English General Baptists during the Seventeenth Century." He aptly summarizes their commitment to Scripture in the following statement:

And there was one point in which they all agreed: they all esteemed the holy scripture as the rule of faith and practice; and manifested a sincere desire to bow with implicit submission to what they judged its dictates. Some of their most striking peculiarities may be traced to a laudable anxiety to follow literally the injunctions of the Bible. They had not yet begun to examine the possibility or rationality of the doctrines of revelation, nor the propriety or justice of its precepts: their highest ambition, in their best days, was, in strict conformity to the letter of scripture, to believe the one and practise the other [p. 358].

BIBLIOGRAPHY

Bradford, William. *History of Plymouth Plantation.* Edited by William T. Davis. New York: Scribner's, 1908.

Braithwaite, William C. *The Beginnings of Quakerism.* London: Macmillan, 1912.

Burrage, Champlin. *The Early English Dissenters in the Light of Recent Research (1550-1641).* 2 vols. New York: Russell & Russell, 1912.

Emmott, Elizabeth Braithwaite. *A Short History of Quakerism.* New York: Doran, 1923.

Grantham, Thomas. *Christianismus Primitivus.* London: Printed for Francis Smith, at the Sign of the Elephant and Castle in Gornhill, near the Royal-Exchange, 1678.

Helwys, Thomas. *The Mistery of Iniquity.* London: Kingsgate Press, 1935 (published for the Baptist Historical Society from a copy presented to King James in 1612 by Helwys).

Lumpkin, W. L. *Baptist Confessions of Faith.* Valley Forge, Pa.: Judson, 1959.

Smyth, John. *The Works of John Smyth.* 2 vols. Edited by W. T. Whitley. Cambridge: University Press, 1915.

Taylor, Adam. *The History of the English General Baptists.* London: T. Bore, Raven Row, Mile-End Turnpike, 1818.

Underhill, Edward B., ed. *Tracts on Liberty of Conscience and Persecution.* London: J. Haddon, 1846.

CHAPTER TWO

"And God . . . Divided the Waters"

The second expression of Baptist life in England also arose from English Separatism. In 1616 a man named Henry Jacob founded a Congregation-alist-Separatist church. The church eventually was known as the Jacob-Lathrop-Jessey Church because the two succeeding pastors were John Lathrop and Henry Jessey. The church members were involved in an ongoing discussion concerning the nature of the church and its ordinances. This necessarily involved an effort to relate properly the practice of baptism to church membership. One question to which they sought an answer was, Who is a proper administrator of baptism? A second and, perhaps, more important question was, Who is the proper recipient of baptism? Free discussion was tolerated and even encouraged.

Church records show that in 1630 a man named Dupper withdrew from this church. He rejected the validity of his baptism because it was from the hands of Anglican clergy. He had answered the first question partially, if only negatively. The Anglican establishment, according to the Separatists, was antichrist. Dupper concluded that the priest of antichrist could not possibly administer a true ordinance of Christ. Therefore, he concluded, he had no true baptism and neither did any other member of the Jacob-Lathrop-Jessey Church. All had received it at the hands of antichrist.

In 1633 a similar withdrawal occurred in the case of Samuel Eaton, who received a "farther baptism." Records do not indicate the reason for this action. Eaton possibly had the same motivation as Dupper—rejection of baptism from the Anglican clergy. However, it is possible that he not only rejected those who administered his baptism but that he also rejected infant baptism itself and advocated believer's baptism. Either way, his action was not merely negative. It represented an effort to reinstitute true baptism. Whether or not this became a true Baptist church depends on Eaton's reasons for seeking a "farther baptism." Because the records do not indicate his motive, historical certainty must delay affirming that the church held a consistent, full Baptist theology at that time.

Finally, in 1638, a group of people from the Jacob-Lathrop-Jessey

Church came to reject infant baptism per se and advocated believer's baptism. They united in a church fellowship under the leadership of a man named John Spilsbery. Historians generally identify this congregation as the first Particular Baptist church in England. Eventually four or five different Particular Baptist churches sprang from the Jacob-Lathrop-Jessey Church. Henry Jessey himself became a Particular Baptist pastor.

Two years later, in 1640, Richard Blunt, a member of Eaton's congregation, became convinced that baptism "ought to be by dipping the Body into the Water, resembling Burial and rising again." Desiring to be as close to Scripture as possible, the congregation sought further information and in 1641 sent Blunt to Holland to be immersed by the Rhinesburg Collegiants. This was a liberal group that, in its exaltation of reason, closely resembled the unitarian Polish Brethren in theology. However, the General Baptists still baptized by pouring, and the Collegiants were the only group the Particular Baptists were aware of that practiced baptism by immersion. Although the Collegiants were unorthodox in their doctrine of Christ, they claimed to be Christian, and their practice of baptism, not their theology, attracted the Baptist congregation. In fact, the Baptists may not have been aware of this doctrinal aberration until Blunt's visit with them. After Blunt returned, he baptized the church's teacher, Mr. Blacklock, and the two proceeded to immerse fifty-one others. Thus, by 1641 Baptists had reinstituted what they considered the scriptural mode of baptism, immersion.

There is good reason for the name "Particular Baptists." These Baptists retained the Calvinistic theology inherited from the Puritans. This included a belief in limited atonement and particular election, thus the designation "Particular." In the first confession of faith published in 1644 by the Particular Baptists, a clear statement of limited atonement appears. Article twenty-one declares:

> That Christ Jesus by his death did bring forth salvation and reconciliation onely for the elect, which were those which God the Father gave him.

Particular election is taught in article three, among other places:

> God had in Christ before the foundation of the world, according to the good pleasure of his will, foreordained some men to eternal life through Jesus Christ, to the praise and glory of his grace, leaving the rest in their sinne to their just condemnation, to the praise of his Justice.

These doctrines present a stark contrast to the teachings of the General Baptists. Other doctrinal differences appear between the two groups of Baptists. A parallel chart will illustrate these differences.

Doctrine	Particular Baptists	General Baptists
Election:	God has elected certain individuals to salvation. Only they will come to Christ, and they come only by God's free and unmerited choice.	All those who believe in Christ are elect. Election is not of individuals but of Christ himself. Any one who comes into Christ becomes elect.
Atonement:	Jesus died for His elect only, and the benefits of His death are applied to the elect when God generates faith in their lives.	Jesus died for all men, and any person may partake of the benefits of Christ's death by accepting Christ when the gospel is preached.
Will:	Man lost free will in the Fall. He has lost any ability to will spiritual good. He cannot convert himself or even prepare himself for conversion, for he is dead in trespasses and sins. Man is wholly passive at the moment of regeneration. The will is made immutably free only in the state of glory.	Although man does not have free will, God's grace, which is the offer of salvation, frees man's will so that he may either choose or reject that grace without being compelled for or against the offer.
Perseverance:	The elect can never finally or totally fall away; they are kept by the power of God unto salvation.	True believers may from lack of watchfulness fall from the grace of God and become withered branches cast into the fire and burned.

Particular Baptists and General Baptists did agree in several key areas, however. They shared a strong affirmation of the full deity and humanity of Christ, even endorsing the orthodox Christological creeds of the church. Both taught His threefold office of prophet, priest, and king. Both groups rejected infant baptism in favor of believer's baptism, and both were deeply involved in the fight for religious liberty, separation of church and state, and liberty of conscience.

In short, both were orthodox in theology and Baptist in ecclesiology, but they held different views on sin and grace.

Their concern to be counted orthodox called forth the 1644 confession from the Particular Baptists. Because of the Particular Baptists' high profile during the revolutionary period 1640-48, many opponents were resurrecting and spreading scurrilous stories about the excesses of the lunatic fringe of Continental Anabaptism, and by implication they accused English Baptists of the same excesses. The publication of this confession, with its sane orthodoxy and Calvinistic theology, surprised many people in London. At many points it reproduces the exact wording of a Separatist confession titled *A True Confession*. One specific accusation put to flight by the 1644 confession was the rumor spread by Richard Baxter that the Baptists baptized women naked. In the confession, Baptists responded:

> The word Baptizo, signifying to dip under water, yet so as with convenient garments both upon the administrator and subject, with all modestie.

This was also the first Baptist confession of faith to advocate baptism by immersion.

VIEW OF SCRIPTURE IN THE 1644 CONFESSION

The doctrine of Scripture, not the least among the splendid doctrinal developments of the 1644 confession, is due primary consideration at this point.

A PREVIEW

The doctrine of Scripture in this confession is thoroughly Trinitarian. The first chapters expound the doctrine of God and the Fall of man. God is wise, constant, truthful, and faithful; and eternal life lies in knowing Him. But we only know Him as the Scripture leads us to Him. Therefore, the Scripture speaks of these qualities and, as God's Word, possesses those same qualities (article seven).

The character and functions of God the Son are revealed in Scripture (article eight). The Son functions as prophet, priest, and king in relating man to God. As prophet He perfectly reveals the whole will of God. In turn the confession teaches that Scripture partakes of the character and shares in the functions of God the Son, thereby perfectly revealing the whole will of God.

The character and functions of God the Holy Spirit are revealed in Scripture. His function is to give the gift of faith to the elect and apply the completed work of Christ to their lives. The faith that He generates becomes the avenue to complete trust in the truthfulness of Scripture (article twenty-two).

Thus a reciprocal relationship between God and Scripture provides the structure for this confession. The writers close with the affirmation that they believe all things that are written in the Law and in the prophets and apostles.

EXPOSITION

Articles seven and eight of the confession provide the key to its view of Scripture.

> The Rule of this Knowledge, Faith and Obedience, concerning the worship and service of God, and all other Christian duties, is not man's inventions, opinions, devices, lawes, constitutions, or traditions unwritten whatsoever, but onely the word of God contained in the Canonicall Scriptures.

> In this written Word God hath plainly revealed whatsoever he hath thought needfull for us to know, beleeve, and acknowledge, touching the Nature and Office of Christ, in whom all the promises are Yea and Amen to the praise of God.

Removed from the context of the entire confession, these particular articles do not appear profound or impressive. However, when viewed in relation to the whole, the concept of Scripture presented here is one of the most full-orbed of any Baptist confession. These articles stand at a strategic position, solidifying and unifying the entire confession. Article seven relates backward to the preceding six articles. Article eight thrusts the reader forward into the remainder of the confession. Periodic references lead the reader to deeper reflections on the nature of Scripture and eventually come full circle to bind the one who adheres to the confession to the absoluteness of "all things which are written in the Law and in the Prophets and Apostles."

Article three, speaking of the decrees of God, contains the first cord that pulls us toward the Scripture. Wisdom, constancy, truth, and faithfulness are listed as characteristics of God. These traits are understood as separate parts of that which we call providence. The accomplishing of God's will in history, especially the redemption of His elect, occurs as a direct result of these four characteristics of His nature. Two of these, constancy and truth, should be considered separately because the writers of this confession define them in terms that relate them directly to the doctrine of Scripture.

First, constancy is defined as "that whereby the decree of God remaines always immutable." God's decisions remain unchanged. His desires for man and the world are eternal and, because of His character, are not open to alteration. Constancy refers to a plan, design, or idea apart from the actual accomplishing of that plan. Faithfulness is that whereby He actually accomplishes His decrees.

Second, truth is "that whereby he declares that alone which he hath decreed, and though his sayings may seem to sound sometimes another thing, yet the sense of them doth alwayes agree with the decree." Truth, then, is that which God communicates about His plans. Because His plans never change, what He says about His plans never changes.

The words employed to describe the manner in which God communicates His truth are significant. He declares. These declarations are called sayings. They communicate definite impressions to our minds in that they "sound sometimes another thing." They have an intelligible meaning in that we can discern the "sense of them" with proper and consistent interpretation.

Evidently the writers of the confession intended the readers to understand that God has communicated His truth in words—the words of Scripture. The writers also affirmed that no contradiction exists in these sayings. What God declares is consistent ("the sense of them doth always agree with the decree") even though at first appearance a declaration may seem to diverge from a previous or later saying. God will not say anything that contradicts His plans. Contradictory ethical standards and erroneous views of God are not taught in any part of Scripture. A unity of truth is present in the sayings of God; thus the attempt to correlate apparent inconsistencies is entirely proper in interpreting the declarations of this constant, truthful God. These characteristics of God must be remembered as the context in which all references to God and His revelation to us are made.

Articles four, five, and six deal with the Fall of Adam and Eve, the results of the Fall on the human race, and the assertion that "Life eternall is to know the onely true God, and whom he hath sent Jesus Christ." At this point the first article on Scripture is inserted. It flows smoothly out of the previous article using the idea of "knowing God" as the connecting concept. The rule of saving knowledge of God is the Word of God contained in the canonical Scriptures. The writers are speaking of the same God as the one previously described in the articles of the confession, the God from whom man has fallen. All that we may know of Him and how we may best serve Him is contained in the Scripture. Thus, Scripture must contain what God has told us about Himself. His sayings and declarations are in Scripture. He has told us that He is constant and truthful and will not contradict Himself in His sayings. These sayings are the Word of God, which contains the way to eternal life and knowledge, faith, and obedience. Thus, the implication of the 1644 confession is undeniable: God's characteristic constancy and truth are expressed in Scripture itself. The Bible is represented as the unchanging norm in which man can recognize God's truth, for the words of Scripture are expressions of His unchanging will.

Some may object that the confession describes the Word of God as "contained" in the canonical Scriptures rather than identified with the canonical Scriptures. However, the wording of the confession does not intend to teach that God's words are intermixed with other words which do not partake of the characteristics of constancy and truth. The intention is to exclude human wisdom, tradition, and dogma (that is, decrees of Roman Catholicism) from the status of divine truth. The phrase "contained in the Canonicall Scriptures" could as well be stated "limited to the Canonicall Scriptures."

The second article on Scripture, article eight, declares that "in this written Word God hath plainly revealed whatsoever he hath thought needfull for us to know believe and acknowledge, touching the nature and office of Christ." This revelation is characterized by both clarity and sufficiency. God has "plainly revealed whatsoever he hath thought needfull." We are pointed forward in the confession to the person and office of Christ.

After discussing with great conciseness the orthodox doctrine of the person of Christ, the confession moves into a discussion of the offices of Christ: prophet, priest, and king. Christ's work as prophet leads us directly to Scripture again. All that we can know or even need to know about Christ as prophet is plainly stated in Scripture. Further, Christ, as prophet, relieves us of the burdensome ignorance about God under which we labor (article fourteen). Next, this ignorance is relieved because Christ as prophet "hath perfectly revealed the whole will of God out of the bosome of the Father, that is needful for his servants to know, believe, and obey." Also, His position of prophet is enhanced by His person— fully divine and fully human. If He had not been God He could not have understood the will of God or revealed it. If He had not been man, "he could not fitly have unfolded it in his own person to man" (article sixteen). All that we know of the offices of Christ is in Scripture, and Christ leads us to know God. Therefore, to our knowledge, the faithfulness of Christ as prophet is limited to the faithfulness of Scripture to the ministry of Christ.

The words that describe Christ's function as prophet are identical to those that describe how Scripture relates us to God: "know, beleeve, and obey." Thus, Scripture relates to our knowledge of God in at least these two ways. First, it speaks of Him directly. Second, it teaches about God as it communicates the nature of the prophetic office of Christ. Conversely, the character of God and the integrity of the prophetic ministry of Christ reinforce our confidence in the veracity of Scripture. The framers of this confession certainly did not believe that Christ ever spoke in ignorance, thereby misleading us. Nor did they believe that He ever purposefully misled us just to avoid unnecessary quibbling with his contemporaries. It was unthinkable to these Baptists that Christ ever spoke or acted out of harmony with His divine nature. His action as prophet in revealing the will of God in both deed and word conformed to wisdom, constancy, truth, and faithfulness. Holy Scripture partakes of the character of Christ in His prophetic office, for "in this written Word God hath plainly revealed whatsoever he hath thought needful for us to know, beleeve and acknowledge, touching the nature and office of Christ, in whom all the promises are Yea and Amen to the praise of God."

The doctrine of Scripture receives further strengthening in the twenty-second article. Predictably, the work of the *Spirit* in relation to faith is the subject.

> That Faith is the gift of God wrought in the hearts of the elect by the Spirit of God, whereby they come to see, know, and beleeve the truth of the Scriptures, & not onely so, but the excellencie of them above all other writings and things in the world, as they hold forth the glory of God in his attributes, the excellency of Christ in his nature and offices, and the power of the fulness of the Spirit in its workings and operations; and thereupon are inabled to cast the weight of their souls upon this truth thus beleeved.

Spirit-wrought faith affirms Scripture for the individual. By that faith a person comes to see, know, and believe the truth of the Scriptures. He sees it; the truth of Scripture is commended to his mind in an external way. He knows; he internalizes the conviction and becomes intellectually persuaded of the truth of Scripture. He believes; he goes beyond intellectual apprehension and commits his will to the truth of Scriptures and their uniqueness among all the writings in the world.

Further investigation of the Scriptures involves even deeper commitment to their truth. Believers are finally "inabled to cast the weight of their soules upon this truth thus beleeved." That which commits the believer to this trust is the subject matter of the writing. The glory of God, the excellency of Christ, and the power and fullness of the Spirit as expounded in the words of Scripture leave the believer with no other alternative but to cast the entire weight of his soul upon this truth. Our eternity depends upon the faithfulness of each person of the triune God, and the triune God consistently testifies to the complete trustworthiness of the written Word of God. For these Baptist theologians, to trust Christ involves, among other things, trusting His Word. One who harbors doubts about the truthfulness of the written Word, according to these Baptists, is to that degree guilty of not trusting Christ.

Not only does the confession claim that Scripture is clear and true, but its articles are written with that assumption as well. The 1644 confession contains fifty-three separate articles of faith. Printed beside each article are Scripture texts purported to support the corresponding statements in the particular article. For example, the exposition concerning the Fall of man (article four) says:

[1]In the beginning God made all things very good, created man after his own [2]Image and likenesse, filling him with all perfection of all naturall excellency and uprightnesse, free from all sinne. [3]But long he abode not in this honour, but by the [4]subtiltie of the Serpent, which Satan used as his instrument, himselfe with his Angels having sinned before, and not [5]kept their first estate, but left their owne habitation; first [6]Eve, then Adam being seduced did wittingly and willingly fall into disobedience and transgression of the Commandment of their great Creator, for the which death came upon all, and reigned over all, so that all since the Fall are conceived in sinne, and brought forth in iniquitie, and so by nature children of wrath, and servants of sinne, subjects of [7]death, and all other calamities due to sinne in this world and for ever, being considered in the state of nature, without relation to Christ.

The numbers in the quotation refer to the list of Scripture passages in the margin. Number one refers to Genesis 1; Colossians 1:16; Hebrews 11:3; and Isaiah 45:12, all of which speak directly of the personal action of God in creation. Number two refers to Genesis 1:26 and 1 Corinthians 15:45-46, which record the creation of man in the image of God (Genesis) and Adam's creation as a living soul (1 Corinthians). Number three refers to Psalm 49:20—"Man that is in honour, and understandeth not, is like the beasts that perish." Number four refers to Genesis 3:1, 4, 5 and 2 Corinthians 11:3. These verses give the historical occasion of the serpent's speaking to Eve and Paul's New Testament reference to it: "as the serpent beguiled Eve through his subtilty." Number five refers to three New Testament passages: John 8:44; 2 Peter 2:4; and Jude 6, each of which mentions Satan and his angels in their fall, who "abode not in the truth," were "cast . . . down to hell," and "kept not their first estate, but left their own habitation." Number six mentions Genesis 3:1-2, 6; Galatians 3:22; and 1 Timothy 2:14. The Genesis passage gives the historical situation in which Eve was tempted by the serpent and fell, and the 1 Timothy passage is a Pauline statement of practice based upon the precise way in which Eve and Adam respectively sinned. Number seven lists Romans 5:12, 18, 19; 6:23; and Ephesians 2:3. The passages affirm two things. First, one man was responsible for the entrance of sin into the human race. Second, death, sin, and the corruption of man's nature are to be explained in terms of that first sin. The wording of the confession is largely an echo of the words of Scripture. The Genesis 3 passage relates directly to these New Testament passages, and no hint appears that the veracity of either is in doubt.

There is no doubt that this particular article of the confession assumes that the events recorded in the Scripture actually occurred in history and were preserved accurately. Events in human history and in the spiritual world are treated with equal certainty. According to the framers of the confession, God created man in His own image in perfect innocence. A serpent used by Satan actually spoke to Eve. Satan is evil because at a point after his creation he sinned and was actually cast out of his first estate. Eve, being deceived, actually disobeyed God in time and space; and Adam, under her influence, willingly disobeyed God also. Our sinfulness, the calamities of the world, and death are due to that historic Fall. The methodology employed indicates clearly that those Baptists who wrote this confession accepted Scripture as God's special revelation that had been given in meaningful, understandable propositions. Even the words of the vernacular version find full approval as capable of expressing the truth of God. These men's use of Scripture is consistent with their confession about Scripture.

Particular Baptists' loyalty to this profession was soon tested by the efforts of the Quakers to call people to reliance on their "inner light." In an effort to refute Quaker errors and show the rest of England that Baptists were not Quakers, the Particular Baptists republished this confession of faith in 1651 and appended an article entitled "Heart Bleedings for Professors Abominations." Specific items of Quaker thought, including the Quaker view of Scripture, were examined and rejected in the article.

One Quaker error the article considered dangerous was the practice of quoting Scripture "without any distinct knowledge of the true meaning of that which is expressed." The writer called this emptiness, confusion, the mystery of a mere nothing, and swelling words of vanity. The Quakers equated their so-called inner light, or Christ within, with words of Scripture and gave the impression of speaking truth (Satan uses the same method), thereby deceiving "many poor souls." However, a "true, distinct, and cleer understanding [of] the sense of what is spoken" would show that the claims of Quakers to be united with Christ were erroneous. Therefore, Scripture is plain when interpreted in proper context and is profitable for reproof of error.

The article also specifically rejects the mystical spiritualizing of biblical passages practiced by the Quakers. By this method they rejected resurrection of the body, eternal judgment, and the second coming of Christ. They also rejected visible churches, visible ordinances, and justification by an external act of Christ. In this way they "mock at the holy Scriptures, those heavenly oracles of God, denying them to be the Word of God." The Scriptures are the "oracles of God," according to "Heart Bleedings."

Included in a list of conclusions are two further statements relative to Scripture. First, the gospel contains "the whole Minde, will, and Law of God, for us and all Saints to believe and practise throughout all ages."

Second, probably because the *Westminster Confession* had done so in 1646, it describes the Scripture as the "infallible Word of God."

> It must also be granted, That the Scriptures which doe declare this great mysterie of Jesus Christ and his Gospel, be the holy Scriptures, and the infallible Word of God, for it could never have entered into the heart of man to have knowne or manifested those hidden mysteries, had not God himself by his owne Word revealed them from Heaven; . . . Therefore dearely beloved brethren, we beg and intreat you, and every one that loves his soule, to fear and tremble at the thoughts of slighting and despising Christ and his Gospel, or any one of his laws, or holy commandments revealed in his word.

SUMMARY AND CONCLUSION

The doctrine of Scripture in the *First London Confession* receives a Trinitarian exposition. Bibliology is not developed in a separate article but pervades the entire structure of the confession. The serious reader cannot escape the startling and positive dependence of each statement upon a Scripture assumed to be true. The confession also exhibits an internal design of interdependence between each person of the Trinity as He relates to Scripture and Scripture as it relates to each person of the Trinity. The character of God, the ministry of Christ, and the effectual working of the Spirit all witness to the utter truthfulness of the Bible.

In their confrontation with the Quakers, the Particular Baptists reaffirmed their commitment to the sole and infallible authority of Scripture. They also stressed the importance of proper interpretation of Scripture, for its words are the heavenly oracles of God. In harmony with the testimony of the confession itself, the closing article of the confession affirms:

> And if any take this that we have said, to be heresie, then doe wee with the Apostle freely confesse, that after the way which they call heresie, worship we the God of our Fathers, beleeving all things which are written in the Law and in the Prophets and Apostles, desiring from our soules to disclaime all heresies and opinions which are not after Christ, and to be stedfast, unmoveable, always abounding in the worke of the Lord, as knowing our labour shall not be in vain in the Lord.

BIBLIOGRAPHY

"Heart Bleedings for Professsors Abominations." 1651.

Lumpkin, W. L. *Baptist Confessions of Faith*. Valley Forge, Pa.: Judson, 1959.

CHAPTER THREE

"And God Saw That It Was Good"

Rapid change in the political and religious life of England characterized the middle decades of the seventeenth century. 1640 began the decade of Presbyterian predominance. Puritan Presbyterians controlled the English Parliament during those years. The 1650s saw the rise of the dissenters and independents, including Baptists, as Oliver Cromwell ruled England as its Lord Protector. 1660 brought the monarchy back to England in the person of Charles II. There was a noticeable renewal of Anglican strength in Parliament.

From 1661 to 1665 a series of legislative acts was passed that greatly inhibited the freedom of all but Anglicans. Parliament enacted four especially important pieces of legislation as parts of the famous Clarendon Code: The Corporation Act, The Act of Uniformity, The Conventicle Act, and The Five-Mile Act.

The Corporation Act limited eligibility for civil office to members of the official Church of England. The Act of Uniformity defined the Church of England in the same way it had been defined during the reign of Elizabeth. The Conventicle Act, passed in 1664 after the uprising of the Fifth-Monarchy Men, prohibited meetings for religious purposes "in any other manner than is allowed by the liturgy of the Church of England." The Five-Mile Act prohibited any dissenting minister from coming within or setting up school within five miles of a corporate town. Thus, Anglicanism became the established faith.

However, because of their number and prestige, dissenters managed to practice some religious activities even in the face of such proscriptions. Theological similarity reinforced the strength of several of the dissenting denominations. Presbyterians were especially strong and expressed their theological stance in the *Westminster Confession*, published in 1646 by the Westminster Assembly.

Congregationalists thought it wise to show as much agreement as possible with the Presbyterians. In 1658, at the Savoy Conference, they made slight alterations in the *Westminster Confession* and adopted it as their. own standard.

SECOND LONDON CONFESSION

CONFESSION

OF

FAITH

Put forth by the

ELDERS and BRETHREN

Of many

CONGREGATIONS

OF

Christians (baptized upon Profession of their Faith) in *London* and the Country.

With the Heart man believeth unto Righteousness, and with the Mouth Confession is made unto Salvation, Rom. 10. 10.
Search the Scriptures, John 5. 39.

Printed in the Year, 1677.

Fig. 2. *Second London Confession*

From Lumpkin's *Baptist Confessions of Faith,* Judson, 1969. Patterned after original 1677 title page.

Particular Baptists followed suit in 1677 by issuing an anonymous version of the same confession. Some necessary changes were made in the articles on the church, the ordinances, the duties of the magistrate, and so forth; but the framers of the Baptist version said that they had "no itch to clog religion with new words." Rather, they stated their willingness to "acquiesce in that form of sound words which hath been in consent with the holy scriptures, used by others before us." This confession was reissued in 1688 and officially endorsed by a general assembly of Particular Baptists in 1689. Thirty-seven messengers signed the confession "as containing the doctrine of our faith and practice."

THE SECOND LONDON CONFESSION

The introduction to the confession—"To the Judicious and Impartial Reader"—manifests a deep reverence for Scripture as the Word of God. In addition to the above-mentioned desire that the teachings be "in consent with the holy scriptures," the confession admonishes the reader to be like the noble Bereans, "who searched the scriptures daily." Each reader was to investigate personally the biblical texts listed in the margin beside each article. The authors believed that the truth of any article was directly dependent upon its correspondence with the clear teachings of Scripture.

Neglect of family worship and failure to catechise the children properly were said to combine to cause "decay of religion, . . . grosse ignorance, . . . instability, . . . [and] prophaneess." Through this confession, the writers urged a redress of those neglected areas. They encouraged diligence in the education of the young:

> that their tender years might be seasoned with the knowledge of the truth of God as revealed in the Scriptures.

This concern is based upon certain assumptions about the nature of Scripture.

One assumption is that "knowledge" can be imparted by Scripture. Scripture does not simply witness to a common human religious experience that one can only know mystically. Bible study results in real cognitive insight into the nature of God.

A second assumption concerns the quality of this knowledge. Scripture is not simply a mixture of different human conceptions of God or thoughts that merely reflect religious genius that one must amend in the light of personal experience and Christian tradition. Scripture is the "truth of God." This can mean God's truth or truth about God. Either way, one may rest secure in the veracity of the teachings of Scripture. Each individual teaching forms a true part of the whole teaching of Scripture on that particular subject.

A third assumption is couched in the word "revealed." The Baptist signers of this confession of faith indicate no hesitancy in accepting the words of Scripture as revelation from God. In fact, one cannot read the confession without becoming solidly convinced that this is the studied opinion of these Baptists. Revelation occurs in the words of Scripture as well as in the acts that are recorded there. The "truth of God" is revealed in Scripture.

OF THE HOLY SCRIPTURES

These implied assumptions about Scripture become explicit in the first chapter of the confession, entitled, "Of the Holy Scriptures." Consisting of ten paragraphs, this extended treatment of the doctrine of Scripture reflects the wording of the *Westminster Confession*. This article contains the clearest confessional statement on Scripture in all of Christendom. Philip Schaff calls it "the best Protestant counterpart of the Roman Catholic doctrine of the rule of faith" (*Creeds of Christendom*, 1:767). That such an article stands at the beginning of these confessions is strong testimony to the place accorded the Scripture by seventeenth-century Baptists and the Protestant denominations generally. The Reformation principle of *sola scriptura* means that Protestant doctrine stands or falls with the veracity of Scripture. Baptists did not differ from their seventeenth-century Protestant brothers in their view of the inspiration and the authority of Scripture. In fact, Baptists are even more explicit than the Westminster divines in their affirmation of Scripture as the only authoritative source of God's revealed truth. This significant article is reprinted below.

———

Chap. I.

Of the Holy Scriptures.

I. The Holy Scripture is the only sufficient, certain, and infallible[1] rule of all saving Knowledge, Faith, and Obedience; Although the[2] light of Nature, and the works of Creation and Providence do so far manifest the goodness, wisdom and power of God, as to leave men unexcusable; yet are they not sufficient to give that knowledge of God and His will, which is necessary unto Salvation.[3] Therefore it pleased the Lord at sundry times, and in divers manners, to reveal himself, and to declare that His will unto his Church; and afterward for the better preserving, and propagating of the Truth, and for the more sure Establishment and Comfort of the Church against the cor-

[1] 2 Tim. 3. 15, 16, 17. Isa. 8.20. Luk. 16. 2), 31. Eph. 2.20.
[2] Rom. 1. 19, 20, 21 etc. ch. 2 14, 15. Psal. 19.1, 2, 3.
[3] Heb. 1.1.

ruption of the flesh, and the malice of Satan, and of the World, to commit the same wholly unto[4] writing; which maketh the Holy Scriptures to be most necessary, those former ways of Gods revealing his will unto his people being now ceased.

2. Under the Name of Holy Scripture, or the Word of God written; are now contained all the Books of the Old and New Testament, which are these,

[4]Pro. 22. 19, 20, 21. Rom. 15. 4. 2 Pet. 1. 19, 20

Of the Old Testament.

Genesis, Exodus, Leviticus, Numbers, Deuteronomy, Joshua, Judges, Ruth, 1 Samuel, 2 Samuel, 1 Kings, 2 Kings, 1 Chronicles, 2 Chronicles, Ezra, Nehemiah, Esther, Job, Psalms, Proverbs, Ecclesiastes, The Song of Songs, Isaiah, Jeremiah, Lamentations, Ezekiel, Daniel, Hosea, Joel, Amos, Obadiah, Jonah, Micah, Nahum, Habakkuk, Zephaniah, Haggai, Zechariah, Malachi.

Of the New Testament.

Matthew, Mark, Luke, John, The Acts of the Apostles, Pauls Epistle to the Romans, 1 Corinthians, 2 Corinthians, Galatians, Ephesians, Philippians, Colossians, 1 Thessalonians, 2 Thessalonians, 1 Timothy, 2 Timothy, to Titus, to Philemon, the Epistle to the Hebrews, the Epistle of James, The first and second Epistles of Peter, The first, second, and third Epistles of John, the Epistle of Jude, the Revelation. All which are given by the[5] inspiration of God, to be the rule of Faith and Life.

[5]2 Tim. 3. 16.

3. The Books commonly called Apocrypha not being of[6] Divine inspiration, are no part of the Canon (or rule) of the Scripture, and therefore are of no authority to the Church of God, nor to be any otherwise approved or made use of, then other humane writings.

[6]Luk. 24. 27, 44. Rom. 3.2.

4. The Authority of the Holy Scripture for which it ought to be believed dependeth not upon the testimony of any man, or Church; but wholly upon[7] God (who is truth it self) the Author thereof; therefore it is to be received, because it is the Word of God.

[7]2 Pet. 1. 19, 20, 21. 2 Tim. 3. 16. 2 Thes. 2. 13. 1 Joh. 5.19.

5. We may be moved and induced by the testimony of the Church of God, to an high and reverent esteem of the Holy Scriptures; and the heavenliness of the matter, the efficacy of the Doctrine, and the Majesty of the stile, the consent of all the parts, the scope of the whole (which is to give all glory to God) the full discovery it makes of the only way of mans salvation, and many other incompar-

able Excellencies, and intire perfections thereof, are arguments whereby it doth abundantly evidence it self to be the Word of God; yet, notwithstanding; our[8] full perswasion, and assurance of the infallible truth, and divine authority thereof, is from the inward work of the Holy Spirit, bearing witness by and with the Word in our Hearts.

[8]Joh. 16. 13, 14. 1 Cor. 2. 10, 11, 12. 1 Joh. 2 2, 20, 27.

6. The whole Councel of God concerning all things[9] necessary for his own Glory, Mans Salvation, Faith and Life, is either expressely set down or necessarily contained in the *Holy Scripture;* unto which nothing at any time is to be added, whether by new Revelation of the *Spirit,* or traditions of men.

[9]2 Tim. 3.15, 16, 17. Gal. 1. 8, 9.

Nevertheless we acknowledge the[10] inward illumination of the spirit of God, to be necessary for the saving understanding of such things as are revealed in the Word, and that there are some circumstances concerning the worship of God, and government of the Church common to humane actions and societies; which are to be[11] ordered by the light of nature, and Christian prudence according to the general rules of the Word, which are always to be observed.

[10]John 6. 45. 1 Cor. 2.9, 10, 11, 12.

[11]1 Cor. 11. 13, 14. & ch. 14. 26 & 40.

7. All things in Scripture are not alike[12] plain in themselves, nor alike clear unto all; yet those things which are necessary to be known, believed, and observed for Salvation, are so[13] clearly propounded, and opened in some place of Scripture or other, that not only the learned, but the unlearned, in a due use of ordinary means, may attain to a sufficient understanding of them.

[12]2 Pet. 3. 16.

[13]Ps. 19.7. and 119.

8. The Old Testament in[14] *Hebrew,* (which was the Native language of the people of God of old) and the New Testament in *Greek,* (which at the time of the writing of it was most generally known to the Nations) being immediately inspired by God, and by his singular care and Providence kept pure in all Ages, are therefore[15] authentical; so as in all controversies of Religion, the Church is finally to appeal unto them[16]. But because these original tongues are not known to all the people of God, who have a right unto, and interest in the scriptures, and are commanded in the fear of God to read[17] and search them, therefore they are to be translated into the vulgar language of every Nation, unto which they[18] come, that the Word of God dwelling[19] plentifully in all, they may worship him in an acceptable manner, and through patience and comfort of the Scriptures may have hope.

[14]Rom. 3.2.

[15]Isa. 8.20.

[16]Act. 15.15.

[17]John 5.39.

[18]1 Cor. 14.6, 9, 11, 12, 24, 28. [19]Col. 3. 16.

9. The infallible rule of interpretation of Scripture is

the[20] Scripture it self: And therefore when there is a question about the true and full sense of any Scripture (which is not manifold but one) it must be searched by other places that speak more clearly.

10. The supream judge by which all controversies of Religion are to be determined, and all Decrees of Councels, opinions of antient Writers, Doctrines of men, and private Spirits, are to be examined, and in whose sentence we are to rest, can be no other but the Holy Scripture delivered by the Spirit, into which[21] Scripture so delivered, our faith is finally resolved.

[20] 2 Pet. 1. 20, 21. Act. 15. 15, 16.

[21] Mat. 22. 29, 31. Eph. 2.20. Acts. 28.23.

EXPOSITION OF THE CHAPTER

Baptists, completely in line with their independent spirit, began the section on Scripture, and thus the entire confession, by adding a sentence not contained in the *Westminster Confession of Faith:*

> The Holy Scripture is the only sufficient, certain, and infallible rule of all saving Knowledge, Faith, and Obedience.

Several well-chosen words qualify "rule" in this sentence. Scripture is this rule; therefore, these adjectives describe Holy Scripture directly. The concepts conveyed by these words are expanded in different places of the article itself.

"ONLY"

"Only" excludes all other sources of religious authority. Several specific alternative sources of authority are alluded to in the article.

Contemporary direct revelations from the Holy Spirit are rejected because "those former ways of God's revealing his will unto his people [have] now ceased" (paragraph one). Paragraph six directly denies the acceptability of claims of present revelation from God. "Nothing at any time is to be added . . . by new Revelation of the Spirit."

One schismatic Christian group in the early days of the church, the Montanists, moved beyond the claims of the Bible in several of their teachings. Their failure to relate the work of the Spirit properly to the work of Christ led them to proclaim the superiority of the present age of the Spirit over the former time of the incarnation. This failure to evaluate properly the uniqueness of the time of the incarnation and the apostolic age prompted them to profess and seek direct revelations from the Spirit.

Various radical groups during the sixteenth and seventeenth centuries claimed direct revelations from the Holy Spirit. On the Continent, some of the radical Anabaptists justified political anarchy by a claim of direct revelation from the Spirit. In England, the Quakers were causing disturbance and justifying odd conduct by their appeal to the work of God through their "inner light." Baptists firmly rejected the equality with Scripture of any other supposed revelation.

"Only" is also used to exclude human tradition. Paragraph six expressly rejects the "traditions of men" as a source of authoritative knowledge of God and His will. Roman Catholics had canonized tradition at the Council of Trent in 1546. Advocating the principle of *sola scriptura,* the Reformers began to shear the tradition from the church by means of the instrument sharper than a two-edged sword. Roman Catholic orthodoxy found its superstructure being challenged at its very foundations. Therefore, to bolster the Roman Catholic Church's sagging doctrinal constructions the Council of Trent stated that the "written books, and the unwritten traditions" were received either by the apostles from the mouth of Christ Himself or from the dictation of the Holy Spirit. God is not only the author of the Old and New Testaments (including the Apocrypha) but also the author of the unwritten traditions. The Roman Catholic Church claimed to have preserved purity of doctrine because of its continuous existence since Peter. The Baptist *Second London Confession* insists, in opposition to this, that the traditions of men are unacceptable, for God has committed His revelation "wholly unto writing" (paragraph one).

The books of the Apocrypha are also rejected by this confession. Paragraph three has as it target the canon accepted by Roman Catholicism. Textual support for the doctrine of purgatory rests in 1 Maccabees. Acceptance of the Apocrypha was therefore important for Roman Catholicism. Protestants rejected that development and reasserted the more historically valid position. The Apocrypha is not authoritative.

"Sufficient"

The *Second London Confession* recognizes that God reveals Himself in ways other than in Scripture. However, those other ways are not equal to Scripture or sufficient for salvation. One way God reveals Himself is identified by the phrase "light of Nature" (paragraph one). The reference is not to a static kind of natural theology but to a "sense of the divine" actively planted by God in the hearts of men. This sense of the divine has remained even after the Fall, although in a defaced form. By common grace God maintains it in each person's life.

The "light of nature" appears three other times in the confession. In paragraph six of this first chapter, the light of nature serves to order "some circumstances concerning the worship of God and government of the Church common to humane actions and societies." However, chapter twenty-two is more specific in stating:

the light of nature shews that there is a God, who hath Lordship . . . and is therefore to be feared. . . . But the acceptable way of Worshipping the true God is . . . so limited by his own revealed will, that he may not be worshipped according to . . . any other way, not prescribed in the Holy Scriptures.

Chapter ten, paragraph four, concerning effectual calling, states:

Men that receive not the Christian Religion [cannot] be saved; be they never so diligent to frame their lives according to the light of nature, and the law of that Religion they do profess.

As it appears in paragraph one of chapter one, the light of nature provides knowledge enough to "leave men unexcusable"; but, in agreement with the statement in chapter ten, it is not "sufficient to give that knowledge of God and His will, which is necessary unto Salvation." However, the knowledge found in Scripture is sufficient to accomplish God's purpose.

Another way God has revealed Himself is in the "works of Creation and Providence" (paragraph one). Separate articles appear on both of these subjects later in the confession. Chapter four is devoted to creation. The first of the three paragraphs in the article states:

In the beginning it pleased God the Father, Son, and Holy Spirit, for the manifestation of the glory of his eternal power, wisdom and goodness to create.

The purpose of creation was to reveal the glory of God's character. The creation continues to fulfill God's intention. It does this simply by being available for empirical investigation. Nature also fulfills God's intention in an active way by responding to the personal God. This natural response from man's perspective is a miracle, a wonder, or a sign.

Providence is expounded in chapter five. The present activity of God in the life of His creation is especially highlighted in this section.

GOD, the good Creator of all things, in his infinite power, and wisdom, doth uphold, direct, dispose, and govern all Creatures, and things, from the greatest even to the least, by his most wise and holy providence, to the end for the which they were created; according unto his infallible foreknowledge, and the free and immutable Councel of his own will; to the praise of the glory of his wisdom, power, justice, infinite goodness and mercy.

God's work in providence, therefore, as well as in creation, magnifies His power, wisdom, and goodness. Yet, because of man's Fall (chapter six), resulting in dullness of mind and rebelliousness of life, the works of creation and providence do not in fact lead a man to submit to God. Creation and providence are sufficient only to condemn man for rejecting what is evident about God. "They are not sufficient to give that knowledge of

God and His will which is necessary unto Salvation." More explicit guidance is needed.

Thus, the light of nature and the works of creation and providence cooperate to reveal the character of God. Man is enabled to respond to the revelation of God's word in his works because of the revelation of the word of God already within man's mind. But more was needed because of the insufficiency of these for man's salvation.

Special revelation occurred, therefore, out of God's concern for man's salvation. God revealed Himself through history in many ways and at different times and declared His will to His church. To preserve the truth better and propagate it more surely, to establish and comfort the church more completely, God was pleased to "commit the same [the revelation] wholly unto writing." Therefore, the written Scriptures are necessary, because they are the only sufficient source of revelation leading to salvation; "those former ways of God's revealing his will unto his people being now ceased."

Further direct confirmation of this confession's affirmation of the sufficiency of the Scripture is found in paragraph six:

> the whole Councel of God concerning all things necessary for his own Glory, Man's Salvation, Faith and Life, is either expressly set down or necessarily contained in the *Holy Scripture.*

The "whole Counsel" refers to a body of information that includes all God cares for us to know about Him. God's glory is the preeminent subject. Holy Scripture honors God; it exalts His character. God shines through every page as the one worthy of worship and adoration. The perfection of who God is provides part of the content of Scripture.

Second to God's glory is man's salvation. The plan of redemption and man's place in it find in Scripture as full an exposition as God intends to give. When someone comprehends all that Scripture says about salvation, he comprehends all that God says about it.

After salvation, belief and practice, called "faith" and "life," necessarily follow. Faith in this context does not refer simply to the act of receiving Christ. The entire scope of what man believes is in question—his entire world view. The reaction to, evaluation of, and involvement in every aspect of thought should be molded by direct scriptural statements or necessary principles derived from Scripture. The Christian's view of history, science, art, music, education, as well as theology is affected by his faith.

"Life" refers to the Christian's manner of living. How people should actually practice loving God and their neighbor is either expressly stated or clearly implied in Scripture. One needs to look no further for knowledge about God, nor should anyone seek Him in any other place. Scripture is marvelously adequate, for it contains "the whole counsel of God concerning all things necessary. . . ."

Another evidence of the sufficiency of Scripture is derived from the doctrine of the clarity of Scripture. As Peter affirmed concerning Paul's letters (2 Peter 3:16), the writers of the *Second London Confession* stated that "all things in Scripture are not alike plain in themselves, nor alike clear unto all." However, the central message of salvation is so predominant and so clearly laid out in Scripture that any person "in a due use of ordinary means, may attain to a sufficient understanding of them."

Again, Roman Catholicism held a different view of the clarity of Scripture. No one was at liberty, relying on his own skill, to interpret the Bible contrary to that sense which the church held to be correct. The Council of Trent had declared that judgment concerning the true sense and interpretation of Scripture is the exclusive obligation and privilege of the church. Interpretation of Scripture was so laden with allegory and tradition that the common man could only be bewildered by an attempt to understand it. Its message was hidden to him. He merely should obey the church, for the church had created the Scripture. Personal faith, as popularly conceived, consisted of obedience to the church by participation in the sacraments. Understanding by the individual was not necessary, for the sacraments were believed to be the means by which God automatically bestowed His grace. The power of the Word had been replaced in Roman Catholic theology by the efficacy of the sacraments.

However, Baptists based salvation upon some degree of comprehension. The New Testament doctrine of justification by faith implies the necessity of a positive personal response to the truth of the Good News. Positive response implies some degree of perception. Therefore, each man must understand the central message of Scripture for himself in order to make his personal response to God. The affirmation of the sufficiency of Scripture implies an affirmation of the clarity of the essential message of the Bible. This confidence also promotes translation of Scripture into "the vulgar language of every nation" (paragraph eight). The plowboy and the professor of philosophy both have a right and an obligation to read the Scriptures and search them that they may worship God in an acceptable manner. Every man, not just the theologian, is able to understand the central message of Scripture and receive comfort and hope from it.

The principle of interpretation espoused by the *Second London Confession* is known as the analogy of faith; that is, Scripture interprets Scripture. Paragraph nine states:

> The infallible rule of interpretation of Scripture is the Scripture itself: and therefore when there is a question about the true and full sense of

any Scripture (which is not manifold but one) it must be searched by other places that speak more clearly.

Roman Catholicism, with its allegorical method, often found three-, four-, or even sevenfold meanings in a single scriptural text. According to the confession, however, that method is fallacious. Any passage of Scripture has only one real meaning. An underlying assumption of this principle is that Scripture contains no real contradictions. The teaching of Scripture on any subject is characterized by unity and consistency, and Scripture thus stands as an infallible interpreter of itself. This interaction of Scripture with itself crystallizes its sufficiency.

Sufficiency should not be identified with exhaustive knowledge. The Baptists who signed the *Second London Confession* did not live under the illusion that they had God in their hip pockets. On the contrary, God is described as "infinite in being, and perfection, whose Essence cannot be comprehended by any but himself." The majesty and holiness of God are protected with some of the most exalted and noble words of the English language. Maintaining God's majesty, however, did not involve rejecting the truthfulness of what He revealed. Even though human comprehension is partial, it is nevertheless accurate; and in addition to being accurate, it is adequate. Therefore, "sufficiency" refers to noncomprehensive but accurate and adequate knowledge about God.

"CERTAIN"

The third term describing the Scripture is "certain." This word is used to mean "sure in its workings or results; dependable; also, unerring" (*Funk and Wagnall's Standard College Dictionary*, 1968). Those things declared in Scripture are found to occur or to have occurred exactly as represented. None of the statements of Scripture fails to represent reality accurately. This is the same idea that is properly conveyed by the word "inerrant" as it is used in scholarly evangelical discussions today. "Certain" refers only to the character of what is actually written. It affirms that nothing misleading or erroneous exists in Scripture.

"INFALLIBLE"

"Infallible" as a descriptive word was not used unadvisedly or ignorantly. The *Oxford English Dictionary* (O.E.D.) gives no less than seven cognates of the word. "Infallible" itself has more than six different uses, including adjectival, substantival, and verbal uses. Its root meaning is the same in all instances. Examples of its employment from the fifteenth through the nineteenth centuries are listed in *O.E.D.*, and its meaning through the centuries is consistent. The *O.E.D.* definition is:

> Exempt from liability to err; . . . unfailing certainty; . . . not liable to be
> deceived or mistaken; incapable of erring; . . . not liable to prove false,
> erroneous or mistaken; . . . most certainly, indubitably; unerringly.

Webster's Unabridged Twentieth Century Dictionary (1952) defines
"infallible" as "not capable of erring; entirely exempt from liability to mistake." The word has communicated essentially the same meaning for at
least five centuries, from the fifteenth through the twentieth. "Infallible"
is far stronger than "certain" or "unerring" in that it communicates a theoretical impossibility of committing error. A person may score 100% on
an exam in English. On that particular exam the person was "certain" or
"inerrant." However, that does not indicate that the person is incapable
of missing a question on an exam. Thus some writing could be certain
without being necessarily infallible. But infallibility, the inability to err,
does guarantee certainty. It is significant that this influential Baptist confession affirms both the certainty and the infallibility of Scripture.

In addition to its use in the introductory sentence, "infallible" occurs two
more times in the section on Scripture. In paragraph five the content of
Scripture is referred to as "infallible truth." Paragraph ten describes Scripture as "the infallible rule of interpretation" of itself.

There is no indication in this confession of faith that the Baptists har-
bored any reservations about the completely errorless nature of Scripture.
It was infallible truth to them—it was incapable of committing an error
or being deceitful. The reason for this is that they considered it to be the
Word of God. "It is to be received, because it is the Word of God" (paragraph four). They accepted Scripture as infallible truth, the Word of
God, because they believed it was inspired of God.

The method of inspiration is not discussed in this confession. The fact
and the result of inspiration are the focus of the description. Four phrases
are employed to emphasize the fact of inspiration. Paragraph two lists all
the books of the canon. Then it adds, "all of which are given by the inspiration of God." Paragraph four rests the authority of Holy Scripture
wholly upon God, who is "the author thereof." Paragraph eight affirms the
final authority in religious controversy to be the Old Testament in Hebrew
and the New Testament in Greek, for they are "immediately inspired by
God." In a similar vein, in paragraph ten Scripture is declared "supream
judge . . . in whose sentence we rest," for it is "delivered by the Spirit."
The Baptists who signed the confession left themselves no room to expur-
gate any portion of Scripture as misleading, incorrect, inconsistent, or representing an untrue viewpoint. To do so would be to doubt the Spirit's
knowledge of the mind of God or to impute a deceitful character to God.

Thus, although the method of inspiration is not discussed, the fact and the product of inspiration are strongly attested. Because Scripture is delivered by the Spirit and immediately inspired by God, Christians may place their confidence in it as infallible truth.

The article on Scripture in the *Second London Confession* is comprehensive in scope. Although geared to disarm the opposition in the immediate context, the theological content of the article is timeless in its application. Couched in ten paragraphs, four things are asserted about Scripture. Scripture is exclusive in its authority concerning man in his relationship to God and the world. Its content is sufficient, containing all God deemed necessary for men to know concerning doctrine and ethics, the Christian life, and God's historical revelation. It is certain—that is, errorless. Furthermore, Scripture is incapable of error—that is, it is infallible—because it is inspired by God. A progressive accumulation of strength is observable in the order of the words used. It is exclusive for it is the only; it is sufficient in its exclusiveness; it is certain in its sufficiency; and it is infallible in its certainty. Seventeenth-century Baptists put their complete trust in the Bible, God's Holy Word.

BIBLIOGRAPHY

Lumpkin, W. L. *Baptist Confessions of Faith*. Valley Forge, Pa.: Judson, 1959.
Schaff, Philip. *Creeds of Christendom*. 3 vols. New York: Harper, 1877.

CHAPTER FOUR

"The Waters Brought Forth Abundantly"

Although confessions of faith are valuable to the historian as portrayals of a denominational consensus during a certain period of time, they do not provide the luxury of feeling the warm breath or hearing the quick footsteps of individuals. Baptist ideology in the seventeenth century attracted an amazing variety of individuals and produced a startling richness of literary expression. Although eager to identify themselves with the theological orthodoxy of Protestantism, Baptists refused to be swallowed by the boredom of sameness in areas where Scripture allowed freedom.

The personalities examined in this chapter are indicative of the unity as well as the creative diversity of Baptist life during this period. Roger Williams, John Bunyan, and Benjamin Keach were personally convinced that the Baptist way was biblical. Each suffered severe repression because of his convictions. Each was innovative and creative. Williams developed a seemingly impregnable defense of liberty of conscience based on Calvinistic theology. Bunyan was the most successful allegorist of modern history and is one notable exception to the contention that Puritanism produced few works of art. Keach labored in the face of strong opposition to bring about positive changes in the practice of Baptist churches in England.

Williams, though personally in sympathy with the Baptists to the end of his days, remained in organic connection with a Baptist church for only three months. He believed that a true church existed only if it reproduced the New Testament pattern for a church and could connect its founding with the apostles by way of historical succession. The Baptists duplicated the New Testament pattern, Williams thought, but all true churches ceased to exist in the Middle Ages, and as a result, no church could find legitimate connection with the apostolic institution. Therefore, according to Williams, no true churches existed in Williams' day.

John Bunyan, though he was pastor of a Baptist church and was personally immersed as a believer, refused to make baptism an issue to exclude pious Christians from membership. Therefore, he maintained a church with open membership and drew censure from Baptists with a stricter ecclesiology.

Benjamin Keach disagreed with Bunyan and Williams. He advocated a stricter ecclesiology and rejected apostolic succession. In his catechism he defines the visible church as "the organized society of professing believers . . . wherein the gospel is truly preached and the ordinances of Baptism and the Lord's Supper rightly administered" (*Baptist Catechism*, p. 41).

Undergirding the diversity of these men is a unanimous agreement on the nature and authority of the Bible. This chapter will demonstrate that each was sure that what Scripture says, God says. All three would also agree with Williams in his affirmation of the importance of maintaining the truth, for all had paid the same price for its propagation.

> Having bought Truth deare, we must not sell it cheape, not the least graine of it for the whole World, no not for the saving of Soules, though our own most precious [*Writings*, 3:13].

ROGER WILLIAMS

Though he was a Baptist officially for only about three months, Roger Williams manifested the spirit of Baptists in his willingness to suffer for truth, his quest for liberty of conscience, his ideological defense of the separation of church and state, and his jealousy for the purity of the worship of God. The banner of "Baptist" flew above the heads of some of the most innovative and creative persons of the seventeenth century. Williams' intriguing odyssey adds to the richness of the Baptist potpourri.

Williams' birthdate, probably between 1603 and 1606, is uncertain because in 1666 a fire destroyed the records of St. Sepulchre Church, his baptismal spot. Through the influence of Sir Edward Coke, in 1621 he attended Sutton's Hospital (a charitable institution for the education of the young) and two years later enrolled in Pembroke College, Cambridge University, receiving his B.A. in 1627. Though he continued working at Cambridge, he did not receive a graduate degree. Apparently he discontinued his academic studies because of his changing theological position. Finding that he could no longer conscientiously stay within the Church of England, he left Cambridge and took a position as chaplain in the household of Sir William Masham, a staunch Puritan. Neither his friendship with Coke nor his Puritanism enhanced Williams' position in the eyes of William Laud, the rising power within the English church.

When Charles I ascended the throne of England in 1625, he initiated one of the most unreasonable and infamous reigns in the annals of Eng-

Fig. 3. Roger Williams
From Cathcart's *The Baptist Encyclopedia*, Evert's 1883. Frontispiece to vol. 1.

lish history. Laud quickly gained the favor of Charles and was responsible for an increasing amount of intolerance in matters of religion. Will Durant records the punishment inflicted in 1628 on the author of *Zion's Plea Against Prelacy*, Alexander Leighton:

> He was put in irons and was kept in solitary confinement for fifteen weeks in an unheated cell "full of rats and mice, and open to snow and rain." His hair fell out, his skin peeled off. He was tied to a stake and received thirty-six stripes with a heavy cord upon his naked back; he was placed in the pillory for two hours in November's frost and snow; he was branded in the face, had his nose slit and his ears cut off, and was condemned to life imprisonment [Durant, 7:189-90].

Soon thereafter Williams decided that England was no longer a safe place for one of his persuasion. In a letter to Mrs. Anne Sadleir, the daughter of Sir Edward Coke, Williams explains why he could remain no longer.

> It was as bitter as death to me when Bishop Laud pursued me out of this land, and my conscience was persuaded against the national church and ceremonies, and bishops, beyond the conscience of your dear father [*Writings*, 6:239].

Williams arrived in Boston on February 5, 1631. The people of the church immediately elected him to the position of teacher, but he rejected their call because they were an "unseparated people." He moved from there to Salem, Massachusetts, where he found that he was unwelcome. Correspondence from Boston warning the Salem church of Williams' tendencies had preceded him. He therefore went to Plymouth to live with the Pilgrims. While there, about two years, he "worked hard at the hoe" and spoke to the church on Sunday and sometimes on weekdays.

Eventually, Williams moved back to Salem and took an active part in the church, though he continued to support himself by farming. He had several disagreements with the Massachusetts Bay authorities during his years at Salem. Liberty of conscience and separation of church and state formed the basis of these disagreements, which ultimately resulted in Williams' banishment from the colony. In January of 1636, rather than be shipped back to England, Williams fled "to winter miseries in a howling Wilderness" because he had been denied "common aire to breath in, and a civill cohabitation upon the same common earth" (*Writings*, 1:319).

Williams, with the help of the Indians, eventually established residence in what is now Providence, Rhode Island. On March 16, 1639, John Winthrop, governor of Massachusetts Bay, recorded a significant event in his journal:

> At Providence things grew still worse; for a sister of Mrs. Hutchinson, the

wife of one Scott, being infected with Anabaptistry, and going last year to live at Providence, Mr. Williams was taken (or rather emboldened) by her to make open profession thereof, and accordingly was rebaptized by one Holyman, a poor man late of Salem. Then Mr. Williams rebaptized him and some ten more. They also denied the baptizing of infants, and would have no magistrates [Winthrop, 1:297].

By July of 1639, however, Williams, had denied the validity of his adult baptism. His reason was that it lacked apostolic authority. Williams had come to believe that the true church could no longer exist on earth since it had become antichrist during the Middle Ages. He did believe that the New-Testament church was a believer's church. Regenerate church membership and believer's baptism were both espoused by Williams. Their practice in this age was invalid, he said, because of the present condition of the church. However, he reaffirmed his basic Baptist convictions in 1649 in a letter to John Winthrop:

At Seekonk a great many have lately concurred with Mr. John Clarke and our Providence men about the point of a new Baptism, and the manner by dipping: and Mr. John Clarke hath been there lately (and Mr. Lucar) and hath dipped them. I believe their practice comes nearer the first practice of our great Founder Christ Jesus, than other practices of religion do, and yet I have not satisfaction neither in the authority by which it is done, nor in the manner [*Writings*, 6:188].

Debate exists concerning the meaning of the last phrase ("nor in the manner"), but it is clear that Williams' sympathies lay with Baptists, for he believed that their practice was nearer than other denominations to the practice of Christ. Had he not been captured by unnecessary views of apostolic succession, his ministry would likely have remained within the context of the Baptist churches. His views on most matters, however, can be taken as fairly representative of Baptist views in the seventeenth century. This is certainly true regarding his view of Scripture.

Williams' view of Scripture is expressed most thoroughly in his debate with the Quakers entitled *George Fox Digg'd out of His Burrowes*. While the Quakers sought to prove the superiority of the "light within," Williams contended that the external, written Word must have preeminent authority.

If one spends any significant amount of time with the *Complete Writings of Roger Williams*, he quickly discerns Williams' intent to be true to Scripture. He defends his views on liberty of conscience, and other matters, from a theology based upon sound biblical exegesis. He approaches his arguments from a biblical base because he believes that Scripture teaches the believer all that he needs to know about God and man. In his debate with the Quakers, Williams asserts that Scripture as opposed to personal revelations, is the judge of all things.

> I urged that this will of God (for this declaration of what Christ said and did, and of all the rest of the Scripture was a Declaration and Revelation of Gods Will to his People and to the whole World) this written and revealed will of God I said was the Judge and Decider of all Questions, the tryer of all Spirits, all Religions, all Churches, all Doctrines, all Opinions, all Actions [*Writings*, 5:140].

When the Quakers objected to Williams' comments and claimed that they used the Scripture in that manner, Williams accused them of calling their own "revilings, cursings, and abominations" the work of the Spirit and therefore Scripture. Again he emphasized the comprehensive authority of the Bible. It is the "square rule" that determines "all knowledge of God and of ourselves." All knowledge of how man should worship God and attain blessedness and salvation is in Scripture and even the Spirit within man is "tryed, determined, approved, and condemned" by Scripture (*Writings*, 5:140).

Williams' main principle of interpretation could be reduced to one concept—"genuine and proper Sense." Even his view of the relationship between the Old and New Testaments is best understood by this principle. For example, John Cotton, a Boston minister and an antagonist of Williams, interpreted the commandments of God to kings of Israel to be binding upon magistrates in the present. Civil officials should enforce attendance at the true church and punish all deviations from orthodox theology, according to Cotton. Williams saw the commandments to kings of Israel as no more than that. They were not commands to any magistrate of any other age—they were simply commandments to Israelite kings. The church is different from Israel, he said, and its commandments are in the New Testament. This interpretive method does not render the Old Testament less true, says Williams, it just enforces the "genuine and proper sense" of the Scriptures.

Williams upbraided the Jews, Roman Catholics, and Quakers for setting up their rabbis, popes, and inner light respectively as the only true interpreters of Scripture. According to Williams, each of those groups superimposes a "forraign and strange" interpretation upon various passages and forces "the holy Scriptures of God to attend and wait upon their Abomination as a Negro Slave and Lacquey" (*Writings*, 5:138).

Williams' method of interpretation allowed quite naturally for literary devices within Scripture. When hyperbole is used it should be interpreted as hyperbole, and when simile and metaphor are used they should be interpreted as such. The "genuine and proper sense" of Scripture could only be discerned through properly observing the rules that govern those devices. In fact, Williams refers to this as the "metaphorical sense" of Scripture.

> As to the Scriptures, the understanding of them is threefold.
>
> First, Literal: who understands not, Thou shalt not kill, Thou shalt not Steal? &c.
>
> The second is Metaphorical, as I am the Dore, I am the Bread, &c.
>
> The third is saving and Spiritual, when it pleaseth God to set home the heavenly Commands, Promises, &c. in particular, Soul Application [*Writings*, 5:387].

Only through study of the original languages can a Christian avail himself of the best way to ascertain the true and proper sense of Scripture. Williams thunders this point into the ears of the Quakers and any who disparage language study.

He maligns the Roman Catholics who set up the Latin Vulgate, "a most defective translation," in the stead of the "first copyes" of the Hebrew and Greek manuscripts. Williams contended that all translations should flow from the original languages, and that all Greek and Hebrew manuscripts should attempt to duplicate the original autographs. The science of textual criticism was not highly advanced in his day, but he seems aware of its existence and usefulness. Any group, like the Roman Catholics, that purposefully removed itself from the original sources invited doctrinal error, according to Williams.

The Quakers also, by removing themselves from the original languages, encountered severe reprimands from Williams. He charged them with the crime of unthankfulness and ingratitude and with "proud laziness" for not studying the original languages themselves. Williams also was not above more severe name-calling in this matter, for he called George Fox a "proud Ignoramus" and his followers "blind disciples." Not only did the Quakers reject the study of the original languages, they also claimed that the spirit within them was superior to the Scripture, and that "if the Scriptures were lost and burnt out of the world, the spirit within them could give new Scriptures" (*Writings*, 5:388, 139).

Williams claimed that we had only two options: follow the Quakers in their rantings or "with Luther and his Associates, Calvin and his followers maintain Learning" by studying the "originals, copyes, and translations" and vindicate their purity and perfection (*Writings*, 5:142).

Words of praise came forth from Williams for those who dedicated themselves to Bible study. Were it not for Tyndale and others who were serious language students and extended themselves to "dig out the knowledge of the Hebrew and the Greek and turn it into French, Dutch, [or] English" we would not even be able to discuss God or His creation. Williams exclaimed that he even knew some "very Eminent men and women, Independents and Baptists, [who] give themselves up to serious study of the Hebrew language" (*Writings*, 5:388).

Bishop Ridley, burned during Queen Mary's reign, "had got most of the holy Epistles in Greek by heart" and concentrated more on them as the days of persecution waxed hot. The study of Scripture in the Greek and Hebrew tongues "confounded and put to flight the Papists," said Williams. Furthermore, according to Williams, during the "42 months of papal reign and darkness" Jesus has given authority to his witnesses to "search after the Holy Records in the Original, Hebrew and Greek Copies, and to bring them forth by translating and preaching the Doctrine of them" (*Writings*, 5:145).

Williams placed such strong emphasis on the study of Greek and Hebrew because he believed in the verbal inspiration of the original writings. According to Williams the writers were "Pens of Heaven writing, and used by the hand of the holy Spirit" (*Writings*, 5:137). He also asserts that Scripture was written "and pen'd by chosen Pen-men as Pens in the hand of [the] Holy Spirit" (*Writings*, 5:141). He states that "every word, Syllable and Tittle in that Scripture or writing is the Word, or immediate revealed will of God" (*Writings*, 5:387).

Therefore, the languages should be learned, for they are the "tongues in which the most wise and most holy Lord pend his letters or writing to us" (*Writings*, 5:387). He likens the language to "golden cups and bowles" in which the King of Kings was pleased to convey the wine of his eternal majesty and goodness (*Writings*, 5:146).

Williams clearly believed that Scripture communicates saving knowledge of God, and that Scripture must sit in judgment on all our opinions. Its meaning is plain and is to be determined by the genuine and proper sense of the words and style. We best understand the sense of Scripture by dealing with it in the original languages. Study of the original languages is profitable, for "the most holy and Infallible Spirit" has inspired the very words of the originals.

JOHN BUNYAN

John Bunyan's baptism as an infant in the parish church of Elstow, near Bedford, England, was recorded on November 28, 1628. He was the first child born to Thomas Bunyan, a brazier, by his second wife. According to Bunyan, his youth was filled with swearing, playing various sports, and indulging in other amusements. Though his opponents accused him of sexual immorality, Bunyan denied that he had ever been immoral in

Fig. 4. JOHN BUNYAN

From *Puritan's Progress* by Monica Furlong. New York: Coward, McCann & Geoghegan, 1976. Used by permission of the Trustees of Bunyan Meeting, Bedford, England.

that way and claimed that "if all the fornicators and adulterers in England were hanged by the neck till they be dead, John Bunyan, the object of their envy, would still be alive and well" (*Grace*, p. 94).

In 1644 Bunyan became a soldier in the Parliamentary army and served until July of 1647. Divine providence spared Bunyan's life on at least one significant occasion when one man stood sentinel in Bunyan's stead and "was shot into the head with a musket bullet, and died" (*Grace*, p. 10).

After leaving the army, Bunyan "changed [his] condition into a married state" with a woman who was as poor as he was and had only *The Plain Man's Pathway to Heaven* and *The Practice of Piety* as an inheritance.

For a while Bunyan continued in his flippant ways until he received a sharp rebuke from a "very loose and ungodly wretch" who upbraided him for being "the ungodliest fellow for swearing that ever she heard in all her life." Bunyan sought personal reformation after that and sought to obey the commandments for his salvation. He stopped swearing, gave up bell ringing (after he had a terrifying premonition that a bell or even the steeple might fall on him), and eventually quit dancing. In his new life style he thought that no man in England "could please God better than I" (*Grace*, p. 15).

However, his conversion to Christ came as a result of his hearing a few poor women of Bedford speaking of the new birth, the work of God in their lives, the comfort they felt when God sustained them in the midst of Satan's attacks, and the abhorrence they felt in their own wretchedness of heart. This talk stayed with him for days and evidently culminated in what he considered to be his conversion.

In 1653, at about twenty-five years of age, he joined the congregation at Bedford under the ministry of John Gifford and was baptized by immersion in the river Ouse. Throughout the rest of his life Bunyan remained Baptist in his personal conviction though he did not espouse an exclusively Baptist ecclesiology. He continued to allow nonimmersed believers to hold membership in the Bedford church after he became its pastor in 1671. In fact, he had much controversy with several of the strict Baptists and in 1673 published his *Differences in Judgement About Water-Baptism No Bar to Communion*. He accepted believer's baptism by immersion as God's ordinance but refused to make "an idol of it."

Bunyan was imprisoned in 1660 for twelve years. He was imprisoned again in 1675 for six months. Both of those arrests issued from his refusal to quit preaching to gatherings of people when he had been forbidden by law to preach to them. He died in 1688 from a severe respiratory problem contracted while on a ministry of reconciliation to London.

His genius and literary accomplishments have been lauded for almost three hundred years by the most revered names in the world of literature.

Monica Furlong says in *Puritan's Progress* that Samuel Johnson, Alexander Pope, Jonathan Swift, William Cowper, Matthew Arnold, John Keats, Robert Browning, Charles Lamb, George Eliot, and Mark Twain all make reference to him and his work. In fact she claims that "he is paid perhaps the greatest compliment given to an author—otherwise reserved in England chiefly for Shakespeare and Dickens—that the characters and events of his masterpiece are known by name even by those who have never read his work" (p. 13).

John Bunyan dealt very little with the theory of Scripture. He showed much greater energy in speaking of the practical use of Scripture. However, certain basic assumptions supported the rich variety of ways he used the Bible, First, one should examine Bunyan's practical use of Scripture. Then one may seek to determine what theory provided the foundation for Bunyan's use of Scripture.

PRACTICE

Bunyan conceived the first function of Scripture as a convicting power. It acts as a law to condemn us and a mirror to show us our "miserable condition." His great allegory, *Pilgrim's Progress*, begins with the pitiable cry of a man under the deep weight of sin.

> I dreamed, and behold I saw a man cloathed with Raggs, standing in a certain place, with his face from his own House, a Book in his hand, and a great burden upon his back. I looked and saw him open the Book, and Read therein; and as he Read, he wept and trembled: and not being able longer to contain, he brake out with a lamentable cry; saying, what shall I do? [*Pilgrim's Progress*, p. 9].

Still in great distress the next day, the man fell into conversation with Evangelist, who asked him why he was crying.

> He answered, Sir, I perceive by the Book in my hand, that I am Condemned to die, and after that to come to Judgement; and I find that I am not willing to do the first, nor able to do the second [p. 10].

After crossing the Slough of Despond ("whither the scum and filth that attends conviction for sin doth continually run"), Christian meets and talks with Mr. Worldly-Wiseman. Christian describes to him the terror of the heavy burden upon his back and how he is seeking deliverance from the burden:

> World. How camest thou by thy burden at first?
> Chr. By reading this Book in my hand [p. 19].

Christian's experience was very much a parallel of Bunyan's own pil-

grimage. In *Grace Abounding to the Chief of Sinners,* Bunyan describes
a vision he had during a period of struggle perhaps early after his conversion. He saw a high mountain upon which there was light, warmth,
and happiness. Surrounding this mountain was a wall which had only a
small fissure that would allow passage. The mountain, to his mind, represented the church of the Living God. The light and warmth were the shining of God's merciful face upon those within the wall. The wall "was the
Word, that did make separation between the Christians and the world,"
and the fissure in the wall was Christ. The Word stood in judgment on all
those without and would not allow passage to the mountains except
through Christ.

Appended to *Grace Abounding* is Bunyan's *A Brief Account of the
Author's Call to the Work of the Ministry.* After some account of his call
to preach and his success in his calling, Bunyan describes his preaching
methodology.

> In any preaching of the Word, I took special notice of this one thing,
> namely, that the Lord did lead me to begin where his Word begins with
> sinners; that is, to condemn all flesh, and to open and allege that the curse
> of God, by the law, doth belong to and lay hold on all men as they come
> into the world, because of sin [*Grace,* p. 85].

It would be impossible to catalogue the immense conflict and trial
wrought within Bunyan by his grappling with individual passages of
Scripture. They stood as sentences of condemnation to him until he could
discern their proper interpretation and application and unite them with
the words of mercy and grace. Scripture points out sin to the Christian
as well as to the non-Christian and teaches us "the insufficiency of all inherent righteousness" (*Grace,* p. 102).

Bunyan was thankful that the Word's second function was as a word
of grace and forgiveness. This grace and forgiveness was communicated
through an explanation of the ministry of Christ. Bunyan professed to
have no valid experience of Christ apart from the ministry of Scripture
and distrusted any feeling or conclusion that could not be verified by Scripture. He did find Scriptures at variance with each other quite often, but
struggled with them, denying neither, until they harmonized in interpretation *and* experience.

For example, the word of grace concerning Christ's sacrifice for sin was
a cause for struggle in Bunyan's pilgrimage.

> I found, that unless guilt of conscience was taken off the right way, that
> is, by the blood of Christ, a man grew rather worse for the loss of his
> trouble of mind, than better . . . Wherefore (I should cry) Lord, let it not
> go off my heart, but the right way, but by the blood of Christ, and by the

application of thy mercy, through him, to my soul; for that scripture lay much upon me, "without shedding of blood is no remission." (Heb. ix. 22).

But that same word, under the preaching of "holy Mr. Gifford," became the source of great comfort to Bunyan. Gifford admonished his congregation not to trust the word of man or make unsound tests upon their souls, "but to cry mightily to God that he would convince us of the reality thereof . . . by his own Spirit, in the Holy Word" (*Grace*, p. 38). Bunyan took that admonition to heart: he began a chronological study through the gospels and found that Christ's ministry procured his forgiveness.

> Truly, I then found, upon this account, the great God was very good unto me; for, to my remembrance, there was not anything that I then cried unto God to make known and reveal unto me but he was pleased to do it for me; I mean not one part of the gospel of the Lord Jesus, but I was orderly led into it. Methought I saw with great evidence, from the relation of the four evangelists, the wonderful work of God, in giving Jesus Christ to save us, from his conception and birth even to his second coming to judgment. Methought I was as if I had seen him born, as if I had seen him grow up, as if I had seen him walk through this world, from the cradle to his cross; to which, also, when he came, I saw how gently he gave himself to be hanged and nailed on it for my sins and wicked doings. Also, as I was musing on this, his progress, that dropped on my spirit, He was ordained for the slaughter (I Pet. i. 19, 20).

> When I have considered also the truth of his resurrection, and have remembered that word, "Touch me not, Mary," etc., I have seen as if he leaped at the grave's mouth for joy that he was risen again, and had got the conquest over our dreadful foes (John xx. 17). I have also, in the spirit, seen him a man on the right hand of God the Father for me, and have seen the manner of his coming from heaven to judge the world with glory, and have been confirmed in these things by these scriptures following, Acts i. 9, 10; vii. 56; x. 42; Heb. vii. 24; viii. 3; Rev. i. 18; I Thess. iv. 17, 18 [*Grace*, pp. 38-39].

Bunyan allows his Pilgrim to gain this same assurance from Scripture. Christian, approached by his neighbors Obstinate and Pliable, seeks to convince them to make the trip with him. They ask where he is going and he replies:

> I seek an Inheritance, incorruptible, undefiled, and that fadeth not away: and it is laid up in Heaven, and fast there, to be bestowed at the time appointed, on them that diligently seek it [*Pilgrim's Progress*, p. 12].

As Pliable halts between the discouraging shrieks of Obstinate and his own desire to continue with Christian, the pilgrim encourages him by showing him the book. "If you believe not, read here in this book; and for the truth of what is exprest therein, behold all is confirmed by the blood of him that made it" (*Pilgrim's Progress*, p. 9).

The third use to which Bunyan put the Scripture was instruction. He held that the only true source of knowledge about God, Christ, our neighbor, and ourselves is the Bible. One person Christian met in his pilgrimage went by the name of Ignorance. Christian took it upon himself to relieve some of that characteristic in the man.

IGNOR. But my heart and life agree together, and therefore my hope is well grounded.

CHR. Who told thee that thy heart and life agree together?

IGNOR. My heart tells me so.

CHR. Ask my Fellow if I be a Thief: Thy heart tells thee so! Except the word of God beareth witness in this matter, other Testimony is of no value.

IGNOR. But is it not a good heart that has good thoughts? And is not that a good life that is according to God's Commandments?

CHR. Yes, that is a good heart that hath good thoughts, and that is a good life that is according to God's Commandments. But it is one thing indeed to have these, and another thing only to think so.

IGNOR. Pray what count you good thoughts, and a life according to God's Commandments?

CHR. There are good thoughts of divers kinds, some respecting ourselves, some God, some Christ, and some other things.

IGNOR. What be good thoughts respecting ourselves?

CHR. Such as agree with the Word of God.

IGNOR. When does our thoughts of ourselves agree with the Word of God?

CHR. When we pass the same Judgement upon our selves which the Word passes: To explain myself; the Word of God saith of persons in a natural condition, There is none Righteous, there is none that doth good. It saith also, That every imagination of the heart of man is only evil, and that continually. And again, The imagination of man's heart is evil from his Youth. Now then, when we think thus of our selves, having sense thereof, then are our thoughts good ones, because according to the Word of God.

IGNOR. I will never believe that my heart is thus bad.

CHR. Therefore thou never hadst one good thought concerning thyself in thy life. But let me go on: As the Word passeth a Judgement upon our HEART, so it passeth a Judgement upon our WAYS; and when our thoughts of our HEARTS and WAYS agree with the Judgement which the Word giveth of both, then are both good, because agreeing thereto.

IGNOR. Make out your meaning.

CHR. Why, the Word of God saith, That man's ways are crooked ways, not good, but perverse: It saith, They are naturally out of the good way, that they have not known it. Now when a man thus thinketh of his ways, I say when he doth sensibly, and with heart-humiliation thus think, then hath he good thoughts of his own ways, because his thoughts now agree with the judgement of the Word of God.

IGNOR. What are good thoughts concerning God?

CHR. Even (as I have said concerning ourselves) when our thoughts of God do agree with what the Word saith of him. And that is, when we think of his Being and Attributes as the Word hath taught [*Pilgrim's Progress*, pp. 142-44].

Bunyan tied himself to Scripture for his personal instruction. During one of his spiritual struggles he was troubled over the question of the person of Christ, "whether the Lord Jesus was both man as well as God, and God as well as man." He wrestled hard with that question, determined not to come to an answer "unless I had it with evidence from heaven." Eventually the "fifth of Revelations" came to his mind: "And I beheld, and lo, in the midst of the throne and of the four beasts, and in the midst of the elders, stood a Lamb" (*Grace*, p. 39).

In the midst of the throne, thought I, there is his Godhead; in the midst of the elders, there is his manhood; but oh! methought this did glisten! it was a goodly touch, and gave me sweet satisfaction. That other scripture also did help me much in this, "To us a child is born, unto us a son is given; and the government shall be upon his shoulder: and his name shall be called Wonderful, Counsellor, the mighty God, the everlasting Father, the Prince of Peace" [*Grace*, p. 39].

Bunyan's confrontation with the Quakers provided further opportunity for the instructional aspect of Scripture to strengthen his life. He claims that God led him into the Scripture, which "did wonderfully maintain" the truth. One essential error of the Quakers which Bunyan opposed was their teaching that "the holy Scriptures were not the Word of God." Other doctrinal points that he examined concerned the nature of the incarnation, the personality of the Holy Spirit, objective atonement, the resurrection of saints, the resurrection and ascension of Christ, and the second coming of Christ. In all of this Bunyan rejoiced that "I was driven to a more narrow search of the Scriptures, and was, through their light and testimony, not only enlightened, but greatly confirmed and comforted in the truth" (*Grace*, p. 40).

This instructional aspect finds specific expression in Bunyan's *Confession of Faith*. The Scriptures, in addition to making us wise unto salvation and making the man of God perfect in all things, are able to "instruct thee in all other things, that either respect the worship of God or thy walking before all men." He makes this further statement: "I believe the great end why God committed the scriptures to writing was; that we might be instructed to Christ, taught how to believe. . . ."

Finally, Bunyan sees Scripture as promise—its truths release the Christian from despondency and help him conquer temptation. The shift from conviction to comfort in the meaning of the Word for a Christian is depicted in striking imagery in one of the most beautiful passages in *Pilgrim's Progress*.

Bunyan describes how Pilgrim struggles on a highway lined by the wall called salvation:

> He ran thus till he came at a place somewhat ascending; and upon that place stood a Cross, and a little below in the bottom, a Sepulcher. So I saw in my Dream, that just as Christian came up with the Cross, his burden loosed from off his Shoulders, and fell from off his back; and began to tumble, and so continued to do, till it came to the mouth of the Sepulcher, where it fell in, and I saw it no more.

> Then was Christian glad and lightsom, and said with a merry heart, He hath given me rest, by his sorrow; and life, by his death. Then he stood still a while, to look and wonder; for it was very surprizing to him, that the sight of the Cross should thus ease him of his burden. He looked therefore, and looked again, even till the springs that were in his head sent the waters down his cheeks [*Pilgrim's Progress*, p. 40].

At that point three shining ones appeared who granted separate blessings to him. The first declared, "Thy sins be forgiven"; the second gave him a change of clothing; and the third set a mark on his forehead and gave him a roll with a seal on it, "which he bid him look on as he ran." This roll represents Scripture as promise and surety from God, a weapon to be wielded in the fight against those forces that would waylay the Christian.

Christian lost the roll as he slept at the bottom of Hill Difficulty and discovered his loss as he "felt in his bosom for his Roll, that he might read therein and be comforted." He ran back, greatly troubled, to the place he slept, and found the roll. "Who can tell how joyful this man was, when he had gotten his Roll again! For this Roll was the assurance of his life and acceptance at the desired Haven" (*Pilgrim's Progress*, p. 47).

The Bible is also a sword in the hand of the Christian. Bunyan's dream involving Apollyon, the prince and god of the City of Destruction who trys to slay Christian, presents a gripping picture of the power resident within Scripture as far as Bunyan was concerned. The monster was covered with scales like a fish, had wings like a dragon, and had feet like a bear; out of his belly came fire and smoke; and his mouth was like the mouth of a lion. Christian withstood his onslaught for half a day ("no man can imagine . . . what yelling, and hideous roaring Apollyon made all the time of the fight") and was on the verge of death, for he had lost his sword and Apollyon had leaped upon him.

> But as God would have it, while Apollyon was fetching of his last blow,
> . . . Christian nimbly reached out his hand for his Sword, and caught it
> [*Pilgrim's Progress,* p. 64].

Christian followed with several well-aimed slices at the fiendish Apollyon till the beast mounted up on his dragon's wings and flew away. Bunyan then remarked concerning Christian, "I never saw him all the while, give so much as one pleasant look, till he perceived he had wounded Apollyon with his two-edged Sword, then indeed he did smile, and look upward" (*Pilgrim's Progress,* p. 65).

Bunyan changes the image from sword to key in his picture of the Bible's power in the life of the Christian. Giant Despair captured Hopeful and Christian when they were asleep on the grounds of Doubting Castle. The Giant drove them into his castle where they were imprisoned for four days "without one bit of bread, or drop of drink, or any light, or any to ask how they did" (p. 112). Christian fell into great remorse and depression, and Hopeful sought to encourage him.

On Saturday night at midnight they began to pray, and a little before day Christian suddenly exclaimed, "What a fool . . . am I thus to lie in a stinking Dungeon, when I may as well walk at liberty! I have a Key in my bosom, called Promise, that will, I am persuaded, open any Lock in Doubting Castle" (p. 113). The two companions then opened every lock and escaped Doubting Castle and its lord, Giant Despair, and began walking again on the King's Highway toward the Celestial City.

If the reader protests that this is a poor literary device because it unfolds only with the aid of a deus ex machina, he is probably grasping Bunyan's meaning. Bunyan considered the promises of Scripture just that—God's entrance into our experience in the form of human words, faith in which delivers us from the prison-house of defeat and despair.

THEORY

All of the above practical uses of Scripture were effective, as far as Bunyan was concerned, because Scripture was both clear and true. Bunyan embraced this theory with great relish and unconditional confidence but exhibited a sense of responsibility in his application of these truths.

Clarity of Scripture for Bunyan did not mean that one could grasp its meaning through a casual and careless reading. On the contrary, Scripture would not open to those who handled it flippantly. Gaius reminds the reader of this as he tells Christiana and her children a poem in part two of

Pilgrim's Progress. He quoted it as they were passing around a dish of nuts.

> Hard Texts are Nuts (I will not call them cheaters),
> Whose shells do keep their kernels from the Eaters.
> Ope then the Shells, and you shall have the Meat,
> They here brought are for you to crack and Eat [*Pilgrim's Progress*, p. 275].

Matthew, Christiana's son, indicated earlier that he already knew that lesson well. At the Porter's House, Prudence had catechised all the children and happened to ask Matthew a question concerning Scripture.

> Prudence: What do you think of the Bible?
> Matthew: It is the Holy Word of God.
> Prudence: Is there nothing Written therein, but what you understand?
> Matthew: Yes, a great deal.
> Prudence: What do you do when you meet with such places therein, that you do not understand?
> Matthew: I think that God is wiser than I. I pray also that he will please to let me know all therein that he knows will be for my good [*Pilgrim's Progress*, p. 232].

Given this difficulty of understanding, in what sense did Bunyan conceive the Scriptures to be clear? First he believed that Scripture should be understood literally in the same way any literary piece should be understood. Those words and phrases that were intended to be understood in a normal, straightforward literal manner, "we understood them so; but for those that were to be understood otherwise, we endeavored so to understand them" (*Grace*, p. 109).

He was pushed into this method of interpreting by the overwhelming spiritual struggles that dominated much of his life. Early in these conflicts he was overcome by individual Scriptures divorced from their context coming in upon his mind and warring with each other, one giving him comfort and peace and the other torment and trouble. He even went so far on occasions as to wish those against him "out of the book." One day he thought, "Lord, if both these scriptures would meet in my heart at once, I wonder which of them would get the better of me." This occurred a few days later: "So they did indeed; they bolted both upon me at a time, and did work and struggle strangely in me for a while." This method of dealing with Scripture proved entirely too unstable and left Bunyan with no greater security. Therefore, during one of his periods of comfort, he took courage and decided "to come close" to the disquieting Scripture passages, "to read them, and consider them, and to weigh their scope and tendency" (*Grace*, p. 69). He then records how he systematically dealt with the words, context, historical situation, and audience addressed in the Scriptures considered. He also began to renew his study of the promises of Scripture and "with careful heart and watchful eye, with great seriousness, to turn over every leaf, . . . to consider every sentence, together with its natural force and latitude" (*Grace*, p. 77). He ceased relying on his emotions and began applying the promises of Scripture to his situation even before he *felt* the comfort of Scripture. He would "labour to take the Word as God had laid it down, without restraining the natural force of one syllable thereof." He began to consider that God had "a bigger mouth to speak with than [he] had heart to conceive with" (*Grace*, p. 77).

The method of interpretation that in Bunyan's opinion best served the interests of clarity was the analogy of faith, or the comparison of Scripture with Scripture. An opponent objected to Bunyan's appeal to Scripture on the ground that "you take the Scriptures one way, and they another." Bunyan answered that the Scripture will open itself if one passage is compared with another rightly.

On several occasions members of the established church confronted Bunyan with his supposed ignorance of Greek and insinuated that he could not know the Scriptures without such knowledge. Bunyan, however, believed that God had chosen the poor and foolish and rejected the wise, mighty, and noble of this world. And if the poor were to be saved, they could understand the Scripture without knowing Greek. On another occasion, Bunyan replied to the upbraiding of an arrogant critic who claimed that his Greek Testament was a true copy of the original, "So do I believe our English Bible to be a true copy of the original" (Philip, *The Life*, p. 587). These retorts by Bunyan should not be understood as deprecation of the Greek text. Rather they are judgments upon the haughtiness of those who would refuse to allow a man like himself to exercise his gift of preaching. Also, the answers serve as witnesses to Bunyan's confidence in the clarity of Scripture. Even the unlearned, under the guidance of the Spirit, with a tenacious mind and an English text can know God's truth.

The second part of Bunyan's theory simply asserts that Scripture is true—it cannot be broken. At bottom Scripture is true because, as he states in his *Confession of Faith*, "all the Holy Scriptures are the words of God." He couches this same conviction in the dialogue of Christian with Pliable. Pliable asked whether the words of the book were certainly true. Christian answered, "Yes, verily, for it was made by him that cannot lye" (*Pilgrim's Progress*, p. 14).

Even in the midst of his greatest struggles, Bunyan knew that the Bible, all the Bible, must stand. He desired to throw some Scriptures away, but the apostles appeared to him and said, " 'All our words are truth, one of as much force as another'. . . . I quaked at the apostles, I knew their words were true, and that they must stand for ever" (*Grace*, p. 66).

Perhaps Bunyan's confidence in the verity of Scripture is best attested in his discourse with the Clerk of Peace, Mr. Cobb, in April of 1661. Bunyan was in jail for violation of an old Elizabethan law newly enforced by Charles II. He was given abundant opportunity to conform and be released from prison but refused his freedom lest he give an example of compromise to those to whom he had been preaching. He could not cease preaching to assemblies without being disobedient to God's Word, which demanded that a man exercise his gift.

> Cobb: But, said he, how shall we know that you have received a gift?
> Bunyan: Said I, Let any man hear and search, and prove the doctrine by the Bible.
> Cobb: But will you be willing, said he, that two indifferent persons shall determine the case, and will you stand by their judgment?
> Bunyan: I said, Are they infallible?
> Cobb: He said, No.
> Bunyan: Then, said I, it is possible my judgment may be as good as theirs. But yet I will pass by either, and in this matter be judged by the Scriptures; I am sure that it is infallible, and cannot err [*Grace*, p. 122].

That is the crux of Bunyan's viewpoint. That is the reason Scripture consumed his life and filled his literature. That is the reason that conviction of sin, reception of Christ, knowledge of God, and comfortable assurance was impossible, in Bunyan's mind, without the written word of God. "It is infallible, and cannot err."

BENJAMIN KEACH

Benjamin Keach was born February 29, 1640, at Stoke Hammond, Buckinghamshire, England, and was baptized as an infant in the parish church on March 6. His parents, John and Fedora Keach, were poor and could give him little education but, somehow, bequeathed to him such unusual genius that he was superior to most and equal to any of the men of his time in strength of mind and application of knowledge.

Scripture study was an early passion of Keach's and led him at an early age to "suspect the validity of the baptism he had received in infancy" (Crosby, 4:2). He joined the General Baptists at age fifteen and was baptized by John Russell. The church was so impressed with Keach's knowledge of the Bible and spiritual sensitivity that, when he was eighteen, they called him to the work of the ministry. From that time forth, he preached.

In 1660 he married Jane Grove, "a woman of great piety and prudence," who bore him five children and died in 1670 at age thirty-one. He remained single for two years and then married a widow, Mrs. Susanna

Partridge. They had five daughters (two of them named Rachel) and lived together for thirty-two years before Keach died. Susanna survived him by twenty-three years.

Keach was seized and carried to jail in 1664 for preaching to a meeting of dissenters in Buckinghamshire. He was released after "suffering great hardships and trouble." He was soon arrested again when it was discovered that he was the author of a little book entitled *The Child's Instruction; or, a New Easie Primmer.*

The trial took place on October 8, 1664. Keach was accused of being a "seditious, heretical, and schismatical person" who did "maliciously and wickedly" have published a "seditious and venemous book" containing certain "damnable positions, contrary to the book of Common Prayer" (Crosby, 2:189).

The specific doctrines Keach affirmed that were considered heretical included believer's baptism and an understanding of the second coming in terms of a literal thousand-year reign upon the earth. The second doctrine was considered dangerous because it was similar to the viewpoint of a radical group called the Fifth Monarchy which was instigating political rebellion.

Despite some reticence on the part of the jury and a technical difficulty with the charge, Keach was found guilty (the judge browbeat the jury into the verdict). He was sentenced to jail for two weeks without bail and ordered to appear twice in the pillory—two hours each time—one appearance at Ailsbury and one at Winslow. He gave a strong witness to those who watched at his first pillory experience. All the copies of his book were burned before his face at the pillory in Winslow. A contemporary testified that Keach's punishment was "a more strict execution than ever he saw in town or country" (Crosby, 2:208).

In 1668 Keach became pastor of a church that met in a private house on Tooley Street in London. He was ordained with prayer and laying on of hands, the first non-Anglican ordination of record since Charles Stuart (Charles II) was restored to the throne of England in 1660. He remained pastor of that congregation until his death.

After he moved to London and gained more opportunity to study, he changed his theological position from General Baptist to Particular Baptist. He was constantly in the forefront of controversy either by defending the Baptist viewpoint on baptism or by taking part in polemical discussion within Baptist life.

His baptismal disputes were mainly with Richard Baxter and Mr. Burkit, rector of Malden in Suffolk. Others also joined the fray; but, according to Crosby, Keach managed to silence his opponents with dispatch.

He had made himself master of this controversy and kept close to the rules of disputation, and avoided all indecent expressions and personal calumnies and generally got the better of his antagonists [Crosby, 4:286].

Keach took an active part in controversies within Baptist life. One controversy concerned the propriety of the practice of laying on of hands at the admission of baptized persons into the church, a practice Keach defended.

Keach was also active, in fact a pioneer, in seeking "due maintenance to those that were employed in the ministry." Baptists had discouraged the idea of a paid clergy, but under Keach's prodding and perseverance they began to make progress in that area.

The practice of hymn singing in worship was another area in which Keach was innovative. "When he was convinced, that singing the praises of God was an holy ordinance of Jesus Christ, he laboured earnestly . . . to convince his people thereof" (Crosby, 4:298). The church eventually agreed to sing the praises of God on every Lord's day, thereby becoming the first Baptist church to practice that exercise of worship. However, Keach was not able to convince all the opponents of hymn singing of its holiness. Some used the unflattering nomenclature of "error, apostacy, human tradition, prelimited forms, mischievous error, carnal forms, and carnal worship" to describe Keach's practice.

Keach periodically debated any who held erroneous doctrine: those who denied the deity of Christ; Matthew Caffyn, who denied the true humanity of Christ; the Quakers; the seventh-day Baptists; and others. He was a prolific writer. No fewer than forty-three separate works of his were published, and he wrote the preface to several others. "He was no idle labourer in his master's vineyard" (Crosby, 4:310).

Keach's continual involvement in dispute should not be attributed solely to an inherently pugnacious spirit. Rather, his activities should be measured by his love for truth, as indicated by his early and independent rejection of infant baptism. Also, his desire for the basic unity of the Baptist cause are manifest in his efforts, along with six other ministers, to call the first general assembly of Particular Baptists in 1689. This assembly approved the *Second London Confession* of 1677 as representative of the theological position of their churches. Keach, at this time pastor of the Horse-lie-down Church (the church on Tooly Street had moved), was assigned the task of producing a catechism on this confession. Entitled *The Baptist Catechism,* it is commonly known as Keach's catechism.

Keach died on July 18, 1704. He had asked Mr. Stennet to preach his funeral sermon from these words: "I know whom I have believed, and am persuaded that he is able to keep that which I have committed unto him against that day" (2 Timothy 1:12).

Although the view of Scripture outlined in the *Second London Confession* sufficiently pictures Keach's personal view, present-day observers need not rest on that assumption. Keach published in 1682 a book entitled *Tropologia: A Key to Open Scripture Metaphors.* Prefixed to this work was a section called *Arguments to Prove the Divine Authority of the Holy Scriptures.* This book was republished by Kregel Publications in 1972 and has had at least two printings in this American edition. Quotations will come from a 1779 London edition.

Keach asserts that his reason for writing his defense of Scripture was not because of any lack of assent to its authority on the part of Christians. Rather he wrote it so that they might know the grounds of that assent, "the true formal reason thereof." He envisions the result of his discussion as a "perfect security to our present and future welfare" by eliciting a reliance on the Bible as "the infallible Storehouse of heavenly Verities" and the only revelation by which God "does inform, rule, and . . . judge the World." Keach believed that if Satan destroys the trust people have in the truth of God's Word "he at the same instant shakes the very foundation of all their hope and religion" (p. vii).

This is the statement Keach intends to defend: "The Scripture, or Book called the Bible, is of divine Original, inspired by the Spirit of God, and therefore of infallible Truth and Authority" (p. viii). He puts this same meaning into the *Baptist Catechism* of 1693 under the question "What is the word of God?"

> The Scriptures of the Old and New Testament, being given by divine inspiration, are the word of God, the only infallible rule of faith and practice.

He offers numerous reasons for such a position.

The contents of Scripture are of such a nature as to defy attributing them to human origin. The doctrines of the Trinity, the incarnation, the substitutionary death of Christ, and the covenant of grace "can be drawn from no other Fountain but Divine Revelation." Its concept of God's law and the comprehensive sweep of its view (past, present, future; heaven and hell; time and eternity) commend the book as having a divine origin. Its threatenings, miseries, and mysteries are of such sweep and grandeur that the reader must ponder "what less than infinite Wisdom can be the supposed Author of such a Book?" (*Tropologia*, p. viii).

The antiquity of the Scripture is evidence of its divine origin, gives evidence that it is the wisest and truest book in the world, and gives evidence that it proceeded from the God of truth," according to Keach. The majesty and authoritativeness of the Spirit of God speaking in it attest to its divinity. Of all the writings in the world, Scripture assumes most unto itself: it claims to be the words of eternal life, it claims to be the testimony of Jesus Christ, it claims to be given by inspiration of God, it claims to be immortal seed, and it holds the terror of "Thus saith the Lord." The Spirit of holiness which dominates the book from beginning to end precludes the possibility of the Bible's origin from the intrigue of polluted or even deluded men and invites the conclusion that the book is from God.

The agreement and harmony of every part of Scripture, though written by different men, from different places, and at different times, leads to the conclusion that the writers were "guided in what they wrote by the supreme Wisdom of that one God, who is always constant to himself." The character of the penmen, their antipathy to self-seeking, and their desire to glorify God are further evidence that the Scriptures are what they claim to be, "viz. the Word of God, dictated to the writers thereof by his Holy Spirit." The exact and punctual fulfilling of prophecy demonstrates that the Scriptures, "which are filled with so many evident and certain Predictions, must certainly proceed from the Finger of God" (pp. xii, xiii).

Also, the writings were confirmed by miracles. The miracles, recorded and attested by trustworthy persons, were performed often and openly and should serve to convince one that the words confirmed by the works are of God. Further, the miraculous preservation of Scripture, in spite of its antiquity and determined efforts on the part of its enemies to destroy it, is evidence that God in His providence assured its preservation. "Heaven and Earth shall pass away, but one Iota or Tittle of his Word shall not pass away." In addition to that, Keach asserted that Scripture not only survived but triumphed over "all the Oppositions of the Devil and the World." That a doctrine so contrary to human desires and espoused by such despised persons should subject so many nations to the obedience of the Cross "shews it to be owned by Omnipotency, and not to be of human Extract" (p. xxi). And not only has Scripture conquered nations, but it has also proved itself the master of men's hearts and consciences.

> Who can speak Words that shall restrain and repel all the Powers of Darkness, when falling to make Havock and Desolation in the Souls of men? That shall be able to give Laws to the Terrors of Death, nay eternal Death, when they have taken hold of the Consciences of Sinners? Are not all these Wonders performed by the holy Scriptures? And do they not often, on the other Side, breathe Thunder and Lightenings? throw down the Mighty from their Seats, and destroy the Thrones of the Proud and confident? Do they not turn the Security of many into Trembling and Horror, and make their consciences to burn as if the Fire of Hell had already taken hold of them? . . . And when should such mighty Operations proceed, but because the almighty Author has endued them with such Virtue through the Spirit, whereby they become the Power of God unto Salvation [p. xvi].

Keach also claims that there is great power and credibility in the testimony of the church in all ages. The universal church from the beginning until his time (the seventeenth century) believed the Christian religion to be divine and "doth also profess that these Books are of God." In fact the testimony has been so consistent, Keach claims, that "whoever rejects the Bible, obliges himself to believe no other Books in the World whatsoever," for no other book has such abundant and reliable attestation of its trustworthiness. For a person to reject testimony with such strong foundations and yet receive a book with less reliable witness brings that person's motivation into question and shows "peevish obstinacy." However, if one does credit the biblical authors with common honesty—that is, if one would trust them to be men who would not knowingly write an untruth—then he cannot refuse to receive the Bible as a book that is divine and infallible, for the writers affirm "that God himself inspired them to write it, and that it was no product of their own, but every part of it the genuine Dictate of the Holy Ghost" (p. xvii).

Attestation of the Bible's infallibility in matters of fact, according to Keach, comes in overflowing supply from its enemies. Such events as creation, the long lives of the patriarchs, the Flood, the existence of Noah, Sodom's destruction, Moses, the Bethlehem star, Herod's slaughter of the infants, and the darkness at noon at the time of the crucifixion are corroborated by secular and pagan historians of the respective times.

Keach further reasons that if a man disowns the Bible to be of divine authority, either he thinks that divine revelation exists somewhere else or he thinks that there is none. If he thinks that there is no divine revelation, he "gives the lie . . . to all Religion" and makes man the most miserable of all creatures, because he alone is unable to fulfill the highest relationship for which he has potential. If he asserts that there is another revelation, let him produce it and compare it with the Bible "for all those glorious Characters and Marks of divine Authority, Power, and Excellency, which we have enumerated" (pp. xxiii, xix).

Another strong argument Keach advances is a syllogism, the major premise of which he believes to be self-evident. He proves the minor premise by using reductio ad absurdum. If formalized, the argument would appear this way:

> The Scriptures are from God or from the devils or from men.
> The Scriptures are not from devils or men.
> Therefore, the Scriptures are from God.

Devils could not have written it, for that would mean Satan was dividing his own kingdom by viciously opposing himself and warning men against himself. If from men, they must be either good men or bad men. Good men would never claim the inspiration of God falsely or hold out such lofty hopes and expectations without foundation. Bad men would never espouse the cause of God and holiness so ardently and villify their own practices in such unmistakable terms. Therefore neither devils nor men are the source of Scripture. Therefore, God is the source of Scripture.

Near the end of *Arguments*, Keach seeks to answer five objections to the doctrine of infallibility. Here are the first four: How were these writings distinguished as infallible in their respective ages? How do we know our canon is complete? Can we trust the integrity of the Hebrew and Greek manuscripts we possess? If only the originals are inspired, what benefit comes from studying a translation? Keach's answer to this fourth question is especially instructive.

> The Word of God is the Doctrine and Revelation of God's Will, the Sense and Meaning, not barely or strictly the Words, Letters, and Syllables. This is contained exactly and most purely in the Originals, and in all Translations, so far as they agree therewith. Now though some translations may exceed others in Propriety, and significant rendering the Originals; yet they generally, (even the most imperfect that we know of,) express and hold forth so much of the Mind, Will, and Counsel of God, as is sufficient, by the Blessing of God upon a conscientious Reading thereof, to acquaint a Man with the Mysteries of Salvation, to work in him a true Faith, and bring him to live godly, righteously, and soberly in this World, and to Salvation in the next [p. xxi].

The fifth objection concerned apparent contradictions in Scripture. Keach gave one example of how so-called contradictions were capable of being harmonized and how they served to demonstrate that there was no corrupt confederacy on the part of men in the writing of the Bible, but that a deep and uncontrived concord existed and "an unanimous tendency towards the great End of the Whole" (p. xxi).

Keach's final argument admits that in spite of the great force of the external arguments "to evince the divine Authority of Scripture," only the internal testimony of the Spirit can create stability and assurance of faith. He states the case succinctly in the *Baptist Catechism*, question five.

> Question 5. How do we know that the Bible is the Word of God?

> Answer. The Bible evidences itself to be God's Word by the heavenliness of its doctrine, the unity of its parts, its power to convert sinners and edify saints; but the Spirit of God only, bearing witness by and with the Scriptures in our hearts, is able fully to persuade us that the Bible is the Word of God.

Fig. 5. BENJAMIN KEACH
From Cathcart's *The Baptist Encyclopedia*, Everts, 1883. 1:637.

BIBLIOGRAPHY

Roger Williams

Durant, Will, and Durant, Ariel. *The Story of Civilization.* New York: Simon & Schuster, 1935-1975. Vol. 7, *The Age of Reason Begins.* 1961.

Williams, Roger. *The Complete Writings of Roger Williams.* 7 vols. New York: Russell & Russell, 1963.

Winthrop, John. *History of New England 1630-1649.* Edited by James Kendall Hosmer. 2 vols. New York: Scribner's, 1908.

John Bunyan

Bunyan, John. *Grace Abounding to the Chief of Sinners and the Life and Death of Mr. Badman.* London: J. M. Dent and Sons, [c. 1910-19].

———. *The Pilgrim's Progress.* London: Constable & Co., 1926.

Furlong, Monica. *Puritan's Progress.* New York: Conard, McCann & Geoghegan, 1975.

Philip, Robert. *The Life, Times, and Characteristics of John Bunyan.* Cincinnati: Moore, Wilstack and Baldwin, 1867.

Benjamin Keach

Crosby, Thomas. *The History of the English Baptists.* 4 vols. London: Printed for the editor, 1738.

Keach, Benjamin. *The Baptist Catechism.* 1693. Reprint of 1794 ed. Grand Rapids: Baker, 1952.

———. *Tropologia; A Key to Open Scripture Metaphors to which are prefixed Arguments to prove the Divine Authority of the Holy Bible.* London: Printed by J. W. Pasham, for William Otridge, 1779.

Fig. 6. JOHN GILL

From Cathcart's *The Baptist Encyclopedia*, Everts, 1883. 1:453.

CHAPTER FIVE

"Be Fruitful, and Multiply"

When William and Mary issued the *Act of Toleration* in 1689, removing many of the burdens and repressive measures from the backs of dissenting groups, one would think that, of all people, Baptists would have flourished. The moment for which they had fought and suffered had arrived. Having developed a strong ideology of liberty of conscience and the necessity of an uncoerced response to the gospel, they could now act upon those beliefs with a degree of freedom. However, the period immediately following 1689, instead of manifesting intense evangelical activity, was characterized by extreme dryness in religion in all of England.

Deism, Socinianism, rationalism in general, and a theology that refused to affirm important distinctives sapped the strength of many of the denominations. The General Baptists were especially affected by Socinianism, a type of Unitarianism. Particular Baptists were rendered ineffective by antinomianism (a rejection of the dutiful observance of the moral law on the part of the Christian) and hyper-Calvinism (which is characterized by refusal to offer invitations for people to receive Christ).

In spite of the extraordinary dullness of the religious vigor, Baptists managed to produce several outstanding leaders during this time. John Gill, blamed by some as the cause of the Particular Baptists' problems, was one of the most brilliant theologians of the age. Andrew Fuller, possessing a broad and loving spirit and a vigorous, uncompromising mind, provided one human stimulus leading to revival among the Particular Baptists. The two men were, however, completely unified in their view of Scripture.

JOHN GILL

According to the respected Baptist historian Thomas Armitage, the deepest impression upon eighteenth-century Baptists in England was made by John Gill of Northamptonshire. John Rippon, the writer of Gill's *Memoir* and his successor in the pastorate, called Gill "one of the greatest and best of men." He was born in 1697. Nineteen years later he gave testimony to his rebirth by submitting to believer's baptism. A few years later

Gill became a Baptist minister at the age of twenty-three. He continued as pastor of one London church for over fifty years, until his death in 1771.

Gill's first movement toward spiritual life took place when he was twelve years old. Mr. William Wallis, pastor of the church in which Edward Gill, John's father, was a deacon, preached a sermon on Genesis 3:9. "And the LORD God called unto Adam, and said unto him, Where art thou?" That text continued to press questions into Gill's mind: "What a wretched state and condition art thou in? How miserable wilt thou be, living and dying in an unconverted state?" (Rippon, p. 6).

As his depravity and sinfulness weighed on his conscience, he also became aware of the free offer of the righteousness of Christ. "And as those sublime truths came to him, not in word only, but in power, and also in the Holy Ghost, and in much assurance, he felt himself free from the bondage of the law . . . and was filled with joy and peace in believing." His public profession and baptism were delayed, however, "by consideration of his youth," until he was almost nineteen years of age (p. 7).

On Thursday, November 1, 1716, Gill made his public profession of faith. The same day, Thomas Wallis baptized him "by immersion in a river, according to the command of Christ and the practice of his apostles, in the name of the Father, and of the Son, and of the Holy Ghost" (p. 8).

On Sunday, November 4, he was received as a member of the church and took the Lord's Supper. That evening, in a meeting at a private home, he read and preached from Isaiah 53. The next Sunday evening he preached again, this time from 1 Corinthians 2:2, "For I determined not to know any thing among you, save Jesus Christ, and him crucified."

In 1718, while teaching young converts in a newly established church, Gill met Elizabeth Negus, a member of the new church, whom he later married. During their forty-six years together they had "many children, all of whom died in their infancy except three" (Rippon, p. 10).

He moved to London in 1719, after a brief period of preaching at Kettering, and "by a very great majority" was called as pastor of the Horse-lie-down Church, Fair Street, Southwark. Benjamin Stinton and Benjamin Keach were the immediate predecessors of Gill as pastor. He remained here until his death, on October 14, 1771.

Gill's friends perceived very early in his life that he had unusual abilities and sought in vain to secure admission for him to one of the universities. Unable to enter a university, he studied under private tutors and became a superior scholar in Latin, Greek, and logic. Through long years of personal study, he also mastered rabbinical Hebrew and became well acquainted with the Targums, Talmud, and other ancient Hebrew writings. Rippon claims that Gill learned Hebrew "without any living assistance, by the help of Buxtorf's Grammar and Lexicon" (p. 5).

As a result of his extensive learning in Hebrew and his then-recent *Exposition of the Whole New Testament* he was awarded a Doctor of Divinity degree in 1748 by Marischal College, Aberdeen. Professor Osborn of the university wrote Gill a letter stating that "on account of the honest and learned defence of the true sense of the Holy Scriptures against the profane attacks of Deists and Infidels" as well as for the scholarship indicated in all his works and the reputation those works procured for him in the scholarly world, "as soon as it was moved in the University to confer the degree of Doctor in Divinity on him, it was readily agreed unto."

When his deacons congratulated him upon the accomplishment of such an honor, he thanked them and added, "I neither thought it, nor bought it, nor sought it" (Rippon, p. 59).

After Gill's death, his intimate friend Augustus Toplady remarked concerning Gill's astuteness:

> If any man can be supposed to have trod the whole circle of human learning, it was Dr. Gill. . . . It would, perhaps, try the constitutions of half the *literati* in England, only to read with care and attention the whole of what he wrote. As deeply as human sagacity enlightened by grace could penetrate, he went to the bottom of everything he engaged in [Rippon, p. 137].

Included among his many volumes of important works are, *The Doctrine of the Trinity Stated and Vindicated; The Cause of God and Truth; An Exposition of the New Testament; Exposition of the Old Testament; A Dissertation on the Antiquity of the Hebrew Language; A Body of Doctrinal Divinity;* and *A Body of Practical Divinity.* Some of them were written simply in Gill's leisure time for his recreation. However, each of them represented his stand for true Christianity and his opposition to infidelity, deism, and inadequate expressions of Christian faith.

Many persons in the generation following Gill did not hold him in quite the esteem his contemporaries did. On a certain occasion Robert Hall and Christmas Evans, a great Welsh preacher, were discussing the fullness and richness of the Welsh language. Evans exclaimed that he wished the words of John Gill had been written in Welsh. To this Hall answered, "I wish they had, sir; I wish they had, with all my heart, sir, for then I should never have read them! They are a continent of mud, sir!" John Fawcett, Hall's contemporary, was criticized by some members of his congregation for not dealing thoroughly enough with some points of predestination. His defense of his ministry took the form of a poem which ended with this couplet:

> To be brief, my dear friends, you may say what you will,
> I'll ne'er be confined to read nothing but Gill.

Doubtless some of the negative reaction to Gill, because he was of such strong opinion, is quite predictable. However, the fact that his name invited such direct and distinct reaction is evidence that his influence was widespread and that many were thoroughly familiar with his work and thought.

Supralapsarianism is the belief that God predestined some to be saved (election) and some to be damned (reprobation) before He created anything. Thus, the sin of man and the Fall were also decreed by God as the means by which He could accomplish the actual saving or damning of men. Armitage records that Gill was "so high a supralapsarian" that he could not invite sinners to receive the Savior. He could preach their guilt and condemnation and their need for new birth. He could preach that Christ died a substitutionary death and rose from the dead. But he held it to be an imposition on the divine prerogative to invite men to Christ. According to Armitage, "under this preaching his church steadily declined, and after half a century's work he left but a mere handful" (Armitage, p. 561).

H. C. Vedder, a competent Baptist historian of the early twentieth century, joins the anti-Gill clamor by asserting that Gill's supralapsarian Calvinistic doctrine served to nullify the Great Commission. Vedder exclaims: "What wonder that a spiritual dry rot spread among the English churches where such doctrines obtained! Could any other result be reasonably expected as the fruits of such a theology?" (Vedder, p. 241).

On the other hand, John Rippon, Gill's successor at Horse-lie-down and his biographer, does not attribute the stagnant condition of Baptists at this time to the influence of Gill's hyper-Calvinism. Gill "never beseiged an error, which he did not force from its strong holds; nor ever encounter an adversary, whom he did not baffle and subdue." His learning and labors were exceeded only by the sanctity of his life as "himself, no less than his writings, demonstrated, that the Doctrine of Grace does not lead to licentiousness." Rippon adds that Gill was "burning with love to God, to Truth, and to Souls." Indeed, if Rippon suspected that the name of John Gill would experience such opposition, he would never admit that such was deserved.

> His Doctrinal and Practical Writings will live, and be admired, and be a standing blessing to posterity, when their opposers are forgotten, or only remembered by the refutations he has given them. While true Religion, and sound Learning have a single friend remaining in the British Empire, the works and name of Gill will be precious and revered [Rippon, p. 140].

After Gill became pastor of the Horse-lie-down church in 1720 he wrote a confession of faith to which each member of the church verbalized assent before each Lord's Supper. The first article of this confession is a very simple and reduced statement of Gill's (and the Baptists') view of Scripture. "We believe that the Scriptures of the Old and New Testament are the word of God, and the only rule of faith and practice." Just how much Gill intended from these few words may be seen by studying his extended exposition of the doctrine of Scripture in his major theological works.

Chapter one of Gill's *Body of Divinity* is an exposition of the being of God: "For if there is no God, religion is a vain thing; and it matters not neither what we believe, nor what we do" (p. 1).

All his early arguments except one proceed upon bases not directly related to Scripture because they merely seek to give strong evidence *that* God is, not *what* God is. However, before proceeding to write about the "essence, perfections, persons, works, and worship and everything relative to him," Gill determines to prove the divine authority of Scripture, because everything to be said about God's nature "will be taken out of the Sacred Scriptures, and proved by them" (p. 11).

His discussion is divided into four major headings: first, the divine authority of Scripture; second, the perfection, or complete adequacy, of Scripture; third, the clarity, or perspicuity of Scripture; and fourth, the necessity of revelation, and especially written revelation, from God.

Under his treatment of the divine authority of Scripture, Gill places two headings: "Prior Considerations" and "Proof of Divine Authority." One prior consideration concerns the meaning of the term the "Word" of God. It does not mean that God necessarily spoke in an articulate voice or wrote with His own fingers, though on occasion He did exactly that. Rather, Scripture is the Word of God because the penmen wrote as they were "directed, dictated and inspired by him" (p. 12). They wrote as they were moved by the Holy Spirit. They did not write out of their own hearts or according to their own will, but according to God's direction.

Second, the interpreter should recognize that many words in Scripture are not directly God's words but are from mistaken men or even from Satan. However, the context makes these situations clear; some examples are speeches of Satan, bad advice from Job's friends, speeches of Pharaoh, Cain, and so forth. They are given by divine authority to show the corruption of human nature and are included in Scripture by God's direction although they are not His teachings. A similar approach will explain the presence of quotations from pagans in Scripture.

Third, "let it be observed, that not the matter of the Scriptures only, but the very words in which they are written are of God." He rejects the contention that only general ideas that could be clothed with the words and style of the writer were given. If that is the case, he contends, "then we should be left at an uncertainty about the real sense of the Holy Spirit, if not led into a wrong one" (pp. 12-13). God is entirely able to direct the use of words that are consonant both with His exact meaning and the genius and circumstances of the writer. In fact, it was recognition of the time-bound nature of some idioms that provoked Gill to his massive study of the Old Hebrew literature.

> He plainly saw, that as the New Testament was written by men who had all of them been Jews, and who, notwithstanding their being inspired, must needs retain and use many of the idioms of their language, and allude to rites, ceremonies, and customs peculiar to that people; so the writings of the Jews, especially the more ancient ones, who lived nearest the times of the apostles, could not but be of use for the better understanding the phraseology of the New Testament, and the rites and customs to which it frequently alludes. With this settled opinion, he set about reading their Targums, the Misnah, the Talmuds, the Rabbot, their ancient Commentaries, the book of Zohar and whatever else, of this kind, he could obtain [Rippon, p. 58].

The fourth prior consideration asserts that only the Scriptures in their original languages, the "original exemplar," are to be considered given by inspiration of God. Every translation is to be brought to the original and by it to be examined, tried, judged, corrected, and amended.

> And if this was not the case, we should have no certain and infallible rule to go by; for it must be either all the translations together, or some one of them; not all of them, because they agree not in all things: not one; for then the contest would be between one nation and another which it should be, whether English, Dutch, French [*Body of Divinity*, p. 13].

Gill continues by pointing out the absurdity of the Roman Catholic adoption of the Latin Vulgate, which "abounds with innumerable errors and mistakes," as superior to the original itself. On the other hand, he provides consolation for those who are able to use only translations. They are made by men highly skilled in the language, pious, and reverent in their esteem for the Word. Therefore, "no momentous article of faith or practice" has been affected by any inadequacies of the translations.

After those considerations, Gill proceeds to his "Proof" of the divine authority of the Scriptures. He gives eight basic proofs of their divinity which are very similar to Benjamin Keach's defense of the divine origin of Scripture.

First, Gill contends that the subject matter is evidence that the Scriptures are from God. Nothing in them is unworthy of God or contrary to His purity. "There is no falsehood nor contradiction in them." In fact, Gill makes the strong claim in this section that "the holy Spirit dictated them, holy men spoke and wrote them, and they are justly called Holy Scriptures" (p. 14). Things naturally unknowable to man (that is, creation and prophecy of the future) and things above reason (that is, the Trinity of persons in the Godhead) all are part of the contents of the Bible and provide evidence that it is from God.

Second, the style and manner, the majesty and authoritativeness, would be daring and presumptuous were Scripture not the word of God.

Third, the writers themselves provide evidence for the divine origin of Scripture. They were men of little education whose writings far exceed what one might normally expect of such men. Both chronological and geographical space separated them and yet they all speak the same sentiment, truths, and doctrine, which shows that "they were dictated and influenced in all by the same Spirit of God" (p. 16). These men were plain and honest, holy and good, and disinterested, not seeking the applause of men or worldly wealth.

A fourth argument is drawn from the effect that the writings have had on the hearts and lives of men. Many have been converted from error, superstition, idolatry, and a "vicious course of life" to embrace the truth simply from reading the Scriptures or hearing them explained.

Fifth, the miracles bear testimony to the divine origin of Scripture.

Sixth, the hatred and opposition of men to the scriptural teachings is no inconsiderable testimony to their supernatural origin.

Seventh, Gill contends that "the awful judgments of God on such who have despised them, and have endeavoured to destroy them are no mean evidence that they are of God." As an example he cites Antiochus Epiphanes, who cut to pieces the book of the Law. Because of this, says Gill, he died of a "violent disorder in his bowels, his body was covered with worms, his flesh flaked off, and was attended with an intolerable stench" (p. 17).

Eighth, the antiquity and continuance of these writings favor the view affirming their divine genesis.

Next, Gill discusses the perfection of Scripture. By *perfection* Gill does not mean that everything God is or has done is written in Scripture. God is more and has done more. Nor does Gill mean that everything Christ and His apostles said and did are contained there. Gill does claim that all things necessary to salvation, everything that must be believed and done, is contained in them. Again, eight reasons are listed in support of this claim. Because God is the true author of the Scriptures, they are free from imperfection (or incompleteness). Because both parts are "testaments," they must contain the whole of God's will and pleasure toward us. If "the law of the LORD is perfect" (Psalm 19:7), how much more could that claim be made of the fuller and clearer teachings of the prophets and apostles? The parts of Scripture, Law and gospel, are per-

fect in their explication of man's duty to God and neighbor and their exposition of Christ's perfect atonement, perfect forgiveness, and complete
righteousness and freedom. The Old Testament was complete in the time
of Christ, as He himself testifies (Matthew 5:18; Luke 16:17; 24:27), and
no one can prove that the same perfection is not true of the New Testament. Also, the perfection of Scripture may be argued from its sufficiency
to answer the ends for which it is written—for doctrine, for reproof, for cor-
rection, and for instruction in righteousness. Ultimately, the perfection of
Scripture is seen in that it makes us wise unto salvation. Indeed, the Scriptures were written for this end: that men "might believe that Jesus is the
Christ, the Son of God; and that believing [they] might have life through
his name" (John 20:31).

Gill's third purpose is to prove the perspicuity (clarity) of the Scriptures. Because they are the rule of faith and practice, they should be plain.
The problem is that all scriptural passages are not equally clear and plain.
In fact, some passages are actually dark and obscure to men's minds.
However, by comparing spiritual things with spiritual, letting clear passages interpret those less clear, they all may be plainly understood. In
addition, neither learned nor unlearned men can understand the Word
apart from the Spirit of God, "the dictator of them" (p. 21).

Nevertheless, the perspicuity of Scripture may be affirmed, because God
is the Father of lights and all that comes from Him is light and clear. The
Scriptures compare themselves to a light, a lamp, and a glass, and its ministers are light to the world. All sorts of people—men, women, children,
strangers, rich, and poor—are exhorted to read them. Were they not plain
and clear, no purpose could be seen in attending to them. Because they
are thus clear and plain, they are a "sure, certain, and infallible rule . . .
yea, must be reckoned infallible, since they are the Scriptures of truth,
and not only contain what is truth, and nothing but truth in them: but
have a true, even a divine testimony bore unto them, and come from the
God of truth, who cannot lie" (p. 22).

The fourth and last area with which Gill deals concerns the real necessity of such a divinely given, infallible rule of faith in the present state of
things. Divine revelation was necessary for Adam even in an unfallen condition (how else would he have known his manner of creation or his
Creator?) and is certainly necessary for fallen men like ourselves. Also
reason itself (even if unfallen) is incapable of constructing the truth about
God, for many of His attributes are above, though not contrary to, reason.
Reason alone can be neither an infallible guide nor a competent, final judge
in such matters.

We may know that God exists by the evidence of nature, but who and
what God is comes only by revelation. Nature teaches us that God is to

be worshiped, but knowledge of how to worship Him comes only by revelation. We know that our response to Him is inadequate, but understanding of our real condition comes from revelation. We know that we should appease Him, but only revelation gives us knowledge of the perfect sacrifice. Knowledge of God's willingness to forgive and how He forgives comes only by revelation. We learn about the Son of God and the nature of His atonement by revelation. We may long for an eternal blissful state, but only revelation sheds light on the resurrection of the body, the immortality of the individual person, and the future state of happiness.

> Let us therefore bless God that we have a better rule and guide to go by; "a more sure word of prophecy to take heed unto:" let us have constant recourse unto it, as the standard of faith and practice and try every doctrine and practice by it, and believe and act as that directs us, and fetch everything from it that may be for our good, and the glory of God [p. 25].

John Gill believed that Scripture is infallible. The Bible itself asserts, he said, that it has no untruth in it. Its very words in the autographs are inspired by the God of truth Himself. Gill does not even shrink from calling the writers penmen and asserting that the Holy Spirit "dictated" (i.e., directed) what they should write, though at the same time he was well aware of the different styles of each human author and the time-bound nature of some idioms. The statement from his 1720 confession that "the Scriptures of the Old and New Testaments are the word of God, and the only rule of faith and practice" was no meaningless platitude to him. It was his joyful affirmation of his total allegiance to that which is absolutely binding on all human thought and action.

Andrew Fuller

Andrew Fuller was born in a village in Cambridgeshire, England, on February 6, 1754. His father, with whom Fuller worked until 1773, was a farmer and died in 1781 at fifty-eight years of age. On the other hand, his mother, Philippa, survived Andrew and died when she was ninety-three or ninety-four. She was a woman of "excellent Christian character" and was the dominant Christian influence on all her children, including two sons in addition to Andrew.

The family attended a Baptist church where Mr. Eve was minister. Fuller described him as a high Calvinist who had "little or nothing to say to the unconverted" and whose preaching "was not adapted to waken my conscience." Fuller read *Grace Abounding to the Chief of Sinners* and *Pilgrim's Progress* by John Bunyan but responded more deeply to *A Gospel Catechism for Young Christians: or Christ All in All in Our Complete Redemption* by Ralph Erskine. Fuller records, "I read, and as I read I wept" (Ryland, pp. 7-9).

Fig. 7. ANDREW FULLER
From Cathcart's *The Baptist Encyclopedia*, Everts, 1883. 1:421.

His tears gave way to "pursuits of folly" followed by great conflicts of mind. He describes his adolescent years in much the same fashion as Bunyan and seems to have been especially fond of swearing, lying, and gambling. However, in November of 1769 the extremity of his unregenerate condition bolted upon him in graphic dimensions.

> The reproaches of a guilty conscience seemed like the gnawing worm of hell. I thought, 'Surely that must be an earnest of hell itself!' The fire and brimstone of the bottomless pit seemed to burn within my bosom. I do not write in the language of exaggeration. I now know that the sense which I then had of the evil of sin, and the wrath of God, was very far short of the truth; but yet it seemed more than I was able to sustain. In reflecting upon my broken vows, I saw that there was no truth in me. I saw that God would be perfectly just in sending me to hell, and that to hell I must go, unless I were saved of mere grace, and as it were in spite of myself. I felt, that if God were to forgive me all my past sins, I should again destroy my soul, and that, in less than a day's time. I never before knew what it was to feel myself an odious, lost sinner, standing in need of both pardon and purification [Ryland, p. 12].

He struggled for some time with these crushing thoughts. Finally he cast himself on the Lord Jesus Christ for salvation "to be both pardoned and purified . . . ; and as the eye of the mind was more and more fixed upon him, my guilt and fears were gradually and insensibly removed" (Ryland, pp. 13-14).

Fuller was baptized in April, 1770 (the example of two young ladies encouraged him in this), and became active in the church at Soham, where Mr. Eve was pastor. During that year, he had his first confrontation with one of the major theological errors of the time, antinomianism (a disregard for God's law as the proper and authoritative guide for the life of a Christian). One of the members of the church had been guilty of drinking alcohol to excess. Fuller went and talked with him and the man responded that he had no power to keep himself from such activity. This excuse enraged Fuller, and he went and told Pastor Eve. The drunkard was dismissed from the church, but an ongoing discussion was taken up in the church concerning "the power of sinful men to do the will of God, and to keep themselves from sin." This discussion resulted in the departure of Mr. Eve, who found himself in disagreement with the majority of the church on the ability of a man to do outward acts in obedience to the law of God. Fuller was greatly agitated over this question but found help from reading John Gill's *Cause of God and Truth* on the difference between natural and moral inability to obey God's law.

Soon after Eve's departure, Fuller began reading the Scripture in worship and commenting on it. In January of 1774 the church set him aside to the ministry. He was publicly ordained in May, 1775, and remained as pastor until 1782, when he went to the Baptist church in Kettering.

His deepening acquaintance with the problem of antinomianism led Fuller into dialogue with another theological position known as hyper-Calvinism. In reading Bunyan and Gill, he noticed that although they seemingly held the same theology, Bunyan advocated a free offer of salvation to sinners without distinction, whereas Gill offered no such invitation. Bunyan's attempt to hold the doctrine of God's unconditional election of individuals to salvation and the doctrine of limited atonement (the conviction that Christ's atoning death was limited in that it was only for those elected to salvation) together with the free offer of salvation to all men (both elect and nonelect) was extremely intriguing to Fuller's creative mind. He made such substantial progress in his understanding of these doctrines that in 1785 he published his conclusions in a book entitled *The Gospel Worthy of All Acceptation.* Fuller's main point in this writing is that it is the duty of all men (whether they are among the elect or not) to repent and believe the gospel. Therefore, those duties must be pressed upon all men by preachers of the gospel. All men are perverse and totally depraved. All men flee from God, and they are, therefore, justly condemned for refusing to do what God requires. That God in mercy elects some and makes provision for them does not lessen the obligation of all to believe.

> There is no contradiction between this peculiarity of design in the death of Christ, and a universal obligation on those who hear the gospel to believe in him, or a universal invitation being addressed to them. If God, through the death of his Son, have promised salvation to all who comply with the gospel; and if there be no natural impossibility as to a compliance, nor any obstruction but that which arises from aversion of heart; exhortations and invitations to believe and be saved are consistent and our duty, as preachers of the Gospel, is to administer them, without any more regard to particular redemption than to election; both being secret things, which belong to the Lord our God, and which, however they be a rule to him, are none to us [*Works*, 2:374].

Fuller's break with high, or "false" as he called it, Calvinism provoked some twenty years of controversy among Particular Baptists. Their strong belief in election had for years kept the Particular Baptists from recognizing their duty to evangelize the world. If God wanted the heathen to be saved, they argued, He would so elect them to be saved; and if God did that, they would all be saved without any help from the Baptists. The controversy begun by Fuller proved to be highly instrumental in the development of the modern foreign-mission movement. The Particular Baptist Foreign Mission Society was formed in 1792 in the home of one of his church members. Fuller was appointed secretary of the society and continued as such until his death in May of 1815. His work as secretary was accomplished in the midst of extremely trying domestic difficulties, duties as pastor of a large church, and a large writing ministry.

W. T. Whitley (writing in 1923) considered Fuller's contribution to Baptist life of his century to be positive and highly significant. He pointed to Fuller as a model for Baptists.

> Fuller thus was able to unite the doctrinal strength that has ever characterized Calvinists, with the evangelistic fervour that had shone forth in Smyth. . . . He stands as a fine type of the Baptist for the nineteenth century and in this period as the ablest theologian yet produced, though Gill's *Body of Doctrinal Divinity* did find publishers till 1815 [Whitley, p. 232].

Fuller did not confine his interests only to the internal concerns of the church as they related to hyper-Calvinism and antinomianism. He was also aware that enemies from outside the church were potentially dangerous and should not go unchallenged. Specific external attacks upon Christian truth were being mounted by Deism (the belief that God is exclusively transcendent, this world having been created to run by itself) and Socinianism (among other things, denial of the Trinity, denial of the total depravity of man, affirmation that man can be saved by imitating the good works of Jesus, and affirmation that the Bible is to be judged by human reason). Their attacks were never to him "a cause of a moment's uneasiness." For if Christianity be of God, one need not be anxious, for the "safety of the vessel which contains his Lord and Master" (*The Gospel*, p. xi). But though truth has nothing to fear, it does not follow that its friends should be inactive.

Deism, particularly of the Thomas Paine variety, was at the peak of its influence during the ministry of Andrew Fuller. Therefore, Fuller aimed his apologetic cannons at this ideology and managed to dismantle it rather handily. Fuller believed that "the controversies between believers and unbelievers are confined to a narrower ground than those of professed believers with one another." Because he intended to focus his attention on "the internal evidence which Christianity possesses, particularly in respect of its holy nature, and divine harmony," his book *The Gospel Its Own Witness* has two parts: the first compares the holy nature of the Christian religion with the immorality of Deism; the second affirms the internal consistency of Christianity and is essentially a discussion of the truth of Scripture.

> If the Scriptures can be proved to harmonize with historic fact, with truth, with themselves, and with sober reason; they must, considering what they profess, be divinely inspired, and Christianity must be of God [*The Gospel*, p. 179].

Fuller's first line of argument concerns the harmony of Scripture with historic fact, specifically in the case of predictive prophecy. He quotes in part several passages of predictive prophecy from Old and New Testament books. These prophecies range from Cyrus's invasion of Judah in Isaiah to the fall of the harlot in Revelation. In each case Fuller cites the fulfillment of the prophecy if it had already occurred (especially those surrounding the appearance and ministry of the Messiah) and asks historians who recorded those events, "Was this a falsehood?"

> Mr. Paine says the scripture prophecies are "a book of falsehoods." Let us examine this charge. Isaiah, above a hundred years before the Captivity, predicted the destruction of the Babylonish empire by the Medes and Persians, and Judah's consequent deliverance. The plunderer is plundered, and the destroyer is destroyed: Go up, O Elam; beseige O Media: all the crying thereof have I made to cease. Ask Herodotus and Xenophon; Was this a falsehood? [pp. 184-85].

The section on the truth of prophecy closes with sober reminders to the Deists that the same book that has proven consistently true in its prophecies, the Bible, also assures a coming judgment on the unbeliever.

> Again, there shall be mockers in the last time, who shall walk after their own ungodly lusts; filthy dreamers, who defile the flesh, despise dominion, and speak evil of dignities; raging waves of the sea, foaming out their own shame; wandering stars, to whom is reserved the blackness of darkness for ever. Let Mr. Paine, and other infidels consider well the above picture, and ask their own consciences, Is this a falsehood? [pp. 195-96].

The second chapter in this section of *The Gospel Its Own Witness* demonstrates the harmony between Scripture and the dictates of an enlightened conscience. The function of Scripture as an instrument of reproof is Fuller's primary consideration here. Scripture does not seek to flatter but goes directly to a man's conscience and shows him what manner of man he is. It serves as a mirror in which one sees himself. The reader knows that the reflection is truer than his uninformed concepts of himself. Like the woman at the well, we exclaim, "Come, see a man, which told me all things that ever I did: is not this the Christ?" (John 4:29).

> Read it but seriously, and your heart will answer to its descriptions. It will touch the secret springs of sensibility, and if you have any ingenuousness of mind towards God, the tears of grief, mingled with those of hope and gratitude, will, ere you are aware, trickle from your eyes [p. 198].

Not only do we see the truth about ourselves in Scripture, but also a true picture of the depravity of human society is painted in the pages of the Bible. The Bible even prepares its readers to expect the idolatry, prac-

tical atheism, and corruptions of Christianity that have become common-
place in the world. Neither are the persecutions in the least surprising to
the one who has heard and believed the words of Jesus. The wars that
have desolated the earth, while they are grievous to a feeling mind, should
not be surprising to the believer. "Men have revolted from God; and yet
think to live in harmony among themselves." The same forces that threw
off divine government will continue to dissolve the bonds of society.

All the facts of the real world are consistent with the biblical witness,
Fuller continues. "We have seen their correspondence with living truth,
or with things as they actually exist in the mind, and in the world."

> If they speak of things as they are; if conscience echo to their changes, and
> fact comport with their representations, they must have been taken from
> life; and you must conclude them to be, what they profess to be, a work
> of truth. And since the objects described are many of them beyond the
> ken of human observation, you must conclude that they are not only a
> work of truth, but, what they also profess to be, the true sayings of God
> [p. 212].

Chapter three of *The Gospel Its Own Witness* defends the assumption of
the internal consistency of the Bible. If the Bible is what it claims to be,
the Word of God, then its contents, style, and spirit must give evidence of
that. Because the books have come through a human medium we may
expect them "to be humanized," but we must also "plainly perceive in
them the finger of God."

Fuller refutes the claim of Paine that there is nothing majestic or worthy
of God in any part of the Bible. Paine said that Isaiah was filled with
"bombast, beneath the genius of a schoolboy" and that Genesis employed
an "imperative manner of speaking used by a conjuror." Both of those
accusations are false, claims Fuller, and Paine produces no evidences to
support his accusations. Bombast only occurs where great swelling words
are used to support little ideas. This is never the case with Scripture,
Fuller avows. The themes discussed are not small, and if any inadequacy
exists, the words are too small rather than too large. Even Rousseau
praised the dignity of Scripture as "so simple and sublime" as to render
the works of other men as mean and contemptible (pp. 214-19).

The Scripture invariably sees the hand of God as the cause of events.
The prophecies are heavy and fearsome even against the nation from
which they arrive. Prophecy serves to point to God's holiness. The miracles recorded are miracles of compassion, benevolence, and purpose,
never of simple ostentation. Fuller suggests that nothing in Scripture is
aimed merely at gratifying presumptuous speculation or idle curiosity.
The Scriptures do not seek to excite levity or folly, though there is much

irony in them; and they are free from affectation and vanity. They respect authority but are never known to flatter.

The writers of Scripture manifest no anxiety to guard against seeming inconsistency, says Fuller. There is no contrived harmony of different writers, yet on intense investigation one discovers a real harmony in all of the accounts. Such a real harmony would be expected if each writer wrote what he knew was true. In such a case he would not need through great care and caution to manufacture a consistency. Furthermore, divine sanction for the claims of Scripture is abundantly available in the signs that accompanied the teachings of Christ and the apostles. The testimony borne by the resurrection itself and by the witnesses of the resurrection should be convincing.

Chapters four and five deal with the harmony between sober reason and the Christian doctrine of salvation through a Mediator, and with the consistency between the doctrine of redemption and the magnitude of creation. Fuller closes his discussion with a statement affirming the superiority of revelation to philosophy.

> Philosophy may expand our ideas of creation; but it neither inspires a love to the moral character of the Creator, nor a well grounded hope of eternal life. Philosophy at most can only place us upon the top of Pisgah: there, like Moses, we must die. It gives us no possession of the good land: it is the province of Christianity to add, All is yours! When you have ascended to the height of human discovery, there are things and things of infinite moment too, that are utterly beyond its reach. Revelation is the medium, and the only medium, by which, standing, as it were, "on nature's Alps," we discover things which eye hath not seen, nor ear heard, and of which it hath never entered into the heart of man to conceive [p. 307].

On June 1, 1796, Fuller preached a sermon before the Baptist Association at St. Albans. "The Nature and Importance of an Intimate Knowledge of Divine Truth" was his subject (*Works*, 1:160-74). He presupposes in this message that all divine knowledge is to be derived from the oracles of God, the Bible. This phrase, "oracles of God," is entirely appropriate, he says, because it is "strongly expressive of their Divine Inspiration and infallibility; in them God speaks."

Fuller has no hesitancy in affirming the complete consistency and truthfulness of all of Scripture. In fact, its harmony is such that its principles can be grasped in a very helpful manner by systematizing them.

> But is the Bible written upon systematic principles; does it contain a system, or does it encourage us to form one? By the Bible being written on systematic principles, I suppose, is meant a systematic arrangement of its contents; and there is no doubt but the contrary of this is true. But then

the same might be said of the book of nature. Though the different species of animals, vegetables, minerals, &c. are capable of being arranged under the respective genera, and so reduced to a system; yet in their actual position in creation they assume no such appearance. It is wisely contrived, both in nature and Scripture, that the objects of each should be scattered in lovely variety; but amidst all this variety, an observant eye will perceive unity, order, arrangement, and fulness of design [*Works*, 1:165].

Fuller advocates systematizing only for the sake of understanding. Any system of doctrine should be under constant revision as new truths present themselves to the believer. "The best criterion of a good system is its agreement with the Holy Scriptures."

Inerrancy is also a necessary correlative of revelation. According to Fuller, revelation naturally implies infallibility, and infallibility determines inerrancy. First, in matters that are beyond human reason, revelation is essential. Revelation was even necessary for Adam in an unfallen state. How much more is it necessary for fallen men with depraved reason. Human reason is entirely insufficient to gain adequate knowledge of God and His will. Also, Fuller continues, without revelation there would be no faith, and with no faith, no salvation. Therefore, revelation being necessary, it must also be entirely truthful or else it is no better than depraved human reason.

According to Fuller, the Bible, having been written by divine inspiration, answers to the necessity of a divine revelation. The biblical writers certainly claimed to be inspired; "we must, therefore, either admit these writings to be the word of God, or consider them as mere imposture." It is an absurdity to pretend that they are authentic records of the dispensation of God and then to deny their inspiration. That posture is inexcusably inconsistent, for it believes "what the writers say of other subjects" but disbelieves "what they say of themselves." "If their writings be not what they profess them to be, they are imposture, and deserve to be rejected. There is no consistent medium between faith and unbelief" (*Works*, 1:699).

Therefore, inspiration is demanded throughout the whole of Scripture. In some cases when a writer is recording matters that he himself has observed, inspiration may be in the form of divine superintendence, "preserving him from error, and from other defects and faults, to which ordinary historians are subject." A higher degree of inspiration accompanied the writing of things not observable by the writer and things concerning the nature of God and salvation. But in whatever degree inspiration occurred, "it requires that a book professing to be a revelation from God should contain truth, and nothing but truth: such particularly must be its history, its prophecies, its miracles, and its doctrines" (*Works*, 1:699).

One characteristic of Scripture Fuller mentions quite often as evidence of its inspiration is its consistency. He claims that it never contradicts itself. As mentioned above, Fuller insisted that this evidence becomes even stronger when apparent contradictions are shown to be in actual harmony. In these cases it is obvious that no contrived attempt at harmony existed in the purposes of the writer, for the writers were convinced that all they wrote was bare truth, and that no amendments were necessary. Fuller demonstrates his commitment to this biblical consistency when he exegetes thirty sets of Scriptures in which apparent contradictions exist (*Works*, 1:667-83). He begins the discussion with an affirmation of the divine authority of Scripture.

> Admitting the Divine authority of the Holy Scriptures, their harmony ought not to be called in question; yet it must be allowed by every considerate reader that there are apparent difficulties. Nor is it unlawful, but laudable, to wish to see those difficulties removed and to aim at a perception of the particular beauty of God's word, as well as a general persuasion of its harmony [*Works*, 1:667].

Not only did Fuller take pains to show the internal consistency of Scripture in the face of apparent contradictions, but he also actively defended the inspiration and infallibility of Scripture in the face of the denials of the renowned Unitarian, or Socinian, Joseph Priestly. In an article entitled "Veneration for the Scripture" Fuller makes the following affirmations:

> If a man venerate the authority of Scripture, he must receive it as being what it professes to be, and for all the purposes for which it professes to be written. If the Scriptures profess to be Divinely inspired, and assume to be the infallible standard of faith and practice, we must either receive them as such, or, if we would be consistent, disown the writers as imposters. . . . New Testament writers bear ample testimony to the inspiration of those under the Old Testament. . . . Nor did the New Testament writers bear testimony to the inspiration of the prophets only; but considered their own writings as equally inspired. . . . As the sacred writers considered themselves as Divinely inspired, so they represented their writings as the infallible test of Divine truth [*Works*, 2:196].

Priestly considered the Scriptures authoritative in the sense that they were eyewitness history. The writers of Scripture were, however, subject to all the limitations of other historians. Priestly said: "I believe them to have been men, and consequently fallible, and liable to mistake with respect to things which they had not given much attention" (*Works*, 2:197).

Fuller, on the other hand, saw clearly the premise from which Priestly worked ("that it is impossible for God himself so to inspire a man as to preserve him from error without destroying his nature") and proceeded to demolish Priestly's argument point by point and reduce it to the absurd. Priestly contended that the apostles were infallible only when they spoke of Christ. Fuller demonstrates the untenable nature of that position by proving its inconsistency with the whole of Priestly's methodology and showing that Priestly refused to function as if the writers were infallible even when they spoke of Christ. Priestly, for example, denied the deity of Christ even though He is called "Lord" and "God" by Thomas.

Fuller summarized Priestly's treatment of Scripture with a satirical plea for the Socinians to publish a Bible with all the error removed.

> In short, if we must never quote Scripture except according to the rules imposed upon us by Socinian writers, we must not quote it at all; not, at least, till they shall have indulged us with a Bible of their own, that shall leave out every thing on which we are to place no dependence. A publication of this sort would, doubtless, be an acceptable present to the Christian world, would be comprised in a very small compass, and be of infinite service in cutting short a great deal of unnecessary controversy, into which, for want of such a criterion, we shall always be in danger of wandering [*Works,* 2:205].

Fuller believed the Bible was revelation from God. Its words are inspired so that they are infallible and free from error. Therefore we should venerate them, study them, and submit all of our thought and deeds to their authority. Whenever Fuller opposed the heresies of his day, or when he was advising his fellow believers, his appeal was always to the truth of Scripture. The Bible is God's word about redemption. It is not a textbook on science, but it is everywhere truthful when properly interpreted with the aid of the Holy Spirit. Scripture undoubtedly warrants our trust and commitment. Fuller believed that a full trust in Scripture would never result in the worship of the Book. To read and believe the Bible is to learn of and trust in Christ. Scripture exalts the Savior. Its simple, popular style speaks to the average common man, and thus all men are commanded to repent and believe the gospel. This emphasis, which Fuller made, soon came to characterize Baptists in England, in India, in America, and around the world.

BIBLIOGRAPHY

John Gill

Armitage, Thomas. *A History of the Baptists.* New York: Bryan, Taylor & Co., 1887 (1977 reprint by James and Klock Christian Publishing Co., Minneapolis).

Gill, John. *Body of Divinity.* Atlanta, Ga.: Turner Lassetter, 1950.

Rippon, John. *A Brief Memoir of the Life and Writings of the Late Rev. John Gill.* London: John Bennett, 1838.

Vedder, H. C. *A Short History of the Baptists.* Valley Forge: Judson, 1907 (eighteenth printing, 1974).

Andrew Fuller

Fuller, Andrew Gunton. *Andrew Fuller.* London: Hodder & Stoughton, 1882.
———. *Complete Works of Andrew Fuller.* Edited by Joseph Belcher. 3 vols. Philadelphia: American Baptist Publication Society, 1845.
———. *Dialogues, Letters, and Essays on Various Subjects.* London: J. W. Morris, 1806.
———. *The Gospel Its Own Witness of the Holy Nature and Divine Harmony of the Christian Religion.* Clipstone: J. W. Morris, 1799.
Ryland, John. *The Life and Death of the Rev. Andrew Fuller.* Philadelphia: American Baptist Publication Society, [1818].
Whitley, W. T. *A History of British Baptists.* London: C. Griffin & Co., 1923.

CHAPTER SIX

"Unto a Land That I Will Shew Thee"

In Baptist circles, William Carey and Adoniram Judson are names synonymous with foreign missions. Carey's zeal for missions was the fruit of the revival among the English Particular Baptists, a revival effected largely through the writings and prayers of Andrew Fuller. Judson, converted from Congregationalism to Baptist views while en route to Burma, was a gift of God's grace to American Baptists. In conjunction with Luther Rice, he motivated Baptists to enlarge their evangelistic vision. Judson urged them to form an organization for the support of mission causes. Baptists responded by establishing the "General Missionary Convention of the Baptist Denomination of the United States of America for Foreign Missions."

Because the majority of the adult lives of both Carey and Judson were spent in missionary service among people unacquainted with intricacies of Christian theology, they had no occasion to deal with the doctrine of biblical inspiration in a technical fashion. Their work was practical and evangelistic. However, one can easily discern the view of Scripture that both held by investigating the place the Bible occupied in their personal lives and in the mission work.

Carey's theory of biblical authority can legitimately be identified with that of Andrew Fuller, for their minds were virtually one. Carey showed sympathetic interest in Fuller's writings against Deism and Socinianism. On occasions Carey related to Fuller how he sought to convince the Mohammedans of the superiority of the Bible to the Koran. Carey showed particular delight in cases in which unbelieving Indians came to embrace the doctrine of the divine inspiration of the Scriptures. Upon learning of Fuller's death, Carey wrote to John Ryland and said, "There was scarcely any other man in England to whom I could so completely lay open my heart" (S. Pearce Carey, *William Carey*, p. 313).

Judson's view could safely be represented by Francis Wayland, one of the greatest supporters of the American mission movement and the editor

Fig. 8. WILLIAM CAREY
From Cathcart's *The Baptist Encyclopedia*, Everts, 1883. 1:182.

of Judson's *Memoirs*. These assumptions need not stand alone, however, for sufficient material exists to allow the men to speak for themselves.

WILLIAM CAREY

The minutes of the business meeting for Hervey Lane Baptist Church in Leicester, England, for September, October, November, December, and January 1792-93 state: "No business of importance except that [as of January] our pastor gave us notice that he should leave us in March, having engaged to go on a Mission to Bengal in the East Indies" (*Biographical Notices*, p. 7). With such an inauspicious notation, the church of which William Carey was pastor recorded the most signal event in the history of modern missions.

Carey, along with Andrew Fuller, John Ryland, Jr., and John Sutcliff, for some time gouged his way through disappointments and rude rebuffs toward the goal of founding a society for the propagation of the gospel among the heathen. Baptists were just beginning to emerge from their anti-outreach cocoon. This new interest in the lost people of the world was prompted primarily by Andrew Fuller's *The Gospel Worthy of All Acceptation*. However, the greatest surge of evangelistic and mission zeal was supplied by Carey. At the request of the minister's fraternal meeting at Clipstone, Carey published in 1791 *An Enquiry Into the Obligations of Christians to use Means for the Conversion of the Heathen*. In May 1792, at Nottingham, he poured heart and soul into a sermon that could be reduced to two great exhortations: "Expect great things from God. Attempt great things for God." The resistance rising from the strict Calvinistic theology of some ministers and the hesitance in the face of such a bold project on the part of those who supported Carey were so strong that even after delivering that great message, Carey personally had to stop the meeting before it concluded and plead with Fuller to call for some action relating to the foreign-mission question. A resolution was passed:

> Resolved, that a plan be prepared against the next Minister's Meeting at Kettering, for forming a Baptist Society for propagating the Gospel among the Heathens.

On October 2, this group of insignificant, rural, English Baptists plunged into a resolution to form the "Particular Baptist Society for the Propagation of the Gospel Amongst the Heathen." A collection of cash and "promises" was taken amounting to thirteen pounds, two shillings, and six pence. The weakness of the external circumstances is illustrated by the fact that one minister had to delay a full year before he could fulfill his pledge of less than one pound. On the other hand, the strength of the inner conviction of the men is illustrated by Andrew Fuller's being elected secretary of the society and William Carey's volunteering to go to India.

William Carey, the first of five children, was born on August 17, 1761. His father, Edmund, was a weaver; but by 1767, through personal initiative and trustworthiness, he had gained appointment to the united offices of schoolmaster and parish clerk. Botany, entomology, and tales of travel were early fascinations for young William. When twelve years old, he left school in order to devote himself to gardening. However, a skin disease became so aggravated by the sun that he was forced to pursue another vocation. His father apprenticed him to Clarke Nichols, a shoemaker in Piddington, and, like Carey's father, a strict English Churchman.

One of Carey's fellow cobbler apprentices, John Warr, a Nonconformist, invited Carey to attend a prayer meeting with a group of Nonconformists in Hackleton. Carey, coming from staunch Anglican stock, had learned to disdain these people who did not care to worship in accordance with the established Anglican Church. He argued with Warr and, though he often had the weaker argument, made up in positive assertion what was lacking in reasoning. Though resistant for a while, Carey eventually relented and accompanied Warr to a meeting. This activity so traumatized Carey that he resorted to attending his parish church three times on Sunday to assuage his feelings of guilt. Warr continued to try to win Carey to faith in Christ. After a period of attempted self-reformation, Carey experienced true conversion in 1779 and joined the Nonconformists.

Soon after Carey had become a Nonconformist, the opportunity for theological debate irresistibly presented itself. His opponent was the leader of a group of devout mystics at Quinton. Though mystical and intellectually unconvincing, Carey's opponent made such an emotional appeal that Carey stated, "I could neither believe his system nor defend my own." He found some solace but little helpful information among some of his Nonconformist friends who merely related personal experiences to Carey, an exercise which prompted Carey to regard human speculation as unreliable. By this means he was forced "to seek a system of doctrines in the Word of God" (*Memoir*, p. 14). In fact, Carey's later reflections on this period of his life represent it as a "state of uncertainty and anxiety about gospel doctrines." Because he had little acquaintance with ministers in his vicinity, for the solution to his problem he was "obliged to draw all from the Bible alone."

Carey's determination to "draw all from the Bible alone" led him to believe that a conflict existed between the practice of infant baptism and the New Testament doctrine of justification by faith. After examining the subject thoroughly, he decided to reject paedobaptism (baptism of infants) in favor of believer's baptism. He conferred about the matter with John Ryland, Sr., who, evidently satisfied with Carey's experience and theology, turned him over to John Ryland, Jr., for baptism. The true significance of the baptism of the cobbler could hardly have been recognized by those present for the ceremony.

During his cobbling days Carey did much more than make and mend shoes. The study of geography and language provided an intellectual alternative to the tedium of cutting, sewing, gluing, and nailing. It prepared the young shoeman for his great calling of the future. *The Voyages of Captain Cook* put the entire world into the mind and prayers of Carey, and zeal for Scripture prompted him to learn Greek, Latin, and Hebrew. He also learned to read and write in Dutch and French. Thus, he was enabled to translate Scripture from the original languages and examine the style and fidelity of translations in Latin, French, and Dutch.

Carey's reliance on and love for Scripture was not accidental, for evidently Scripture reading at school and home was a regular part of his daily life in childhood. He did not resent it; rather, he was grateful for the advantages it afforded him:

> It is still a matter of thankfulness that I had so general a knowledge of the Bible when I was a child. By that means my mind was furnished with a body of subjects, which, after I had more acquaintance with evangelical truth, were ready upon every occasion, and were often influential upon my heart when I had but little leisure to read [*Memoir*, p. 18].

This knowledge of Scripture so informed and comforted Carey that he had no hesitancy in prescribing a similar remedy to others. His sister wrote him in the winter before he moved from Piddington to become pastor at Moulton. She was under deep conviction and asked Carey for guidance. His remedy: "Sister, read your Bible" (*Memoir*, p. 32).

Though he profoundly subscribed to that course of action, Carey was neither naive of nor oblivious to the value of other books. However, other books, in Carey's opinion, aided the reader to the degree that they were faithful to biblical teaching and brought truth clearly before his mind. Robert Hall's *Help to Zion's Travelers* was such a book for him:

> Mr. Skinner one day made me a present of Mr. Hall's *Help to Zion's Travelers;* in which I found all that arranged and illustrated which I had been so long picking up by scraps [through personal Bible study]. I do not remember ever to have read any book with such raptures as I did that. If it was poison as some then said, it was so sweet to me that I drank it greedily to the bottom of the cup [*Memoir*, p. 16].

It would be impossible to overestimate the importance of Carey's understanding of the authority of Scripture for the organization and implementation of the mission to India. Carey considered the Great Commission of Matthew 28:19-20 to be the direct words of Jesus and thus a binding revelation upon the present generation as well as those under the "immediate inspirations of the Holy Ghost." No evidence could be presented to refute its perpetual nature. In fact, if the implied command to baptize and the promise of God's presence were still in force, the command to make disciples was of equal power (*Enquiry*, pp. 8-9). "Every believer in divine revelation" must concede that the "sacred scriptures assure us" that Christ will conquer all nations and that the kingdoms of this world will become the kingdoms of our Lord and of his Christ (*Periodical Accounts*, 1:12). Therefore, Carey called for the organization of a foreign mission society.

Among the first communications the society received from India was a request from Shree Parbotee, an Indian Christian. He referred to the Bible as the *shaster* (official religious teachings) of God and stated, "Now it is our wish that this great Word was translated into Bengalee. . . . Send preachers into this country, and them that will help forward the translation" (*Periodical Accounts*, 1:34). This request coincided perfectly with the intentions of the society. They sent a response to Shree Parbotee assuring him that the society would send William Carey and John Thomas, who "will labor to translate the Bible as fast as they are able" (1:42).

Carey and Thomas did not belie the promise of the society. They immediately set themselves to learn the Bengali language in order to translate the Word of Life into that language. In 1796 Thomas wrote:

> I would give a million pounds sterling, if I had it, to see a Bengal Bible. O most merciful God, what an inestimable blessing will it be to these millions! . . . Methinks all heaven and hell will be moved at a bible's entering such a country as this. O Lord! send forth thy light and thy truth [1:292-293].

Carey periodically reported on the progress of the translation and in 1796 requested financial assistance for the purpose of printing the Bible. In December of that year, Carey gave expression to his conviction of the preeminence of the translation of Scripture:

> The translation of the Scriptures I look upon to be one of the greatest desiderata in the world, and it has accordingly occupied a considerable part of my time and attention; and through great mercy the New Testament is now so near completion, that I hope to have the translation and first revision of it finished by the end of March [*Periodical Accounts*, 1:345].

In March of 1797 he wrote that only two obstacles impeded the progress of the gospel in any part of the earth: first, a want of the Scriptures and, second, the depravity of the human heart. "The first of these God has begun to remove."

The committee members in England responded favorably to Carey's request for financial assistance and informed their constituency of the need. Money designated specifically for the translation of Scripture entered the financial accounts in 1798, when more than £ 824 was specified for translation. In 1799, £ 200 was given. More than £ 1,142 was earmarked for that purpose in 1800.

In an effort to speed the actual distribution of Scripture, the committee suggested that "some select parts of the sacred scriptures, be first translated and published" (*Periodical Accounts,* 1:305). The book of Genesis, the first twenty chapters of Exodus, Messianic predictions from the Psalms and the Prophets, and the whole of the New Testament ought to receive earliest attention, according to the committee.

Carey pulled the last page of the Bengali New Testament off the press on February 7, 1801. By March 5, 1801, it was bound, and Carey laid it on the Communion table. William Ward, a fellow missionary since 1800, recorded in his journal that "this evening we had Thanksgiving for the finishing of the New Testament." Joshua Marshman, who, along with Carey and Ward, composed the famous Serampore trio, wrote a hymn to celebrate the event:

> Hail, precious Book divine!
>   Illumined by thy rays,
> We rise from death and sin,
>   And tune a Saviour's praise:
> The shades of error, dark as night,
> Vanish before thy radiant light!
>
> Now shall the Hindus learn
>   The glories of our King:
> Nor to blind gurus turn,
>   Nor idol praises sing;
> Diffusing heavenly light around,
> This Book their Shastras shall confound.
>
> Deign, gracious Saviour, deign,
>   To smile upon Thy Word;
> Let millions now obtain
>   Salvation from the Lord:
> Nor let its growing conquests stay,
> Till earth exult to own Thy sway.
>
> [S. Pearce Carey, *William Carey,* p. 199]

Eventually, through an ingenious method of implementing the talents of the indigenous people under his own supervision, Carey was responsible for translating the Bible, whole or in part, into thirty-six distinct languages. These Herculean feats were often met with scorn and ridicule by those in England who opposed the "enthusiastic" efforts of the "mechanic preachers." *The Quarterly Review,* a journal devoted to propagating the interests of High Anglicanism, defended the Baptist missionaries from these unjust pejoratives and celebrated their translation achievements in dithyrambic tones.

> These low-born and low-bred mechanics have translated the whole Bible into Bengalee, and have by this time printed it. They are printing the New Testament in the Sanscrit [etc.]. . . . Extraordinary as this is, it will appear more so, when it is remembered, that of the three men one was originally a shoemaker, another a printer at Hull, and a third the master of a charity school at Bristol. Only fourteen years have elapsed since Thomas and Carey set foot in India, and in that time have these missionaries acquired the gift of tongues; in fourteen years these low-born, low-bred mechanics have done more towards spreading the knowledge of the Scriptures among the heathen, than has been accomplished or even attempted by all the princes and potentates of the world [*Biographical Notices,* p. 42].

When the New Testament was printed, the missionaries began to distribute it carefully. William Ward and Krishna Pal, the first convert of the mission, distributed some tracts and one Bengalee New Testament in a village near Calcutta named Ram Krishnapur. When Ward gave the villagers the New Testament, he instructed that it should be given to the person who could read best. That person was then to read it aloud to all who desired to hear. The villagers followed his instructions.

After continuing this practice for about three years, several from the village walked to Serampore and sought help from Carey and his associates. They asked "How may we obtain the fruits of Christ's death?" Reading the Scriptures in the manner prescribed convinced them of the foolishness of idol worship and brought them to trust in Jesus Christ for salvation.

Krishna Pal, upon questioning them, expressed surprise at the knowledge they had obtained, for they had "no other means, it seems than a New Testament and a few pamphlets" (*Periodical Accounts,* 3:174). In November 1805 about eleven of the villagers were baptized.

Five Kulin Brahmins were converted in 1812. Their faith also was provoked by the unaided study of the Scriptures. According to those Brahmins there were one hundred others in their district who sought the truth as well. It is a significant insight into Carey's theology to realize that he and his compatriots expected that Scripture alone would accomplish these things. William Ward, nearing completion of the task of printing the New Testament, expressed the convictions of all the missionaries in a letter to a friend in Hull:

> Before you get this, we shall most likely have published the New Testament in Bengalee, and the 2,000 copies will be putting [sic] into the hands of the natives. I love England, I love you, and many more friends at Hull; but to give to a man a New Testament, who never saw it, who has been reading lies as the word of God; to give him those everlasting lines which angels would be glad to read; this, this is my blessed work. If it should be long on the earth, it will bear a precious crop sooner or later. If a man should not know the value of it immediately, a leaf, a verse, may sometime be more precious to him than a load of hay. It may, it will enlighten the ignorant, convert the froward, raise the ruined, comfort the distressed and support the dying. Blessed Book! In India it shall be said and sung, "The Gospel bears my spirit up" [*Periodical Accounts*, 2:70-71].

Carey's trust in Scripture was undiminished in times of personal trial. Soon after arriving in India, his wife became mentally ill. She remained in this condition until her death. Probably referring to this trial, Carey wrote in 1794 of his perplexity about "various temporal concerns" but assuaged his worries with his conviction that "the word of God is sure, which abundantly promises all I can want" (*Periodical Accounts*, 1:164). Later the same year Carey was overwhelmed with the innumerable obstacles obstructing effective work with the Indians. His only solace: "I have God, and his word is sure; . . . my hope, fixed on that sure word, will rise superior to all obstructions" (1:175).

In March, 1812, a fire ripped through the mission printing works, destroying invaluable manuscripts of translations, dictionaries, and grammars, including the magnum opus of Carey's linguistic life, his *Dictionary of Sanskrit and its Indian Cognates.* Over fifteen hundred reams of paper were destroyed, along with 4,400 pounds of English type, many fonts of English-cast Hebrew and Greek, and type for printing in fourteen Eastern languages. Yet Marshman could write to John Ryland that God's Word was still as "firm as the pillars of heaven." God would certainly work all things for good, as He had promised.

After Andrew Fuller died, the society in England became more aggressive and grasped for greater control of the foreign enterprise. Carey responded: "We will never consent to put power over these premises and over ourselves into their hands, at a distance of a quarter of the globe's circumference. . . . We will carry on our work, subject to no control but his [God's] most holy Word" (S. Pearce Carey, *William Carey*, p. 318).

Part of the mission effort of the Serampore missionaries was expressed in programs of education for the nationals. Their theory of education clearly demonstrates their commitment to the entire trustworthiness of Scripture and their belief in the unity of all truth. Their task, as they conceived it, was not simply to give theological or biblical instruction, though "the importance of imparting to them the words of everlasting life is fully acknowledged," but also to offer a comprehensive education to prepare the students for a rich life free of superstition. This type of study would discipline the intellectual capacities of the students and "make them enter thoroughly into the beauty and glory of the Sacred Oracles [the Christian Scriptures]" (*Periodical Accounts*, 5:497).

Not only were Carey, Marshman, and Ward convinced that general education would increase one's appreciation of the biblical material, they also believed that true learning would reveal the perverseness of false religion. If religion is true, then it must be consistent with every other established truth. God, who is both Creator and Redeemer, will not design His creation so that it opposes His revelation of the necessity and means of redemption. God does not contradict or oppose His own works. Sound education would reveal several untenable features of pagan religion and at the same time greatly enhance one's openness to true Christian faith, according to the missionary trio.

On this basis they recommended the following courses of study:

(1) A simple and concise introduction to arithmetic. This was proposed simply for the sake of increasing the business acumen of the nationals and sharpening their minds. At that time, "an expert accomptant among the Hindoos will be several minutes in resolving a question in simple multiplication which a well-instructed English lad would do almost in the twinkling of an eye" (*Periodical Accounts*, 5:497).

(2) A concise system of geography. The Indians, completely ignorant of geography, had their entire religious system built upon or interwoven with this ignorance. Soomeroon, their holy mountain, was in their teaching the seat of a multitude of heavens and the focal point of seven continents and seven seas which extend from the mountain like root hairs from an onion. A study of geography would render this belief untenable, according to Carey (5:498).

(3) A study of general history. This would also throw a "flood of light on the minds of Hindoo youths." Both ancient and modern history should be covered. Especially anything "worthy of remark" concerning the history of India would increase the usefulness of such a course. This study would "furnish them with knowledge of greatest value when they come to read the Sacred Scriptures" (5:498).

(4) Practical Hindu wisdom. Using the practice of the apostle Paul when addressing the Athenians, Carey proposed that a "selection of the best ideas found among Hindoo writers relating to the duties of life" should be counted as part of the course. Any correlation between these teachings and "the law of righteousness" would be extremely helpful, and

"their deficiency might be improved to the highest advantage, by shewing the necessity of a better guide" (5:498).

(5) The Holy Bible. The final recommendation included items related directly to Scripture. "Selections from the Sacred Oracles," both the Old and New Testament, should be a part of the required course. An introduction of the whole of Scripture would prove overwhelming to children so little accustomed to reading; therefore, strategic selections from the whole "still retaining the language of inspiration" would be made.

Some selections would be made from Old Testament history, beginning with creation and ending with the captivity of Israel. These would be dated and correlated with the dates of the general history studies.

Other selections would come from scriptural passages concerning ethics. Special attention was to be given to a study of the nature, attributes, and law of God. The direct concern of these studies was to show how these revealed truths relate to sin, man, redemption, and future judgment. These sections would in turn be compared to the best teachings from the Hindu writers "certainly not to the disadvantage of the Sacred Oracles."

The last biblical section would include all the prophecies relative to the coming of the Messiah into the world together with a complete history of Jesus taken from the gospels. To this would be added selections from the book of Acts and such passages from the epistles that exhibit the doctrine of salvation by faith in Christ (5:499).

Serampore College was founded with the same basic purpose in mind. The college was open to Christians of all denominations and Indians of all castes. The missionaries envisioned that it should be a school, "so scientific, thorough, and open air" as to prepare men to judge between truth and falsehood. They desired that Serampore be to India what the University of Halle was to Germany.

The curriculum would make the Indian scriptures, classics, and science available to all who came, as well as the Christian Scriptures and Western science. On this basis the students would be qualified to make a comparative judgment of the worth of the options. Only in this way should India raise up its own Christian scholars to fight ignorance and spiritual darkness as England had produced its own warriors in Wycliff and Tyndale.

> They would lay open to them the Vedas, Upanishads and Puranas side by side with the Christian Scriptures in their own vernaculars enabling them to prove all things, and hold fast whatsoever they judged to be good [S. Pearce Carey, *William Carey*, p. 329].

Carey found encouragement in the fact that even the Reformation progressed slowly and made its permanent gains on the strength of thorough

Fig. 9. ADONIRAM JUDSON

From *The Life of Adoniram Judson* by Edward Judson. Philadelphia: American
Baptist Publication Society, 1883. Frontispiece.

education. If progress out of corrupted Christianity were slow, then progress out of pagan darkness would be slower. However, the instruments of progress would be the same: unswerving fidelity to the Bible as the Word of God, who cannot lie, and a subjection of all learning to its truth.

Adoniram Judson

Adoniram Judson (born August 9, 1788) was recognized as a precocious child. By the time he was four years old, he was regularly gathering the neighborhood children around him and preaching sermons that he had heard in church. At seven, little Adoniram became obsessed with the question, Does the sun move at all? Somehow, even at the age of seven he had learned to require positive proof rather than naively to trust his senses. Judson was also noted for his extraordinary ability to solve charades and riddles. By the age of ten he had gained a widespread reputation for his ability in arithmetic, and he began to study navigation with a Captain Morton. He had also become quite proficient in Greek and was fond of reading books of theology, novels by Richardson and Fielding, and plays by Ben Johnson.

In 1804, Judson entered Providence College, subsequently called Brown University. He began his work at the age of sixteen, and he graduated with highest honors in 1807. This achievement is all the more remarkable in that he missed six weeks of his senior year because he was teaching school in Plymouth.

In the fall of 1807 Judson opened a private academy in Plymouth in which he taught for nearly a year. He wrote two textbooks for the classes there: *The Elements of English Grammar* and *The Young Lady's Arithmetic*. Ava Messer, president of Providence College, wrote a letter to Judson indicating his appraisal of the grammar. Messer said:

> It exhibits a fresh instance of the ingenious literary enterprise and perseverance of its author; and should you conclude to give it to the public, it will, we hope, meet as it merits, a generous patronage [*Memoir*, 1:16].

Throughout his childhood and youth, Judson had maintained his membership in a Congregational church. While Judson attended Providence College, however, he became enamoured with Deism (a form of Theistic liberalism that affirms that God created the world but denies that God ever miraculously intervenes in history). During those days Judson became, at least professedly, an unbeliever. One particular young man whom Judson's sister described as "amiable, talented, witty, exceedingly agreeable in person and manners, but a confirmed Deist" had an unusual influence upon Judson. Strangely enough, Judson's admiration for this person,

simply called E_____ in Judson's biography, gave rise to the occasion
of Judson's conversion to Christianity.

After teaching at Plymouth, Judson set out on a tour through the Northern states with some cronies. Judson said, "We lived a reckless, vagabond
life, finding lodgings where we could, and bilking the landlord where we
found opportunity" (*Life*, p. 11). One night Judson stopped at an inn
where he was placed in a room next door to a young man who was dying.

> Sounds came from the sick-chamber—sometimes the movements of the
> watchers, sometimes the groans of the sufferer; but it was not these which
> disturbed him. He thought of what the landlord had said—the stranger
> was probably in a dying state; and was he prepared? Alone, and in the
> dead of night, he felt a blush of shame steal over him at the question, for
> it proved the shallowness of his philosophy. What would his late com-
> panions say to his weakness? The clear-minded, intellectual, witty
> E_____, what would he say to such consummate boyishness?
> But still his thoughts would revert to the sick man. Was he a Christian,
> calm and strong in the hope of a glorious immortality? or was he shudder-
> ing upon the brink of a dark, unknown future? Perhaps he was a "free-
> thinker," educated by Christian parents, and prayed over by a Christian
> mother. The landlord had described him as a young man; and in imagina-
> tion he was forced to place himself upon the dying bed, though he strove
> with all his might against it. At last morning came, and the bright flood
> of light which it poured into his chamber dispelled all his "superstitious
> illusions." As soon as he had risen, he went in search of the landlord,
> and inquired for his fellow-lodger. "He is dead," was the reply. "Dead!"
> "Yes, he is gone, poor fellow! The doctor said he would probably not sur-
> vive the night." "Do you know who he was?" "O, yes; it was a young man
> from Providence College—a very fine fellow; his name was E_____"
> [*Life*, pp. 12-13].

That same fall, in November of 1808, in an autobiographical record of
dates and events, Judson recorded how he "began to entertain a hope of
having received the regenerating influences of the Holy Spirit." By December, he recorded that he made a solemn dedication of himself to God.

Judson's interest in foreign missions was prompted in September 1809
by his reading *Star in the East*, a sermon preached in the parish church
in Bristol, England, by Claudius Buchanan. In 1810 Judson, along with
several other young men, led in the formation of the American Board of
Commissioners for Foreign Missions, sponsored by the Congregational
Church. In that same year he "commenced an acquaintance with Ann
Hasseltine." His intensity of interest in both missions and Ann is seen
in this New Year's letter, 1811:

> May this be the year in which you will change your name; in which you
> will take a final leave of your relatives and native land; in which you will

cross the wide ocean, and dwell on the other side of the world, among a heathen people. What a great change will this year probably effect in our lives! How very different will be our situation and employment! If our lives are preserved and our attempt prospered, we shall next new year's day be in India, and perhaps wish each other a happy new year in the uncouth dialect of Hindostan or Burmah. We shall no more see our kind friends around us, or enjoy the conveniences of civilized life, or go to the house of God with those that keep holy days; but swarthy countenances will every where meet our eye, the jargon of an unknown tongue will assail our ears, and we shall witness the assembling of the heathen to celebrate the worship of idol gods. We shall be weary of the world, and wish for wings like a dove, that we may fly away and be at rest. We shall probably experience seasons when we shall be "exceeding sorrowful, even unto death." We shall see many dreary, disconsolate hours, and feel a sinking of spirits, anguish of mind, of which now we can form little conception. O, we shall wish to lie down and die. And that time may soon come [*Memoir*, 1:34-35].

Judson and Ann Hasseltine were married February 5, 1812, and set sail on February 19 to be Congregationalist missionaries in Calcutta. On board ship Judson gave himself to an intensive study of the Baptist position on baptism, because he knew that he would soon meet William Carey, Joshua Marshman, and William Ward. He felt that he would have to defend his sentiments favoring infant baptism. His study, however, was so exhaustive and so strictly biblical that he came to the conclusion that the Baptists were right, and that he had been wrong about the doctrine of baptism. In a personal letter to Carey, Marshman, and Ward concerning his change of mind, Judson requested true Christian baptism from them.

My inquiries commenced during my passage from America, and after much laborious research and painful trial, . . . have issued in entire conviction, that the immersion of a professing believer is the only Christian baptism. . . . Feeling, therefore, that we are in an unbaptized state, we wish to profess our faith in Christ by being baptized in obedience to his sacred commands [*Massachusetts Baptist* 3 (March 1813):266-67].

After informing the American Board of Commissioners for Foreign Missions that he could no longer follow their instructions to baptize "credible believers and their households," on September 27 Judson preached a sermon entitled "Christian Baptism," in which he defended believer's baptism in light of his thorough knowledge of the theology of infant baptism. The sermon was published as a book of 111 pages and enjoyed publication in at least five American editions.

Later, Luther Rice, another early Congregationalist missionary, underwent the same conversion to Baptist theology. Judson wrote to Lucius Bolles, an American Baptist, and made an appeal to Baptists in America that they form a foreign mission society. Carey and Ward also wrote to America to encourage the Baptists to accept these newly baptized missionaries as gifts from God.

Some small societies were formed immediately to support the Judsons and Rice. The financial support, however, was limited. Eventually Luther Rice returned to the United States to report directly to the churches about the needs on the mission field. He was instrumental in the founding of the General Missionary Convention. The *Massachusetts Baptist Missionary Magazine* in 1813 recorded:

> Our esteemed brother Rice . . . has returned from India, and is now visiting our brethren of the south, for the purpose of uniting them with us in this great object [*Massachusetts Baptist* 3 (December 1813):353].

In May 1814, at the First Baptist Church of Philadelphia, a group of thirty-three men met for the purpose of adopting a plan for "eliciting, combining, and directing the energies of the whole denomination in one sacred effort, for sending the glad tidings of Salvation to the Heathen" (*Massachusetts Baptist* 4 [September 1814]:66). They approved a constitution which named the body "The General Missionary Convention of the Baptist Denomination in the United States of America, for Foreign Missions." They determined to meet every third year to conduct their business. The group was therefore commonly known as the Triennial Convention.

At the first regular meeting, in September of 1814, the convention resolved that "Rev. Adoniram Judson, Jun. now in India, be considered as a Missionary, under the care and direction of this Board."

He was advised of this action and admonished to begin pious labor in such places as, in his judgment, appeared most promising.

The first center of Judson's missionary activity was in Rangoon, the principal seaport of Burma. He began work there in 1813 but did not see his first convert until May of 1819. Judson baptized Moung Nau on June 27, 1819. In a letter dated June 2 of that year, Mrs. Judson described the eagerness with which the new convert absorbed Scripture.

> It is peculiarly interesting to see with what eagerness he drinks in the truths from the Scriptures. A few days ago, I was reading with him Christ's Sermon on the Mount. He was deeply impressed and unusually solemn. "These words," said he, "take hold on my very liver; they make me tremble." . . . Mornings and evenings he spends in reading the Scriptures, and when we all meet in the hall for family worship, he comes and sits with us;

though he cannot understand, he says he can think of God in his heart [*Memoir*, 1:225-26].

Judson was not afraid to enter into philosophical disputation with the Burmans to prove the superiority of the Christian religion, and indeed prove it to be the only true religion. He was quite adept at demonstrating the reasonableness of the orthodox Christian doctrines. In fact, he did so well at showing one Burman how sin and eternal misery are reconcilable with the character of an infinitely wise, holy, and powerful God that his inquirer could not refrain from laughing out of pure mental delight and repeating all that Judson said to those around him (*Memoir*, 1:275). Judson records other conversations in which the subject of science and religion formed the core of the discussion. Judson made it clear that he believed that the Copernican system of astronomy was incompatible with Buddhism but that it was perfectly consistent with biblical Christianity (1:310).

However, in no way did Judson consider rational demonstration to be superior to the word of Scripture. Moung Shwa-gnong, a teacher, disputed with Judson regularly. Often the conversation centered its attention on the truth of the Christian Scriptures. On one occasion Moung Shwa-gnong fully admitted the truth of the existence of an eternal being. Judson then records:

> The latter part of the day we were chiefly employed in discussing the possibility and necessity of a divine revelation, and the evidence which proves that the writings of the apostles of Jesus contain that revelation [*Memoir*, 1:234].

Further discussion with Moung Shwa-gnong led to even stronger statements regarding the authority of Scripture. After several hours of "metaphysical cavils" the inquirer said that he believed in God, in His Son, Jesus Christ, and in the atonement. Judson, knowing the Deistic tendencies of Shwa-gnong, continued pressing him.

> "Do you believe all that is contained in the book of Matthew that I have given you? In particular, do you believe that the Son of God died on a cross?" "Ah," replied he, "you have caught me now. I believe that he suffered death, but I cannot admit that he suffered the shameful death of the cross." "Therefore," said I, "you are not a disciple of Christ. A true disciple inquires not whether a fact is agreeable to his own reason, but whether it is in the book. His pride has yielded to the divine testimony. Teacher, your pride is still unbroken. Break down your pride, and yield to the word of God." He stopped and thought. "As you utter those words," said he, "I see my error. I have been trusting in my own reason, not in the word of God." Some interruption now occurred. When we were again

alone, he said, "This day is different from all the days on which I have visited you. I see my error in trusting in my own reason, and I now believe the crucifixion of Christ, because it is contained in the Scripture" [*Memoir*, 1:242].

Moung Shwa-gnong drew the conclusion that because revelation was necessary for us to know the true God and because the writings of the apostles are that revelation, all that Scripture says must be believed.

In February of 1819, Judson again talked with Moung Shwa-gnong. The Burman inquirer was eager to know if he could yet be considered a disciple. Judson records his confession of faith:

> I believe in the eternal God, in his Son Jesus Christ, in the atonement which Christ has made, and in the writings of the apostles, as the true and only word of God [*Memoir*, 1:263].

Shwa-gnong goes on to explain that he had seen and renounced his former error of trusting his own understanding above the divine Word. Moung Shwa-gnong submitted to believer's baptism on July 18, 1819.

Other converts also bear strong testimony to the importance and power of Scripture in their lives. Moung Byaa and Moung Thahlah presented a written document to Adoniram and Ann Judson in which they expressed their Christian faith. They explained how they had been convinced that there is one eternal God; that there is a divine Son, the Lord Jesus Christ; and that they knew that He suffered death on a cross in their stead. They were under deep conviction "on account of [their] many sins." While they remained in this lost condition the "two teachers produced the sacred system from the Scriptures," by which the inquiring Burmans became disciples of the divine Son, Jesus Christ" (1:238-39).

Judson finished his translation of Ephesians in April of 1820. By May he had begun to distribute copies (probably handwritten) to the Burmans. Judson remarked that "one characteristic trait in these people is a particular love for the Scriptures." He had given one copy of Ephesians to three visitors from Nan-dau-gong who came to the mission quite often. They so loved its message that they quarreled with one another for that copy. According to them it was much plainer and more early understood than the translation of Matthew, a fact quite pleasing to Judson, for he had translated Ephesians without the help of anyone. He was determined to give these Burmans another copy of Ephesians as soon as one was available (1:277).

Ann and Adoniram Judson conceived of their ministry as a direct outgrowth of their commitment to the truth of the Bible. First, they came to Burma under biblical authority and they considered their main job to be the teaching of Scripture. Second, the success of their undertaking was dependent on the effectual power of Scripture. Third, the growth of individual Christians and the continuance of the work depended on the availability of Scripture in the language of the people.

Their audience with the monarch of Burma is illustrative of their sense of obedience to biblical authority. In January of 1819, the Judsons appeared in Ava before the king of Burma to seek a guarantee of freedom from government molestation in their mission work. After answering several questions regarding their customs, dress, intentions, and so forth, they heard Moung Zah, the private minister of state, read their petition to the monarch. The petition described the function of the missionaries as "teachers and explainers of the contents of the sacred Scriptures of our religion." It also stated that their coming to Burma was in obedience to the Scriptures so that "both those who teach and those who receive the religion will be freed from future punishment, and enjoy, without decay or death, the eternal felicity of heaven" (1:255).

Their trust in the power of the Word is seen in many ways. After the first convert came to Christ, Mrs. Judson wrote of the hope that this "single trophy of victorious grace" had given them.

> This event has convinced us that God can and does operate on the minds of the most dark and ignorant, and that he makes his own truths, his own word, the instrument of operation [*Memoir*, 1:225].

The Bible in the native language was indispensable for the growth of the new disciples and for the continuance of the mission. Judson therefore steadily worked on the translation of the Bible into the Burman language, in addition to his regular preaching, teaching, and debating. He intensified his translation efforts during periods of government intimidation; he had more time to spend on translating, for few inquirers came to hear him preach during those times. While Mrs. Judson visited America in 1821-23, he devoted himself with redoubled energy to the work of translating.

Prince M., brother to the king of Burma, encouraged Judson to finish his translation. Judson had presented the last three chapters of Matthew to the prince in December of 1822 because the Prince had especially asked to have an account of the death and resurrection of Jesus. In January the Prince asked Judson to bring him all the Christian Scriptures and translate them into Burman, "For I wish to read them all." On August 5, 1823, Judson sent a letter to Daniel Sharp in America.

> It is with real satisfaction that I am able to inform you of the completion of the New Testament in Burman, about six weeks ago; since which I have added, by way of introduction, and epitome of the Old Testament, in twelve sections, consisting of a summary of Scripture history from the creation to the coming of Christ, and an abstract of the most important proph-

ecies of the Messiah and his kingdom, from the Psalms, Isaiah, and other prophets. I trust this work will be found as valuable at present as the preaching; for though not, strictly speaking, the word of God, it is compiled almost entirely in the words of Scripture, is received by the converts with great eagerness, and found to be peculiarly interesting and instructive, and forms, moreover, a sort of text book, from which I am able to communicate much information on the history, types, and prophecies of the Old Testament in a systematic manner [*Memoir*, 1:325].

The members of the board of the General Missionary Convention expressed their desire that Judson continue with his translating until the Old Testament was also complete. As the number of inquirers increased, so did the frustration of the translator.

Our house is frequently crowded with company; but I am obliged to leave them to Moung En . . . in order to get time for the translation. Is this right? Happy is the missionary who goes to a country where the Bible is translated to his hand [*Memoir*, 1:523].

However, Judson did realize that he was uniquely qualified to pave the way for others in this endeavor. Though the task was often grueling, his confidence in its value never decreased. The importance of having the Scripture in the reading tongue of each person was pressed upon Judson in a conversation with a new convert in December of 1827.

After worship, he inquired with feeling, "What shall I do to be saved?" "Believe on the Lord Jesus Christ." "I do believe. I do believe. This religion is right. I have been all wrong. What shall I now do?" "If you have begun to believe, let your faith increase. Attend worship. Keep the Lord's day. Become the Saviour's servant. Do all his will. Give yourself, soul and body, into his hands. Will you do so?" "I will, I will. But I do not know all his will." "Read the Scriptures." "I can read Talaing only, not Burman." "Come then, and we will read to you. Come every day to worship, and at all times of day, and we will instruct you" [*Memoir*, 1:440].

After this conversation Judson adopted a new missionary method. He set up an open, covered building, a Zayat, in an accessible public place in which he employed one of the native Christians to read the Scriptures each day.

Judson wrote that he had two great objects toward which he labored in Burma. First he desired to establish a church. The conversion of the local people was his primary concern. But the second great goal of his missionary work was the translation of the Bible into the language of the people (*Memoir*, 2:192).

In June of 1832, Judson concluded that it was his duty to confine himself exclusively to the work of translating. According to his calculations, this course of action would allow him to complete the task in two years. He begged the prayers of his friends that "in my seclusion, I may enjoy the presence of the Saviour, and that special aid in translating the inspired word" (2:50).

On December 31, 1833, Judson wrote the corresponding secretary of the General Missionary Convention that

> I did hope, at one time, to have been able to insert, under this date, a notice of the completion of the Old Testament; but, though I have long devoted nearly all my time to that work, I have found it so heavy, and my health (as usual this season) so poor, that, though near the goal, I cannot yet say I have attained [*Memoir*, 2:75].

Judson delayed mailing the letter for one month. Just before finally sealing the envelope, he wrote a postscript.

> P.S. January 31, 1834. Thanks be to God, I can now say I have attained. I have knelt down before him, with the last leaf in my hand, and imploring his forgiveness for all the sins which have polluted my labors in this department, and his aid in future efforts to remove the errors and imperfections which necessarily cleave to the work, I have commended it to his mercy and grace; I have dedicated it to his glory. May he make his own inspired word, now complete in the Burman tongue, the grand instrument of filling all Burmah with songs of praise to our great God and Saviour Jesus Christ. Amen [*Memoir*, 2:75-76].

Judson also desired to begin a seminary for the native preachers. He had no desire to carry them through a long course of study "until they are able to unravel metaphysics, and calculate eclipses, and their souls become as dry as the one and as dark as the other." His desire was to see them "thoroughly acquainted with the Bible from beginning to end." He wanted to teach them the related theological disciplines only so far as it was necessary for them "to understand the Scriptures." He particularly wanted them to study a course in systematic theology. New preachers also needed to be instructed in the art of communicating their ideas intelligibly.

Judson's view of the inspiration of Scripture and its irreplaceable, infallible authority as revelation from God is best summed up in his own words to the American and Foreign Bible Society in 1845.

> The word of God is the golden lamp hung out of heaven, to enlighten the nations that sit in darkness, and to show them the path that leads from the confines of hell to the gates of paradise. The Bible, in the original tongues, comprises all the revelation now extant which God has given to this world. It is, in all its contents, and parts, and appendages, just the book, the one book, which infinite wisdom saw best adapted to answer the end of a writ-

ten revelation. It may not be reducible to the rules of human philosophy or logic, for it transcends them all. It is just as clear and obscure, just as copious and scanty, has just as many beauties and blemishes, is replete with just as many difficulties and apparent contradictions, as infinite wisdom saw necessary, in order to make it, like all the works of God, perfect and unique. This one perfect book is the sacred deposit in the hands of the church. It has been deposited with injunction, "Freely ye have received, freely give." Woe be to that man who withholds the treasure from his neighbor. Woe be to him who attempts to obscure the light of the lamp of heaven. It is the peculiar glory of the last half century that the Christian world has awaked to the duty and importance of giving the sacred word "to all lands." Praised be God for Bible and Missionary Societies, the peculiar institutions of modern times. May their efforts be continued and enlarged a hundred fold, until their work is consummated—until the Bible is translated and published in every language under heaven, and a copy of the sacred volume deposited in every palace, and house, and hut inhabited by man [*Memoir*, 2:236-37].

BIBLIOGRAPHY

William Carey

Biographical and Literary Notices of William Carey. Northampton: The Dryden Press, Taylor & Son, 1886.

Carey, Eustace. *Memoir of William Carey.* London: Jackson & Walford, 1836.

Carey, S. Pearce. *William Carey.* New York: Doran, 1924.

Carey, William. *An Enquiry Into the Obligations of Christians to Use Means for the Conversion of the Heathens.* Leisester: printed and sold by Ann Ireland, 1792.

Periodical Accounts Relative to the Baptist Missionary Society. Vols. 1-5. London: printed by J. Morris, 1800-15.

Adoniram Judson

Judson, Edward. *The Life of Adoniram Judson.* Philadelphia: American Baptist Publication Society, 1883.

Massachusetts Baptist Missionary Magazine. Vols. 3-4 (1813-14).

Wayland, Francis. *A Memoir of the Life and Labours of Adoniram Judson.* 2 vols. Boston: Phillips, Sampson & Co., 1853.

CHAPTER SEVEN

"They Separated Themselves the One from the Other"

The seeds of division between Baptists in the North and Baptists in the South were sown as early as 1619, when the English crown introduced slavery into the colonies over the protests of the Virginia colonial government. The harvest began in 1833, when English Baptists, heady from victory in procuring legislation against slavery in the British West Indies, enthusiastically encouraged Baptists in America "to seek, by all legitimate means, its speedy and entire destruction" (*Source Book*, p. 88).

This letter was received by an officer of the General Missionary Convention and after some delay was presented to the Baptist Board of Foreign Missions. This board referred the matter to a committee whose members discussed the matter thoroughly and finally answered the letter on September 1, 1834. Lucius Bolles, corresponding secretary, penned the letter.

Bolles first explained the nature of the United States government, absolving it of any guilt, for it had "no power nor right, to adopt any direct measures in reference to the emancipation of the slaves in the Southern States" (pp. 88-89). The Constitution made no provision for the national government to interfere in the matter.

Second, Bolles reminded the British Baptists that the insistence of their own sovereign brought about the existence of slavery in America and that part of the grievances of the Revolution was "that the King of England had steadily resisted the efforts of the colonies to prevent the introduction of slaves" (p. 89). At present, Bolles said, many states have no slavery and others are seeking its entire extinction.

Finally, Bolles appealed to the sense of unity among the Baptists of America and assured the Englishmen that "our brethren at the south would rejoice to see any practicable scheme devised for relieving the country from slavery" (p. 89).

We have the best evidence that our slaveholding brethren are Christians, sincere followers of the Lord Jesus. In every other part of their conduct, they adorn the doctrine of God our Savior. We cannot, therefore, feel that it is right to use languages or adopt measures which might tend to break the ties that unite them to us in our General Convention, and in numerous other benevolent societies; and to array brother against brother, church against church, and association against association in a contest about slavery [p. 89].

This reply, however, was most unsatisfactory to some other Baptists in America. In May of 1835 a group met in Boston and sent an alternate reply to the English Baptists. It stated that no attempt should be made to exonerate the nation from the charge of upholding slavery. "We are verily a guilty nation before God, touching the inalienable rights of many of our fellowmen" (p. 90). They then pledged themselves "to labor in the use of weapons not carnal but mighty through God to the overthrow of this as well as every other work of wickedness."

Convictions concerning this subject became more intense until in 1839 Baptists in the North formed the American Baptist Anti-Slavery Convention. In April of 1840 this convention published an address to Southern Baptists. After presenting an argument against slavery, the address concluded with an impassioned appeal to concerned Baptists to forsake the South and move to the prairies on the frontier. If the Southerners chose to reject both the warnings and the entreaties given and still cling to the present system the Convention members said,

> we cannot and we dare not recognize you as consistent brethren in Christ; we cannot join in partial, selfish prayers, that the groans of the slave may be unheard; we cannot hear preaching which makes God the author and approver of human misery and vassalage; and we cannot, at the Lord's table, cordially take that as a brother's hand, which plies the scourge on woman's naked flesh—which thrusts a gag into the mouth of a man,—which rivets fetters on the innocent,—and which shuts up the Bible from human eyes. We deplore your condition; we pray for your deliverance; and God forbid that we should ever sin against Him by ceasing so to pray [p. 94].

Tension continued to increase between North and South until in 1844 relationships reached the breaking point. Vows of neutrality had been taken in 1841 by the Home Mission Society and the General Missionary Convention. However, Georgia Baptists were not convinced of the integrity of such vows in light of the abolitionist activity of leaders of the Home Mission Society. Therefore, in 1844 the Georgia Baptist Executive Committee, of which J. L. Dagg was a member, submitted the name of James E. Reeve to be appointed by the Home Mission Society as a missionary.

With his application the information that he was a slaveholder was included. The Executive Board of the Society answered:

> In the opinion of several members of the Board, the application seeks the appointment, not in the usual manner merely of a Missionary, but of a slaveholder, and is designed as a test whether the Board will appoint a slaveholder as a Missionary, and this (in the language of the Society's resolution) "in direct contravention of the whole letter and spirit of the Constitution" introduces the subject of slavery. . . .
>
> Resolved, that taking into consideration all the circumstances of the case, we deem ourselves not at liberty to entertain the application for the appointment of Rev. James E. Reeve [p. 106].

Alabama Baptists, upon hearing of the answer to Georgia, were unwilling to allow the missionary agencies to skirt what they considered a vital issue. Therefore, under the influence of Basil Manly, Sr., they sent a document of resolutions to the Board of Managers of the General Missionary Convention asking for specific information. One resolution read:

> Resolved, that our duty at this crisis requires us to demand from the proper authorities in all those bodies to whose funds we have contributed, or with whom we have in any way been connected, the distinct, explicit, avowal that slaveholders are eligible, and entitled, equally with non-slaveholders, to all the privileges and immunities of their several unions; and especially to receive any agency, mission, or other appointment, which run within the scope of their operation or duties [p. 107].

The upholders of the Alabama resolutions also determined to withhold any funds from the societies unless a satisfactory answer was forthcoming.

The Board of Managers responded promptly. They stated regret that such a "demand" was made upon them in a situation entirely hypothetical. However, an explicit answer was given:

> If, however, any one should offer himself as a Missionary, having slaves, and should insist on retaining them as his property, we could not appoint him. One thing is certain; we can never be a party to any arrangement which would imply approbation of slavery [p. 109].

To the possibility of the South's withholding funds, the Board replied that the principles espoused were "dearer to us than any pecuniary aid whatever."

This answer prodded Virginia Baptists to take action. The Virginia Baptist Foreign Mission Society considered the Board's reply, though it had been provoked by "exciting and embarrassing circumstances," clearly to be "an outrage on our rights." The decision was inconsistent with certain admissions made in the reply, unjust, and unwise, the Vir-

ginia Society said. It indicated refusal to appoint slaveholders yet willingness to receive and use their money. Therefore, in view of the lack of full
cooperation with slaveholders and the supposed infringement of the constitution and rights of Southerners, the Virginia Baptist Foreign Mission
Society issued a call for a convention to discuss the best means for Southerners to promote the foreign mission cause. The meeting was held in
Augusta, Georgia, in May of 1845.

Because of its separation from the General Missionary Convention, the
North accused the South of clinging to and cherishing slavery "in prefer-
ence to everything else." Obviously the South denied the charge.

> Southern Baptists [do] not "cling to and cherish slavery in preference to
> everything else." Slavery has been inherited by her; it clings to her; she
> feels it to be a burden and a curse; and gladly would she get rid of it,
> if she could do so without inflicting greater mischiefs than those which
> she would attempt to remove. Such, at least, we believe to be the senti-
> ments of a large majority of professing Christians and considerate men in
> the South ["An Examination," pp. 134-35].

The South claimed that the constitution of the General Missionary Convention had been violated by introducing a novel qualification, nonslave-
holding, for approval as a missionary. As a result of this, the missionary
outlet for Southerners was clogged and, in their opinion, they had no other
option than to form a separate convention. Also the rights of the churches
had been bypassed by the Board's introduction of a new moral criterion
without either the direction or the approval of the churches. The separation was complete, and the South pleaded for a unity of purpose even
though there was a division in the mission organizations.

> Henceforward, let there be no strife between North and South. We are
> brethren. Our interest is one and indivisible. Entertaining similar views
> of the kingdom of Christ, we should vie with each other in labors and
> sacrifices to extend and perpetuate it ["An Examination," p. 135].

It is evident, and none has ever denied it, that the separation did not
take place as a result of theological differences. North and South were in
unison theologically, in union in their zeal for missions, and in union in
their view of Scripture. The ground of the separation lay in other issues,
most of which centered on the existence of slavery in the South. That such
unanimity existed can easily be demonstraed by examining the doctrine
of Scripture of the two groups. One of the most prominent and influential
theologians in the North at that time was Francis Wayland. In the South,
John L. Dagg carried out a formative teaching ministry. Those two men
are representative of the Baptist viewpoint in those days of organizational
crises.

FRANCIS WAYLAND

On March 11, 1796, Sarah Moore Wayland gave birth to a child who became the namesake of her husband, Francis. The couple had moved from England to New York and had arrived in the New World September 20, 1793. They had been Baptists in England and soon after arriving in New York united with Fayette Street Church. Mr. Wayland was chosen a deacon. His association with the church's deacons form some of the earliest religious impressions that young Francis Wayland recalled.

> My father's associates seem to me to have been far better acquainted with the Scriptures and with the doctrines of the gospel, and more thoroughly religious, than we commonly find professing Christians at the present day. Fuller, Gill, Booth, Romaine, Hervey, Toplady, and Newton were much more frequently quoted by them than such writers are by Christians among us. My father's peculiar treasure was a copy of Cann's Bible, with marginal references. This he unceasingly studied, and never relinquished it, until it was actually worn out by daily and almost constant use [*Memoir*, 1:13].

Evidently Mr. Wayland was a keen businessman, and through his astute business practices the Waylands "soon became prosperous to such an extent as satisfied their ambition" (1:13). However, in 1805, through the influence of systematic Bible study and sessions devoted to the practice of exhortation, "he decided to close his business and devote himself exclusively to the ministry" (1:16). He became pastor of a church in Poughkeepsie in that year, and four years later, in 1811, he moved to Albany and then to Troy.

In 1811 young Wayland entered Union College at Albany, New York. His course of study was somewhat dissatisfying there because of what he considered to be unfortunate methods of instruction. He also records in a letter to his mother a significant spiritual struggle he was experiencing.

> I know that nothing but the blood of Christ applied to my soul can cleanse me; but how can this blood be applied? . . . I try to pray, but I know that I can do nothing to help myself. I think I can say that God would be just, were he to send me to hell; but I know that he alone can save me [*Memoir*, 1:35].

After his graduation, in July 1813, he began the study of medicine in the offices of two prominent physicians. During this time Wayland was converted—two times. One conversion occurred in his intellect. The second conversion made him a new creature.

Wayland describes his first conversion as a "remarkable change . . . in my intellectual condition" (1:41). Although he read well and had an "unlimited command of books," he subsided into reading for amusement—

Fig. 10. Francis Wayland
From Cathcart's *The Baptist Encyclopedia*, Everts, 1883. 2:1220.

novels, travels, and works of humor. He enjoyed only narrative and found didactic and abstract writing uninteresting and tiring. His style changed suddenly, however, and that sudden change colored his philosophy of education and preaching.

> I remember with perfect distinctness, the time when I first became conscious of a decided change in my whole intellectual character. I was sitting by a window, in an attic room which I occupied as a sort of study, or reading-place, and by accident I opened a volume of the Spectator—I think it was one of the essays forming Addison's critique on Milton—it was, at any rate, something purely didactic. I commenced reading it, and, to my delight and surprise, I found that I understood and really enjoyed it. I could not account for the change. I read on, and found that the very essays, which I had formerly passed over without caring to read them, were now to me the gems of the whole book, vastly more attractive than the stories and narratives that I had formerly read with so much interest [*Memoir*, 1:42].

Far outweighing this experience in importance is the second conversion—his rebirth. His own testimony of his salvation experience spans eight pages of small print in his biography. The following is a greatly reduced edition of that autobiographical account.

> I believed the truths of religion, for ought I know, as fully as I do now. But my heart was unmoved. . . . At times the Spirit of God strove powerfully with me. I saw my danger. . . . I do not remember any sermon that did me any good. The preaching, then as now, seemed to me to be too theological . . . with but little of that warm interest in man's salvation that appears suitable in the herald of a free and finished redemption. . . . I believed all that the Bible said of my condition and my danger. Jesus Christ came to save sinners; yet I had never sought his forgiveness [*Memoir*, 1:52].

Wayland at that point devised a plan whereby he would seek salvation and "do nothing else until I had secured the salvation of my soul." He even marked out a plan through which his conversion must come. It did not work. As he described the situation, God "disappointed me, and made me willing to accept his grace in any manner he should choose to bestow it" (1:53). Finally Wayland heard Luther Rice preach on the text "the glorious gospel of the blessed God" (1 Timothy 1:11).

> For the first time in my life, I was constrained to believe that the sentiments of my heart were in harmony with the gospel; that I loved God and all that God loved; and that it would be a pleasure to me to devote all my life to his service [*Memoir*, 1:54].

After his conversion, the doctrine of election, offensive to him earlier, became a source of great comfort.

> My mind at one time rebelled against the doctrine of election. It seemed
> to me like partiality. I now perceived that I had no claim whatever on
> God, but that if I were lost it was altogether my own fault, and that if I
> were saved, it must be purely a deed of unmerited grace. I saw that this
> very doctrine was my only hope of salvation, for if God had not sought me,
> I should never have sought him [*Memoir*, 1:55].

Coincident with his call to salvation, Wayland decided that he could
ask God's blessing on his activity in no enterprise save the gospel ministry.
Therefore, in 1816 he entered Andover Theological Seminary and studied
for one year before returning to Union College as a tutor. After four years
at Union he accepted a call to First Baptist Church in Boston as pastor.
The members of that church had heard him preach four Sundays (he
had only eight sermons) and had extended a call to him on the basis of a
fifteen to ten vote. Wayland's friends encouraged him to accept the call,
for "the cause here absolutely and imperiously demands a man like you,
who has a depth of exegetical lore, who can meet the Unitarians on ground
where he is not liable to feel his inferiority, or be put to the blush" (1:119).
Wayland accepted the call ("I don't think much of these unanimous calls.
It looks as though people did not judge for themselves.") and set out for
Boston in early August 1821. He was ordained on the twenty-first of
August and entered into his responsibilities with fear and trembling.

> I could not but reflect that in all human probability . . . I should be the
> cause of the eternal salvation or damnation of many souls. The doctrines
> which I should preach, the behavior which I should exhibit . . . was to
> have henceforth a bearing upon eternity. Who was sufficient for these
> things? I certainly was not. I could only find consolation in looking to
> that Name which is above every name, renewedly dedicating myself to his
> service, and praying that he would make me faithful unto death [*Memoir*,
> 1:120].

In his first message to the congregation, Wayland revealed his spirit of
total submission to Scripture. A minister "may not add to the word of God
his own inference nor the inferences of other men," and he is certainly
"forbidden to take anything from the Word of God." Even if there are
apparent inconsistencies in the doctrines of Scripture, it is the duty of the
minister "to preach them both, fully and clearly, as they are revealed in
the Scriptures." God is doubtless consistent with Himself, "but he has
never appointed us judges of his consistency" (1:121-23).

He maintained that attitude to the end of his days. In 1858 he wrote
a letter to a student in which he set forth his opinions on the subject of
how preaching should relate to Scripture.

> I apprehend that when we give up the account of our ministry, one of our
> greatest failures will be found to be that we have so often neglected the

Word of God. It looks strange that the Son of God has left heaven to teach us, and has promised his Spirit to accompany his Word, and has set us to preach it, and that we should have anything to preach that we like better, or that we should merely take a start from the Bible, and go on with our own imaginings [*Memoir*, 2:230].

In 1827, Wayland accepted the presidency of Brown University. The situation he inherited was less than ideal.

The condition of the college was not encouraging. The number of undergraduates was small. Discipline had been neglected. Difficulties had arisen between the president and the trustees, and between the president and some members of the Faculty. In point of fact the college had not a high reputation in the community, and probably did not deserve it [*Memoir*, 1:205].

Wayland, by creative and reasonable methods of discipline and instruction, raised the quality and prestige of the university to match that of any in the land at that time. He resigned the presidency in August of 1855, twenty-eight years after he had accepted the position, terminating a highly innovative and successful term of office. He stated that one of the factors of his success was his knowledge of Scripture. "Whatever of knowledge I have of men or mind, I have gained from the New Testament of our Lord Jesus Christ" (2:150).

In 1857 Wayland, upon the death of Rev. Granger, pastor of First Baptist Church, Providence, was "requested to undertake the performance of ministerial and pastoral labors for the time being, and until it may be thought best to make some other arrangement" (2:185). His compensation was twenty-five dollars a week. In 1858 he was invited to become permanent pastor of the church, but did not accept the invitation. During the year a great revival had taken place and Wayland had baptized fifty-one people. However, in May, after sixteen months of labor, he terminated his peculiar relationship with the church because of increased demand on his decreasing physical strength.

He spent the remainder of his days in intermittent preaching, speaking to patriotic assemblies, writing, and voluminous correspondence. He died on Saturday, September 30, 1865. On the Sunday before he died he talked very openly with a close Christian friend.

I feel that my race is nearly run. I have, indeed, tried to do my duty. I cannot accuse myself of having neglected any known obligation. Yet all this avails nothing. I place no dependence on anything but the righteousness and death of Jesus Christ. I have never enjoyed the raptures of faith vouchsafed to many Christians. I do not undervalue these feelings, but it has not pleased God to bestow them upon me. I have, however, a confident hope that I am accepted in the Beloved [*Memoir*, 2:360].

Among the many books written by Wayland is an ethics text entitled *The Elements of Moral Science,* first published in 1835. He reveals much about his view of the authority of Scripture as he states, in his preface to the first edition of the book, his hopes for the success of his writing.

> Entertaining those views of the Sacred Scriptures, which I have expressed in the work itself, it is scarcely necessary to add here, that I consider them the great source of moral truth; and that a system of ethics will be true, just in proportion as it develops their meaning. To do this has been my object; and to have, in ever so humble a manner, accomplished it, I shall consider as the greatest possible success.

Wayland divides his volume into book one, on theoretical ethics, and book two, on practical ethics. In book one, chapter seven, Wayland investigates the subject of natural religion. In one section he discusses the "manner" in which one learns his duty by the light of nature. A second section discusses "how far" one may learn his duty by the light of nature. The third section of this chapter mentions the defects of the system of natural religion and concludes that "there seems to exist a great need of some additional moral force, to correct the moral evils of our nature" (p. 121). Therefore it is certainly not improbable that a merciful Creator would have given additional instruction concerning man's duty.

Chapter seven discusses the relation between natural and revealed religion. Wayland argues very carefully for the unity of truth in this section. Theological statements cannot be affirmed as true if they directly contradict irrefutable and obvious truth from nature.

> It is granted that natural religion does teach us some unquestionable truths. Now, no truth can be inconsistent with itself. And hence it might be expected, that whenever natural and revealed religion treated upon the same subjects, they would teach in perfect harmony. The second instructor may teach more than the first; but so far as they give instruction on the same subjects, if both teach the truth, they must both teach the same lesson [*Elements,* p. 122].

A revelation would also give us greater and clearer information on the subject of duty, present us with motives to virtue, and furnish us with truths which could not be communicated by natural religion. The Old and New Testaments fully realize all of those expectations, according to Wayland. Thus, the evidence favors an a priori judgment that "the Author of the universe—that is, of natural religion—is also the Author of the Scriptures" (p. 124).

Wayland also discusses the possibility of revelation occurring in language. He exhibits no reticence in affirming that many elements of revealed religion could not possibly be communicated by either general laws or personal experience but must be made known by language. The doctrine of the resurrection, of a universal and impartial judgment, of the atonement, and of the way in which a man benefits from the atonement are all of great practical importance; "and yet, all of them being of the nature of facts, they could be made known to man in no other way than by language" (p. 125).

On this basis—the coincidence of what one might reasonably expect from the God of nature and what one actually confronts in Scripture—Wayland concludes that the barrier to belief in Scripture as a revelation from God should be removed.

> And hence we conclude that a revelation of the will of God by language is not as many persons suppose, an event so unlikely, that no evidence can be conceived sufficiently strong to render it credible; but, that it is, on the contrary, an event, from all that we know of God already essentially probable; and that it is, to say the least of it, as fairly within the limits of evidence as any other event and . . . is as much entitled to belief as any other event [*Elements*, p. 126].

Wayland's submission to Scripture is evident in the divisions of this book as well as in the ethical principles he espouses. He considers all ethical questions in book two on practical ethics under two headings—"Love to God" and "Duties to Man." This division arises naturally from the scriptural teaching concerning the greatest and second greatest commandments.

Biblicism did not make Wayland ignore contemporary problems but rather raised his sensitivity to the obligation of seeking solutions to them. The most obvious example of his grappling with knotty problems rests in his analysis of slavery.

Slavery, in Wayland's day, was the most common violation of personal liberty. After stating certain political and economic disadvantages of slavery, Wayland says: "Let us inquire what is the doctrine of Revelation on this subject" (p. 200). He then proceeds to demonstrate how slavery violates the commandment to love one's neighbor and Jesus' command to treat others as you would have them treat you. Thus, the moral precepts of the Bible are diametrically opposed to slavery.

Also, God, in Scripture, has imposed obligations upon man which are inconsistent with domestic slavery. Slavery, by repressing the intellectual liberty of the slave (e.g., by forbidding reading), violates the Great Commission, because it limits the means by which a man may come to know God. Slavery, by interfering with conjugal, parental, and filial relations, renders the Scripture's precepts regarding family life an impossible attainment for the slave. Thus, these considerations make one conclude that the

Scripture indirectly forbids slavery, and "what is indirectly forbidden in the Scripture, is as truly forbidden as though it were directly forbidden" (p. 203).

Wayland discusses the implications of slavery further and carefully interprets the passages outlining the duties of slaves to masters. He concludes:

> The manner in which the duty of servants or slaves is inculcated, therefore, affords no ground for the assertion, that the gospel authorizes one man to hold another in bondage, any more than the command to honour the king, when that king was Nero, authorized the tyranny of the emperor [p. 205].

Throughout this section, Wayland takes great pains to discuss the subject thoroughly in its biblical context, examining each facet of the arguments that allow slavery. He does not construct a straw man for the sake of his argument but sets forth the strongest points in the pro-slavery position and then systematically dissembles each point by careful exegesis of Scripture. His method is never sarcastic or unfair but is always designed to ascertain truth. He attacks no person but aims his weapons at inadequate interpretations of Scripture that lead to immoral, unbiblical conduct.

Wayland is not deluded as to the complexity of the situation (whether it be slavery, church and state, freedom of the press, or any number of matters he addresses) and does not provide simplistic answers. In fact he is quite aware of the objection raised by many Southerners during this time that it is better to keep the slave and provide for him than manumit him to a hopeless freedom. Wayland concedes that that is a possible condition and allows for a moral alternative to immediate emancipation.

> I answer, supposing such to be the fact, it may be the duty of the master to hold the slave; not however, *on the ground of right over him,* but of *obligation to him,* but of obligation *to him* for the *purpose of accomplishing a particular and specified good.* And, of course, he who holds him for any other purpose, holds him wrongfully, and is guilty of the sin of slavery [p. 206].

He even outlines the biblical teaching concerning the duties of slaves to masters and considers them, as revelation from God, binding. However, he is insistent that obedience, fidelity, submission, and respect proceed on the ground of duty to God and to man. Admonitions to slaves do not legitimize slavery; they merely provide a method by which a slave "may exhibit a sublimity and purity of moral character" (p. 207). In fact, the Bible insists that a slave disobey and suffer the consequences if a master commands him to do wrong. If opportunity to gain freedom arises, and if the welfare and safety of others are not jeopardized, it may be the slave's obligation to seize his freedom and withdraw personal service from the master. Wayland lists 1 Corinthians 7:21 as a text supporting that option.

It should be clear that in practice as well as theory Wayland believes that a system of morality is true to the extent that it reflects the biblical teaching on any subject.

Wayland was deeply concerned about the vitality of Baptist churches and Baptist preaching. In 1856 a series of letters on Baptist life appeared in *The Examiner* over the signature of "Roger Williams," a pseudonym for Wayland. The letters were published as a book in 1857 under the title *Notes on the Principles and Practices of Baptist Churches*, by Francis Wayland. Preaching is a subject he addresses often. In the course of these letters Wayland tells many things a preacher should not do. Two warnings concern how a man prepares to preach:

> A strong temptation frequently assails a man, when preparing a sermon, to look around for helps. He can easily find a book of skeletons made to his hand, and it seems to him very convenient to make use of it. Let me urge every brother, as he values his self-respect, his honesty, his ministerial usefulness, as he values his own soul and the souls of others, to resist this temptation at the outset. If he have any of these crutches, let him commit them at once to the flames, or he will never learn to walk. The habit is absolutely fatal [*Principles*, p. 283].

Wayland warns against a second devastating practice in a book entitled *Letters on the Ministry of the Gospel*:

> In fact, there was, for a considerable period within my recollection, a prejudice against an educated ministry. It was supposed that an education far in advance of their brethren induced a reliance upon learning rather than on the Spirit of God. This was frequently carried to a ludicrous extreme. Some people believed that a man should not prepare for the pulpit by studying at all; and ministers would sometimes, in the way of boasting, declare at the commencement of a discourse that they did not know until they entered the pulpit from what text they should address the audience. The result was such as might be expected. They either spoke at random, without any object, and tending to no result, or else they had become familiar with one or two trains of thought, which they easily fell into, no matter what text they might happen to select [*Letters*, p. 18].

Of greater concern to Wayland was the source of authority for the preaching. In *Principles and Practices* he proposes the question "Why take a text at all?" which he proceeds to answer.

> It proceeds upon the supposition that the Bible is the word of the living God; the only manifestation that has been made to us of the will of our Creator and our Judge, the only record of what he has done for our sal-

vation; the only volume on whose pages are inscribed the conditions on
which we may escape eternal wrath, and enter into the rest which remain-
eth for the people of God. This is the truth which the minister of the gospel is sent forth to utter. This is the beginning, and the middle, and end
of his teaching. He comes to us with a message from on high. He claims
to be an ambassador. It is meet, therefore, that he should take for his
subject, not merely as his motto, some part of the revelation from God,
so that when he speaks to us, we may know that he keeps within the limits
of his commission. It is this truth alone which God has promised to accompany with that energy of Holy Spirit, without which we know that no soul
is ever made wise unto salvation [*Principles,* pp. 297-98].

Wayland asked the question "Why take a text?" a second time in his
book *Letters on the Ministry of the Gospel.* The answer is predictable:
"Simply because we profess in preaching to unfold some idea of inspiration, and, on the authority of God, enforce it on our hearers." At this
point Wayland makes a statement which, taken out of context, could
mislead the reader concerning Wayland's view of inspiration. He states,
"It is not enough that we take for our text the words; we must take the
ideas of the sacred Scriptures" (p. 64). This echoes a statement Wayland
made eleven years earlier (1853) in his book *The Apostolic Ministry.* At
that time, concerned with the biblical knowledge of the Baptist ministry,
Wayland wrote: "the revelation given to us consists of ideas, and not of
words" (p. 69). On first glance these statements seem to reject the idea
of verbal inspiration. However, that is precisely what Wayland did not
intend to reject. His desire was that the interpreter might "ascertain the
precise idea communicated by the Spirit of God in that particular passage."
He would have the preacher preach the truth revealed to us by God, not
some idea merely analogous to the text. Wayland would not allow a man
to preach on one word of a text if the direction of the message moved
away from the meaning of the text and toward a general discourse using
that word as a theme. That is what Wayland meant by asserting that the
revelation of God was of ideas, not words. For example, if a man chose
the word "repent" from the text "Except ye repent, ye shall all likewise
perish" (Luke 13:3) and presented an oration (for Wayland would not
call it a sermon) on "repentance," complete with etymological studies, historical illustrations, and contemporary applications, so that it could be
"laid away in a safe place, and become one of the stock-discourses of the
author" (p. 69), and yet failed to deal with the idea of repentance as it is
explicitly presented in that text of Scripture, he would not have presented
the revelation from God.

For Wayland, the sermon must be "the text expanded, and the text the
sermon contracted" (*Letters on the Ministry,* p. 71). In preaching the
thoughts of Scripture one preaches the thoughts of God. "Without doing

this he can never expect the blessing of God upon his labors, nor can he say, when he has finished his course, 'I am free from the blood of all men.'"
Revelation of ideas, for Wayland, binds the preacher to the true meaning of Scripture and excludes fanciful excursions into nonrevelatory areas.

He manifests the same thought in discussing kinds of preaching. The first kind he mentions is doctrinal preaching. The object of doctrinal preaching "is to explain and prove some truth of revelation" (p. 284). This kind of sermon falls naturally into two divisions: first, the exposition of the truth, and second, the proof of it.

> The proof of any truth of revelation must be essentially revelation itself. God has not made a revelation of that which has been already made known by natural religion. The highest authority for our belief of any truth, is that God has said it. Why, then, should we go to the weaker evidence to support the stronger? We may present the texts in the Bible which affirm the truth directly, showing by a brief exposition that this is their exact and legitimate meaning. We may adduce other truths from Scripture which harmonize with what we affirm, or which take it for granted. We may appeal to the experience of inspired men, who have relied on this truth as the foundation of their trust and hope, and thus, from every inspired source, derive confirmation and proof of what we affirm to be true. . . .

> There has seemed to me a growing disposition to omit the proof of a revealed truth from revelation, and attempt the proof from every other source than the Bible. Why should this be? If the Bible be true, why should we ignore its evidence? To do thus may seem more philosophical, and may be more pleasing to unregenerate men, but is it really according to the mind of the Spirit? Do we not thus practically lead men to the conclusion that there is a higher authority than the word of God, by which it is to be judged, and to which its teachings are to be subjected [*Principles*, pp. 285-86]?

The preceding discussion reveals several characteristics of Wayland's view of Scripture.

One, he considered the teachings of Scripture true. Scriptural truth is consistent with all other truth. Two, he identified God's revelation with the written word of Scripture. Scripture is a revelation from God. Three, the precepts of Scripture are morally binding. A person commits intellectual and moral error to the degree that he departs from scriptural teaching. Four, there is no authority by which one can sit in judgment on Scripture. Rather, Scripture judges all things.

John L. Dagg

John Leadley Dagg can easily be viewed as a representative Southern Baptist of this period. He was born in Loudoun County, Virginia, on Feb-

Fig. 11. J. L. Dagg

From *Manual of Theology* by John L. Dagg. Charleston, S.C.: Southern Baptist
Publication Society, 1859. Frontispiece.

ruary 13, 1794, the son of Robert and Sarah Davis Dagg.

Though Dagg had little formal education, his scholarly achievements are unquestionable. He was highly motivated to learn. Through personal tenacity (and careful parental guidance) he conquered Hebrew, Greek, and Latin almost singlehandedly. Dagg learned the greatest amount of Hebrew after he lost his eyesight. His abilities were so obvious to those around him that at the age of fifteen, he became the teacher at a school in Landmark Hill, four miles from Middleburg, Virginia. Of the twenty-seven students he taught, several were older than he was.

Soon after accepting that position, Dagg became deeply concerned about his salvation. In his autobiography he records the events leading to his conversion.

> On the night of February 12th, after I had gone to bed, I thought much on the words of Christ, "Blessed are they that hunger and thirst after righteousness; for they shall be filled." A glimmer of hope, feeble and transient, now first entered my mind. The next day was my birth day; and on my way to school, I prayed that as I had been born on this day into the natural world, so the Lord might bring me this day into the spiritual world. In the evening after returning from school, I took up Boston's *Fourfold State,* and read until I came to a passage, "Think not of want of time, while the night follows the busy day; nor of want of place, while fields and out houses may be got." I rose, and retired behind the corn-house. Here, while in prayer to God, my soul was relieved by a joyful sense of divine acceptance. The prayer of the morning seemed to be answered; and the following words, though originally spoken in a far higher sense, appeared applicable to my case: "Thou art my son; this day have I begotten thee" [*Autobiography*, p. 9].

Three years later, after a period of study related to the question of the baptism of infants, Dagg concluded that the arguments supporting infant baptism were weak logically and even weaker biblically. Thus in the spring of 1812 Dagg presented himself to Elder William Fristoe, who baptized him into the Baptist church at Ebenezer, Virginia.

In an effort to determine his life's work, Dagg pursued various vocational interests. His father's occupation, making saddles and harnesses, occupied his early years. He studied medicine under Dr. E. B. Grady from 1811 until 1814, when he entered the army for the last part of the War of 1812. Because both his father and his stepmother died the year the war ended, he had to arrange for the support of his brothers and sisters. He began teaching as a private tutor in the family of Cuthbert Powell. Powell was so impressed with his abilities that he urged Dagg to study law. Dagg relates the event that prompted this encouragement.

> Being the only Baptist in the family, or among their connections, my re-
> ligious opinions were often brought under discussion. On one occasion,
> when on a visit to Major Burr Powell, he put Mason's *Essay on the Church*
> into my hand, pleasantly remarking that he wished to convert me to the
> Pedobaptist faith. I received the book thankfully; and, after reading it
> with care, wrote a review, in which I controverted his positions, and main-
> tained Baptist principles. This he read; and, at least, became satisfied that
> there was very little encouragement to labor for my conversion. Mr. Cuth-
> bert Powell asked permission to read this manuscript; and, after perusing
> it, favored me with some criticisms on it; and took occasion to advise, that
> I should turn my attention to the legal profession. Suspecting that I was
> inclined to the christian ministry, he remarked, that it was not every man's
> duty to minister at the altar, and that he thought my talents were specially
> adapted to the bar. I replied, that though I could not decide to give myself
> to the gospel ministry, I was unable to go in a contrary direction [*Auto-
> biography*, p. 19].

The apparent status, success, and affluence that accompanied the legal
profession were obvious enticements to Dagg. However, to paraphrase
C. G. Finney, Dagg had a retainer from a higher authority.

> Over against those I contemplated the reproach of being a Baptist minis-
> ter, and the poverty to be expected. In full view of the contrast, my heart
> said, give me reproach and poverty, if I may serve Christ and save souls.
> From that hour I never doubted my call to the ministry [*Autobiography*,
> p. 20].

Dagg suffered from extreme physical disabilities most of his adult life.
He was lame, blind, and hoarse during his most productive years. His
lameness resulted from a series of aggravations to his legs. In 1819 he
was forced to jump from a window when a floor in a building in which he
was preaching collapsed. The building was situated on an incline and
Dagg, having entered the building at night from the front, did not realize
how far the ground was from the window he exited. The ground was fully
fifteen feet below, and he wrenched his ankle severely. The ankle evidently never healed properly and the debility was compounded in 1823
when Dagg attended the fourth meeting of the Triennial Convention and
walked an inordinate amount. He used a crutch the remainder of his life.

That same year, 1823, two additional tragedies further complicated the
life of John L. Dagg—his wife's death, and severe damage to his eyesight.
He suffered the loss of his wife a few weeks after she gave birth to their
fourth child, in August. Dagg described this as "the severest blow I had
ever received." His wife's mother took charge of the "four helpless babes"
left behind, and Dagg was enabled to assume the responsibilities at his
school (*Autobiography*, p. 25).

Also, as a result of the duties he had recently taken on as principal at Upperville Academy he began to lose his eyesight. Teaching Greek constituted a part of his load at the academy. He arose early in the morning and studied Greek by the light of burning pine knots or candles until daybreak. By summer he found that his eyes were failing. The impairment eventually became so advanced that he was forced to wear bandages over his eyes much of the time. According to his testimony, his faith was severely tried: "Lame and blind, how could I be useful, and how provide for the wants of my children?"

Despite these handicaps he was called to the pastorate of Fifth Baptist Church in Philadelphia in 1825. Missions, temperance, and benevolences occupied his energies in addition to his preaching ministry. Dagg was instrumental in founding the Pennsylvania Missionary Association, which became the Pennsylvania Baptist Convention. His steady ministry of preaching and teaching gave rise to soreness in this throat which physicians were unable to remedy. In April of 1834 his voice completely left him. He was never able to speak much above a whisper after that time.

After losing his voice, he continued his ministry in a series of college presidencies and finally a writing ministry. From 1834-36 he was president of Haddington College, near Philadelphia. There he began his career as a professor of theology. In 1836 he accepted the presidency of Alabama Female Athenaeum, in Tuscaloosa, Alabama, where he remained until 1844, when he was appointed professor of theology and president of Mercer University. He went to Mercer on the strength of a recommendation by Basil Manly, a prominent Baptist preacher who was at the time president of the University of Alabama. Ten years later, in 1854, when he was sixty years old, he resigned the presidency of Mercer but continued as professor of theology until 1856.

His first volume of the *Manual of Theology* appeared in 1857. His pamphlet on "The Origin and Authority of the Bible," written in 1853, was included as a part of this. A second volume of his *Manual*, on "Church Order," was published in 1858. For the purpose of writing these books, Dagg invented a writing board, a device that enabled him to write without the aid of an amenuensis (though Dagg was virtually blind). The board held the paper firmly, and a guide could be shifted down one line at a time by turning a crank. He would write a line, turn the crank, and write another line without using his eyes.

Dagg's work called *Moral Science* was completed in 1859 after about one year of writing. He acknowledged his indebtedness to Francis Wayland but disagreed with Wayland on the subject of slavery and its necessity for the present society.

His next endeavor was entitled *The Evidences of Christianity* (1869).

His premise in that book is that pure Christianity is defined solely in terms of the Bible, its only source for doctrine. Also he implies that an impartial and accurate reading of Scripture would lead one naturally to assert that Christianity is the way of life taught there. Therefore, he seeks, in ten chapters, to demonstrate the entire trustworthiness and truthfulness of Scripture and thus establish the truth of the Christian faith. Chaper five constitutes an attempt to demonstrate the inerrancy of the Bible in matters of history.

The labors of J. L. Dagg would have been outstanding for a man of extraordinary physical vigor and endurance. When one considers that such significant pastoral, administrative, educational, and literary contributions proceeded from a man who could not see, could not walk, and could not talk, the accomplishment is all the more astonishing.

The enduring respect that Dagg enjoyed among Southern Baptists and the implicit acquiescence of Baptist leadership to his theological viewpoint is quite plainly revealed in an action taken at the Southern Baptist Convention of 1879. W. H. Whitsitt offered the following resolutions:

> Resolved, That a catechism be drawn up, containing the substance of the Christian religion, for the instruction of children and servants, and that brother Jon. L. Dagg be desired to draw it up.
>
> Resolved, That brethren Jeter, Mell, Winkler, Gambrell and Boyce be requested to assist brother Dagg in this work, in the capacity of a Committee of Revision.
>
> Resolved, That in case brother Dagg is unable to accede to the request of the Convention, the brethren of the Committee of Revision be desired to draw up the said catechism.
>
> Resolved, That the brethren in question be desired to publish the said catechism as soon as convenient after it is prepared [*SBC Annual,* 1879, p. 15].

The following morning at ten o'clock the resolutions were discussed and passed unanimously. Evidently Dagg, in failing health, was unable to fulfill this assignment. Subsequent Convention annuals make no mention of it, and E. C. Starr in his Baptist bibliography does not list a catechism among the works of Dagg. Further evidence that Dagg did not write this catechism appears from the fact that in 1891 John Broadus was commissioned by the new Sunday School Board to write a catechism (because one was still not available). Nevertheless, this convention action of 1879 stands as eloquent testimony to the widespread theological respect enjoyed by J. L. Dagg.

In the South, Dagg's volumes eventually replaced those of Francis Wayland as texts in Baptist colleges. John A. Broadus, in his *Memoir of James P. Boyce*, indicates his personal estimation of Dagg's contribution.

> Dr. Dagg was a man of great ability and lovable character. His works are worthy of thorough study, especially his small volume, 'A Manual of Theology' (Amer. Bap. Pub. Soc.), which is remarkable for clear statement of the profoundest truths, and for devotional sweetness. The writer of this Memoir may be pardoned for bearing witness that after toiling much, in his early years, as a pastor, over Knapp and Turrettin, Dwight and Andrew Fuller, and other elaborate theologians, he found this manual a delight, and has felt through life the pleasing impulse it gave to theological inquiry and reflection [pp. 112-13].

However, transcending all of his accomplishments in the work of the schools, churches, and the denomination was the genuine Christian spirit of J. L. Dagg. This element of his life is captured in a paragraph in his autobiography written "by request, for the perusal of his family, and not for publication."

> To excite their gratitude to God, I wish to make mention of the Lord's kindness to our family. All my five children professed Christ. Two of them are gone to heaven; and the remaining three are on the way. Of my grand children, seventeen have professed Christ, and are, I hope, true disciples. If all of these twenty-two are heirs of the incorruptible inheritance, worth more than all the kingdoms on earth, what a rich family are we! Let us all unite in gratitude to God for his unspeakable blessings. But let us not forget that there are still nine grand children and eight great grand children who need Christ and his great salvation. For them let us pray fervently that they all may be brought into the fold of Christ, and may serve him faithfully on earth, and be united with the rest to make an unbroken family in heaven [*Autobiography*, p. 53].

Origin and Authority of the Bible, by J. L. Dagg, was first published in 1853 as a joint project of the Southern Baptist Publication Society of Charleston and the Virginia Baptist Sunday School and Publication Society of Richmond. In 1858 it was included as an appendix to chapter one of Dagg's *Manual of Theology*. In only thirty-two pages, Dagg gives a sufficient and clear discussion of his intended topics. Just as the title of *Origin and Authority of the Bible* indicates, the pamphlet is divided into two parts. Part one gives attention to the origin of the Bible, and part two discusses its authority.

Dagg expanded the thoughts of *Origin and Authority* in a work entitled *The Evidences of Christianity*, published by J. W. Burke and Company in 1869. The claim of this book is that "Christianity is the religion which is taught in the Bible" (*Evidences*, p. 13). For Dagg, the supreme evidence of Christianity was the inspiration of Scripture.

> The evidences of Christianity are the proofs that the Bible possesses the
> authority of God, binding men to believe the doctrines which it teaches,
> and perform the duties which it enjoins. These proofs are abundant and
> conclusive. . . . The question whether the Bible comes to us with evi-
> dences of Divine origin and authority, falls properly under the investiga-
> tion of reason; and men do not sin against God, when they examine this
> question as rational beings. To reject God's word when he speaks to us,
> or to close the eyes against the proofs that it is God who speaks, is offensive
> to the Supreme Majesty [*Evidences*, pp. 13-14].

Dagg's concern in both of these works is the origin and authority of the
Bible. He believes that an investigation of those themes will produce the
best evidence for the truth of Christian faith. The following summary
and analysis of Dagg's thought will be patterned after the outline of
Origin and Authority. Where it is necessary or helpful, this outline will
be expanded or supplemented by material from his *Evidences of Christianity*.

Dagg begins *Origin* by observing that all rational beings naturally inquire as to the origin of the works of God and men, especially those that
have greatly influenced our civilization. The natural question then follows, "Whence came the Bible? Is it from Heaven, or from men? If it is
from men, is it the work of good men, or of bad men?" (p. 5). Dagg concludes that it is from good men because its moral standards are holy and
its denunciations of evil and iniquity are clear and strong. In fact Dagg
claims that "the morality taught in the Bible is perfect, and bears the impress of Divine Holiness" (*Evidences*, p. 42).

> It cannot be that wicked men conceived so pure a system; that by every
> utterance which they made they condemned their own fraud; and that they
> have preserved others from perpetrating like iniquity by denunciations so
> terrible that the very imagination of them is unwelcome to the minds of
> transgressors. The Holy Bible cannot be the work of unholy deceivers
> [*Evidences*, pp. 52-53].

In Scripture we have both the perfect precept and, in Jesus Christ, the
perfect example "perfectly adapted to the work of establishing a pure religion in the world."

However, these good men who wrote it make another claim for the origin
of Scripture which, if not true, will condemn them as terrible liars. The
writers claim that the Bible is "inspired of God," the "commandments of
the Lord," and "never . . . brought by the will of man, but . . . by the
Holy Ghost" (*Origin*, p. 6). If it is objected that this allows the Bible to
speak for itself and thus begs the question, Dagg answers that we do the
same for any man of integrity. However, we need not rely on the testimony

of the inspired men that the Bible is from God; we can examine the evidence of many other decisive proofs.

Dagg claims, first of all, that the character of God as exhibited in the Bible cannot be of human origin. Gods of human creation, even of the most enlightened civilizations, have been the supreme patrons and examples of vice. Even the infidel, Rousseau, admitted that "the most contemptible divinities were served by the greatest men" (*Origin*, p. 9). But the God of the Bible is different. He is of purer eyes than to behold iniquity. His form cannot be represented, and He must be worshiped in the beauty of holiness. The God of the Bible is not the creation of man's ingenuity; the truths have come from the voice of God Himself.

Second, the account of the life and character of Christ in the gospels is not a fiction of human invention. Even the most refined of classical writers never invented a character so simple, sublime, and fascinating as Jesus of Nazareth. And yet these writers were simple men and could never have foisted such an overpowering fiction on the whole of world history. The marks of truth are so strong that, were the subject merely a fantasy, the inventor would be a more astonishing character than the hero. Dagg draws a strong conclusion from this argument.

> If the gospels give true account of Jesus Christ, he was a teacher from heaven, and both the doctrine which he taught, and the Scriptures, **to** which he often appealed as of divine authority, are from God [p. 13].

Third, the method of salvation revealed in the Bible is not a human device. The cross is unattractive to both Jew and Greek, a stumblingblock to one and foolishness to the other. If the plan were the product of man's cunning, it would not employ something so offensive as its unalterable core, the cross of Christ.

Fourth, the change the Scripture brings in the morals, art, and learning of continents, nations, and individuals that embrace its teachings witnesses to its goodness and its divine origin.

Dagg at this point discusses the presence of obscurities in the Bible and their relationship to the nature of language. According to some, these obscurities represent imperfections. Even if they were imperfections they would not destroy the usefulness of Scripture, just as spots on the sun do not destroy its warmth. However, these imperfections are not in any sense errors or contradictions; they only reflect the inadequacy of the medium used for the revelation.

> So God may make revelation of Himself to the pure intelligences of heaven in language free from human imperfection; but when He speaks to mortals on earth, He uses the language of mortals; and whatever may be the im-

perfection of the medium, this revelation of God displays his glory in the brightest light in which human eyes can behold it [*Origin,* p. 16].

In addition to this defense of Bible language, Dagg proceeds eventually to reject any notion that biblical obscurities are imperfection at all. Just as so-called sunspots are fuel for the light of day and dark clouds are the rich source of earth's fertility, even so "some of the obscurities of the Bible are the deep things of God" (p. 17). When these mysteries are dissipated in the clear light of God's revelation, they provide unmeasured blessing. Dagg says that some obscurities have given occasion to some critics to charge the Bible with contradictions.

> But a careful examination of the inspired word has not only served to repel the charge of reconciling the apparent discrepancies, but it has added new proof that the Scriptures were written by undesigning and honest men, without any collusion; and that there is perfect harmony in their statements, even when apparently most discordant [*Origin,* p. 18].

Dagg reiterates this point in *Evidences* in discussing a point called "undesigned coincidences." Undesigned coincidences are proof of authenticity to the degree that they can prove that the coincidence of teaching is in fact undesigned. A proverb which alludes to this truism is: "Great minds run in the same train." Dagg contends that coincidences under the appearance of contradictions have the highest possible proof of being undesigned.

> Hence if it can be shown that the alleged inconsistencies are apparent only, and that real harmony lies beneath them; they furnish a very strong argument for the truth of the gospel history, and leave the question of its inspiration free from all objections [*Evidences,* p. 228].

Using that as a rationale, Dagg applauds all attempts by harmonists to find ways to reconcile apparent discrepancies. He even includes in *Evidences* an appendix of nine pages in which he gives viable answers to fourteen apparent discrepancies in the gospels.

> A candid mind, after contemplating the overpowering evidences of Christianity, would decide that the alleged disagreements of the evangelists cannot furnish a valid objection to the divine origin of the religion, even if the apparent disagreements could not be harmonized. But patient investigation converts these apparent inconsistencies into undesigned coincidences, and finds, in the very ground of infidel cavils, a firm foundation for Christian faith [*Evidences,* p. 230].

Evidence for the divine origin of the Bible comes also from the miracles performed in confirmation of revealed truth. Though we have not seen these miracles personally, the evidence in their favor is overwhelming and compelling, according to Dagg.

That Moses and the prophets, Christ and his apostles, performed works truly miraculous, is as well attested as any ancient fact whatever. The character of the works attributed to them, their number, the circumstances in which they were performed, the absence of every thing indicating fraud or imposture, the sufferings by which the witnesses demonstrated their sincerity, the credence which their testimony obtained rapidly and extensively, and in the face of bitter persecution, and the absence of all counter testimony; all these considerations compel the belief that miracles were wrought, and if wrought, the revelation which they attest must be from God. The evidence, though it may be less impressive, is not less decisive than it would have been if we had personally witnessed the miracles [*Origin*, p. 20].

Another phenomenon witnessing to the divine origin of the Bible is the prophecy it contains. In fact, Dagg claims that the design of prophecy is not to satisfy our curiosity or "make us prophets"; rather, by its accuracy it is to establish our faith and prove the benevolence as well as the prescience, or foreknowledge, of God. These prophecies must have proceeded from infallible knowledge, according to Dagg, or both their content and their purpose would fall to the ground.

The argument from prophecy commends itself so heartily to Dagg that he values it as a proof of the "plenary" inspiration of Scripture. He states: "Many of these predictions were not understood by the prophets who delivered or recorded them; and therefore they must have proceeded wholly from the Spirit which dictated them" (*Evidences*, p. 222).

Dagg discusses a number of other prophecies (a full fifty pages in *Evidences*) and indicates confidence that prophecies yet unfulfilled will certainly be fulfilled so that "the prophetical evidence now constantly accumulating will be complete" (*Origin*, p. 26). "The whole taken together forms an immense mass of evidence, establishing conclusively the divine origin of the Bible" (*Evidences*, p. 152).

Dagg completes his discussion of the origin of the Bible with a jealous admonition worthy of the most intense evangelist.

Unhappy infidel! Is there a God? Hast thou an immortal soul? Until thou canst, with unfaltering hardihood, answer No to both these inquiries, do not cast away from thee the Bible, the Book of God, the Light of Immortality [*Origin*, p. 27].

Dagg begins his second section, on "Authority," with an unmistakable affirmation that the authority of the Bible is a divine authority.

Though the Bible was written by inspired men, they are to be regarded merely as the instruments chosen, fitted, and employed by God, for the production of this work. God himself is the author of the Bible. When we read its sacred pages, we should realize that God speaks to us, and when we suffer it to lie neglected, we should remember that we are refusing to listen to God, when he proffers to instruct us on subjects of infinite moment [*Origin*, p. 28].

Evidently some people objected that such a thoroughgoing view of God's activity in the writing of Scripture eliminated the human element. We must affirm, they claimed, some errors in Scripture if men had any part at all in its production. Not so, Dagg replied. The mistake in that objection is that it assumes inspiration to be a compound made of two distinct elements. However, inspiration is not a compound but a single process, which God designed and for which He created the method. Man is introduced simply as an instrument, not a partner. His instrumentality differs significantly from that of an unconscious pen ("the mental powers of the sacred writers were not set aside, but the divine wisdom has used them, and all the peculiarities of style, and modes of thought, that distinguished the several writers"), but it is still instrumentality.

The whole of revelation is the work of God as the author; the whole is the work of man as the instrument; and the whole has perfection, that it exactly fulfills the design of him who designed it [*Evidences*, pp. 222-24].

Dagg also encountered the objection that because the Spirit's activity in sanctification is effective without being infallible, it is not necessary that the Scripture be infallible even though it is inspired.

It is objected that inspiration is positive, not negative, imparting truth to the minds of the inspired, without banishing their errors; and that, in this particular, it is like the ordinary influences of the Spirit, which have a sanctifying effect on the believer without annihilating his depravity. It is a fundamental error in this objection, that it contemplates inspiration as designed merely for the benefit of the inspired: whereas it is clear that God gave his word to be spoken and written by prophets and apostles for the instruction and benefit of other men, who were required to receive it, not as the word of man, but as in truth the word of God, attested by miracles. Positively, it is divine truth; negatively, it is not human error [*Evidences*, p. 224].

Dagg also makes this claim for inerrancy in discussing the relative clarity and value of the New Testament in relation to the Old. He had affirmed that Christ and the apostles accepted the Old Testament as divinely inspired and therefore infallible. The New Testament teachings were certainly superior to those of the Old from the moment they were first orally proclaimed. "But whatever may have been the superiority of the New Testament revelation at its outset, it could not have equalled that of the Old Testament in permanent advantage, if it had not been committed to writing without human error" (*Evidences*, p. 216).

Dagg's knowledge of Greek and his interest in the many New Testament manuscripts that had been discovered made him aware of the (mostly minor) textual variants from one manuscript to another. Biblical authority resides only in the Bible, not in some inadvertent slip of the pen or in some scribal addition or omission. That which is binding upon the Christian is that which the prophets and apostles actually wrote under the guidance of the Holy Spirit. Where textual variants exist, divine authority is not to be assigned to the variant but to the original text. Therefore, Dagg rightly attributed infallibility and divine authority to the autographs (original writings) only. He strongly encouraged the science of textual criticism, because "it is our duty to employ whatever means may be in our power for approaching as nearly as possible to the precise language and meaning of the inspired originals" (*Evidences*, p. 227).

The Bible is the testimony of God, according to Dagg, and we call God a liar when we refuse to receive the testimony in His holy Word. The Bible reveals the moral standards of God, and thus we rebel against the supreme lawgiver of the universe when we refuse to obey the precepts of the Bible. The Bible contains the promises of God and is therefore a rule of hope, for it is impossible for God to lie.

The authority of the Bible is supreme in all of these areas and endures above conscience, testimonies of men, or promises of nature. "God never deceives. . . . When the Bible speaks, all else may be silent, and its decisions leave no room for doubt and admit no appeal" (*Origin*, p. 29-30).

According to Dagg, the authority of the Bible is independent, receiving nothing from its writers, transcribers, or printers. "It possesses authority simply because it is the word of God" (*Origin*, p. 30). The authority of the Bible is immediate. Its message moves directly from God to the mind of each reader. No one can understand the Bible for us or obey its precepts in our stead, but each person must say for himself, "Speak, Lord, for thy servant heareth."

Dagg concludes his study of the origin and the authority of the Bible with another impassioned plea for belief in Scripture.

> For myself I realize that I am standing on the shore of the boundless ocean, with but an inch of crumbling sand remaining. I hear the shrieks of the dying infidel at my side, to whose view all is covered with impenetrable darkness. He, too, has come to the brink, and would gladly refuse to proceed, but he can not. Perplexed, terrified, shuddering he plunges in and sinks, he knows not whither. How precious at this trying moment, is the Book of God! How cheering this Light from heaven! Before it I see the shades retiring. The Bible lifts its torch—nay, not a feeble torch, such as reason may raise, to shine on the darkness and render it visible; the Bible sheds the light of the noonday sun on the vast prospect before me, and

enables me, tranquil and joyful, to launch into eternity with the full assurance of hope. Mortals hastening to the retributions of eternity, be wise; receive the revelation from heaven presented to you in the Bible; attend diligently to its instructions and reverence its authority, as the word of the final Judge before whom you will soon appear [*Origin*, p. 31].

Though they separated from one another during their earthly lives, when Wayland and Dagg appear before the "final Judge" they will stand united and with one voice will be able to say, "We have believed the Bible as Your own Word. We have treated it as if it were without error, for Thou, O Lord, art the God of truth, and cannot lie."

BIBLIOGRAPHY

Baker, Robert A. *A Baptist Source Book: With Particular Reference to Southern Baptists.* Nashville: Broadman, 1966.

A Southern Baptist. "An Examination of the Review of the Minutes of the Southern Baptist Convention." *The Christian Review*, May 1846, 41:114-35.

Francis Wayland

Wayland, Francis. *The Apostolic Ministry: A Discourse.* Rochester: Sage & Brother, 1853.

———. *The Elements of Intellectual Philosophy.* New York: Sheldon & Co., 1854.

———. *The Elements of Moral Science.* London: The Religious Tract Society, 1835.

———. *The Elements of Political Economy.* Boston: Gould, Kendall & Lincoln, 1837.

———. *Letters on the Ministry of the Gospel.* Boston: Gould & Lincoln, 1864.

———. *The Limitations of Human Responsibility.* New York: Appleton, 1838.

———. *Notes on the Principles and Practices of Baptist Churches.* New York: Sheldon, Blakeman, & Co., 1857.

Wayland, Francis, and Wayland, H. L. *A Memoir of the Life and Labors of Francis Wayland, D.D., LL.D., Late President of Brown University.* 2 vols. New York: Sheldon, 1867.

John L. Dagg

Broadus, John A. *Memoir of James Petigru Boyce, D.D., LL.D.* New York: A. C. Armstrong & Son, 1893.

Dagg, John L. *Autobiography of Rev. John L. Dagg.* Rome, Ga.: J. F. Shanklin, Printer, 1886.

———. *The Evidences of Christianity.* Macon, Ga.: J. W. Burke & Co., 1869.

———. *Origin and Authority of the Bible.* Charleston: Southern Baptist Publication Society. Richmond: Virginia Baptist Sunday School and Publication Society, 1853.

Part Two

"A NEW KING . . . WHICH KNEW NOT JOSEPH"

Pierre Antonie de Machy, *Démolition de l'église-Saint-Jean-en Greve.*
Courtesy of the Musées Carnavalet, Paris. Photo by Lauros-Giraudon.

CHAPTER EIGHT

"Their Gods Shall Be a Snare"

During the last one hundred fifty years or so, vast changes have swept the Christian world. Belief or unbelief, paganism or Christianity: those were the clearly defined options throughout much of Christian history. But in these latter days a major shift in basic attitudes and viewpoints occurs. In the following chapters of this book, questions are seriously debated that in earlier days would have been settled by common consent. This present chapter is an attempt to explain why the shift in thinking occurs and exactly what the shift is. To summarize the intellectual content of these changing ideas in so few pages will demand some oversimplification perhaps, but not a false analysis, one hopes. The emphasis of this chapter will fall on the nineteenth century, but ideas usually do not appear *ex nihilo* nor do they rapidly self-destruct. Thus the proper starting place for real understanding of the modern scene is somewhat earlier than 1800.

People not inclined toward the study of philosophy or the history of ideas may find this chapter hard to follow. But it should be said that those who do not understand these intellectual changes will not likely be those who find lasting solutions to the problems that threaten to shatter Baptist unity in the present day. As a noncreedal denomination, Baptists will find their lasting unity only in a total allegiance to Jesus Christ as He is revealed in Scripture and as His work is interpreted there. However, the foundations of biblical authority have been attacked on a massive and unprecedented scale since the nineteenth century. Why did that happen, and why was it so successful? Must informed Christians give up the views of Scripture held by their forefathers? Is the modern "critical" approach to the Bible the necessary one for theology today? Baptists need answers to these and other relevant questions. However, answers are found only when the questions are clearly understood. Why would anyone even ask if modern Baptists could hold the same beliefs as those which former Baptists held? That is the question that will be treated in this chapter. What has happened to make Baptists even consider changing their views on Scripture?

BACK TO THE BIBLE

One can hardly study history and fail to see the importance of the tremendous cultural phenomenon that closed out the Medieval period. This cultural revolution took a secular form in Italy and a religious form in Germany. The Italian Renaissance truly was a rebirth of the ancient classical forms, especially in art and architecture. The German Protestant Reformation revived the authority of ancient Scripture and opposed the traditionalist theology of the dominant Roman Catholic Church in favor of apostolic and patristic theology. Despite the hundreds of books on the subject, no one really understands all the factors that brought about this change in mood throughout Europe.

The idea of making Scripture alone normative for theology was at the very heart of the Protestant reaction to Roman Catholic dogma. This theological stance may well have been influenced by various historical, psychological, and sociological factors. But Luther and Calvin attempted to justify this theological authority-structure by an appeal to Scripture itself. They said that God is the only absolute and infallible authority. Therefore, what God says is true, and what God reveals is to be believed. Based on a lengthy and comprehensive study of the claims and the evidence, and based upon the apparent work of the Spirit of God in the human mind, the great Protestant theologians taught that God mediated His revelation to mankind through the written Scripture. What Scripture teaches is what God says to us. God's Word is truth.

How was one to know the truth of God's doctrine or how could one discover God's moral standards? Such knowledge came only by properly interpreting the Holy Scripture. Proper interpretation included a study of the original languages, the grammatical forms, the historical context, and the theological relationships between various passages on the same subject. Once the biblical position was discovered, the true believer was automatically expected to believe it. No one accused the Scripture of teaching falsehood or of leading the believers into erroneous doctrinal positions. When different theologians came to different doctrinal conclusions, they blamed it on human weaknesses and prejudice. They did not suggest that Scripture might be wrong just because two careful theologians came up with some different interpretations. In any case, the differences were over details. Essential doctrines in their main forms—doctrines like the deity of Christ, the substitutionary atonement, the eternal Trinity, justification by faith, and the necessity of repentance—were accepted by most Protestant theologians.

This appeal to biblical authority rather than to traditional dogmas did not produce a perfect society nor did it solve all problems. Looking back at the Reformation, one may even find instances of human cruelty among the very Reformers who were holding the Bible highest in their thinking. It has been known for some time that both Luther and Calvin had gout, a particularly uncomfortable form of arthritis. Who knows what influence pain and discomfort may have had on their actions or on their thinking at various times? But speculations of this sort are mostly unprofitable. Physical discomfort or other similar factors are not likely to have radically shaped their deepest intellectual conclusions.

Why they misunderstood some aspect of what Baptists consider to be Christian truth (such as the idea of a regenerate church membership, the liberty of conscience, or the separation of church and state) is interesting to talk about but not always easy to discover with assurance.

Nevertheless, one can hardly overemphasize the importance of the Protestant Reformation in the history of Western civilization. It was a giant step forward theologically. The Roman Catholics were not unaffected by all of this, and reform did come in many ways throughout the Christian world.

The Reformers believed Scripture to be God's Word written. It was trusted, not doubted. It was studied, not ignored. It was taken as the final authority with regard to those matters on which it spoke or made affirmations. God had not revealed everything. The Bible did not expressly contain all the truth that could be known. But what the Bible did teach was believed to be completely trustworthy. Truth in any other area would not contradict biblical truth. Starting from Scripture, one could find the true knowledge of reality.

What Is Truth?

The great extent of the cultural shift produced by the European Renaissance can be recognized by studying the philosophical developments of this period. The British philosophers such as John Locke and George Berkeley strongly emphasized the empiricist method of coming to know truth, while European scholars such as René Descartes and George Leibniz clearly took a rationalist approach.

Empiricist methodology began with the assumption that a child is born with a blank mind. An infant starts with no knowledge. All ideas enter the mind from outside. This process is called experience. Every experience registers with the mind, and the collective experiences together with mental reflection on those experiences make up one's thought-life. John Locke said, for example, that we come to know that God exists because of rational reflection on experiences that we have.

Rationalistic methodology began with the assumption that a child is born with an undeveloped mind but not a "blank tablet" mind. Every mind starts with some inherent or innate ideas. All truth can be deduced from those basic ideas, which serve as the common assumptions of man's mental life. René Descartes said that we can know that God exists because the idea of His existence has all the essential characteristics (clarity and distinctness) of an innate idea.

These philosophical systems appeared in an age that was new in many ways. The science of the Medieval period had been exploded by the scientific ideas of Copernicus, Galileo, and Newton. The overseas expansion brought Europeans into contact with alien cultures. The Renaissance had revived a knowledge of the ancient skeptical philosophers. Slowly but surely skeptical ideas spread through Europe. God still played an important part in these modern systems of thought, but His role was secondary. Theology no longer dominated the intellectual world.

The invention of the microscope is simply one illustration of the advancement in the sciences during the seventeenth century. Francis Bacon proclaimed a "novum organum," a new inductive way of thinking that made the study of nature (rather than the study of God) the "queen of the sciences." Knowledge began to be valued not for its own sake but for its utilitarian value. Seventeenth-century science, however, went out of its way to show that scientific work was in fact a religious enterprise. Isaac Newton said that the scientific study of the universe was the way to "think God's thoughts after him." Yet the inductive method started not with God but with the observation of nature. It purposefully omitted assumptions about the manner of creation or even the "whether" of creation. Thus the study of nature began to be done without thinking of God at all. The universe began to be conceived as a giant machine. Everything was thought to be explainable by unalterable natural law.

One could choose, as Newton and Kepler did, to view natural law as God's law, but someone else could just as easily treat nature as an impersonal cause-and-effect chain. The implications of this new scientific method became increasingly clear. Pascal challenged the growing unbelief of his day by an appeal not to scientific evidences or to metaphysical speculations but rather to reasons of the heart and history.

Philosophers generally saw their main task not as providing support for theology but as trying to understand and explain the new scientific views about nature. Nevertheless, the seventeenth century is characterized correctly as a period in which there was relative peace between science, philosophy, and religion. The famous painting *The Triumph of the Eucharist* by Peter Paul Rubens pictures Religion triumphantly leading the way, with Science, Philosophy, Nature, and the New World following along behind. Rubens may have been slightly idealistic, but religion did still

Fig. 12. Peter Paul Rubens, *The Triumph of the Eucharist.* Courtesy of the Musées Royaux de Beaux-Arts, Brussels.

exert a considerable influence over the whole realm of human intellectual life.

The seeds of religious doubt and skepticism were growing, however. The tendency at first was not to challenge specific Christian doctrines but rather simply to restrict theology to the area of faith and morals. As the secular world began to establish autonomous spheres of thought, the religious world began to feel the pressure. The existence of God was not so much doubted, but disagreement rapidly began to grow over the question of God's nature. As naturalistic science grew in its explanatory power, God was increasingly pushed out of the universe. He became that original force which set the universe in motion, the one who in the distant past wound up the great mainspring, the ancient architect of this vast and complex machine. At the same time, however, God was more and more being identified with beauty in the universe. God was conceived of as literally filling the universe with His presence. He was imagined as actually existing in some substantial sense throughout space. Spinoza so identified God with the whole of nature that God became depersonalized. God and nature were two words describing the same reality, reasoned Spinoza.

Thus God's nature, not His existence, became the point of controversy. Conservative Christian theology, of course, resisted all of these departures from orthodoxy. Perhaps the most significant aspect of this orthodox resistance is the Puritan movement. Puritan leaders, such as Cartwright, Johnston, Smyth, Cotton, Winthrop, Bradford, and Mather firmly believed that they were simply completing the Reformation. They were "purifying" the church. Others, such as Browne, Barrow, Penry, and Greenwood gave up any hope of reforming the organized church and thus became leaders of the early Separatist movement. Baptists, such as Smyth, Helwys, Busher, Murton, Williams, Clarke, and Goold fought to preserve or restore what they believed to be the true biblical faith. They were radically committed to New Testament Christianity. But the handwriting was already on the wall. Richard Baxter may have preached as a "dying man to dying men," but fewer men were listening.

The Turning Point

The Enlightenment, as the eighteenth century has so often been designated, was the hinge on which Europe turned from the Middle Ages to the Modern Era. Christianity had dominated the earlier centuries (that were now being called the Dark Ages). As men were "enlightened," said the philosophers, reason would gradually liberate their minds. The supernaturalistic and authoritative mentality of the earlier centuries rapidly gave way to a more scientific (naturalistic) and individualistic way of thinking.

Rationalism of the seventeenth-century variety began to fade. Reason could not operate apart from sense experience, claimed the eighteenth-century thinkers. Thus reason alone could never penetrate the world of appearances. Immanuel Kant, one of the most important thinkers of the modern era, tried to synthesize the theories of rationalism and empiricism. The mind is not blank at birth, he maintained, but it does not contain innate ideas either. The mind contains inherent categories. The actual ideas arise from sense perception, he said, but the ideas are unintelligible apart from the active mind that shapes, arranges, and interprets the "raw" experience. The mind interprets sensory perceptions in terms of categories such as space and time, not because the world necessarily exists in space and time but because the human mind is structured to think that way. No one can get outside of his own head, says Kant. No one can know with absolute certainty whether things actually are the way he thinks things are. Each man sees the world through his own mental glasses. Things surely appear to be in space and time, but how things appear is no proof of how things are.

Thus Kant claimed to be able to point out a basic fallacy in all the classical proofs for the existence of God. It may be true that the observation of cause and effect patterns in nature leads a man to believe that there must be a First Uncaused Cause (God), but that proves only that human minds are innately structured to think that way. It does not prove, says Kant, that such a God actually exists. Design leads men to suppose a Designer, but again, the mind is inevitably led to that conclusion by its own logic. What proof is there that what man is inherently forced to think is necessarily true in fact? Is the rationally inescapable conclusion always an absolute truth about reality? How can man ever get beyond his own perceptions to the reality that lies behind those perceptions?

This "critical," or "analytical," approach to truth and knowledge resulted in the destruction of time-honored principles not only in religion but in political, social, and scientific thought as well. Yet for Kant, criticism and analysis were the necessary first steps toward true enlightenment. For Kant, God was a necessary postulate of "practical reason," deduced from man's moral nature. But God was clearly unknowable in any philosophical or scientific sense.

The common vocabulary of eighteenth-century thinkers included references to the "limitations" of man's knowledge and the "mysteries" of nature. Hope for a unified system of thought that would include all of reality in its harmony slowly slipped away. Even Diderot and D'Alembert, the authors of the famous *Encyclopedie*, tried to make cross references throughout the work, offered generalized conclusions, and constructed a "tree of knowledge"; nevertheless, they had no illusion about offering the only possible system of thought and knowledge. As Diderot perceived it, nature was constantly changing, the facts were not all in, and the former unity of the arts and sciences was disintegrating.

Even more significantly, theology in Diderot's "tree of knowledge" was clearly in subordination to history and philosophy (human memory and human reason). More and more, the eighteenth century saw the sciences becoming autonomous and thus secular. Moral philosophy and political theory separated themselves from their former alliance with theology.

One must not misunderstand this trend toward secularization. It is not as though the eighteenth century could be characterized as being religiously indifferent. Quite the opposite is true. The religious debates were endless. Did God exist, and how could one know? If God exists, what is He like? But the very fact that these questions were the subjects of debate shows that the supernatural increasingly seemed remote to the general public. God's existence, God's nature, and the fact of God's revelation of Himself in Scripture had in previous centuries been assumed. Now those concepts seemed to be the very things most likely to be questioned. For the eighteenth-century man, it was nature that seemed to be predictable and familiar. Ideas about miracles and the supernatural were the ideas that strained the boundaries of credibility. Men became uncomfortable with the thought that God might truly be able to influence the regularities of nature. Such a view seemed to make science impossible, for who could know when God might decide to interfere and change natural law. Thus nature would be unpredictable.

David Hume not only challenged the belief in miracles, but he also offered a new theory of the origin of religion. The original religion was polytheism (belief in many gods), he said, and through fear and superstition men were guided toward monotheism (belief in one God). Baron d'Holbach, the "personal enemy of God," was far more radical than Hume. He popularized all of Hume's skeptical ideas, but added his own thought that matter was eternal and inherently in motion. Thus God became an unnecessary hypothesis.

From the latter part of the eighteenth century, the Romantic movement has continued to have a profound impact upon philosophy, art, literature, and religion. The so-called "cultivated" people began to admire the development of emotions (especially sympathy). The wise man was the one who left the king's court, the pressures of civilized society, and took up the unambitious, peaceful pleasures of rural life. In the past, education had been viewed as the chief restraint on passions. The orderly Newtonian universe had symbolized the ideal for government and society. But the Romantics grew tired of rigid structures and desired excitement.

Essentially, Romanticism substitutes aesthetic for utilitarian standards.

"Tiger, tiger: burning bright," wrote Blake. Who before had thought of tigers as beautiful? The Romantics preferred Gothic architecture. Their novels were filled with storms, dangerous journeys, mountainous cliffs, and other violent and useless things. It seems that the Romantic movement has had a permanent effect. Any evening spent watching modern television, or any casual glance at the movie advertisements will demonstrate the importance modern people place on emotion, action, terror, sex, violence, and excitement.

Jean-Jacques Rousseau is often called the first great figure in the Romantic movement. Reacting against his Calvinistic parents, Rousseau argued that man was basically good (not inherently a sinner). Institutions made people bad. This was quite the opposite of any theories of salvation through the church.

Since the days of the ancient Greeks, theologians had believed it to be an important part of their responsibility to offer intellectual reasons why people should believe in God. Rousseau is at least partly responsible for the change in viewpoint that has occurred. Today there is widespread ignorance and lack of concern about rational proofs. Many modern Christians base their faith upon some form of emotion, a sense of mystery or awe, or a feeling of love or acceptance. That shift from rational proofs to simple experience is a product of the Romantic movement Rousseau initiated.

Francis-Marie Arouet, better known by his pen name, Voltaire, did much to discredit the Roman Catholic Church in the eyes of the intellectuals of the eighteenth and nineteenth centuries. Between 1817 and 1829 Voltaire's collected works sold over three million volumes. Because of Voltaire's influence, France went directly from the Renaissance to the Enlightenment. It never really experienced the Reformation. But Voltaire, though a critic of the church, was no atheist. "I shall always be convinced," he wrote in 1741, "that a watch proves a watch maker, and that a universe proves a God." Yet he struggled with the problem of evil. Rousseau and Voltaire both died the same year, 1778. Both lived through the same historical events. Both came to respect the other's point of view, but they never learned to agree.

Lisbon—9:40 a.m., November 1, 1755, All Saints Day. A massive earthquake occurred that in six minutes destroyed thirty churches and one thousand homes. Fifteen thousand people were instantly killed and another fifteen thousand were fatally injured. John Wesley preached a sermon about it called "The Cause and Cure of Earthquakes." He considered sin to be the ultimate cause. Rousseau suggested that civilization was the problem. Had people been scattered throughout the countryside rather than located all together in the city, very few if any would have been

killed. Voltaire maintained a belief in God, but came to believe that the
Christian teaching about God must be false. Surely the all-good and all-
powerful God of Christian theology could not exist, for if He did exist He
would not have allowed such a tragedy to occur. Thus Voltaire, for reasons
different from those of Rousseau, nevertheless accelerated the general
trend toward a minimal theology. God was still "there," but He left no
scientific or historical tracks that could lead one with certainty to discover
His nature. For many people, God became an unknown and an unknowable entity.

Deism (an early form of liberal Christian theology) also assaulted
revealed religion in the eighteenth century and substituted a natural religion in its place. As early as 1696 John Toland had published *Christianity
not Mysterious*. Thomas Woolston claimed that biblical accounts of miracles were pious hoaxes. Men should believe in God, these deists affirmed,
but that belief must be purged of myth and mystery. God created the
universe, but He then left it to run by rational and scientific principles.
Thus man can have and should have a fully rational religion, but he must
give up all supernatural mythology. The deist attack grew to the point
where the credibility of biblical facts was readily challenged. The arguments against biblical infallibility began to grow in apparent strength.
How could the true biblical faith be preserved at all? The eighteenth
century also saw the beginning of modern biblical criticism. Jean Astruc
in 1753 suggested that Moses may have compiled Genesis from two
sources. This French physician had noticed that Elohim and Yahweh
were both used as divine names in the Pentateuch. If that could be understood as indicating two literary sources, a whole new approach to biblical
criticism would open up. The first task would be to locate and separate
those sources in order to get back to the original theology of the earlier
documentary sources. Scholars in the eighteenth century began those
studies, but the roots produced mature trees only in the nineteenth century.

In 1778 Gotthold Ephraim Lessing published the *Wolfenbüttel Fragments* written by Henry Samuel Reimarus (1749). Reimarus was a pure
Deist. He denied all miracles except the one miracle of creation. He
attempted to advance natural religion by contradicting revealed religion.
Revealed religion is simply unintelligible, he said. So again, how could
the true faith be preserved?

Lessing himself offered one answer that had an enormous influence on
later theological developments. He suggested that faith is not based on
history. "Accidental truths of history can never become the proof of
necessary truths of reason," he contended, and thus Lessing dug an "ugly,
broad ditch" between history and theology. Christianity was a marvelous

ethical system, he believed, able to transform men through love, but it could not be established by evidence based upon history or scientific facts. Faith is one thing. Fact is another. The one needed no support from the other. Men could believe in God and Christ by faith and still believe in the "factual" scientific theories offered by naturalistic thinkers. There is a distinction that should be made, said Lessing, between faith, which is spiritual truth, and history, which is scientific, rational, or empirical truth. History cannot contradict faith, but for the same reason it cannot support faith, according to Lessing's theory.

Not everyone, however, was swept into this divided theory of knowledge. Not everyone was persuaded that faith and history should or could be so separated. The eighteenth century is undoubtedly an age of faith as well as of skepticism. No one can deny that the "universal obsession" with the pursuit of earthly happiness (for example, in America's "Declaration of Independence") signifies a conscious revolt against the otherworldliness of traditional Christianity. Nevertheless, one can also find a great religious revival in the eighteenth century. Pietism developed as a protest against the rigid formalism and creedalism of many churches. A devotional use of the Bible increased and personal conversion began to be stressed. In one sense this religious individualism was fully consistent with the general tendencies of the age, but, of course, it was not based on a skepticism about the supernatural.

John Wesley went into "the highways and the hedges" to preach. His messages were not the formal orations of the professional clergy. Rather he preached in "plain speech." He frequently used simple biblical illustrations in his messages, and he literally shook England with the gospel. Jonathan Edwards and George Whitefield spoke of the wholeness of truth under God. Edwards was by far the greatest American theologian of his day. Revival was real and effective. Yet it was not the dominant movement of the times.

In France the order of the day was revolution, not revival. Pierre Antonie de Machy clearly illustrated the eighteenth century as an age of unbelief. His painting *Démolition de l'église-Saint-Jean-en-Greve* shows the slow, casual, and yet deliberate destruction of a thirteenth-century cathedral. It symbolized the destruction of Christianity itself, at least in its Medieval form. [See p. 172.]

CURRENTS OF COMPLEXITY

It is almost a cliché to say that the nineteenth century is the most complex, the most "critical," the most disunited century of the modern era. Men began consciously to think of themselves as living in an age of continuous transition. Matthew Arnold spoke of the "strange disease of mod-

Fig. 13. Francisco Goya, *The Dream of Reason Produces Monsters*

Collection of The Art Institute of Chicago. Courtesy of The Art Institute of Chicago.

ern life" which he called "multitudinousness." Reason, that which had offered hope for a new, unified world, now had forsaken man. As Francisco Goya's famous engraving expresses it: *The Dream of Reason Produces Monsters.*

In 1818 Mary Shelley published her now famous *Frankenstein,* an allegorical prophecy of Romanticism far more profound than most people have recognized. Baron Frankenstein uses the best hands, the best legs, and the best brain, and builds what he hopes will be the perfect man. The creature is at first a gentle, loving being, anxious for human affection. But he is ugly, and his ugliness inspires horror in those who see him. Their violent reaction to him drives him to hatred and violence.

When normal human society refuses to love him because of his looks, the creature demands that Frankenstein make a female for him to love and to be loved by. When the request is refused, the monster murders one by one those whom Frankenstein loves. Finally, the man created by man murders his creator. Standing over the dead body of Frankenstein, the monster's emotions pour out:

> That also is my victim! in his murder my crimes are consummated; the miserable genius of my being is wound to its close! Oh, Frankenstein! generous and self-devoted being! What does it avail that I now ask thee to pardon me? I, who irretrievably destroyed thee by destroying all that thou lovedst. Alas! he is cold, he cannot answer me. . . . When I run over the frightful catalogue of my sins, I cannot believe that I am the same creature whose thoughts were once filled with sublime and transcendent visions of the beauty and the majesty of goodness. But it is even so; the fallen angel becomes a malignant devil. Yet even that enemy of God and man had friends and associates in his desolation; I am alone.

Though the population rapidly expanded, nineteenth-century man was lonelier than ever before. There was more of everything available, and yet there seemed to be less of that which matters.

Several factors must be included in any adequate analysis of this age of crises. For one thing the development of Western thought now expanded geographically. America and Russia, as well as Europe, made their contributions, and the philosophy of India and the Far East began to have an impact upon European philosophy. More significantly, however, the social structure of the Western world was profoundly altered by the rapid production of machines and inventions.

Prince Albert spearheaded a Great Exhibition (1851) that brought together at the Crystal Palace in London a "living picture" of man's achievements. On display there were newly invented instruments that enabled the blind to write. People came and were impressed by artificial teeth carved from hippopotamus ivory, universal drills for tooth decay, an improved double truss for hernia, and a train that laid its own track! But science boasted of bigger conquests than those, especially in the fields of chemistry, geology, and biology. No one science, however, proved to be strong enough to resist the growing fragmentation of knowledge. Particularism, or specialization, seemed necessary if truth were to be found, but the result of this division of knowledge into highly specialized disciplines was anarchy, not unity. The spirit of unfettered inquiry produced the most extremely varied and antithetical ideas. Moreover, this individualism was no longer limited just to the uncommon minds. The average working man gave up the ideal of being a jack-of-all-trades and began to concentrate on one job. Each man thought of himself as an expert in his own field.

Beginning with Kant, Germany achieved and maintained an intellectual predominance. England and France had dominated Enlightenment culture because the Thirty Years' War had destroyed German unity in the post-Reformation era. Only Prussia had successfully resisted the power of France in the eighteenth century. Even Prussia fell to Napoleon, however. Its revival under Bismarck was like a resurrection of the days of Charlemagne. Berlin became a cultural center, and Germany finally united under Prussian leadership.

Georg W. F. Hegel provided the culmination of the philosophy of Kant. Hegel's thought is perhaps the most difficult to understand of all the German idealist philosophers. But it may also be that his philosophy was the most powerful expression of the true spirit of the age. From his youthful interest in mysticism, Hegel supposed that fragmented knowledge was not truth. Nothing is ultimately and completely real, he said, except the whole. But the whole (which he called the "Absolute") is not a simple substance. Rather, it is a complex system, an organism. It is an illusion to think of truth as if it were found in the separateness of things. Actually each thing is a greater or a lesser part of reality, which Hegel identified as being the wholeness of all things together. The reality consists of the whole.

Naturally this view could only be accepted if one could, with Kant, accept the possible unreality of space and time. If space and time were actually real, rather than simply being subjective mental categories, then separateness and multiplicity would also be ultimately real. Because man has no way of ever getting at the actual, physical, existing aspect or aspects (the "noumena") that compose the universe, and because man cannot get outside his own mind, it must be proper, reasoned Hegel, to define reality for man in terms of his thought life. The "real is the rational," Hegel affirmed, "and the rational is the real." Empirical, individual, scientific or historical facts were not real in and of themselves. No fact can stand alone, he said. Facts are real only when they become rational—that is, when they are viewed in context as being a part of the whole. Facts become real when they begin to "make sense." A man does not believe that some fact is real unless he understands it or at least until he becomes convinced that rational understanding is possible.

Because, for Hegel, only the whole was real, truth must be defined as statements about the whole (the Absolute). But any such statement would turn out to be self-contradictory. Suppose someone were to affirm that the Absolute is Pure Being ("pure" meaning "only," or "nothing but"). "Pure Being" would mean that the Absolute simply is, that it exists. Yet such a bare existence is impossible. Pure Being would be something that could not be described. No adjectives could be used. The word "pure" is intended to exclude any possible descriptive characteristics. The Absolute is not round, or big, or red, or hot, or anything. It is just existing in a "pure" nondefinable state. No qualities at all are included in the statement that the Absolute is "Pure Being." However, something with no defining qualities is not something after all. If it cannot be described, it does not exist. Thus the Absolute of Pure Being turns out upon reflection to be Nothing. If the Absolute is Nothing, then it is not "being" at all.

To discover truth, says Hegel, one must include the whole of reality in the statement. Thus, if the Absolute is to be affirmed as Pure Being, it must also be affirmed as Nothing (Non-Being). The more accurate affirmation, then, is that affirmation which resolves this seeming contradiction. Therefore, the original statement now must be changed to say that the Absolute is Becoming (a synthesis of Being and Non-Being). Becoming is, however, a process, not a static substance. On this point Hegel believed that he had discovered a new and yet a basic insight into the nature of reality. That which was real did not simply exist, it grew. Reality was not fundamentally a substance, it was a moving process. It was not a static thing, it was a thinking mind.

The process of discovering truth is never ending. People can never know the whole of reality, because it is always changing. Truth will always be relative to that which is not yet known about reality. In a sense truth disappears in Hegel's philosophy except as a goal or as an ideal. Truth and falsehood are no longer thought of as absolute opposites. For Hegel, no individual idea is wholly false, nor can one know any particular or individual idea that is wholly true. Knowledge and reality are essentially ongoing processes. They never stand still. They never remain the same. What is true today in this situation and context, may not be true tomorrow in a new situation or a new context. Truth is no longer an absolute concept. It is not a stable factor. The key words in this new philosophy are relationship and process.

If there is no final, absolute truth, then one must conclude that the Bible is not absolutely true. Scripture is a product of the process of history just as other ancient literature is. What Scripture says is what the authors believed that God had said in their day. But times have changed. Things are different now. What Scripture says cannot be literally binding and normative for modern people. The most certain fact for Hegel and for those who followed him was that everything was developing and changing and thus no individual idea was absolutely, unchangeably true. Philosophically speaking, this view is a dialectical theory. The common man, however, just called this process "evolution." Most people were fully convinced that everything was definitely changing. This process was quite generally seen as change from simple to complex. The theory was applied to theology as well as to biology and history.

For Hegelianism, Christ could not be the final and unchanging revelation of the Father. No single individual could be the embodiment of absolute truth. The cross may have been a decisive event, but the theology of the atonement held by Peter or Paul would be normative only in the sense that their views were early, original theories. Later theologians had years and centuries to reflect on the significance of the cross, and their more modern theories of the atonement were "closer to the truth" because they included more data. Modern theories did not claim to be final statements of the truth, of course. In future years an even larger synthesis would be possible. Truth must include everything, and thus it grows and changes as the years continue to pass.

Every biblical doctrine is equally affected by this open-ended theory of truth. Biblical theology itself was reinterpreted by German higher critics along these same lines. Simple ideas were classified as being early. Complex theological ideas were designated as being late. If simple and complex ideas were found together in Genesis, for example, the critic would suppose that this reflected the work of an editor living near the end of the pre-Christian era. Documentary theories of the origin of the Pentateuch did not develop because of any manuscript evidence for the existence of these documents. The supposed documents were defined in terms of stylistic, literary criteria as well as theological criteria.

Scripture then became not the authentic and infallible record of God's true Word as expressed in his revelatory activity; rather, the Bible was viewed as a book of primary sources describing the experiences of godly men and women. It is not that theologians consciously applied Hegel's theories to Scripture. It is that Hegel expressed the general consensus of the age. What Hegel said, many were feeling. Truth was not static. Progress was inevitable. Change was the fundamental reality. Scripture was a collection of devout human opinions. These biblical ideas were to be respected as primary, firsthand testimonies of religious experiences. But the Bible must now be treated, said modern critics, as a purely human book. Hegel's dialectical philosophy did not create these attitudes so much as it simply expressed what many had come to believe.

For Hegel, the human race was a reflection of the free development of the great rational Idea. Karl Marx employed this dialectical process of Hegel, but he did it in an even more characteristically nineteenth-century fashion: materialistically. The process was still at the heart of the system, but rather than attributing this dialectic to reason, Marx based it in economics. The whole was "becoming," Marx agreed, but now the "whole" meant "society" and the goal was a classless unity. Hegel's necessary conflict between opposing ideas (which led to rational synthesis) became the class conflict between rich and poor, the haves and the have-nots (resulting in the Communistic classless society). In fact, Marx offers a secularized plan of salvation. Divine providence becomes the dialectic process, original sin is private property, and sinners are capitalists. Confidence in man rapidly replaces confidence in God.

Scientifically, man achieved the climactic vindication of his new philosophical world view in Charles Darwin's theory of biological evolution. One frequently reads that Darwin is to the nineteenth century what Galileo and Newton were to the seventeenth century, but that is far too flattering. Darwin's actual scientific accomplishments are rather ordinary and unimpressive. His academic credentials, such as they were, were in theology. He became a botanist almost by accident. In school he had read the 1789 *Essay on the Principle of Population* by a clergyman named Thomas Malthus. This study attempted to demonstrate that population will always increase faster than the means of subsistence. Thus the majority of mankind is inevitably destined for poverty and misery. The struggle for existence seemed to be an accepted fact.

When Darwin was twenty-two years old he began a five-year voyage on the *Beagle* as the ship's naturalist. He took along a copy of Charles Lyell's *Principles of Geology* to read. Lyell's work had been published the previous year (1830). For the first time, geology was seriously being interpreted by a theoretical system known as "uniformitarianism." Basically Lyell argued that the traditional theories which assumed a recent creation were at least unnecessary and more likely false. Geologic change should not be interpreted, said Lyell, in terms of sudden "catastrophes" such as the biblical Flood in Noah's day but rather in terms of wholly natural causes working at a uniform rate throughout an endless amount of time. In other words, Lyell emphasized the slow yet constant change through which nature was going. He offered the hypothesis that the earth was far older than just several thousands of years (as the Bible seemed to teach). Catastrophism (the traditional theory that explained earth's geological features in terms of several major catastrophes that could have produced geological strata through rapid deposition) seemed to be able to account for most if not all observable geologic changes in a time span of only a few thousand years, but Lyell claimed that the proper interpretation of geological evidence demanded millions or even billions of years. Thus Darwin, who already had the concept of a struggle for existence, now had an apparently limitless amount of time for that struggle to continue.

In the South Pacific Islands, Darwin noticed that small changes within animal and plant populations occurred from one generation to the next. These changes were very small and seemingly insignificant. But if one considered that these tiny changes had continued to accumulate for millions and millions of years, these changes would become major. Those animals or plants best suited to survive, he theorized, those best adapted to the changing environment, would continue to exist. Thus from generation to generation giraffes' necks must have grown longer, and deer must have run more swiftly, he speculated. This process, given enough time, could even explain the supposed development from molecules to man. In a radical way Darwin historicized nature.

Thomas H. Huxley spoke of nature itself as the "cosmic process." Nature was not designed; it simply evolved. Design was an illusion created by the process of natural selection. Nature seemed to work according to a free competitive economy. Thus American businessmen sought to achieve the marvelous evolutionary success of nature by imitating the "natural" laws of survival of the fittest in their economic practices. Monopolies developed as one company survived by destroying all weaker companies. But business was only one area where evolutionary theories made their social implications felt.

If animals and men had a common ancestry, and if these changes were slow and gradual, then when did all men begin to be equal? Why should not apes (or rats or shrimp for that matter) have civil rights? The simple answer suggested that rights belonged only to the "civilized." Slavery was easily justified by some on the basis of "property rights." Others simply came to believe that some people were inherently (by nature) an inferior race. This would surely be a reasonable conclusion if evolution were true. Perhaps they had not yet evolved enough to even have a soul. Many Christians claimed that slavery resulted from Noah's curse on a son of Ham. The overriding factor, however, seems to be the assumption that some people were simply destined by nature to exist in poverty or slavery. It seems that even Charles Dickens, for all his generosity, took a kind of sadistic pleasure in describing the horrors of poverty. In 1859 Lyell wrote that what alarmed philosophers and theologians most about the theory of evolution was their fear that the dignity of man would be lost.

The first biologist to use evolution theory was Jean Baptiste Lamark. He published *Philosophie Zoologique* in 1809. Basically, Lamark tried to argue that acquired characteristics could be inherited, thus explaining how evolution happens. Darwin does not mention Lamark's theories in his *Origin of Species*, but his purely speculative theory of "pangenes" which supposedly migrate from various parts of the body to the reproductive system is a clear attempt to utilize Lamark's ideas. Lamark is a direct philosophical descendant of the materialist philosophers of the French Age of Reason. The German August Weismann in 1893 published a refutation of Darwin's theory of "pangenesis," showing that no scientific observation or experiment could be found to support any Lamarkian method. By this time, however, the "fact" of evolution was already accepted and was thus maintained, despite the loss of any acceptable theory concerning the method by which it could happen.

The readiness of the intellectual world to accept this new evolutionary theory is not properly explained by representing *The Origin of Species* as the triumph of science over superstition. In fact, naturalistic evolution was not so much a step forward as it was a leap backward into the pagan pantheism of the ancient world. Modern Darwinism is scarcely different in its basic world view from the cosmology of the pre-Socratic Greeks. If anything, the Greeks were more dynamic, less mechanical, and more open to the possible divinity of the universe than was Darwin. But their "eggs" are all in the same "basket."

More than any other factor, Darwin's theories contributed to the demise of traditional religion and the rise of a new, secular Europe. As Lord Acton described it in 1887, unbelief in the shape of "doubt" yielded to unbelief in the shape of "certain conviction." Huxley coined the term "agnosticism" to express this modern doubting attitude. The world now seemed to be without design, and all men were without a soul. Nietzsche even declared the death of God in an 1882 book called *The Joyful Wisdom*.

Of course, religion did not roll over and play dead while all this was going on in the secular intellectual world. Liberal theologians began to emphasize a new "doctrine" of evolution. This was expressed at first simply in terms of a belief in progress. The liberal theologians tried to build their interpretations of the biblical testimony around ideas of slow, continuous development. They tried to emphasize the dynamic and personal rather than the mechanistic aspects of the Darwinian theory. But the impersonal materialism upon which the theory most consistently rests could not be suppressed.

They soon began to work out a new natural theology. But this new theology built itself upon an entirely new foundation, quite different from traditional methods of interpretation. Biblical history suddenly became radically evolutionary. Higher criticism began to rewrite scriptural history in evolutionary patterns. Science, not revelation, became the standard for truth. The origin of man, the origin of the various races, and the natural development of theology all were explained by secular not biblical (super-natural) criteria. Men were not directly created, they evolved. Thus Genesis had to be poetry at best or mythology at worst. The races were sociological and ecological, not providential and tribal. Religion, the critics said, was a natural human quest. Religions grew out of historical and cultural circumstances.

Religious mythology of all kinds would eventually become outmoded. Especially the first eleven chapters of Genesis seemed obviously out of touch with the new evolutionary "reality." Biblical history could not be true. Hegel would have said that biblical history could not be true if for no other reason than because it was not the whole of history. Change had become the new reality for most philosophers. All changes were increasingly being accounted for on naturalistic assumptions. Science said that biblical history could not be true for specific reasons. Scripture spoke of a recent creation, of a universal Flood, of a burning bush that was not consumed, of a miraculous crossing of the sea, of the sun standing still, of men living through a fiery furnace, of a virgin birth, of a bodily resurrection, of a return to earth of Jesus from heaven. Scientifically, those kinds of things, of which Scripture was full, simply were impossible.

If Christianity developed as all other religions developed, then it grew out of an animal-like, savage superstition, said the modern critics. The gruesome biblical theology of sacrifice was surely not compatible with modern ideas. The cross could no longer be viewed as a substitutionary, blood sacrifice. Rather, for modern Christians the cross of Christ should be reinterpreted as a significant, moral example of self-giving love. The cross must be retained in Christian theology as the temporal, historical form by which one comes to know of God's forgiveness, but the New Testament theology of the atonement as expressed by Paul or Peter or of the book of Hebrews is now outdated and no longer of normative or final significance. Thus saith evolution. Thus saith human reason. Thus saith modern biblical criticism.

James Frazer, author of *The Golden Bough* (1890), believed that religion was passing from the scene. Just as religion had superseded magic, so science would soon supersede religion. Religion was simply a temporal expression of a particular culture. By the same reasoning, ethical systems were also limited by their historical and cultural origins. Ethics became

Fig. 14. Caspar David Friedrich, *Man and Woman Contemplating the Moon*

Courtesy of Nationalgalerie, Staatliche Museen Preussischer Kulturbesitz, Berlin (West). Photo: Jörg P. Anders.

that which was useful for survival. Biblical infallibility seemed to be an extremely outdated concept.

The Genesis account of creation was apparently incompatible with the new scientific theories. Thus Genesis was doubted historically and scientifically. Perhaps the theological teaching could be true even if the history were false, but at best this demanded a reduction in theological content to a bare minimum: "God did it," but science decides not only "how" but "what" He did. The Old Testament is primitive; the New Testament is a moral advance; the Holy Spirit can lead even beyond that to new and more acceptable theories in the modern day. Thus reasoned the nineteenth-century liberal theologians.

Optimism and progress dominated the thought life of nineteenth-century men and women. The so-called New Enlightenment viewed science as the great hope for mankind. History became the only acceptable category of final explanation. Progress seemed to be an inevitable law.

The Romantic movement also continued into the nineteenth century as a parallel development in the intellectual world. One of the outstanding Protestant Romantic theologians was Friedrich D. E. Schleiermacher, who individualized religion around a deep psychological experience of dependence upon some indefinable Reality. God was found by looking deep within man's emotional nature, Schleiermacher said. But God could not actually be known. He could only be "felt" by experience. Caspar David Friedrich painted *Man and Woman Contemplating the Moon* (1819) to express the sense of religious awe that could be experienced through looking at a simple landscape. For the two humans in the picture, nature and God seem as near as the twilight is to both night and day. Yet this romantic thirst for the Infinite was simply swallowed up by the Darwinian emphasis upon autonomous nature.

By the end of the nineteenth century the mixture of ideas floating around in the intellectual sea was almost indescribable. On the one hand there was a growing skepticism, on the other an idealistic optimism. The new philosophical emphasis fell upon man's irrationality rather than upon his freedom. Irrationality may be interpreted in either an optimistic or a pessimistic manner. Nevertheless, irrationality apparently was there at the heart of reality. Man did not always pursue happiness after all, it seemed. Sometimes man deliberately chose chaos and destruction. Nietzsche said that man sometimes lies even to himself. This is irrational, yet it seemed undeniably to be the normal pattern of life in the world.

By the end of the century a full-scale revolt against reason was under way. One place where this reaction is clearly seen is in the historical philosophy of Wilhelm Dilthey. History was not science, he maintained.

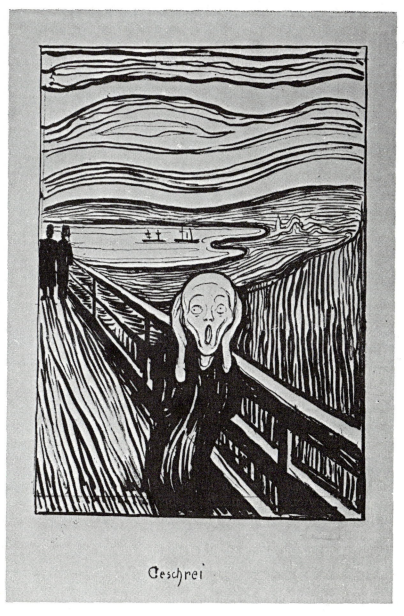

Fig. 15. Edward Munch, *The Scream*

Collection of The Art Institute of Chicago. Courtesy of The Art Institute of Chicago.

History was a human study. It did not concern physical reality and thus was not subject to physical laws. History is made up of individuals and values and must be mentally "relived" in order to be understood. Benedetto Croce called history an art rather than a science. Yet no one seemed able to decide where this line could be legitimately drawn.

By the end of the century, mystical-idealist philosophy had begun an attack on positivist science. Samuel Butler accused science of becoming as much of a religion as any traditional religion ever had been. Science had its own "ritual," its own "priests," and its own "doctrine." Henri Bergson contended that intuition, not intellect, would lead us to truth. Bergson, in *Creative Evolution* (1907), spoke of a mysterious élan vital that accounted for the constant and continual flux of nature. But man is also a part of this continuous change. Edward Munch painted *The Scream* in 1893. The screaming figure seems to be blending in with the landscape surrounding him. He is merging into the total process, and out of deep anxiety over this loss of his uniqueness, he almost cries out from the canvas for help. Men were becoming fearful, lonely, and panic stricken over their loss of identity.

Yet Pierre Auguste Renoir's *The Luncheon of the Boating Party* reminds us that for many in the nineteenth century there was no awakened conscience, no Nietzsche, no Marx, no anxiety, just simple pleasure in daily life. The people in Renoir's painting are playing with dogs, falling in love, carrying on casual conversations, eating, drinking, and being merry.

Herman Melville described the nineteenth-century American as a Captain Ahab who fully believed that he must and could conquer Moby Dick (either nature or God). But it is the captain, not the whale, who is destroyed by his own self-confidence and egomania.

The wonders of Thomas Edison's inventions were just the tip of the coming technological iceberg. The praise heaped upon Edison was just a part of the hymns of praise for man and his achievements that were heard as the century closed. Man could now take the power of Niagara Falls and use it in his home miles away. Buildings twenty stories high were in use. Telegraph messages could now be sent without wires. The Atlantic could be crossed in six days. People miles apart could speak into a special device and be heard and recognized by each other as they carried on a casual conversation. The God of Scripture was a fond memory, but he had long since been bid adieu. The church was soon to divide over the same issues that had come to dominate the non-Christian world.

The Baptists' radical commitment to the New Testament held them together for a while. But soon some of their finest scholars were persuaded by the German Higher Criticism. Their basis of authority shifted to personal religious experience and away from the grammatical-historical inter-

Fig. 16. Pierre Auguste Renoir, *The Luncheon of the Boating Party*
Used by permission of The Phillips Collection, Washington, D.C.

pretation of Scripture. The question became, "How do I explain my experience?" not, "How does Scripture explain reality?" The search was for that
which was useful, not that which was true. Those who tried to preserve
biblical authority were ridiculed as "Fundamentalists," while the so-called
Modernists moved ahead with what they considered to be a useful and a
more contemporary theology.

But as the nineteenth-century optimism crashed into the twentieth-
century First World War, and from that tumbled into the Great Depression,
and from that fell into the Second World War, which was characterized
by the systematic slaughtering of six million Jews and ended in a blast
of extermination, to say the least, the key word became "disenchantment."
Despair faces twentieth-century men at every hand. The Cold War, the
Korean Conflict, the Vietnam War, to mention only those things in which
America was engaged, have left the general public alienated from the
world and even from other citizens of their own country.

Baptists have recognized the growing diversity within their own ranks.
Some have tried to glory in the diversity, but that always rings hollow after
carefully and honestly reading the first chapter of Galatians or the seventeenth chapter of John. Unredeemed political democracy can never serve
as an adequate model for church polity, nor can unredeemed civil courts
serve as an adequate substitute for Christian ethics or church discipline.
The issues are what they have ever been. No man can serve two masters.
Jesus says, "Follow me." God's Word is truth.

BIBLIOGRAPHY

for further reading

Baumer, Franklin L. *Modern European Thought: Continuity and Change,
1600-1950.* New York: Macmillan, 1977.

Becker, Carl L. *The Heavenly City of the Eighteenth-Century Philosophers.*
New Haven: Yale U. Press, 1932.

Brown, Colin. *Philosophy & the Christian Faith.* Downers Grove: InterVarsity,
1968.

Bury, J. B. *The Idea of Progress.* New York: Macmillan, 1920.

Chadwick, Owen. *The Secularization of the European Mind in the Nineteenth
Century.* Cambridge: at the University Press, 1975.

Clark, Kenneth. *Civilization.* New York: Harper & Row, 1969.

Dictionary of the History of Ideas. 4 vols. New York: Scribner's, 1973.

Durant, Will, and Durant, Ariel. *The Story of Civilization.* 11 vols. New York:
Simon & Schuster, 1935-75.

Flew, Antony. *An Introduction to Western Philosophy: Ideas and Argument
from Plato to Sarte.* Indianapolis: Bobbs-Merrill, 1971.

Flower, Elizabeth, and Murphey, Murray G. *A History of Philosophy in America.* 2 vols. New York: Putnam, 1977.

Gay, Peter. *The Enlightenment.* 2 vols. New York: Knopf, 1966, 1969.

Gundry, Stanley N., and Johnson, Alan, eds. *Tensions in Contemporary Theology.* Rev. ed. Chicago: Moody Press, 1979.

Hazard, Paul. *The European Mind, 1680-1715.* New Haven: Yale U. Press, 1953.

Kuklick, Bruce. *The Rise of American Philosophy: Cambridge, Massachusetts, 1860-1930.* New Haven: Yale U. Press, 1977.

May, Henry F. *The Enlightenment in America.* New York: Oxford U. Press, 1976.

Randall, John Herman, Jr. *The Career of Philosophy.* 2 vols. New York: Columbia U. Press, 1962, 1965.

Russell, Bertrand. *A History of Western Philosophy.* New York: Simon & Schuster, 1945.

CHAPTER NINE

"Come, and Let Us Go to Gilgal"

"The requisites for an institution of learning are three b's—bricks, books, brains. Our brethren usually begin at the wrong end of the three b's; they spend all their money for bricks, have nothing to buy books, and must take such brains as they can pick. But our brethren ought to begin at the other end of the three b's." These words, spoken by Rev. Thomas Curtis of South Carolina in 1858, accurately represented the sentiments of young James Petigru Boyce as he reported on the progress of obtaining the necessary funds for the opening of a new theological seminary in Greenville, South Carolina.

In 1845, J. L. Dagg and Francis Wayland had advised young Basil Manly, Jr., to enroll at Princeton Theological Seminary. No institution in the South existed that offered a full theological course, though several Baptist colleges had theology departments. Southern Baptists, however, began in that year to discuss the benefits that would flow from having a seminary in the South within reach of the men called to the ministry. Indeed, many people believed that such an institution was essential if Southern Baptists were to have a ministry competent to meet the needs of the time. However, the discussion of the need was punctuated with jeremiads. Many people were convinced of the impossibility of such a venture. Therefore, progress toward establishing a full-fledged seminary was slow at best.

In 1849, Basil Manly, Jr., stated his views on the necessity and advantage of establishing a single, central theological seminary in the South. Such an institution would allow the professors to concentrate and develop expertise in one area. Also, the influence of several professors would promote a well-rounded rather than a one-sided development of students. One central institution bringing together students from all over the South would serve to promote contact between different sections of the country and minimize sectional peculiarities and jealousies. Such a metropolitan situation, in Manly's opinion, would prove to be a great stimulus to study and would

201

Fig. 17. James P. Boyce
From Broadus's *Memoir of James Petigru Boyce*, Armstrong & Son, 1893.
Frontispiece.

enhance the opportunity for enjoying the advantages of higher culture, a needed benefit for Baptists of the South. Basil Manly, Jr., and J. P. Boyce had enjoyed such a situation at Princeton.

Boyce's active role in pursuing the formation of a seminary commenced in 1856—while he was teaching in the theology department at Furman—when he served on a committee and wrote the committee report asking for concrete information about funds available and a possible location for "the common institution." Later that year, Boyce proposed that the seminary be located in Greenville, South Carolina. South Carolina Baptists would raise a $100,000 endowment, including $30,000 already allotted for Furman's theology department, provided that the other Southern states could raise $100,000 among them. The South Carolina Convention agreed to the plan.

J. P. Boyce, Basil Manly, Jr., J. A. Broadus, E. T. Winkler, and William Williams were appointed by Basil Manly, Sr., as the Committee on Plan of Organization for the new seminary. Boyce chaired the committee. He appointed Basil Manly, Jr., to write an abstract of doctrinal principles for the new school. Boyce himself made the legal and practical arrangements regarding trustees and professors. Broadus prepared the outline for a course of instruction. Their plans were completed in August 1857.

In May of 1858 the last of a long series of meetings related to the establishing of the common theological seminary was held in Greenville, South Carolina. Boyce presented the plan for organization of the seminary—brains, books, then bricks. The seminary would be housed, without rent, in the recently vacated house of worship of the Greenville Baptist Church. In that way, the instructional life of the school would be secured before indebtedness accrued on account of "bricks." The committee for nominating professors also reported: James P. Boyce and Basil Manly, Jr., owned the first set of brains acquired by the new Southern Baptist Theological Seminary.

J. P. BOYCE

James Petigru Boyce, born January 11, 1827, was the first of five children born to Ker Boyce and his second wife, Amanda Jane Caroline Johnston. Ker Boyce had three children before his first wife, who was the older sister of Amanda Jane, died in 1823. Of the eight children, however, James is by far the most famous.

James Petigru Boyce was reared in Charleston, South Carolina. Basil Manly, Sr., was his pastor until Boyce was ten years old. At Manly's death

Boyce remarked, "After a lapse of more than thirty years I can yet feel the weight of his hand, resting in gentleness and love on my head. I can recall the words of fatherly tenderness, with which he sought to guide my childish steps" (*Memoir,* p. 17).

Business enterprise played an important role in the life of Boyce. His father was a successful merchant in Charleston, and apparently Boyce inherited financial expertise as well as a large sum of money from his father. During a severe financial crisis in 1870, Boyce pledged both his business ability and his money to salvage Southern Baptist Theological Seminary. Boyce's business acumen received a well-intended but ill-worded compliment in 1847 after he declared his intentions to be a minister. One of his father's partners exclaimed, "Well, well, why don't he follow some useful occupation? If he would only have stuck to business, he would have made one of the best merchants in the country" (*Memoir,* p. 54).

Boyce entered Princeton in September of 1847, two years after his boyhood friend, Basil Manly, Jr., had finished there. Broadus records that "the most influential of Boyce's instructors at Princeton was Dr. Charles Hodge" (*Memoir,* p. 74). Though he fastened his favor on the study of systematic theology, Boyce had natural gifts for organization and administration. Even as a student he gave many hours to the process of systematizing the results of his reading and conversations. He did not receive the Princeton diploma, though, because he omitted several required courses. He was nevertheless personally satisfied that he learned more by the curriculum he did pursue.

In 1851 he accepted the call to be pastor of the Baptist Church in Columbia, South Carolina, at that time a city of seven thousand. He began his ministry there October 1 and was ordained in November. A member of the ordaining council, Dr. Thomas Curtis, asked Boyce if he intended to make preaching a lifelong matter. Boyce answered, "Yes, provided I do not become a professor of theology" (*Memoir,* p. 88).

He got his chance to become a professor of theology in 1855 when the trustees of Furman University elected him to the faculty in their theology department. At the end of his first year of teaching, he delivered an inaugural address entitled "Three Changes in Theological Institutions" before the board of trustees at their regular precommencement meeting. They immediately elected a committee to contact Boyce in order to request the privilege of publishing the address.

The content of that presentation played a formative role in the establishment of the spiritual and academic structure of Southern Baptist Theological Seminary. First, Boyce suggested that a Baptist theological school ought not limit its enrollment only to college graduates but should provide theological opportunities for men having only "a plain English education"

(*Three Changes,* p. 18). The church would not be abundantly supplied with ministers unless this change from the common practice in other theological schools was adopted. The course of study should be so constructed "as to train the mind to habits of reflection and analysis, to awaken it to conceptions of the truths of Scripture, to fill it with arguments from the Word of God in support of its doctrines, and to give it facility in constructing and presenting such arguments"(p.18).

The second change Boyce proposed from the current Baptist ideas about theological education involved providing courses of study that would prepare some men to be teachers and authors. The training was to be of such quality that it would free the students from dependence upon foreign scholarship "in which much of error has been mingled with truth, owing to the defective standpoint occupied by their authors" (p. 28). Theological institutions, in Boyce's opinion, were already performing admirably in the area of the relationship between science and the Bible. Boyce commended those efforts and indicated his agreement with their purpose and with their view of Scripture that provoked such an endeavor.

> But this seems to be already accomplishing among the many who, having like Christian sympathies with us, regarding the Bible as a book not to be interpreted in any way fancy may direct, and believing equally in the verbal inspiration of its writers, occupy such positions in connection with our Colleges and scientific schools, as lead them to devote their attention to this subject, and to stand forth as champions of the Scriptures—abating in no respect their authority, showing their true relations to science, and holding forth increasing evidences of their inspiration in the language upon their pages, which accords with the exactest discoveries of modern science, and confirms our conviction that the men who wrote it when these discoveries were unknown, were guided in their very language by Him to whom are "known all His works from the beginning of the world," "who looketh to the ends of the earth and seeth under the whole heaven" [p. 27].

Boyce did not recommend that a Baptist seminary needed to pursue original research on the subject of science and Scripture, for the field was adequately covered by others. A general course directing students to readings in the area would be sufficient.

His primary concern centered on original studies in philology and history. In the past, Baptists had been "overlooked, ridiculed and defamed." They could no longer be content with that position, said Boyce, and they were "bound to show an adequate reason for the differences between us and others." He stated that Baptist theological education should produce at least some men who could write scholarly, technical studies that would demonstrate that "we have not made the gross errors in philology and criticism, which we must have made if we be not right." Even Baptist

missionary enterprise, which largely depended on the degree to which
Baptists are able to give doctrinal training to the natives of a land, would
benefit greatly from the higher quality of education, according to Boyce.

The third change in theological institutions that Boyce proposed involved the "adoption of a declaration of doctrine to be required of those
who assume the various professorships." Boyce was adamant on this point:

> His agreement with the standard should be exact. His declaration of it
> should be based upon no mental reservation, upon no private understand-
> ing with those who immediately invest him into office; but the articles to
> be taught having been fully and distinctly laid down, he should be able to
> say from his knowledge of the word of God, that he knows these articles to
> be an exact summary of the truth therein contained . . . for better is it that
> the whole endowment be thrown aside than that the principle be adopted
> that the Professor sign any abstract of doctrine with which he does not
> agree, and in accordance with which he does not intend to teach. No pro-
> fessor should be allowed to enter upon such duties as are there undertaken,
> with the understanding that he is at liberty to modify the truth, which he
> has been placed there to inculcate [p. 35].

Boyce expected some people to object that such a confession of faith is
not required of the church in Scripture. His answer was that even if that
were true, a theological institution is not a church and must conform to
"such laws as human wisdom can best devise, to carry out the laudable
designs of its founder" (p. 39). But Boyce did not in fact grant that such
a test was without warrant even in the church. He points to several instances in which confessions were employed as tests of true faith during
the ministry of Jesus and during the period of the apostles. The purpose
of those New Testament creeds, as he names them, was twofold: "the
declaration of faith and the testing of its existence in others" (p. 41). This
same pattern continued through the Fathers of the first three centuries,
"evidencing, by the Providence of God, that He intended them, like all
other blessings conferred upon the churches, to be continued in use to the
remotest ages" (pp. 42-43).

Not only had creeds been employed by the New Testament and ante-
Nicene church, but, according to Boyce, "by the Baptists of all ages, creeds
have been almost universally used, and invariably in this twofold way"
(p. 43). Boyce stated that some people had misconstrued the Baptist
stance on liberty of conscience to indicate absence of creed, and in his
day many Baptists had "given countenance to this opinion by misstatements of our practice." However, the same concept of the spirituality of
the church that led Baptists to assert liberty of conscience "impressed upon
us the necessity of excluding those who have violated the simplicity which
is in Christ" (pp. 43-44). In view of this discussion, Boyce affirmed the

legitimacy of adopting the "test of doctrine I have suggested to you" (p. 44).

Boyce first printed his *Abstract of Systematic Theology* privately in 1882 for use in his classes at the seminary. The American Baptist Publication Society printed the first public edition in 1887. The method of his writing was determined by the assumptions with which he approached the task. In his preface, Boyce states, "The Author . . . believes in the perfect inspiration and absolute authority of the divine revelation, and is convinced that the best proof of any truth is that it is there taught" (p. vii).

After discussing the science of theology and the being of God, Boyce turns to the subject "Reason and Revelation." The question he actually treats is "How has God made himself known?" Boyce's answer includes both reason and revelation as mediums through which God is made known.

When Boyce refers to reason as a source of knowledge distinct from revelation, he refers to information attained from natural phenomena as distinguished from information attained from supernatural phenomena. Reason involves an employment of all the faculties of mind together—that is, consciousness, observation, intuition, instincts, and deduction. There are no innate ideas, according to Boyce. All knowledge arises from the "exercise of proper thought and reflection, in connection with some perceived facts" (p. 47). By this method, man should learn certain basic concepts about God. Among the truths thus perceived are the existence of God, our dependence upon Him for our existence and well-being, our duty to reverence and love Him, and a sense that our full duty has not been discharged. Some people may even deduce the existence of a future state characterized by rewards and punishment.

However, knowledge derived from reason is imperfect (or incomplete) and must be supplemented by knowledge from special revelation. Boyce observed that this was probably true of man even in innocence and has been compounded as a result of man's Fall from innocence. Thus, we would expect this revelation to exhibit certain minimal characteristics.

> It must come from God, the source of all our other knowledge. No other could give it, and it is fit that no other should do so.
>
> It must be suited to our present condition, confirming the truth already known, and teaching what is practically useful to man as a sinner before God.
>
> It must be secured from all possibility of error, so that its teachings may be relied on with equal, if not greater, confidence than those of reason.
>
> It must come with authority, claiming and proving its claim to be the word of God, who has the right to command, and to punish those who disobey his command; with authority also, that man may with confidence believe and trust the promises and hopes of pardon and peace it may hold out.

That it will be accompanied by difficulties and mysteries is what may be expected, since these are found frequently attending the knowledge derived from reason [p. 48].

The question arises, given the necessity and the characteristics of a divine revelation: How will it be recognized? Boyce concluded that certainty in recognizing revelation comes from an accompanying miracle and from its concurrence with past revelation.

In any new revelation the prophet of God must present a doctrine perfectly consistent with every past revelation and with the knowledge conveyed by nature, and must, at the same time, confirm by miracles his authority as a teacher from God. Without the miracle the new truth has no evidence that it is not simply the product of human reason or imagination. The coincidence in doctrine is necessary to protect against pretended miracles and the tricks of unprincipled men. . . . No truth ever taught by God can be opposed by any new truth from him. . . . It may be more abundantly or clearly revealed . . . but whatever God has once given as truth must so remain forever, as changeless as his own life [p. 50].

Boyce demonstrates his commitment to this unity of truth throughout his *Abstract*. The chapter on creation provides an especially strong example of this. He discusses, first of all, the relation between mind and matter and demonstrates the reasonableness of the biblical teaching that the universe arose out of the mere will and power of God. Mind (God's mind) preceded the existence of matter. Matter is not eternal, nor is it an emanation from God, nor is it a subject upon which God has simply acted in the production of the universe. God preceded matter and brought it into being. "The creation of the world out of nothing is the plain teaching of Scripture" (p. 170).

Boyce then faces the challenge to the truth of the first chapters of Genesis from the science of the nineteenth century. He carefully avoids claiming that Scripture, when properly interpreted, is found to be in perfect alignment with contemporary science. He just as carefully avoids being more dogmatic than the Scripture itself is. Thus, he allows some flexibility of interpretation in the Genesis account and concludes, concerning various objections, that they "seem not to render impossible the absolute verity of this Genesis account of Creation" (p. 173).

Boyce, in the light of his commitment to the unity of truth, also sets forth two principles the reader of the Bible must bear in mind when confronting scientific questions in Scripture. First, the Scripture uses phenomenal language when describing scientific matters. This is the only method possible for a book intended for all ages. Had it been written with the language and insights of today's science it would be obsolete within fifty years. Had it employed the science of its own day it would only be laughable now, and "age after age would have rejected it as false" (p. 173). Thus, it describes natural events only as they appear to the observer. This language of appearance is timeless and is just as true in the modern world as it was in the ancient.

A second principle calls the reader to recognize that, in spite of phenomenal language, the Bible "often gives underlying evidence that God its author knew truths of science, that could not have been known to the science of that day" (p. 173); for example, light appears before the sun and moon in Genesis 1, a view that is much closer to modern cosmological theories than to ancient ones.

Interpreters should be extremely reticent to impute error to Scripture, according to Boyce. We are very careful to guard the integrity of trustworthy men among our present acquaintances and are willing to accept plausible explanations for what appears on the surface to be inconsistent behavior. How much more should one be open to plausible explanations for difficulties within the text of Scripture. Boyce employed this principle when dealing with the biblical creation account.

> It is enough that there are possible means of such reconciliation, and that any one, or more of them, may be true. The veracity of Scripture is otherwise abundantly proved. . . . They are charged with error. It is enough to show one possible explanation. But, in this case, we can show several. This would suffice. But we are justified in challenging those who deny inspiration to account for the many coincidences with the scientific teaching found in this narrative [p. 174].

Boyce's method remains the same throughout his *Abstract of Systematic Theology*. Wherever theology and observable phenomena are coincident, he treats the Scripture as if it were perfectly consistent with and foundational to truth in all other areas of knowledge. At times he asserts the truth of Scripture in the face of objections from other disciplines. For example, in spite of evolutionary theories to the contrary, he maintains the personal and individual existence of Adam and Eve as a necessary historical fact. Only if they had a fully historical existence, just as Genesis teaches, could we finally justify our doctrinal beliefs regarding the unity of the race, the dignity of all people, and the universal sinfulness of man. The analogy of Christ to Adam also necessitates a real first man or else the intent of the analogy is without strength and does not in any way explain the relation of Christ to the redeemed (pp. 190-94; 230-34; 252-58).

Boyce is still remembered for his concern and emphasis upon the highest quality in theological education. He gathered the first seminary faculty ever assembled from within the Southern Baptist Convention. As president of the first Southern Baptist seminary, he faced the first major theological controversy in Southern Baptist life (in the late 1870s, the Toy

Fig. 18. Basil Manly, Jr.

From "The Dollar Roll," Centennial Commemoration Certificate, July 4, 1876. Printed by Southern Baptist Theological Seminary, Louisville, Kentucky. Personal copy of Tom J. Nettles.

case). Without a doubt Boyce shaped Baptist theology in a profound way. His commitment to the Bible as the unique source of religious authority is obvious in everything he wrote. He unhesitantly asserted that Scripture is without error. According to Boyce, the surest proof of any teaching is that it is taught by Scripture.

BASIL MANLY, JR.

Basil Manly, Jr.'s father, Basil Manly, Sr., took part in several significant developments in Baptist life in the South. He was the preacher for the meeting in which the mother of J. P. Boyce, Mrs. Ker Boyce, was converted to Christ (1830). In 1844 his influence was largely responsible for the resolutions passed by the Alabama Baptist Convention that led to the eventual separation of Baptists, North and South. The zeal of Manly, Sr., for ministerial education was a significant factor in the founding of Furman University, in South Carolina. As early as 1835, Manly, Sr., at that time pastor of the First Baptist Church of Charleston, South Carolina, began to call for the founding of a Southwide theological seminary. Those efforts came to fruition in 1859, when Southern Baptist Theological Seminary had its beginning in Greenville, South Carolina.

Basil Manly, Jr., though deeply influenced by his father's commitment to the work of the Lord, attained prominence and recognition out of the force of his own commitment to Christ and his unusual intellectual power. Not only was he one of the original four professors at Southern Seminary in Greenville, but he was also selected to draw up the "Abstract of Principles" that still endures today as the confession of faith signed by tenured Southern Seminary professors. Manly left the seminary in 1863 to serve as the first president of the newly formed Southern Baptist Sunday School Board. Under his leadership the Board soon established itself upon a sound philosophical and theological base. When C. H. Toy resigned from Southern Seminary in 1879, President Boyce sought out Manly to resume his former post as the new professor of Old Testament.

Upon returning to the Seminary, Manly was asked to deliver a formal opening address. He delivered the address on September 1, 1879, and it was printed in full in the September 4, 1879, issue of the *Western Recorder*. Manly's title for the address was "Why and How to Study the Bible." He began by reminiscing about the commitments and trials of the past that had "tinged our locks with gray." Then he presented a challenge for the job of the present and sounded a victorious note for the future. He spoke of falling into line and marching on together "as tried soldiers in the conflicts and successes that await us." The great point of the academic theological enterprise, as far as Manly was concerned, was that professors and students be "mighty in the Scriptures."

There are three grades of Bible study, he said. First there is devotional study, and second there is exegetical study of the English Bible. But Manly pleaded for Bible study "in the original tongues" in which God had given the Bible. He bemoaned the fact that few Baptists in the South were able to "weight an elaborate critical argument upon a question of New Testament Philology." Even fewer could do that with regard to the Old Testament, and still fewer could present original and personal research that would add to the sum total of theological science, he continued.

Although Baptists treasure their dependence on God to qualify His called ones for the spiritual task, Manly said, the minister must not forget that the task is sublimely intellectual as well as spiritual, and ministers "should strive to understand the Word of God for [themselves], as God from heaven gave it to [them]." They must study the very languages in which "his blessed truth was to become incarnated," treasure the "heaven-sent documents," and refuse to "content [themselves] indolently with some cheap substitute for God's own revelation." This attitude toward Scripture expressed in Manly's formal opening address had been the basis of his work in establishing the Sunday School Board, and it was to become the driving force behind his work at the seminary.

In 1888 Manly published his only major volume, entitled *The Bible Doctrine of Inspiration*. In the preface, he writes that this book represents his studied opinion. The views expressed in the book were the product of more than a quarter of a century of discussion on the subject of inspiration. His sense of the importance of the subject had increased each year, he says, until he finally determined to present a study of it to the public "specially from a Biblical standpoint" (p. iii).

In his preliminary considerations, Manly discussed, among other things, the deficiencies of an uninspired Bible. First, an uninspired Bible would "furnish no infallible standard of truth," and would leave us open to the mistakes and errors in judgment of the human authors. "It would furnish no principle of accurate discrimination between the true and false, the divine and the human" (p. 15). On this point Manly quoted with approval the Rev. D. Douglas Bannerman, who said:

> The existence or not of an infallible standard of right and truth is a difference of kind, and not of degree, and therefore a fundamental difference. The more or the less of human error, the greater or less degree of man's fallibility, is a difference that sinks into unimportance in comparison with it [p. 15].

Chapter two of the book contains several pages discussing the fact that inspiration implies both human and divine authorship.

> The divine origin and authority of the Word is not to be affirmed, so

as to exclude or impair the reality of the human authorship, and the peculiarities resulting therefrom. The Bible is God's Word to man, throughout, yet at the same time it is really and thoroughly man's composition [p. 27].

Manly rejected any idea of partial inspiration or partial human authorship and partial divine authorship. Rather it is all of God and all of man. "It is all by singular and accumulated evidence declared to be the Word of God; all written by man, all inspired by God. Both points are proved by separate and sufficient evidence" (p. 29).

However, the human authorship does not necessitate error, according to Manly.

> This full recognition of the human authorship of the Scriptures is of prime importance; for much of the force of the argument against a strict doctrine of Inspiration consists in proving this human authorship of the sacred writings, which we think is undeniable, and then inferring from that their fallibility. 'Human, therefore, fallible,' they say; 'fallible, therefore false in some measure.' But this favorite line of argument seems to us to be more plausible than powerful. It is a mere assumption that their being human forbids their being also divine; that God cannot so inspire and use a human being as to keep his message free from error; that the human origin, under divine control, necessarily involves either falsity or fallibility. This seems to be perfectly plain: yet this fallacy underlies whole pages of vigorous denunciation and confident appeal [pp. 29-30].

In chapter three, Manly summarizes various views of inspiration. The first he discusses is the mechanical theory of inspiration. This view has been espoused by some people, but more people have been accused of it than have actually held it, says Manly.

Another concept of inspiration is what he calls partial inspiration. This view considers the doctrinal teachings inspired but not the narrative or emotional parts. Things naturally unknown were divinely communicated to the writers, but in all other matters natural inaccuracies ordinarily occur. Ideas in general are inspired, but not the language, illustrations, and allusions. The kernel is divine, but the shell is human and imperfect. This view includes those people who would change the statement "The Bible is the Word of God" into "The Bible contains the Word of God."

Manly rejects those views and names his own view of inspiration "Plenary Inspiration." He gives a short definition of this view in chapter three but reserves its defense for the last two hundred pages of the book.

> The doctrine which we hold is that commonly styled Plenary Inspiration, or Full Inspiration. It is that the Bible as a whole is the Word of God, so that in every part of Scripture there is both infallible truth and divine authority.

These two characteristics are distinguishable. Statements might be true, exactly true, yet not conveyed to us on divine authority. The union of absolute truth and divine authority constitutes the claim of the Scripture to our faith and obedience.

This brief statement comprehends the whole of our doctrine on the subject. Nevertheless, in order to promote the clearer understanding of our view, it may be desirable to present some explanations and distinctions, and to exhibit the doctrine both negatively and positively [pp. 59-60].

Chapter four involves thirty pages of explanation as to what the doctrine is not. Manly, in a thorough fashion, refutes ideas that "have often been imputed to the doctrine commonly held, but not justly" (p. 68). Inspiration does not imply that those "who enjoyed it had perfect knowledge on all subjects, or on any subjects, but only that they had infallibility and Divine authority in their official utterances" (p. 78).

Inspiration does not preclude personal growth in knowledge, either.

Not only might one know more than another, yet not be any more truly inspired, for there are no degrees in infallibility; but the same man at one time would know more than he himself knew at an earlier time. Thus there were all diversities of gifts, but the same Spirit [p. 80].

Inspiration does not imply the propriety of actions recorded but not approved. Nor does inspiration imply that all opinions or sayings recorded in Scripture are true, for some things are recorded that Satan said or that other liars said. However, it is true that they said those things, and the words are recorded in order to provide the actual historical context for other implied truths.

The Bible is truly the Word of God, having both infallible truth and divine authority in all that it affirms or enjoins.

The Bible is truly the production of men. It is marked by all the evidences of human authorship as clearly and certainly as any other book that was ever written by men.

This twofold authorship extends to every part of Scripture, and to the language as well as to the general ideas expressed.

Or it may be summed up in one single statement: The whole Bible is truly God's Word written by men [p. 90].

A very important part of Manly's argument for inspiration consists in what he calls the "Presumptive argument for Inspiration" (pp. 93-104). Granted revelation, it is not incredible that God would inspire the record—"that is, control, protect from error, authorize its utterance." Rather, it is likely that God would do so. This contention is enforced by several considerations. First, the nature of God, the nature of man, and the necessity of redemption demand that clear, accurate, and authoritative information concerning truth and duty be available. This information must also be authenticated as coming from God. Second, the permanence and extent of the object in view (redemption and eternal life) demand this kind of inspiration. All men of all eras must be able to discern the truth concerning salvation in its fullness.

A third presumptive argument takes into account two other supernatural acts connected with the giving of Scripture. The following stages of divine activity are involved:

> a. God communicating to the prophet the truth—Revelation.
> b. God controlling the record or utterance of this revelation by the prophet—Inspiration.
> c. God attesting it by divine signs so as to confirm the authority of the prophet as a divine messenger—Evidential miracles [pp. 95-96].

Bible-believing scholars who differ with Manly on the exact nature of inspiration concede the first and the third steps of this procedure. Why then, asks Manly, cannot the middle step be as easily conceded so that the revelation comes to us unbroken by "human frailty and the liability to mistake"? It is evident throughout Manly's discussion that his concept of inspiration extends to the very words of the entire canonical Scripture. They were all written under God's direction.

> If God works a supernatural wonder in giving revelation, and others to authenticate it, then it is not improbable, but likely, that He would exercise such control, and give such supernatural aid as might be necessary to secure the accurate transference of the revelation into human speech, so as to make it just what He meant it should be [p. 96].

However, as stated in Manly's preface, "the Bible statements and the Bible phenomena are the decisive considerations in the case." Thus, the main content of Manly's doctrine is built not from the presumptive arguments but from the "direct proofs of inspiration" in Scripture. In this sixty-five-page section he discusses the general manner in which Scripture writers themselves and the Lord Jesus quoted Scripture. Manly concludes that they never suggest anything to have been erroneous in the previously written Scripture but only add to the continuing revelation of God culminating in Jesus Christ.

> In the similar expressions found in Matthew xi. 13, and Luke xvi. 16, 17, our Saviour reiterates the same teaching. Until John, the law and the prophets had remained the one grand source of divinely authorized information; now, they are to be, not superseded, condemned to failure, but retained and completed. Not an item is to be lost, not a jot, not a tittle [pp. 120-21].

He also discusses passages implying the inspiration of the Bible as a whole (for example, Matthew 22:29; John 10:35; Galatians 3:8; 2 Timothy 3:16), declarations of the inspiration of particular persons and passages, and promises of inspiration to the sacred writers. In this latter instance, Manly treats, along with other passages, John 14:25-26:

> These things have I spoken unto you, being yet present with you.
> But the Comforter, which is the Holy Ghost, whom the Father will send in my name, he shall teach you all things, and bring all things to your remembrance, whatsoever I have said unto you.

This passage applied specifically to the apostles, Manly says, and guaranteed that the record of Jesus' life and teachings would not be left "to the fallible memory of the men who heard them."

> These precious deposits are to be insured, repeated, presented afresh, in more condensed form, in more perfect light, in clearer relations to all else that they knew, and especially to the advancing providence and revelations of God [p. 152].

The Spirit was to guide them into all truth (John 16:13), thus completing what they were unable to understand and communicate even in the presence of the incarnate Lord. Manly remarks from this that "we see the necessity that this added, advancing influence should be given, to finish the unfinished work" (p. 154). However, he reminds the reader that

> the imperfection and inferiority freely acknowledged in the Old Testament as compared with the New, and even in the earlier of the progressive communications of our Lord, or in those of the promised Spirit itself, do not conflict with their being thoroughly divine, and exactly true, as far as they went [p. 155].

Manly continues the chapter by discussing the assertions of inspiration which the writers themselves made and by expounding passages that recognize the union of human and divine authorship in the Scripture. He concludes this section by stating:

> It remains only to submit our minds frankly and lovingly to the combined influence of all God's words about his Word, and to join with peaceful confidence in the prayer and the assurance of our Lord Jesus—"Sanctify them in the truth: Thy Word is truth" [p. 175].

In the third part of the book, Manly seeks to answer objections to inspiration. He discusses objections from Scripture, objections from the existence of difficulties, objections from alleged discrepancies or mistakes, objecti ns on moral grounds, objections on critical grounds, objections on scientific grounds, and objections from insignificant details.

The section on objections on critical grounds includes discussions of both textual criticism and higher criticism. One objection from textual criticism questions the practicality of a doctrine of verbal inspiration when the original autographs no longer exist. The copies that do exist have discrepancies and have performed their task admirably well without being inerrant. Therefore, one might ask, what is gained by strenuous argument for the exact inspiration of the words? Manly's answer is simple and unpretentious.

> A truly divine original, even if copied with no more than ordinary human care and fidelity, is vastly superior to an original, however accurately preserved, that never had divine authority. And obviously the fact that it was recognized and accepted as from God would serve greatly to insure its being preserved with more than ordinary care [p. 227].

Manly touches upon several items relating to higher criticism. He initially chastises the "conceited confidence" of the higher critics and warns against the impression left by such phrases as "the verdict of criticism" (p. 229). He then rejects the "cool assumptions" of many critics.

> For instance, the views of Graf and Kuenen are avowedly based on the denial of anything really supernatural, the ignoring of any actual miracle or prophecy [p. 229].

These, along with the Tübingen school, Manly said, have sought to revise the history of divine manifestation by omitting the divine. The efforts are parallel to performing "the play of Hamlet with Hamlet left out" (p. 230).

Manly also reminds the reader that the question of the extent of the canon must not be confused with the question of its inspiration, nor should some questions of authorship be confused with the integrity of the text of those books. However, the Mosaic authorship of the Pentateuch was an extremely important question for Manly:

> It is so thoroughly assumed and recognized elsewhere in Scripture, that to deny it leads naturally, we think, to a denial of the reality of Old Testament history, and to a subversal of the whole scheme and system of divine revelation. If the Pentateuch, as we are told by some is "not a work, but a growth," of exceedingly composite authorship and mainly post-exilian origin; if it is a compound of Babylonish legends and pious frauds, whether gotten up for selfish interest, or class aggrandizement, or with broader and more patriotic purpose; if it not only gives indications, as we think it does, of diverse sources traditional or documentary, employed under divine direction by Moses himself, but also contains, as we think it does not, contradictions and marks of falsehood; if Moses himself is, as some contend, a mythical personage, and the Exodus never actually occurred as de-

scribed;—we can scarcely vindicate the verity of the subsequent history, or the allusions of Jesus and the Apostles to these writings [p. 233].

In his conclusion, Manly indicates his hope that his investigation of the doctrine of inspiration would be helpful to many people who had a general conviction of the divine authority of Scripture "but did not see how this was to be reconciled with some of the conclusions of modern scholarship" (p. 257). Having investigated the subject candidly, knowing that truth has nothing to fear from critical inquiry, he submits his studies "in the humble hope that they may convince opponents, and reclaim the doubting to a real and rejoicing faith in the Bible as God's Word to Man" (p. 258).

In the fall of 1887, as he sought to aid a friend in trouble, Manly was struck on the head by a robber. He never regained full health after that incident. According to A. T. Robertson, the blow resulted in a valvular disease of the heart which, when complicated by pneumonia, brought on his death on January 31, 1892.

At the funeral, John A. Broadus eulogized Manly with many fair words. "He was the most versatile man I ever met," said Broadus. "I never saw him try to do anything that he did not do it well. The worth of such a man only God can measure" (*Life and Letters,* p. 398).

C. H. Hudson wrote to Broadus on February 2, 1892, about the untimely death of Manly.

> The daily papers of this morning announce the death of two eminently godly and useful men—Rev. Charles H. Spurgeon, of London, and Dr. Basil Manly, of Kentucky. The Baptist world mourns their loss. Their voices are now hushed in the sleep of death. Their words live on, and will continue to live, till they themselves shall awake to newness of life [*Life and Letters,* p. 400].

Hudson's prophecy that Manly's words would continue to live were not ill said. An outline of his theology is preserved in Southern Seminary's *Abstract of Principles* and has doubtless extended his influence into the lives of literally thousands of Baptists. Although his book, *The Bible Doctrine of Inspiration,* has long been out of print, its teaching is firmly established in the tradition of Southern Baptists through article one of the *Abstract of Principles:*

> The Scriptures of the Old and New Testament were given by inspiration of God, and are the only sufficient, certain and authoritative rule of all saving knowledge, faith and obedience.

BIBLIOGRAPHY

James P. Boyce

Boyce, J. P. *Abstract of Systematic Theology*. Philadelphia: American Baptist Publication Society, 1887.

———. *Three Changes in Theological Institutions*. Greenville, S.C.: C. J. Elford's Book & Job Press, 1856.

Broadus, John A. *Memoir of James Petigru Boyce*. New York: A. C. Armstrong & Son, 1893.

Basil Manly, Jr.

Manly, Basil, Jr. *The Bible Doctrine of Inspiration*. New York: A. C. Armstrong & Son, 1888.

———. "Why and How to Study the Bible." *Western Recorder*, September 4, 1879.

Robertson, Archibald Thomas. *Life and Letters of John Albert Broadus*. Philadelphia: American Baptist Publication Society, 1901.

CHAPTER TEN

"O My Son Absalom"

Among the severest pains of life are those that involve conflict between pleasure and principle. This pain is multiplied when pleasure is in the form of a happy relationship with a dear friend and when principle demands an ideological and professional separation from that friend. In Southern Baptist life, this phenomenon is best illustrated by the controversy at Southern Seminary over the higher critical methodology of C. H. Toy. The deep personal friendship and admiration running through the years of this theological controversy lend an irony and pathos to the event reminiscent of the Old Testament story which gave rise to the title of this chapter.

Several pertinent observations may be derived from this study. First, personal friendship does not necessarily blind one to the demands of principle. Second, theological disagreement may occur without personal rancor. Third, "meanness" of spirit does not necessarily accompany conservative and even fundamental theology.

The chapter begins with a cameo of John A. Broadus during the years of his acquaintance with Toy. This includes a summary of Broadus's view of the divine inspiration of the Bible and demonstrates his unanimity of mind with Boyce and Manly. Then the chapter proceeds to unfold some of the complexities involved in the Toy affair before, during, and after the critical months leading to his resignation.

John A. Broadus

John Albert Broadus was born January 24, 1827, in Culpepper County, Virginia. In 1851 and 1852, while he was pastor of the Charlottesville Baptist Church, he also served as a tutor in Greek at the University of Virginia. The combined load became so heavy for him that he was forced to surrender his position at the university in 1853 and invest all his time in the ministry through the church at Charlottesville. Crawford H. Toy, a close friend and associate, wrote that this decision was "greatly regretted in university circles," for it was believed that had he remained a teacher, Broadus would have eventually become an eminent Greek scholar. While

Fig. 19. JOHN A. BROADUS

From *Baptist Principles Reset*, J. B. Jeter, ed. Edited by *The Religious Herald*.
New edition. (Richmond: The Religious Herald Co., 1902), opposite p. 72.

Broadus continued as pastor he was instrumental in the founding of Albermarle Female Institute. This school built an excellent academic reputation. It was especially noted for its elevation of English studies to the level of the "ancient classics and cultured tongues of modern Europe" (*Life and Letters,* p. 121).

When Southern Baptists established their first seminary, in 1858, John A. Broadus, James P. Boyce, Basil Manly, Jr., and E. T. Winkler were elected as professors. Storms of protest assaulted Broadus from his church members, who were determined that he should not quit his position as pastor. Leave the teaching to men "who can't hold out in preaching," said one loyal church member. After all, this layman continued, theological education teaches few preachers, "many of whom are made worse by it, and none benefitted." (Some of these rather humorous ideas seem to have immortal souls.) This same church member suggested that Broadus's influence upon Albermarle would achieve greater good than all the theological seminaries in the nation (*Life and Letters,* p. 148).

Another formal protest contended that no one could replace Broadus as pastor of Charlottesville, for no one would have the same influence on the university and "the great mass of mind there, sanctified and unsanctified." The paper continued by asserting that Broadus was unaware of the great influence he was exerting over the young men in the church "in leading them in the way of Christian duty, and preparing them for future usefulness" (*Life and Letters,* p. 149). This protest was signed by C. H. Toy.

After a great personal struggle, numerous conferences with friends, and a significant amount of correspondence with Boyce, Manly, and Winkler (who declined the professorship), and with William Williams (who was elected in Winkler's stead), Broadus did become the Professor of New Testament Interpretation and Homiletics at the newly formed seminary in the fall of 1859. The spring of 1860 saw Broadus undergo some severe physical difficulties, so much so that he was required to stop teaching for a period. However, he resumed his teaching duties before the spring was over. During that semester, C. H. Toy boarded with Broadus, and their deep friendship and mutual scholarly appreciation began to grow.

The American Civil War interrupted the early progress of the seminary. The faculty became engaged in preaching to Confederate troops and ministering to rural churches. Broadus also served as corresponding secretary of the new Sunday School Board at Greenville. The Board had been established in 1863 largely through the influence of Broadus and Basil Manly, Jr., its first president. Broadman Press, the publishing house affiliated with Southern Baptists, was named in honor of these two devout Baptist scholars.

The seminary reopened on November 1, 1865, with just seven students.

Broadus had only one student in homiletics, William J. Lunn; however, A. T. Robertson reports that Broadus's careful preparation to teach that one student led to the writing of *On the Preparation and Delivery of Sermons* (first published in 1870). Lunn was blind, and he lived less than four years after taking the course under Broadus. Evidently he never graduated from the seminary.

A man of gigantic intellect, Broadus had a very simple and yet profound basis for his scholarship—the divine inspiration of the Bible. This basis is stated most clearly in two particular writings. The first was a sermon preached before the American Baptist Publication Society in 1887. It was published in tract form that year, entitled *Paramount and Permanent Authority of the Bible.* The second is a catechism published jointly by the Sunday School Board of the Southern Baptist Convention and the American Baptist Publication Society in 1892, entitled *A Catechism of Bible Teaching.* The language of this catechism was designed for students from ten to fifteen years of age.

The printed sermon, *Paramount and Permanent Authority of the Bible,* addresses itself to people who believe that the Bible is the word of God. Broadus makes it clear that he does not mean "merely that it *contains* the word of God, which wise persons may disentangle from other things in the book, but that it *is* the word of God." Broadus insists that the Bible has always been and must remain the supreme authority in Christian faith. Other options have vied for this position, but all must be rejected in favor of Holy Scripture. Reason cannot be the Christian's authority, nor can we accept Schleiermacher's contention that Christian consciousness is authoritative. The "tendency of the times" must not rule Scripture, nor should contemporary culture overshadow the authority of God's Word. The church, elevated above Scripture by some groups, must always come under the judgment of Scripture. Also, according to Broadus, the Christian must beware of claims concerning present-day individual inspiration and be ready to subject his own ideas to the teachings of the Bible.

Several advances in philology and archaeology have helped the expositor toward more precision in his interpretation, says Broadus, so that "those who dislike orthodoxy cannot now be so loose in their exegesis; and consequently they have become more loose as to the authority of the Bible." Another help in our understanding of the Bible, according to Broadus, has been the movement of divine providence in history. For example, some of the indecision discernible in the first-century church concerning circumcision is no longer problematic for the simple reason that many elements of the ritual became impossible in light of the destruction of Jerusalem. In the same way, the heat generated in antebellum America concerning the biblical teaching on slavery had cooled considerably during the postwar decades. "Providence changes our standpoint, and we see Scripture in a different light."

However, not all biblical teaching is subject to revision on the basis of cultural change. As an example of a clear teaching not subject to change, Broadus chooses the doctrine of eternal punishment. Some theologians in his day argued that man would receive a postmortem opportunity for salvation called secondary probation. Broadus rejects the concept of a secondary probation because it is "contradicted and forbidden by plain teaching of the Bible." This doctrine did not arise from ambiguity in the Bible, according to Broadus, but from a nineteenth-century humanistic concept of fair play. While contemporary moods may provoke us lawfully to investigate the meaning of Scripture in the light of current opinion, "it is not lawful to put anything as authority above God's word." Broadus contends that even the slightest departure from the teaching of Scripture will be logically devastating to a true and consistent biblical theology. A small fissure in the top of a levee, he says, eventually results in a great crevasse allowing the destructive waters to pour through and render the fair land desolate. "Let us stop the beginnings of departure from the teachings of God's word," he pleads.

The catechism, of course, was not written to be preached as such but to be taught to and memorized by new converts. Here the language is brief but carefully and consciously stated with some precision. Section three is devoted to questions and answers on "The Word of God." Part one of this section, consisting of ten responses, concerns the books of the Bible. Part two is entitled "Inspiration and Authority of the Bible." Below are some of the questions and answers on that subject as they were written by Broadus.

11. Were the books of the Bible written by men? The books of the Bible were written by men, but these men were moved and guided by the Holy Spirit. 2 Peter 1:21; 1 Cor. 14:37.
12. What special proof have we that the entire Old Testament is inspired? Christ and his apostles speak of "Scripture," or "the Scriptures," as inspired by God, and we know that they meant exactly what we call the Old Testament. John 10:35; 2 Tim. 3:16.
13. Does the Bible contain any errors? The Bible records some things said by uninspired men that were not true; but it is true and instructive that these men said them.
14. What authority has the Bible for us? The Bible is our only and all-sufficient rule of faith and practice. . . .
20. With what disposition ought we to study the Bible? We ought to study the Bible with a hearty willingness to believe what it says and do what it requires. John 7:17. . . .

"Advanced Questions"

(b) What promise did our Lord give his apostles as to the Holy Spirit? Our Lord promised his Apostles that the Holy Spirit should bring all his teachings to their remembrance, and guide them into all the truth. John 14:26; 16:13.

(c) Did the inspired writers receive everything by direct revelation? The inspired writers learned many things by observation or inquiry, but they were preserved by the Holy Spirit from error, whether in learning or in writing these things.

(d) What if inspired writers sometimes appear to disagree in their statements? Most cases of apparent disagreement in the inspired writings have been explained, and we may be sure that all could be explained if we had fuller information.

(e) Is this also true when the Bible seems to be in conflict with history or science? Yes, some cases of apparent conflict with history or science have been explained quite recently that were long hard to understand.

(f) Has it been proven that the inspired writers stated anything as true that was not true? No; there is no proof that the inspired writers made any mistake of any kind.

From this catechism one sees several specific points related to biblical inspiration that might never have been addressed by Broadus apart from the tumult of the time.

First, he made a special point of affirming the full inspiration of both the Old and New Testaments. His answers to questions eleven and twelve in the regular section and question b in the advanced section give explicit answers related to the work of the Holy Spirit in assuring the truthfulness of the message recorded by the writers of both testaments. He also refers to Scripture passages to support his position.

Second, Broadus asserted without equivocation the inerrancy of Scripture. Question thirteen introduces this issue in the section of regular questions, and advanced questions c, d, e, and f pursue it in more detail. Scripture, according to Broadus, was inerrant not only in theological areas but also in other areas. Phenomena of common observation recorded by the biblical writers were without error, for the writers "were preserved by the Holy Spirit from error." Apparent contradictions are not errors but "could be explained if we had fuller information." This is the case also in areas of science and history. Scripture must not be accused of error; it will certainly be vindicated in the future as it has been in the past. In short, "there is no proof that the inspired writers made any mistake of any kind."

The theme of biblical authority evidently stayed on his mind until the last day he taught. C. L. Corbitt attended the last class that Broadus taught in English New Testament. Broadus was lecturing on Apollos:

Young gentlemen, if this were the last time I should ever be permitted to address you, I would feel amply repaid for consuming the whole hour in endeavoring to impress upon you these two things, true piety and, like Apollos, to be men "Mighty in the Scriptures." Then pausing, he stood for a moment with his piercing eye fixed upon us, and repeated over and over again in that slow but wonderfully impressive style peculiar to himself, "Mighty in the Scriptures," "Mighty in the Scriptures," until the whole class seemed to be lifted through him into a sacred nearness to the Master. That picture of him as he stood there at that moment can never be obliterated from my mind [*Life and Letters*, p. 430].

Broadus died March 16, 1894. Of all the eulogies which marked that event, one delivered by W. H. Whitsitt placed Broadus in historical context more appropriately than any other.

The Lutherans speak of their great pair of twins, Luther and Melancthon. The Reformed point with pride to Calvin and Beza. Southern Baptists may find their twins in Boyce and Broadus, who will stand side by side in our history till the end of time [*Life and Letters*, p. 434].

CRAWFORD H. TOY

As indicated above, John A. Broadus did not develop his pointed statements concerning the inspiration and authority of Scripture in a vacuum. Rather, they issued from his direct involvement with a colleague of a different persuasion, Professor Crawford Howell Toy of Southern Baptist Theological Seminary. Broadus had respected Toy's scholarship at least since 1860, when Toy was but twenty-four years old. In a letter to Miss Cornelia Taliaferro, Broadus stated, "Toy is among the foremost scholars I have ever known of his years, and an uncommonly conscientious and devoted man" (*Life and Letters*, p. 173). In fact, Toy had been appointed to mission service in Japan. The Civil War interrupted those plans.

At one time Toy and Lottie Moon, the famous Southern Baptist missionary to China, seriously considered marriage to each other. However, she rejected his proposal in 1879 because she considered his theological position untenable. She had carefully read the books recommended to her by Toy, as can be seen from marginal notations in her copies of the books. She was also aware of the problems caused at Southern Seminary by Toy's views. When asked by a relative in later years if she had ever been in love, she answered, "Yes, but God had first claim on my life, and since the two conflicted, there could be no question about the result" (*Our Ordered Lives*, p. 99).

When it became clear that Toy had in fact begun to teach the historical-critical theories of Scripture, President James P. Boyce called upon him to teach without referring to those views. That, of course, proved impos-

Fig. 20. CRAWFORD H. TOY

From "The Dollar Roll," Centennial Commemoration Certificate, July 4, 1876. Printed by Southern Baptist Theological Seminary, Louisville, Kentucky. Personal copy of Tom J. Nettles.

sible, and Toy finally offered the trustees his resignation in May of 1879. Upon hearing that the resignation had been accepted, Broadus sighed:

> Alas! The mournful deed is done. Toy's resignation is accepted. . . . Poor bereaved three; we have lost our jewel of learning, our beloved and noble brother, the pride of the Seminary. God bless the Seminary, God bless Toy, and God help us, sadly but steadfastly to do our providential duty [*Life and Letters,* p. 313].

George William Gardner was a student at Southern in the fall semester of 1876. That was the last semester in which the seminary was located in Greenville, South Carolina. (It moved to Louisville, Kentucky, the next year.) Gardner heard Toy's lectures on the Old Testament during that fall and kept a very detailed book of class notes that has been preserved in the Fleming Library at Southwestern Baptist Theological Seminary, Fort Worth, Texas.

Based on those notes, it is possible to reconstruct some of the ideas being presented by Toy at that stage of his teaching career. Lecture number one, delivered September 5, 1876, dealt primarily with the differences between Genesis 1 and 2. Toy made reference to the use of two different divine names. He went on to elaborate on other stylistic differences. Chapter one is elevated and poetic, while chapter two is prosaic, he said. Only results are emphasized in the first chapter, while the second mentions processes. Toy concluded that these chapters present two separate, conflicting creation accounts.

Toy rejected any attempt to make the Genesis account reflect a scientific version of the origin of all things. He specifically rejected the so-called "age-day" theory which is based on making the Hebrew word for "day" represent a long period of time or perhaps a geological age. According to Toy, the Hebrew word when used in a context such as this never means anything except a twenty-four-hour day. Even if the word could mean a period of time, the days in Genesis 1 do not correspond with the geological records. Toy went on to deny other theories, such as the "history of maximum development" view (in which the writer is thought to have treated the periods only at their highest peak) or the "gap theory" (in which Genesis 1 is interpreted as belonging only to the latest period of earth history). Simply stated, Toy did not believe that Genesis 1 could be in any way compatible with modern science.

Moreover, Toy also rejected the theory that Genesis 1 is simply a theological statement and not a historical narrative. He opposed the idea that Genesis 1 teaches only the theological truth that God made all things. Gardner notes Toy as saying:

> This is true in itself. Science could never have made the discovery. But this chapter is a narrative exegetically. This theory, therefore, cannot stand.

The Bible intends to teach a plain six-day creation, Toy said. The Bible is simply in error at that point. It is, of course, true that God did make all things, but to argue that this was the only intended teaching of the biblical writer is to misread the text, according to Toy.

To accept the biblical account as a true and factual presentation of what actually happened was not even an option that Toy would consider. Truth was not a necessary characteristic of Scripture for him. The truth-value of Genesis 1 must be judged by the current scientific theories, which were based on human observation. This, of course, is one of the basic assumptions of the historical-critical method. Though he did not state it as such, Toy apparently believed that human observation should take priority over divine revelation as the normative source of truth. Or to describe his position more accurately, Toy believed that human observation could distinguish those parts of the Bible that were inspired by God from those parts that were not inspired. Reason judged revelation.

On September 6, 1876, Toy's second lecture picked up with a study of Genesis 2. Again he denied any possibility of finding scientific information in the narrative. To paraphrase from Gardner's book of notes: Darwinism and evolution are unimportant issues for biblical studies. If modern science proves that the Darwinian theories are true, then they should be accepted. Toy believed that they had no bearing on the Bible at all. The literal meaning of the Bible seemed to oppose evolutionary theories, but that did not matter. The Bible was not intended to be a scientific textbook. It may well be mistaken in its scientific statements. The Bible teaches that God created man, but it is up to the scientist to find out how that was done.

Later on in the series of lectures recorded by Gardner, Toy indicated his belief in a dual-source theory for the Flood account. "The fact that the author took his account from two sources is not at all opposed to inspiration," he said.

Toy taught that Abraham had received his monotheism from some existing human source in Chaldea. "There is no special reason for supposing that the idea [of circumcision] was conveyed by God to Abraham," said Toy. Other contemporary cultures practiced it already. "God simply told him to adopt it." These ideas, of course, all come from Toy's growing interest in the historical-critical method of biblical interpretation.

Higher criticism is a total system of Bible interpretation. It has clear implications for the study of Genesis, but it is also used throughout the Bible. Toy was consistent with his method when he denied that Isaiah wrote the whole book attributed to him and when he taught that Daniel did not write his book at all. Many of the messianic prophecies were reinterpreted by Toy. For example, Toy specifically mentioned Genesis 49:10:

> The sceptre shall not depart from Judah, nor a lawgiver from between his feet, until Shiloh come; and unto him shall the gathering of the people be.

This Scripture has no messianic implications, according to Toy. "I would translate it—until he come[s] to Shiloh." Toy says that the verse simply means that Judah should retain the supremacy until he should come to the place at Shiloh where the Ark was.

At the beginning of Toy's tenure at Southern, he gave no indication that he would eventually pursue this critical method of interpretation. Had it been known, he would never have been elected to the faculty. Toy was not dishonest, however. His original views were openly and honestly conservative in every way. On his induction into the professorship of Old Testament interpretation at the seminary in 1869, he presented an inaugural address entitled "The Claims of Biblical Interpretation on Baptists."

The speech was unusually lengthy (sixty-one pages of small print) and was as brilliant as it was long.

Toy began by indicating that accurate biblical interpretation was especially necessary for Baptists because they reject all human authority and depend upon the Bible, "and it alone," for their religion. The bulk of his address was devoted to a survey of the history of biblical interpretation. The treatment contains some exceptionally insightful analyses of the contributions and inadequacies of the methods developed in the past. Toy goes on to affirm that the grammatical-historical method of biblical interpretation is the most scientific and accurate method yet devised. The purpose of this method is to allow the true text of Scripture to say what it truly means. No effort is made to alter the plain meaning of the Scripture by means of alien presuppositions.

Toy strongly criticized Philo, Origen, and Augustine for their fantasizing and allegorizing of the text. He chastised the subjectivity of Schleiermacher and Neander by indicating that "of late, a supposed Christian consciousness has been made the instrument of destructive error."

He even dealt with the problem of science and Scripture in this 1869 address, offering the age-day theory of the six days of creation as a legitimate interpretation of certain passages. Toy affirmed his confidence that when science reaches a satisfactory conclusion regarding these questions relating to ultimate origins, "we may rest in the assured conviction that it will not be in conflict with the inspired record." His contention concerning much of the language of the Bible is that it describes things merely as they appear. The Bible, says Toy, "conforms its language to that phenomenal observation which will probably last to the end of time, as is demanded of a book intended for all time." This is, of course, one of the basic insights upon which almost all conservative Bible-believing scholars agree today.

Some of the most interesting features of Toy's inaugural address are those paragraphs and sentences in which he strongly implies a view of inspiration that extends to the very words of the text. Toward the end of his address, while affirming the necessity of language study, Toy states:

> Suffer us, however, to make a special appeal in behalf of the study of the original languages of Scripture—the Greek and the Hebrew. Some of us are not without inclination to question the wisdom of the Divine Providence in selecting these languages in which to record the truth, and secretly think it would have been better if English had been employed. We shall not now enter into a defense of the Divine scheme. . . . It is an undeniable, and unchangeable fact that God has spoken specifically in two particular languages.

Notice the phrase Toy uses to describe the original-language manuscripts in this sentence from his address:

> There are circumstances, perhaps, which make it right that a servant of God should pass by the original utterances of the Holy Spirit, and accept, instead, the translations of men.

Later, in remarks concerning the relative value of different translations, Toy defends the words as well as the doctrine of the Bible:

> We add that the text, like the doctrine, is committed by God to our keeping, not as a heritage of sloth, but as a discipline of our watchfulness, sobriety, humility, and honesty. So also we ought to feel about the original languages of the Bible. It is inconceivable that a Christian man should not rejoice in any studies or discoveries which give us a greater mastery over the original expression of the words of God.

The relationship between this strong view of inspiration and the grammatical-historical method of interpretation was clearly defined in Toy's thinking. He had no hesitancy about stating his conclusion:

> The method indicated above takes for granted a theory of inspiration, namely, that under the absolutely perfect guiding influence of the Holy Spirit, the writers of the Bible have preserved each his personality of character and intellect and surroundings. Here we do no more than refer again to the fact that the theory of inspiration affects the system of interpretation, and that a fundamental principle of our hermeneutics must be that the

Bible, its real assertions being known, is in every iota of its substance absolutely and infallibly true.

These strong statements approving full inspiration of the biblical text and infallibility "in every iota of its substance" were undoubtedly careful statements of a well-reasoned position. However, as indicated in George Gardner's notes, by 1876 Toy had changed significantly in his approach to biblical interpretation. He no longer accepted "the real assertion" as infallible truth and even asserted that there was no way to reconcile the conflict between the Bible and science in certain areas; thus, the Bible must yield.

Toy himself admitted that he had changed. His written resignation to the trustees in 1879 began with these now famous words:

> Dear Brethren,—It having lately become apparent to me that my views of inspiration differ considerably from those of the body of my brethren, I ask leave to lay my opinions before you, and submit them to your judgment.

Regarding the statement on Scripture in the seminary's articles of faith, he said: "I have always taught, and do now teach in accordance with, and not contrary to it."

It was in the details of the subject that Toy found himself diverging from the majority.

> The divergence has gradually increased in connection with my studies, from year to year, till it has become perceptible to myself and others.

A committee of five trustees, apparently including J. B. Jeter, chairman of the board and editor of *The Religious Herald,* and J. C. Hiden, then editor of *The Baptist Courier,* met with Toy and unanimously recommended that his resignation be accepted. The full board accepted the resignation with only two dissenting votes (probably cast by J. A. Chambliss, an associate editor of the *Courier,* and W. C. Lindsay, pastor emeritus of the First Baptist Church of Columbia, South Carolina, who first published Toy's statement).

The main contention of his resignation treatise, stated in many forms and supported by several illustrations, is this:

> When discrepancies and inaccuracies occur in the historical narrative, this does not invalidate the documents . . . as expression of religious truth.

This position was a definite change from his prior reverence for the "words" as well as the doctrine. He had come to believe that the Bible did contain discrepancies and inaccuracies. He was convinced that one must admit that errors do exist in Scripture. But he was equally convinced that this admission would never affect the essentials of true doctrine.

According to Broadus in his *Memoir of James Petigru Boyce* (published in 1893), by the end of the first Louisville session "certain views in the historical and literary criticism of the Old Testament . . . were found to have been adopted and taught by our justly honored and dearly beloved colleague, Dr. Toy." Broadus described this as a "painful difficulty" for Dr. Boyce.

On pages 260-64 of the *Memoir*, Broadus describes the process of change in Toy's views. This passage includes the famous story of the final encounter at the railway station. Also, Broadus is very clear about the reason for Toy's eventual resignation. The entire passage is reprinted below.

> Dr. Toy had entered upon the study and teaching of the Old Testament with the idea that it was very important to bring the Scriptural references to physical phenomena into recognized harmony with all assured results of physical science. He had himself been, while chiefly devoted to language and kindred subjects, an eager student of various physical sciences. During his first years as professor in Greenville, he made earnest attempts, upon one or another line of theory, to reconcile the existing views of geology and astronomy with Old Testament statements, and afterwards to bring the tenth chapter of Genesis into harmony with the current ethnological views. None of these attempts were entirely satisfactory to his own mind. Some persons think that such theoretical reconciliation between sciences still inchoate, and interpretations still incomplete, must of necessity be only tentative, and the matters left to grow clearer for men of the future. But our young professor could not be content without every year renewing his efforts. About that time appeared the most important works of Darwin, and Dr. Toy became a pronounced evolutionist and Darwinian, giving once a popular lecture in Greenville to interpret and advocate Darwin's views of the origin of man. About the same time he became acquainted with Keunen's works on the Old Testament, presenting the now well-known evolutionist reconstruction of the history of Israel, and relocation of the leading Old Testament documents. These works, and kindred materials coming from Wellhausen and others in Germany, profoundly interested Dr. Toy. They reconciled Old Testament history with the evolutionary principles to which he had become attached in the study of Herbert Spencer and Darwin. If the Darwinian theory of the origin of man has been accepted, then it becomes easy to conclude that the first chapter of Genesis is by no means true history. From this starting point, and pressed by a desire to reconstruct the history on evolutionary principles, one might easily persuade himself that in numerous other cases of apparent conflict between Old Testament statements and the accredited results of various sciences the conflict is real, and the Old Testament account is incorrect. This persuasion would seem to the critic to justify his removing various books and portions of books into other periods of the

history of Israel, so as to make that history a regular evolution from simpler to more complex. For example, it is held that the laws of Moses cannot have arisen in that early and simpler stage of Israelitish history to which Moses belonged, but only in a much later and more highly developed period,—all of which might look reasonable enough if we leave the supernatural out of view. Then the passion grows stronger for so relocating and reconstructing as to make everything in the history of Israel a mere natural evolution; and the tendency of this, if logically and fearlessly carried through, must be to exclude the supernatural from that history altogether. These views would of course be supported by certain well-known theories to the effect that the first six books of the Old Testament were put together out of several different documents, as indicated by certain leading terms, and other characteristic marks of style and tone.

Near the end of the Seminary's first session at Louisville it became known to his colleagues that Professor Toy had been teaching some views in conflict with the full inspiration and accuracy of the Old Testament writings. By inquiry of him, it was learned that he had gone very far in the adoption and varied application of the evolutionary theories above indicated. Dr. Boyce was not only himself opposed, most squarely and strongly, to all such views, but he well knew that nothing of that kind could be taught in the Seminary without doing violence to its aims and objects, and giving the gravest offence to its supporters in general. Duty to the founders of the institution and to all who had given money for its support and endowment, duty to the Baptist churches from whom its students must come, required him to see to it that such teaching should not continue. From the first he saw all this clearly, and felt it deeply. Anxious to avoid anything that might look like an official inquisition, he laid these convictions before Dr. Toy through a colleague who had been the latter's intimate friend from his youth. Dr. Toy was fully convinced that the views he had adopted were correct, and would, by removing many intellectual difficulties, greatly promote faith in the Scriptures. Besides opposing that opinion, it was urged upon his consideration that these ideas could not be taught in the Seminary, and moreover that the great majority of the students were quite unprepared for fitting examination of any such theoretical inquiries, and needed to be instructed in the Old Testament history as it stands. He was entreated to let those theoretical questions alone, and teach the students what they needed. He promised to do this; and in entering upon the next session, of course tried faithfully to keep his promise. It was fondly hoped by his colleagues that in quietly pursuing such a course he might ultimately break away from the dominion of destructive theories. But some students had become aware of ideas he had taught the previous session, which excited their curiosity, and kept asking questions which he felt bound to answer. So, as the session went on, he frankly stated that he found it impossible to leave out those inquiries, or abstain from teaching the opinions he held.

It was hard for Dr. Toy to realize that such teaching was quite out of the question in this institution. He was satisfied that his views would promote truth and piety. He thought strange of the prediction made in conversation that within twenty years he would utterly discard all belief in the supernatural as an element of Scripture,— a prediction founded upon knowledge of his logical consistency and boldness, and already in a much shorter time fulfilled, to judge from his latest works. Some of us are persuaded that if any man adopts the evolutionary reconstruction of Old Testament history and literature, and does not reach a like attitude as regards the supernatural, it is simply because he is prevented, by temperament or environment, from carrying things to their logical results. While not himself perceiving that the opinions he was teaching formed a just ground for his leaving the Seminary, Dr. Toy concluded to send to the Board of Trustees at its approaching session in Atlanta, May, 1879, a statement of the views that he had adopted, and of his persuasion that by teaching them he could do much good; and, in order to relieve the Board from restraints of delicacy, he tendered his resignation.

After due consideration, the Board voted almost unanimously to accept the resignation. The regret at this necessity was universal and profound, and perhaps deeper in the Faculty than anywhere else. Dr. Toy had shown himself not only a remarkable scholar, and a most honorable and lovable gentleman, but also a very able and inspiring teacher, and a colleague with whom, as to all personal relations, it was delightful to be associated. Some of his attached former pupils and other friends thought that there was no necessity for losing him, and that his views were not really in any high degree objectionable, and began vehement remonstrances in private or in the newspapers. This proceeded in a very few cases from sympathy with his opinions; in most cases from lack of acquaintance with the real nature of those opinions and their necessary outcome. Dr. Boyce's personal grief at the loss was shown by a slight but impressive incident. When Dr. Toy returned to Louisville, and made his preparations to leave, his two colleagues who were here went to the railway station. The three happened to stand for a little while alone in a waiting-room; and throwing his left arm around Toy's neck, Dr. Boyce lifted the right arm before him, and said, in a passion of grief, "Oh, Toy, I would freely give that arm to be cut off if you could be where you were five years ago, and stay there."

After a year or two given to literary pursuits in New York City, Dr. Toy was elected Professor of Hebrew in Harvard University. A letter of inquiry from the celebrated Ezra Abbot had led one of the Louisville professors to send a most cordial recommendation, with the explanation that Dr. Toy's leaving the Seminary was due to nothing whatever but his holding views like those of Kuenen and Wellhausen—to which there would, of course, be no objection in Harvard.

Toy's resignation was first announced in the May 21, 1879 issue of *The*

Journal and Messenger, the Baptist state paper published in Cincinnati, Ohio. The editor wrote:

> We are glad to believe that there is a certain unwritten creed in vogue among Baptists that is even more definite than is that article in the [New Hampshire] *Confession,* and that no man can maintain good standing in a Baptist Seminary who does not find more of Christ in the prophecies of Isaiah than Prof. Toy does. Baptists greatly prefer the doctrines of Philip and Paul and Jesus to those of Prof. Toy.

The next day, May 22, several other Baptist state papers carried the announcement. In Georgia, *The Christian Index* expressed deep regret at the loss of Toy but went on to affirm that it was manifestly right for him to submit his resignation and that it was right for the trustees to accept it. The trustee meeting had been held in Atlanta because the Southern Baptist Convention was meeting there.

When Toy's resignation statement was published in the South Carolina *Baptist Courier* (November 11, 1879), several articles began to appear either defending or attacking Toy's views. This led into a general discussion of theories of biblical inspiration. From January through April 1880, *The Religious Herald,* the Virginia Baptist paper, carried six articles by Toy treating revelation, inspiration, criticism, Genesis and geology, and so forth.

Many people wrote articles supporting Toy's views. I. W. Wingo, from Pendleton, South Carolina, wrote in the January 8, 1880 *Baptist Courier:*

> I regard Dr. Toy the safest interpreter of Scripture I have ever learned from. It seems to me that he stands on the firmest ground against the attacks of skeptics and would-be-scientist[s].

Toy's articles in *The Religious Herald,* however, are very revealing as to the exact nature of the controversy. Toy claimed that his resignation paper had spoken only of "results, not processes." He assumed divine inspiration, but the question dealt with the "nature and the extent" to which inspiration was expressed in a "truly human form." Specifically, this human form referred to the "outward human shape of the thought."

In an article published April 22, 1880, entitled "Destruction for Reconstruction," Toy wrote that an old house must be torn down if a new one is to be built. Jesus had to destroy Jewish traditionalism in order to proclaim the gospel of the spiritual kingdom. The Jews built their case upon the basis of Scripture. "Their argument was simple: We know that Moses is right, and therefore this man who opposes Moses must be wrong." Christ asked them to look at the evidence and seek truth rather than bind themselves to a tradition. Toy wrote:

Our Lord's habit was to use the Old Testament not as a petrified statute-book, not as an infallible authority, but as a record of the spiritual experience of Israel, as a divinely inspired, but fallible body of religious and ethical truth. . . . The lesson that we are to learn from Christ's teaching is that our main concern is not with the fallibility or infallibility of a book, but with the truth of God. The truth is something spiritual, which appeals to the soul, and is impotent except in so far as it is received and incorporated into the soul. A book is nothing in itself. Words, spoken or written, are material things, that in themselves have no religious or other power; they are useful only as instruments for bringing ideas into contact with the soul, and the glory of the Bible is its idea. If the soul be thereby brought into union with God, what does it matter whether the book has some errors of date, or astronomy, or some legendary matter mixed with its history? The Samaritan woman, receiving the life-giving message from the strange teacher, whom she believed to be from God, was not scandalized because he sat in human weariness on the well; and one whose eyes are open to see the everlasting truth need not stop to ask whether its soul is encased in a feeble earthly body.

In parting from his disciples, Jesus said nothing to them of being enlightened and guided by a book. He spoke of the Holy Spirit that was to lead them into all truth. He did not say that the Spirit was to be confined to the twelve apostles; he gives us to understand that it will be the advocate and enlightener of all his followers. He meant by this to point to the inward spiritual life as the essential thing—he meant to turn our eyes from all things outward and material, and fix them on the individual spiritual development as the true aim and the true source of power of his people. They were no longer to be (as the Mohammedans call the Jews) "the people of the book"—they were not to be children walking in darkness with pottering steps, but sons of God, having a light in themselves, revering and loving the Scripture, but loving it for the spiritual truth it teaches, which they should perceive and comprehend by their own spiritual instinct. It would not particularly concern them if all the non-spiritual part should be thrown away. Who would be the worse off religiously if the book of Esther and the Song of Songs were left out of the Old Testament?

In cutting away tradition and everything external, Christ was thus elevating the spiritual—he was destroying the worse that he might build up what was better. His followers have to try to imitate him in this.

Another article, "Genesis and Geology" (May 6, 1880), restated his conviction that Genesis clearly taught a creation that took place in six twenty-four-hour days (which, according to Toy, was scientifically untenable); and that age-day theories raised more problems than they solved. Thus, it was necessary for him to decide that Genesis was not in any sense a scientific statement. Scripture still had a religious purpose that it could fulfill apart from any attempts to relate this religious purpose to the disciplines of secular learning.

Once Toy had concluded that personal spiritual insight was finally more authoritative than the written words of Scripture, he rapidly found his insight leading him to find more and more errors in the Bible. From matters of science and history he began to move toward the rejection of theological concepts as well.

For example, his book entitled *The History of the Religion of Israel* was first published in 1882 by the Unitarian Sunday School Society. By this time Toy had become a professor of Hebrew language and literature at Harvard University. Writing on the biblical account of Moses and the Exodus, he states:

> The story in Exodus tells us of the events as pious Israelites long afterwards thought of it, but we cannot be sure their recollection was correct. Many of the particulars given in the narrative are improbable [p. 18].

Later he claims that "there are many reasons why we cannot think that this [biblical] narrative gives a veritable history of the events." Concerning the origin of the Law, Toy wrote, in accordance with the then-current conclusions of historical-critical theories, that

> the law grew up gradually, and hundreds of years after Moses, when pious prophets and priests gathered together the religious usages of their times, they thought that it must all have been revealed in the beginning by the God of Israel, and so they came to believe that their great deliverer from Egyptian bondage had received it all at once [p. 20].

Through the years there has been an unusual interest in the Toy case. John R. Sampey, the Professor of Old Testament Interpretation at Southern Seminary in the early twentieth century, has been reported as saying that Broadus had noticed "marked Unitarian tendencies in [Toy's] thinking" and that this supposed Unitarianism was the real reason his resignation was accepted. Irwin T. Hyatt, Jr., reports that Toy did in fact join the Unitarian Church when he went to Harvard to become Hancock Professor of Hebrew and other Oriental Languages (*Our Ordered Lives*, p. 99).

However, the explanation for Toy's resignation that is given by Broadus seems sufficient to explain the entire phenomenon. The nature of the controversy, as it developed in the lengthy discussions in *The Religious Herald* and *The Baptist Courier* in 1880, was exactly what Toy said: The question was the "nature and the extent" of the human element in biblical inspiration.

J. B. Jeter, the editor of *The Religious Herald*, the first president of the Southern Baptist Foreign Mission Board, and, at the time of the Toy controversy, chairman of the seminary trustees, was a staunch advocate of full biblical infallibility. His untimely death in February 1880 may have been related to the stress he was under regarding the inspiration question. It was reported in *The Religious Herald* (February 26, 1880):

> During his sickness, his mind dwelt more frequently upon the subject of "INSPIRATION" than upon any other theme. He was at times delirious, and yet during his delirium he would discuss this question with the most logical precision.

Jeter was an outstanding Baptist leader, as were many of the people who opposed his views by supporting Toy. *The Baptist Courier* was filled with articles opposing biblical infallibility. The December 4, 1879, issue contained an article by W. J. Alexander on "The Safety and Conservatism of Dr. Toy's Position." F. C. Johnson, from Marietta, Georgia, wrote that "Toy's views could not contradict the views of the majority, for the majority had no views to be contradicted as to the manner of inspiration."

Perhaps the brief article quoted below comes as near as anything printed in those days to describing accurately the general feeling and opinion of most Baptists in the late nineteenth century regarding the controversy touched off by the resignation of Toy. It was published in *The Religious Herald*, March 4, 1880, and was signed simply "H." It was entitled "Dr. Toy's Theory and the Baptist Courier."

> It would seem from various communications to the *Baptist Courier* that Dr. Toy's "views" meet the needs of a great many "perplexed" minds. This perplexity I think, however, is experienced principally by our cultivated and advanced ministers. The rank and file are not troubled about it, except when their leaders persist in pressing their theory upon them. The great body believe that the whole Bible was given by inspiration of God, and are willing to wait until the next life, if necessary, to understand about "the difficulties." They see that the gospel has gone on for 1800 years in the great work of redemption without the aid of that theory. Plain people would be inclined to the opinion that, if a theory of inspiration was or would be at all important, Christ or his apostles would have given us one. But they have been silent to us about that and about still greater mysteries. We have nothing explanatory of the Trinity or the Incarnation, or of other important truths. "The secret things belong to the Lord our God; but those things which are revealed belong unto us and to our children." Now, if the Bible tells us that all Scripture is given by inspiration of God, but gives us no explanation of the mysterious process by which divine truth is communicated through human channels, is not that one of the secret things which

belong not to us, and which we had better not meddle with? The men of Bethshemesh were smitten because they looked into the ark of the Lord.

All that Christ or his apostles said about inspiration was dogmatic. The Savior sent his apostles to preach (not to prove) the gospel. The gospel proves itself in every believer's case. "The difficulties" may remain unexplained, enemies may continue their assaults, friends make concessions which they are not authorized to make, but the gospel will be unchecked in its triumphal progress. The millions who have believed it to be the blessed word of God will go on multiplying until the whole world shall be full of his glory.

BIBLIOGRAPHY

John A. Broadus

Broadus, John A. *A Catechism of Bible Teaching.* Philadelphia: American Baptist Publication Society, 1892.

——. *A Memoir of James Petigru Boyce.* New York: A. C. Armstrong & Son, 1893.

——. *Paramount and Permanent Authority of the Bible.* Philadelphia: American Baptist Publication Society, 1887.

Robertson, Archibald Thomas. *Life and Letters of John Albert Broadus.* Philadelphia: American Baptist Publication Society, 1901.

Crawford H. Toy

Gardner, George William. "Class Notebook for Old Testament Interpretation under C. H. Toy," fall 1876. This is preserved in the treasure room of Fleming Library at Southwestern Baptist Theological Seminary.

Hyatt, Irwin T., Jr. *Our Ordered Lives Confess.* Cambridge, Mass.: Harvard U. Press, 1976.

Toy, C. H. *The Claims of Biblical Interpretation on Baptists.* New York: Lange & Hillman, Steam Book and Job Printers, 1869.

——. *The History of the Religion of Israel.* Boston: Unitarian Sunday School Society, 1894.

CHAPTER ELEVEN

"That the Lord May Continue His Word"

W. T. Whitley, in his *History of British Baptists* (1923), was guilty of a serious historical oversight when he gave only slight attention to John Clifford and Charles Haddon Spurgeon, two important British Baptist figures of the previous century. Clifford, who died in 1923 at eighty-seven years of age, is mentioned in passing on only two pages. Spurgeon, perhaps the most famous of all Baptist preachers, is also mentioned only twice. However, those two men, though they were personal friends, represent two different stances in relation to the intellectual currents of the nineteenth century. John Clifford, who sought to blend evolutionary hypotheses and the conclusions of higher criticism with Christian piety, represents the progressive liberal party of English Baptists. Charles H. Spurgeon, only two years older than Clifford, rejected those hypotheses and conclusions as destructive of true biblical Christianity.

CHARLES H. SPURGEON

Charles Haddon Spurgeon (1834-92) arose from independent stock. His grandfather and his father had been ministers of so-called independent church congregations. One of the best known facts of his life is his conversion to Christ. On January 6, 1850, he attended a morning preaching service at a Primitive Methodist Chapel. Actually he had been on his way to another church, but a fierce and bitter snowstorm forced him to turn down a side street where he found the little chapel. Few people were there. Even the minister was absent. Spurgeon says that he supposed that the minister was "snowed up." Finally a "very thin-looking man" got up to preach; "a shoemaker, or tailor, or something of that sort."

Spurgeon recounts in his *Autobiography* (pp. 105ff.) that this man was "really stupid. He was obliged to stick to his text for the simple reason that he had little else to say." His text was Isaiah 45:22, "Look unto me, and be ye saved, all the ends of the earth."

"It ain't liftin' your feet or your finger," the impromptu preacher began. "It is just 'Look!'" After some ten minutes or so of preaching that men

243

Fig. 21. Charles H. Spurgeon

From picture on file in Fleming Library, Southwestern Baptist Theological Seminary, Fort Worth, Texas. Used by permission of the Mansell Collection, London.

should look to Christ, he fixed his gaze on young Spurgeon sitting under the gallery.

"Young man, you look very miserable."

"Well, I did," writes Spurgeon, "but I had not been accustomed to have remarks made from the pulpit regarding my personal appearance."

"And you always will be miserable," the preacher continued, "miserable in life, miserable in death—if you don't obey my text. . . . Young man, look to Jesus Christ. Look! Look! Look! You have nothing to do but to look and live."

Spurgeon recalls, "I saw at once the way of salvation. . . . The clock of mercy struck in heaven the hour and moment of my emancipation, for the time had come."

His study of the Scripture led him to accept immersion as the only proper form of baptism. On May 30, 1850, his mother's birthday, he walked with Mr. W. H. Cantlow, a Baptist deacon, from Newmarket to Isleham Ferry, where the Rev. W. W. Cantlow, a former missionary to Jamaica, baptized him in the River Lark. In his *Autobiography* (pp. 148ff.), Spurgeon speaks of his decision to become a Baptist.

> I had attended the house of God with my father, and my grandfather; but I thought, when I read the Scriptures, that it was my business to judge for myself. I knew that my father and my grandfather took little children in their arms, put a few drops of water on their faces, and said they were baptized; but I could not see anything in my Bible about babes being baptized. I learned a little Greek; but I could not discover that the word "baptize" meant to sprinkle; so I said to myself, "They are good men, yet they may be wrong; and though I love and revere them, that is no reason why I should imitate them." And they acknowledged, when they knew of my honest conviction, that it was quite right for me to act according to my conscience. I consider the "baptism" of an unconscious infant is just as foolish as the "baptism" of a ship or a bell; for there is as much Scripture for the one as for the other. Therefore I left my relations, and became what I am to-day, a Baptist, so-called, but I hope a great deal more a Christian than a Baptist. . . .

> If I thought it wrong to be a Baptist, I should give it up, and become what I believed to be right. The particular doctrine adhered to by Baptists is that they acknowledge no authority unless it comes from the Word of God. They attach no importance to the authority of the Fathers,—they care not for the authority of the mothers,—if what they say does not agree with the teaching of the Evangelists, Apostles, and Prophets, and, most of all, with the teaching of the Lord Himself. If we could find infant baptism in the Word of God, we should adopt it. It would help us out of a great difficulty, for it would take away from us that reproach which is attached to us,—that we are odd, and do not as other people do. But we have looked

well through the Bible, and cannot find it, and do not believe that it is there; nor do we believe that others can find infant baptism in the Scriptures, unless they themselves first put it there.

While still a student, Spurgeon began preaching as a lay preacher and then became minister to a small church at Waterbeach in 1852. In 1854 he was called to New Park Street Church in London. The building had to be enlarged immediately because of Spurgeon's popularity. Soon the enlarged version became too small. Therefore, the Metropolitan Tabernacle was constructed to seat six thousand and became Spurgeon's bailiwick from 1861 until his death in 1892.

In 1857, *The Texas Baptist* printed a description of Spurgeon as recorded by the London correspondent of the *Banner and Advocate*. Spurgeon was not yet twenty-three years old.

Mr. Spurgeon is of the middle size—thick set in figure, with a deep, capacious chest, and a throat, and tongue, and lip, all formed for vehement oratory. His hair is black, over a tolerably wide forehead; his eyes dark and deep set. . . . He reads the psalm abruptly; he prays with startling rapidity. . . . Then comes an exposition of the chapter. What a torrent of words! What striking remarks, quaint and pithy! And how well he knows his Bible! It is not a lecture. The English will not stand that. But it is a rapid, running commentary, which in my mind, when well done, is the perfection of an expository reading before, and as preparatory to the sermon. Next comes the sermon itself. . . . Listen, tho, to his language. How thoroughly English, vernacular: scarce a Latinized or Greek borrowed term. Is it any wonder with this, and the rich, full, old doctrine of the Puritan age—election defended, asserted, sovereign grace vindicated and glorified; Christ set forth as crucified and slain, pictures, anecdotes—that, in spite of extravagances and much of self, the common people hear him gladly. . . . He does take liberties with his audience; he does deal too much in stimulants; but anything better than these myriads of London allowed to perish unwarned, and anything better than that miserable negation of truth, which our younger preachers are setting forth as a new and better gospel. Spurgeon preaches the doctrine of grace with great courage and fullness: and like Paul, like Whitefield, like Berridge, and Romaine, he freely invites all to our Saviour.

One year later, in 1858, Francis Wayland, in retirement, commented on the young Spurgeon in a letter to one of Wayland's former students:

I have been reading several sermons in Spurgeon's new volume. I am struck with several things; first, the manifest truthfulness of the man, arising from his perfect belief in all that he says. The truths of religion are as much a verity to him as his own existence. Second, his intimate acquaintance with the whole Bible. It bubbles up everywhere as soon as he begins to speak. He uses it with great power to express his own ideas. Third, as a result of this, is his manner of making a sermon. He does not draw an abstract truth out of the text, but expands and illustrates the very text itself. It opens to him a train, or several trains of thought, which he illustrates from everything around him. It is owing to this that he has so great variety. Were he to deduce abstract propositions, he would of necessity often repeat himself. Fourth, he takes the very range of the thoughts of his hearers. They, therefore, all follow him. And then again, while he is accused of egotism, he seems to me to forget himself and his reputation more than any man I know of. He seems not to care what people say of him or do to him, if he can only convert them [*Life and Labors of Francis Wayland*, 2: 231-32].

The first observer, quoted from *The Texas Baptist*, spoke of a tendency which he called "that miserable negation of truth." Thirty years later, in 1887, Spurgeon dissolved his ties with the Baptist Union because that very tendency had become an open reality. Beginning in March of 1887 a series of three articles and several notices appeared in the *Sword and Trowel*, Spurgeon's monthly newspaper, describing what Spurgeon called the "Downgrade." He contended that elements of doctrinal error existing in all the major denominations would soon cause their demise. He was especially concerned about these tendencies among the Baptists.

The entire first article on the "Downgrade" and one-half of the second deals with the gradual encroachment of Arianism and Socinianism into different denominations. Both of those heresies deny, in differing degrees, the eternal deity of Jesus Christ. Spurgeon even asserts that the "Darwinian tadpole" was hatched in a church teaching Socinian doctrine.

In the last part of the second article he identifies the source of those theological errors as "a want of adequate faith in the divine inspiration of the sacred Scriptures." On the other hand, he says, people who accept the Holy Scripture as "an authoritative and infallible rule of faith and practice" never wander "very seriously" from historic Christian truth. Mischievous errors creep in where full confidence in Scripture is weak, Spurgeon claims (*Sword and Trowel*, April 1887, p. 170).

Spurgeon contends that the "new religion" initiated by this view of Scripture is "no more Christianity than chalk is cheese." By this new religion "the Atonement is scouted, the inspiration of Scripture is derided, the Holy Spirit is degraded into an influence, the punishment of sin into fiction, and the resurrection into a myth" (*Sword and Trowel*, August 1887, p. 397). All of those doctrines are reinterperted by the new knowledge, he says, and the traditional understanding of them has changed. When that occurs, Spurgeon says, Christianity in the biblical sense, and, as far as he was concerrned, Christianity in *any* sense, disappears.

Both positive and negative responses to Spurgeon's Downgrade articles ensued. He became the champion for many and the object of derision for others. The Metropolitan Association of Strict Baptist Churches counted themselves among the supporters of Spurgeon's position, and on October 11, 1887, passed unanimously the following resolution:

> Resolved, that this meeting of Pastors and Delegates of the Metropolitan Association of Strict Baptist Churches, recognizing and deeply deploring the present widespread and awful departures from revealed truth, and believing the same to be largely traceable to the bold proclamation of error from some pulpits of various denominational bodies, desires to express its sympathy with Mr. C. H. Spurgeon, in the position he has taken in defense of truth, and his uncompromising exposure of the evils referred to in his articles recently published, entitled "The Down-Grade," considering his action worthy of the highest commendation of all who are anxious to preserve and maintain the truths we hold in common [*Sword and Trowel*, November 1887, p. 598].

However, the majority of his own denomination was unwilling to follow his lead. Many of them believed as he did theologically but apparently preferred unity above the maintenance of doctrinal purity. To them, Spurgeon replied, "First pure, then peaceable; if only one is attainable, choose the former." Again he asserted, "Fellowship with known and vital error is participation in sin," and "to pursue union at the price of truth is treason to the Lord Jesus." Fidelity to God is to be preferred to fraternity among men.

> We who believe the Holy Scripture to be the inspired truth of God cannot have fellowship with those who deny the authority from which we derive all our teaching. We go to our pulpits to save a fallen race, and believe that they must be saved in this life, or perish for ever: how can we profess brotherhood with those who deny the fall of man, and hold out to him the hope of another probation after death [*Sword and Trowel*, November 1887, p. 559].

He called for those of like mind to join him in his struggle against heterodoxy. As far as Spurgeon was concerned this was no mere Arminian-Calvinist debate, as some sought to depict it. It was a conflict over truths central to all believers, "the eternal verities—those foundation truths which belong not exclusively to this party or to that" (*Sword and Trowel*, December 1887, p. 642). Though the foes were strong and the conflict seemed too dear, he encouraged those like-minded with the assurance that the truth for which they fought would ultimately be victorious.

> If for a while the evangelicals are doomed to go down let them die fighting, and in the full assurance that their gospel will have a resurrection

when the inventions of "modern thought" shall be burned up with fire un-quenchable [*Sword and Trowel,* August 1887, p. 400].

Convinced that the theological trend of the Baptist Union was to the left, realizing that the Union itself had no way to enforce theological cor-rectives, and contemplating the further union of the General Baptists with the Particulars, Spurgeon withdrew from the Baptist Union in October 1887. He announced this publicly in the November edition of the *Sword and Trowel:* "We retire at once and distinctly from the Baptist Union." He had already announced this to his church in October and had received a sympathetic and encouraging resolution from his elders and deacons at Metropolitan Tabernacle which they passed with "unanimous and unhesi-tating concurrence." They assured him of their confidence that he had done good service by his affirmation of the inspiration of the Holy Scrip-tures, preaching the doctrines of grace, and preserving an uncorrupted and simple worship in their midst. Their resolution closed with the prayer that his protests against "modern thought" would promote the unity of the churches of Christ throughout the World.

Spurgeon's resolve to "retire at once and distinctly from the Baptist Union" did not mean that he quit his Baptist position. Concomitant with the announcement of withdrawal, he affirmed: "We are in nowise altered in our faith, or in our denominational position. As a baptized believer, our place is where it has ever been" (*Sword and Trowel,* November 1887, p. 560).

In opposition to the prevailing sentiment of his day, Spurgeon found very little in the discipline of higher criticism that he considered edifying. In fact, even those who were not actually a part of the "downgrade school" but who nevertheless acquiesced to some of its influence lost some of their savor in exegesis of Scripture, according to Spurgeon. In August of 1888 Spurgeon published in the *Sword and Trowel* a review of "The Gospel of John" in the *Pulpit Commentary.* Each volume of this commentary has multiple authorship and is divided into sections of exposition, homiletics, and homilies. Spurgeon said that the authors performed "very well, as books run nowadays" or "as far as they go," but the "good men" have cer-tainly not erred "on the side of too spiritual an interpretation."

The modern spirit has a tendency to dry up the Scriptures, and leave them like the skins of the grapes when all the juice has been trodden out in the wine press: though these writers are not of the Down-Grade School, they evidently felt a measure of its influence. . . . Commentators of the present age may be more critical than their predecessors, but they are not more edifying nor improving. . . . We are improving backwards. On the table of spiritual food the joints are finer in bone and scantier in meat. There

Fig. 22. JOHN CLIFFORD

From picture on file in the Treasure Room, Fleming Library, Southwestern Baptist Theological Seminary, Fort Worth, Texas. Used by permission of Fleming Library.

are more stones in the pie, but there is less flavor in the fruit [*Sword and Trowel*, August 1888, p. 493].

Spurgeon's opponents, who considered him incurably obscurantist because of his views on the higher criticism, claimed that the Bible necessarily contained errors because the divine revelation was mediated through human writers. They also accused him of forgetting the human side of inspiration. To those critics he addressed a short article in the October 1889 edition of *Sword and Trowel* (p. 551) entitled "The Human Side of Inspiration."

One might suppose that believers in Plenary Inspiration were all idiots; for their opponents are most benevolently anxious to remind them of facts which none but half-witted persons could ever forget. Over and over they cry, "But there is a human side to inspiration." Of course there is; there must be the man to be inspired as well as the God to inspire him. Whoever doubted this? The inference which is supposed to be inevitable is— that imperfection is, therefore, to be found in the Bible, since man is imperfect. But the inference is not true. God can come into the nearest union with manhood, and he can use men for his purposes, and yet their acts may not in the least degree stain his purposes with moral obliquity. Even so he can utter his thoughts by men, and those thoughts may not be in the least affected by the natural fallibility of man. When the illustration of the Incarnation is quoted, we remark upon it that the Godhead was not deprived of any of its moral attributes by its union with manhood; and even so, in the union of the divine and human in the inspired Word, the thoughts of God are in no degree perverted by being uttered in the words of men. The testimony of God, on the human as well as the divine side, is perfect and infallible; and however others may think of it, we shall not cease to believe in it with all our heart and soul. The Holy Spirit has made no mistake, either in history, physics, theology, or anything else. God is a greater Scientist than any of those who assume that title. If the human side had tainted the lesser statements we could not be sure of the greater. A man who cannot be trusted as to pence is hardly to be relied on in matters which involve thousands of pounds. But the human side has communicated no taint whatever to Holy Scripture. Every Word of God is pure and sure, whether viewed as the utterance of man or as the thought of God. Whatever of man there is in the enunciation of the message, there is nothing which can prevent its being implicitly received by us, since the man saith nothing on his own account, but covers his own personality with the sacred authority of, "Thus saith the Lord." C.H.S.

"Downgrade theologians" also accused Spurgeon of a lack of charity in his deportment toward the new theology. To that Spurgeon replied, "The largest charity towards those who are loyal to the Lord Jesus, and yet do not see with us on secondary matters, is the duty of all true Christians"

(*Sword and Trowel*, November 1887, p. 559). But those who deny the inspiration of Scripture, the vicarious sacrifice, and justification by faith, he said, are enemies of the cross of Christ. True charity toward such people will be "to refuse to aid and abet them in their errors." Furthermore, if the "downgraders" had shown to Spurgeon and his followers the charity they had demanded for themselves, "they might not have driven us out from among the people to whom we naturally belong, wrote Spurgeon (*Sword and Trowel*, December 1887, p. 642).

Spurgeon's worst fears relative to doctrinal decline were illustrated by an essay entitled "Church of the Future," by a Mr. Stead. The *Sword and Trowel* of February 1891 quotes a section of Stead's writing concerning this "church."

> My ideal church will include atheists. . . . Why should the church not include atheists? Surely the Church below ought to be as broad as the Church above! Atheists will be there we may be sure. . . . Of all men of whom I have known, J. S. Mill most nearly approximated to the life of Christ. All of the Church-members of the future must be Christs. . . . If an atheist came to me, and said, "I don't believe in God, or creeds, but your church does good works, and I want to work with it;" of course I would employ him. That man is a real Christian.

Beneath this passage Spurgeon printed some replies to Stead's description of the church of the future, including this one by John Clifford:

> I am completely sympathetic with the spirit and aim out of which his theory grows, and see in them and it a return to the Christianity of Christ Jesus. . . . I doubt not, we are being led by the Divine Spirit who rules the ages in that world redeeming and world-regenerating direction.

Spurgeon exercises great restraint by not taking issue with Clifford's endorsement per se and by not professing "to measure the exact distance to which the Baptist Union Doctor goes." However, his opinion of Stead's church is unmistakable. In Spurgeon's judgment it "is so grotesque, and so defiant of Biblical teaching, as to suggest a ponderous joke rather than a sublime conviction." He further concurs with the evaluation that "the heterogeneous conglomeration" Stead proposed, "is nothing better than a social and religious chaos, from which the good Lord deliver us!"

Even to his death Spurgeon remained unmoved from his position. When some people contended that he would have become more irenical had he lived longer, and indeed that before he died he had regretted his bold defiance of the forward movement in theology, Mrs. C. H. Spurgeon countered in uncompromising tones: "Never once did he regret or swerve one iota from the position he took during the Downgrade Controversy." Although she considered him the most loving and forgiving of men when personal injury was involved, she indicated that he had "no love to spare for those who perverted God's Word." His life was shortened by the conflict of the great controversy, but Mrs. Spurgeon was confident that "he never sorrowed over the sacrifice, or repented that he had been 'faithful unto death'" (*Sword and Trowel*, August 1892, p. 468).

His stance regarding the nature and the authority of the Bible always remained as he said in his *Autobiography* (pp. 164-65):

> Before my conversion, I was accustomed to read the Scriptures to admire their grandeur, to feel the charm of their history, and wonder at the majesty of their language; but I altogether missed the Lord's intent therein. But when the Spirit came with His Divine life, and quickened all the Book to my newly-enlightened soul, the inner meaning shone forth with wonderous glory. I was not in a frame of mind to judge God's Word, but I accepted it all without demur; I did not venture to sit in judgment upon my Judge, and become the reviser of the unerring God. Whatever I found to be in His Word, I received with intense joy.

JOHN CLIFFORD

John Clifford (1836-1923) was pastor of the Baptist Church at Praed Street and Westbourne Park in London from 1858 to 1915. He was instrumental in founding the Baptist World Alliance and was its president from 1905 to 1911. He was known worldwide for his benevolent and liberal spirit and was honored with degrees of distinction by universities in both England and America. A. T. Robertson characterized him as a hero of religious liberty for his stance against religious repression in England (*Heroes and Martyrs*, p. 257).

Clifford played a major role in the developments leading to the founding of the Baptist Union between General and Particular Baptists in 1891. The theological changes among Baptists that made the Union possible, and the laxness of doctrinal standards characterizing the Union caused Spurgeon to describe this whole state of affairs as a movement that was on the "downgrade." Although Spurgeon and Clifford were personal friends and never engaged in direct conflict during Spurgeon's lifetime, that to which Spurgeon objected was most ably stated by John Clifford. However, one should note that Clifford's views did not appear until after Spurgeon's death.

While he was a pastor in London, Clifford also studied at the London University, where he received the Bachelor of Science degree. He won several honors in science, philosophy, and law as he sought to complement his theological training. He made a concentrated effort to prepare himself and his church to deal not only with ecclesiastical problems but with civic and social problems as well. As late as 1906 Clifford wrote, "We cannot, then be surprised that, like our fellows and predecessors, we are still confronted by the ultimate problems of Christianity, and are trying to obtain and express a scientific conception of Christianity in the light of the new knowledge and of the new needs of our time" (*Ultimate Problems*, pp. 7-8).

Clifford's approach to Scripture is derived first of all from the theory of evolution, which he applies to biblical studies as a principle of interpretation. In his book *The Inspiration and Authority of the Bible*, Clifford writes:

> Hence it follows that the latest portion of Revelation is the final and supreme judge of all the rest. . . . Christ Himself expressed and endorsed the evolutionary idea of Revelation; . . . expressly abrogated some of the enactments of Moses, and represented Himself as "*The* Way, *the* Truth, and *the* Life." . . . The theory of evolution, dreaded by some, has certainly become the gracious deliverer of many a student of the Word [pp. 15-16].

In the context of defending what he calls the "scientific method" of interpreting Scripture, Clifford uses the term "evolution" in two ways. First, he uses it to mean the progressive and cumulative process of revelation. "David's Bible was not as copious as that of Malachi." Isaiah's oracles followed one another in chronological order, and Jeremiah added to "his words many like words." Paul knew more Scripture than Moses; thus, "evolution is in the Bible as blood is in the race of man" (p. 30).

However, the second way he uses "evolution" is in the scientific sense as a principle of interpretation.

> Science has pushed the deist's god farther and farther away, and at the moment when it seemed as if he would be thrust out altogether, Darwinism appeared, and, under the guise of a foe, did the work of a friend. . . . So science, through its theory of evolution applied to historical studies, has brought the Bible, which is part of the history of the living God, from the regions remote from our whole human life to which it had been carried, and placed it at the very center of the every-day life of man [p. 32].

In another book, *The Ultimate Problems of Christianity*, he claims that only under the influence of the teaching of evolution was the essence of Christianity, the Fatherhood of God, recaptured in his own time (*Ultimate Problems*, p. 265). He also interprets the biblical "fall" of man in terms of evolutionary theory.

> The evolution of the higher factors and spiritual qualities has been definite and decided. Not, indeed, always direct. Far from that! And though the records of the scientist do not tell of an instantaneous catastrophe or "fall" from a full-orbed perfection of character, . . . yet there have been many fatal deviations and degradations, from the better to the worse, from the

higher to the lower . . . ; in short, not one "fall of man," but a succession of falls [p. 269].

Clifford assumes, however, that evolution, in addition to contributing to the several "falls" of man, would eventually be responsible for irrepressible spiritual and moral ascent.

The men who read the pages of the oldest writing of all, the Book of Nature, discover in its earlier chapters prophecies of the coming man, and assurances of his ascent to moral and spiritual greatness [*Inspiration and Authority*, p. 97].

A second principle of interpretation Clifford uses could be called the rational principle. Nothing can be accepted merely on the force of authority but must first commend itself to the bar of man's reason.

He can find out for himself what Christianity is without testing this or that document, or determining whether Christ said or did not say this particular word, or do this special deed; he can know of the teaching whether it is true or not, by experience; . . . and so he can secure the consent of himself to himself, which is the first condition and foundation of certitude [*Ultimate Problems*, p. 37].

However, Clifford does not identify "knowing by experience" with subjectivism. On the contrary, he rejects subjectivism as incapable of satisfying the larger demands made by the mind of man. Clifford wants to avoid "caprice and exaggeration, misconception and distortion." Experience, for Clifford, is best defined as "common sense at its best—i.e., rigidly accurate in observation and merciless to fallacy in logic." Man's reason, heightened by the teachings of evolution, will be able to see facts as they are without "the distortion of prejudice" (*Inspiration and Authority*, p. 21).

Clifford is confident that man's reason will be able to discern the voice of truth even when it is mixed with the voice of error. For instance, he accepts the idea that the gospel records contain distorted and embellished accounts of the ministry of Jesus. The gospel writers became so carried away that they quite often attributed words and deeds to Jesus that He may never have said or done. Nevertheless, Clifford is persuaded of the importance of knowing the exact teachings of Jesus, for only on that basis can we establish what real Christianity is, says Clifford. It would seem that the lack of exact knowledge and yet the necessity for that knowledge would lead to an insoluble dilemma. Clifford, however, is confident that truth can be found. Somehow man's mind can discern the difference, he claims.

> So that if there are admixtures in our Gospel story, it will not be difficult to tell where Jesus ceases and the editor or reporter begins; where we are listening to the voice of the great Teacher, and where we have the echo of the community [*Ultimate Problems*, p. 58].

Some people may wonder why it will "not be difficult" to discern between the voice and the echo. Clifford's answer is simple and plain. Man's mind can function, he says, completely unencumbered by external ideas that may be brought to the text. Apparently Clifford believed in man's ability to approach the interpretation of the Bible from a neutral standpoint and yet always end up with conclusions that are true to the Christian faith.

> Provided that we face the fact of Christ in these documents, frankly and fearlessly, taking nothing for granted, and setting down nothing from our presuppositions, holding nothing back through bias, but seeing the fact steadily, and seeing it whole, we shall be able to keep severely apart, the Christ of history, and the Christ of faith, and only join them where they are radically and undeniably one [*Ultimate Problems*, p. 58].

Clifford's final vindication of this method rests in his claim that this was the method of Jesus, who "encouraged men to trust in the voice of the Spirit, which is never silent in the heart of him who is prepared to listen thereto and not to dogmas externally imposed" (*Ultimate Problems*, p. 38).

It goes without saying that Clifford rejected the inerrancy of Scripture. "It is not God's way to give us an absolutely inerrant Bible, and he has not done it" (*Inspiration and Authority*, p. 49). He likes the process of revelation to the processes of history and science. We do not reject the stamp of God's providence on history and in the lives of individual men simply because men and nations make mistakes and struggle through troublous times. Nor have the errors of science in the past stopped us from continuing our investigation of the material universe. The achievement of truth is often a process of trial and error, he says. Therefore, it should not surprise us if God gives revelation in the same way, and we must struggle in the same way to comprehend it. The errors mixed in with the truth do not lessen the Bible's value. When critical study has failed in clearing up difficulties or accounting for errors, it still leaves "in unimpeachable integrity, the saving ideas and central facts of the Christian Revelation" (*Inspiration and Authority*, p. 54). Clifford recalls that Samuel Rutherford once said:

> Though there be errours of number, [or] genealogies, . . . yet we hold Providence watcheth so over it, that in the body of articles of faith, and

necessary truths, we are certaine with the certainty of faith, it is that same very Word of God [*Inspiration and Authority*, p. 48].

Not only does Clifford affirm that essential truths are not lost when one denies inerrancy, he also claims that the defense of inerrancy is actually destructive to the Christian faith. A defense of inerrancy, he contends, causes the interpreter to engage in such exegetical gymnastics as to render the central message of the Bible incredible. "We seriously imperil the authority and limit the service of Scripture every time we advocate its absolute inerrancy" (*Inspiration and Authority*, p. 63). Thus, one chapter of Clifford's *The Inspiration and Authority of the Bible* is devoted to refuting "The Three Defences of an Inerrant Bible" (pp. 59-78).

The first defense of inerrancy rejected by Clifford concerns the theory that the autographs, or original manuscripts, are free from errors. Such a theory, Clifford claims, is incurably hypothetical, does not take the present results of textual criticism seriously, overlooks the victories won by the present Bible, and accuses God of carelessness in not preserving the disputed autographs. Moreover, he says, the fact that the originals were probably without punctuation "is fatal to the plea for verbal inspiration" (p. 63). He concludes that the autograph theory is "as unwarranted as it is useless, and as mischievous as it is unwarranted" (p. 64).

The second defense of inerrancy that he seeks to destroy is the claim that the Bible witnesses to its own inerrancy. Clifford asserts that none of the words of Jesus, given their fair and full explication, can be used to support either verbal inspiration or inerrancy. He discusses several pivotal passages, such as Matthew 5:17-18 and John 10:35, finding them not to be making the strong claims advocated by defenders of verbal inspiration. "If, therefore, a theory of 'verbal inspiration' can be proved at all, it must be from sources outside the teaching and example of our Lord," he concludes (p. 70).

Nor do the words of the apostles support either inerrancy or verbal inspiration, according to Clifford. He does not concede that either Peter or Paul is correctly quoted in defense of strict biblical infallibility. It is more consistent with all we know to believe that men moved by the Holy Ghost should not be error-proof, says Clifford. He even leaves the door of the canon open to Ecclesiasticus and Maccabees, for the "breath of God" is there too, and parts of them are profitable for instruction in righteousness. So if one pleas for inerrancy, say, "No! This yoke of literalism cannot be put upon us in the name of the Apostles" (p. 74).

The third defense of inerrancy opposed by Clifford is the claim of its inherent necessity as a foundation for Christian doctrine. In short, the argument states, "Scripture is the criterion of Christian doctrine, and if the criterion is at fault, then how trustworthy is the teaching derived from it?" Clifford replies that the history of the church is filled with accounts of those who have received the word concerning Christ simply upon the testimony of a preacher of the cross. Nine out of ten of the first-century believers found little value in the Old Testament, according to Clifford; and the tenth one only used it to see how Jesus, in whom he already trusted, fulfilled the word of the prophets. Furthermore, the teaching of inerrancy is not a doctrinal safeguard at all, but the opposite. In an age when accuracy and factuality are the passions of men, anything that appears to be shuffling or subterfuge is an affront to reason. Thus, to set forth a doctrine of inerrancy alongside the true Revelation of God and imply that the two stand or fall together is "one of the surest ways of frustrating the redeeming purpose for which the Revelation of the Christ is given" (p. 78).

If Clifford so adamantly rejected the inerrancy and verbal inspiration of Scripture, wherein lay its authority for him? The answer is really very simple. The authority of Scripture lies in man's encounter with the living Christ in its pages. Critical investigation has made this encounter easier to attain, for it has helped us to recognize and remove all those parts of the gospel that are superfluous. We see Christ more accurately as He was and is. We can sense His spirit of justice and pity more keenly and partake of His grace and righteousness more fully.

> If the authority of the truth of the Bible is in the keeping of the Jesus who dwells therein, then never was authority more absolutely secure. The errancy of Scripture neither touches Him nor His work [*Inspiration and Authority*, p. 86].

Clifford viewed the Spirit of Christ (somehow spiritually recognized by the readers of the Bible) as the decisive factor in discerning the authority of Scripture.

> He and He alone, holds the throne of the Divinely authoritative element in religion, and speaks of the human element, i.e. to our spiritual consciousness, so as to secure its immediate response [p. 116].

Christ is the "Soul of the Bible," the "only Master" of the Bible, the life and indestructibility of the Bible, and the inexhaustible element of the Bible. Thus, we need not fret over the mistaken notions about God in either Testament, or over the low morality and vengeful spirit often espoused in the name of God, or over the "outbursts of unrestrained hate in the imprecatory Psalms" or over the mechanical Deism of parts of the Old Testament; because "Jesus is the final test of the morality, and also of the doctrinal teaching of the Old Testament" (p. 135).

Willis B. Glover, in an article in *Foundations* in 1958, is accurate when he characterizes Clifford as an "anti-intellectual" because of his emphasis on experience over knowledge as a source of religious authority. Lack of theological precision, inadequate doctrinal support for Christian activity, and a decline in systematic presentations of objective Christian truth were all signs of strengths to Clifford. According to Clifford:

> Even the aid [Christianity] renders the reason in constructing a philosophy of God is conferred through the higher ministries of the conscience and emotions. . . . for no doubt our theological apathy is due first and mainly to the overshadowing importance accorded in our systems to the regenerate life. . . . Systems of doctrine are trifles light as air to souls that see God face to face in intimate fellowship with the eternal Spirit ["Baptist Theology," *Contemporary Review* 53(1888):505-6, cited by Glover, p. 43].

Thus, the authority of the Bible in all matters is not "in the letter of Scriptures alone, but in Christ Jesus, dwelling and ruling in the conscience and reason of Christian man by and through the Scriptures" (*Inspiration and Authority*, p. 137). According to Clifford, the "post-Reformation theory" of biblical inerrancy is the Protestant counterpart to papal infallibility. It lifts the letter of Scripture above Christ and deposes Him from His throne. The alternative Clifford offers is that Christians should emulate the apostles, who proclaimed Christ, not a book, as the Alpha and Omega of their ministry.

BIBLIOGRAPHY

Whitley, W. T. *A History of British Baptists.* London: Charles Griffin, 1923.

C. H. Spurgeon

The Autobiography of Charles H. Spurgeon. Compiled from his diary, letters, and records by his wife (Susannah Spurgeon) and his private secretary (the Rev. W. J. Harrald). 4 vols. Philadelphia: American Baptist Publication Society, 1897-1900. Pages quoted in this chapter are from vol. 1.

Spurgeon, C. H., ed. *The Sword and Trowel: A Record of Combat with Sin and of Labour for the Lord,* 1887-1900.

The Texas Baptist, "Spurgeon in the Pulpit," 7 January 1857, p. 1.

Wayland, Francis, and Wayland, H. L. *Life and Labors of Francis Wayland.* 2 vols. New York: Sheldon & Company, 1867.

John Clifford

Clifford, John. *The Inspiration and Authority of the Bible.* 3rd ed. London: James Clark & Co., 1899.

———. *The Ultimate Problems of Christianity.* London: The Kingsgate Press and James Clark & Co., 1906.

Glover, Willis B. "English Baptists at the Time of the Downgrade Controversy." *Foundations* 1 (July 1958): 41-51.

Prestridge, J. N., ed. *Modern Baptist Heroes and Martyrs.* Louisville: The World Press, 1911.

Fig. 23. A. H. STRONG

From *The Rochester Theological Seminary Bulletin, The Anniversary Volume (The Record).* 76th year, no. 1, May 1925.

CHAPTER TWELVE

"All His Days They Departed Not"

Late nineteenth-century Baptist life in the northern United States was filled with productivity, dedication, and devotion. A major Baptist commentary on the Bible was produced under the able direction of Alvah Hovey, who for many years served on the faculty of Newton Theological Institution and then as its president. A. H. Strong was a commanding intellectual leader who served many years as president of Rochester Theological Seminary.

The American Civil War had been fought mostly in the territory of the southern states. While the South still struggled to regain the basics, the North's more settled and stable society allowed the churches to develop rapidly.

Theologically, the nineteenth century had been one of rapid change. The documentary theories of Old Testament composition had become a prominent viewpoint with many scholars, and serious challenges were put forth against the traditional views of biblical authority. Baptists needed strong philosophical and biblical theologians, and they found them in Strong and Hovey.

A. H. STRONG

Augustus Hopkins Strong was born on August 3, 1836. His father had been converted under the preaching ministry of Charles G. Finney during his Rochester evangelistic campaign. There was a strong spiritual emphasis in the Strong home from that time on. Strong sometimes spoke of his spiritual experiences as a child (his mother taking him into a dark closet to pray or his father walking with him to church even in a snowstorm), but he never made a personal commitment to Christ in those days. At fourteen he did experience an intellectual awakening of sorts when his lifelong interest in literature began.

One March afternoon during his junior year at Yale, Strong was standing in front of the chapel by Wilder Smith, one of his closest college friends. Just as the college bell rang for evening prayer, Smith put his

261

hand on Strong's shoulder. "O Strong," he said, "I wish you were a Christian." Those words burned deeply into his heart, and he could never forget them.

Spring vacation brought him home, and to his delight it also brought a visit from his young lady cousin. She invited him to hear Finney preach.

> I do not remember what the sermon was, but I do remember that great, stalwart man standing up at the close of the service, with his eyes fixed apparently upon me, and saying: "If there is anyone in this congregation who thinks he ought to begin to serve God, let him rise out of his place and go down the aisle into the basement. There will be some ministers there who will talk with him on the subject of religion." It was like a thunderbolt to me. I did not expect anything like that. But I somehow felt that my hour had come [*Chapel-Talks*, p. 12].

Yet he could not get the spiritual peace he desired. He read his Bible, earnestly prayed, and faithfully attended the prayer services, but nothing changed. He gave himself to personal witnessing. He gave up bad habits. He did all that he knew to do, but for those weeks he was in an endless spiritual struggle.

One night at a college prayer meeting he spoke out to the group. "My friends, I am not a Christian; I do not pretend anything of the sort, but I want to be; can you do anything to help me?"

Several students tried to help him through prayer and spoken encouragement. Still he had no peace. That evening by lamplight he poured over the Scripture, seeking a word from God. Turning the pages of his Bible, he came to Paul's second letter to the church at Corinth, chapter six.

> Wherefore come out from among them, and be ye separate, saith the Lord, and touch not the unclean thing; and I will receive you, and will be a Father unto you, and ye shall be my sons and daughters, saith the Lord Almighty [2 Corinthians 6:17-18].

From that moment, he felt the spiritual tie between himself and God for which he had sought. He graduated from Yale in 1857 and immediately enrolled in Rochester Theological Seminary. His teacher, Ezekiel G. Robinson, was definitely Calvinistic, and Strong began to shift away from the Arminian context of his early Christian experience.

It was Strong's hope to serve as a foreign missionary, but he had a hemorrhage of the lung and was forced to change his plans. He did travel widely, spending some time in Germany. Some evidence exists to suggest that he might have actually pursued some formal study at the University of Berlin. On August 31, 1861, he was ordained at Haverhill, Massachusetts, and he pastored the First Baptist Church there until 1865. From there he was called to "the Rockefeller church," the First Baptist Church of Cleveland, where he served until being called back to Rochester Seminary in 1872 to be its president and to teach biblical theology.

In 1876 Strong printed his *Lectures on Theology.* He did not use the published lectures of Robinson at all. He was afraid that Robinson's influence on him would be so strong that he would become a mere copyist. So this first printing is of significant historical interest. It represents Strong's attempt to construct his own system of theology.

On July 23, 1878, Strong delivered an address entitled "The Philosophy of Evolution," in which he argued that a principle of development was clearly taught in Genesis and had been recognized by Origen, Augustine, and Anselm. However, Strong did not use his evolutionary principles to play down the miraculous in Scripture. On October 23 of that same year he read an essay entitled "The Christian Miracles" to a Baptist pastors' conference in New York state. Miracles authenticate the divine revelation and serve as an external proof of the divine origin of the scriptural truths, he said.

The Examiner, in October, 1880, published an essay by Strong entitled "The Method of Inspiration." He relied heavily on the views of Dorner, a German Lutheran scholar, regarding man's capability of being interpenetrated by God's Spirit. The effect of this union between God and man is not a loss of man's powers of intellect, emotion, and will, but rather a heightening of them. Man is never more fully himself than when God works through him, says Strong. Divine inspiration, then, is not men writing God's words given to them from without; rather, it is as from within. The biblical writers did not react passively. They were in the "fullest conscious possession and the most exalted exercise" of their mental abilities. The Scriptures are the product "equally of God and man." (By 1885 Strong had changed his wording slightly so as to say "just as truly" the product of God and man.) There is no question, however, about Strong's belief that inspiration secured the infallible transmission of divine truth.

During the years prior to the publication of his enlarged and amended edition of his lectures, now called *Systematic Theology* (1886), Strong came to accept higher critical theories of the Pentateuch which found various documents underlying the present text. Though he did still insist on Mosaic authorship of the present text, he increasingly emphasized the necessity of accepting an evolutionary development in the Genesis account of creation. In 1888 he published *Philosophy and Religion,* which included the essays mentioned above plus many others. His *Systematic Theology* was thoroughly revised (but with no substantial change in theological perspective) in 1889. A third edition appeared in 1890 and a fourth in 1892, still with no significant change.

However, the turning point came in 1894. That year Strong read E. G. Robinson's *Christian Theology* for the first time. Also he began writing a series of articles for *The Examiner* that were later published in *Christ in Creation and Ethical Monism* (1899). He proposed an idealistic view called "ethical monism" which became the organizing principle of his later theology and most obviously affected his ideas about the doctrines of perseverance and of the atonement. Essentially "ethical monism" is a theory that explains how humanity's sin could be imputed to Christ. Strong believed that Christ was immanent in creation and was united with man biologically and not just forensically through a covenant. Christ is the principle of evolution, writes Strong.

The 1896 fifth edition of Strong's lectures began to show the changes caused by the adoption of this idealist emphasis. He became increasingly convinced that evolution is the method of the immanent God, though in his mind this still did not imply any reduced belief in the miraculous.

That man did have an animal ancestry is clearly Strong's position by 1898, as can be seen by his address before the Baptist Congress in Buffalo, New York, in November of that year. Strong did not see this as incompatible with a proper doctrine of the Fall. Yet there was no hesitancy on Strong's part to apply this developmental hypothesis everywhere, even to Scripture itself. The immanent Spirit of Christ, working in common evolutionary fashion, he says, moved the biblical writers from within. Inspiration was distinguishable from the normal activity of their own minds only in retrospect (*Christ in Creation*, p. 203). In fact, documentary theories of critical scholarship may not be destructive at all, Strong concludes. The more composite the human authorship, the more apparent it becomes that one divine mind must be behind the whole process. Inspiration "does not guarantee the inerrancy of Scripture in every historical and scientific detail," yet when Scripture is properly interpreted, inspiration does make it "infallible for its purpose of communicating moral and religious truth" (*Christ in Creation*, p. 205). If Christ were the animating force behind all ethical evolutionary development, then the inspiration of the Bible would be expected to follow an evolutionary pattern just as the higher critics claim.

Christ, however, is the ultimate source of all religious authority, Strong says. The purpose of the Bible is not to teach math but to set forth the words and works of Christ. Scripture is the witness to Christ's historical work in both the old and the new dispensations (*Christ in Creation*, pp. 132-33).

Strong personally denied the presence of errors in the autographs of Scripture, but he would not impose the doctrine of absolute inerrancy on his students (*Christ in Creation,* p. 127). The issue is not important enough, says Strong, to exclude others from Christian fellowship over this matter. If someone should in the future prove some real error in historical detail, that would not necessarily affect our faith, he says, though one should be cautious so as not to identify a seeming problem with a real error. Whatever is discovered about historical or scientific imperfections in Scripture, "we can never admit that there are imperfections in Christ" (*Christ in Creation,* p. 134).

The final revision of Strong's *Systematic Theology* came in 1907. This was a revision and an enlargement of the 1886 work, and it now represented his mature conclusions. It was published while Strong was serving as the president of Rochester Seminary and as president of the Northern Baptist Convention. (He was at Rochester from 1872 to 1912 and was the Convention president from 1905 to 1919.) Probably an even more thorough revision in the light of his monistic emphasis would have been forthcoming had he lived longer. He died in 1921, but his final work, *What Shall I Believe?*, published in 1922, shows a thoroughgoing acceptance of evolutionary and higher critical theories. He claimed to be the middle ground of reconciliation for both higher critics and Fundamentalists.

Perhaps the finest study of Strong's entire theological position that takes his developing ideas into account is Carl F. H. Henry's dissertation at Boston University on "The Influence of Personalistic Idealism on the Theology of A. H. Strong." It was published in 1951 as *Personal Idealism and Strong's Theology.*

In what follows, the emphasis is on the doctrine of biblical authority as it is expressed in the final and most influential revision of *Systematic Theology* (1907). Whatever Strong may have come to believe personally, it is the wording of the 1907 revision that has influenced modern Baptist life so significantly. Before looking at Strong's views on biblical revelation, it may be of interest to examine certain points included in his section on the doctrine of man (*Systematic Theology* [1907], pp. 465ff).

Scripture opposes the idea that man is the product of unreasoning natural forces, says Strong. The actual method of man's creation, however, is not specifically taught in Genesis. Strong raises the question of whether the biblical material teaches that man's body was immediately created or whether the text can be legitimately interpreted to allow the idea that man's body was formed through evolutionary processes (understanding those processes to be directed by God). He concludes that man came *through* the animals but not *from* the animals (p. 467).

On the other hand, Strong is careful to point out that it has never been demonstrated that the body of a man ever actually developed from lower animal forms. He states that a theory of natural descent "apart from the direct agency of God . . . can be regarded only as an irrational hypothesis" (p. 470).

Strong would concede an animal ancestry for man's body if such could ever be shown to be the case scientifically, but he does not on that account deny the historical character of the Genesis material. On page 476 he enters into a discussion of the unity of the human race. The Scriptures teach that all people have descended from a single pair. Strong supports this not only from Genesis but also from Romans 5:12 and 1 Corinthians 15:21-22. He finds this truth about man's origin to be basic to Paul's theology of salvation. Acts 17:26 is also used by Strong to emphasize the corollary doctrine of man's brotherhood.

On pages 476-77 Strong describes the controversy over the possibility of the existence of a pre-Adamic race of men. He finds the theory attractive in many ways because it seems to solve certain problems; but ultimately Strong rejects it because "it treats the Mosaic narrative as legendary rather than historical." The theory of a pre-Adamic race of men would make Genesis 3:20 (Eve the mother of all living) a direct error in the text. Thus, Strong rejects the theory because he did not believe that any such errors existed in Scripture. That Cain married his own sister is found by Strong to be the most reasonable solution to that age-old exegetical problem.

Part three of Strong's *Systematic Theology* is entitled "The Scriptures A Revelation from God." In his "Preliminary Considerations" he gives several reasons, first, for expecting a revelation from God. Then he outlines some of the characteristic marks that man could look for in order to identify a revelation from God. Strong discusses miracles and prophecy in this context, for he believed that those two realities served to attest divine revelation. He further presents an extended discussion of the historical evidence supporting the concept of revelation.

These general considerations give way to "Positive Proofs that the Scriptures are a Divine Revelation." In this section Strong points first to the genuineness of the documents—that is, he gives evidence to show that the biblical documents actually do come from the age and from the men to whom they are ascribed. As a part of this lengthy discussion, Strong analyzes and denies the validity of rationalistic theories on the origin of the gospels as suggested by men such as Strauss, Baur, Renan, and Harnack. However, Strong was not greatly upset by and even favored a modified form of the standard JEDP theory of pentateuchal criticism. This view "simply shows God's actual method in making up the record of his revelation," he says (p. 172). Strong does conclude that "a larger portion of the Pentateuch" (p. 169) was written by Moses himself, but he believes that Deuteronomy was composed in the days of King Josiah (621 B.C.), in accordance with standard critical theories. Genesis 1 and 2 represent two differing accounts of creation, he maintains, and thus some form of higher criticism must be accepted.

When defending the credibility of the writers of Scripture, Strong concentrates on the gospel writers, "for if they are credible witnesses," he argues, "the credibility of the Old Testament, to which they bore testimony, follows as a matter of course" (p. 172). The teaching of the Bible is of a supernatural character, he continues. The Bible is the work of one mind (p. 175), its moral teachings are unsurpassed (p. 177), and the conception of the person and character of Christ cannot be accounted for on purely human assumptions (p. 186). Christ claimed to teach absolute truth and to be one with God. This too cannot be accounted for on the assumption that Scripture is a purely human witness (p. 189). The final proof comes from the historical results of the propagation of biblical doctrine (p. 191). All of this leads Strong to affirm that the Scripture is a divine revelation from God.

Having thus proved that God did make a revelation of Himself to man, Strong devotes a full chapter to the doctrine of the inspiration of the Scriptures.

> Since we have shown that God has made a revelation of himself to man, we may reasonably presume that he will not trust this revelation wholly to human tradition and misrepresentation, but will also provide a record of it essentially trustworthy and sufficient; in other words, that the same Spirit who originally communicated the truth will preside over its publication, so far as is needed to accomplish its religious purpose [p. 198].

Strong's definition of inspiration is quite specific and clear. He defines inspiration as

> that influence of the Spirit of God upon the minds of the Scripture writers which made their writings the record of a progressive divine revelation, sufficient, when taken together and interpreted by the same Spirit who inspired them, to lead every honest inquirer to Christ and to salvation [p. 196].

Inspiration, then, is not defined by its method but by its result. According to Strong, the method varied from one instance to the next. It may include revelation. It may include illumination. It may involve neither. For example, Luke's gospel, he says, is an instance of inspiration without revelation (because Luke 1:1-3 says that the information was gathered by research). The prophets had inspiration without illumination (1 Peter 1:10-11).

Strong says he agrees that:

> The men are inspired, as Prof. Stowe said. The thoughts are inspired, as Prof. Briggs said. The words are inspired, as Prof. Hodge said [p. 198].

Jesus Himself vouches for the inspiration of the Old Testament (p. 199), Strong says, and He promised the apostles the same Holy Spirit who worked through the prophets (pp. 199-200). The apostles claimed to have received this promised Spirit, and thus they wrote with the same level of authority as the Old Testament writers (p. 200). However, the ultimate proof of inspiration, Strong avows, is the internal characteristics of the Scripture as the Holy Spirit would disclose them to sincere inquirers (p. 201).

Strong specifically denies the "intuition theory," which makes inspiration simply a higher development of natural insight. This theory does not give adequate significance to the fact that revelation is necessary because of man's inherent fallibility, he says. It is incorrect, according to Strong, because various intuitive claims to inspiration contradict each other. Not only is such a theory subjective, he says, but also it denies a personal God who is truth, and it makes man's intelligence supreme.

The "illumination theory," which says that the Bible "contains" but not that the Bible "is" the Word of God, and which makes only the writers and not the writings inspired, is also directly denied by Strong. Such a method cannot be a source of new revealed truth, and it could not "secure the Scripture writers from frequent and grievous error." Strong believes that Scripture contains "imperfections of detail in matters not essential to the moral and religious teaching of Scripture," but he finds the illumination theory to be logically indefensible in that it includes no basis for originating the revealed truth that is subsequently illuminated.

The "dictation theory" views the writers of Scripture as passive instruments, "pens not penmen" of God. Of course there are some instances in which God's revelation took the form of an audible voice and words, but this "partial induction" should not be generalized into an overall theory. This view, says Strong, "reminds us of the old theory that God created fossils in the rocks, as they would be had ancient seas existed." He describes the dictation theory by attributing it to the post-Reformation reaction to the Council of Trent. The Swiss Formula of Consensus in 1675 declared even the Hebrew vowel points to be inspired, and "some theologians traced them back to Adam." He mentions Louis Gaussen's famous book

Theopneustia as an example of a scholarly book that in Strong's opinion teaches the dictation theory of inspiration.

Strong contends that Scripture does not claim that the immediate communication of words was the universal method of inspiration. One verse often quoted in favor of dictation is 1 Corinthians 2:13:

> Which things also we speak, not in the words which man's wisdom teacheth, but which the Holy Ghost teacheth.

This does not mean dictation, argues Strong. He quotes Basil Manly as saying, "Dictation to an amanuensis is not teaching."

Strong says that dictation theories cannot adequately account for the peculiarities of style among the human writers, and that they cannot explain the "variations in accounts of the same transaction." Why employ eyewitnesses at all? asks Strong. Was there one beggar or two (Matthew 20:30; Luke 18:35)? Did they row twenty-five or thirty furlongs (John 6:19)? Strong understood the claim of complete biblical inerrancy to be incompatible with the actual imperfection of the text regarding these details and others like them. He quotes George Eliot's famous sentence in this context: "God cannot make Antonio Stradivari's violins, without Antonio."

The true view, says Strong, is the "dynamic theory." By this Strong meant that "inspiration is characteristically neither natural, partial, nor mechanical, but supernatural, plenary, and dynamical." Clearly the term "dynamic" is used by Strong as an alternative to the term "mechanical dictation." However, it was not intended to emphasize the human element as being in any way opposed to the fully divine nature of Scripture. He illustrates his view by suggesting the picture of two circles, one inside the other. The small circle, symbolizing the human element in Scripture, is within the large circle, symbolizing the divine element. At every point Scripture is God's work as well as man's. The area bounded by the small circle is equally a part of the area bounded by the large circle. God works from within as well as from without.

> As creation and regeneration are works of the immanent rather than of the transcendent God, so inspiration is in general a work within man's soul, rather than a communication to him from without [p. 211].

Strong defended the dynamic theory, but he made it very clear that he did not regard his theory as being of any essential importance. The true theory, he says, must come from a strict induction from the Scripture facts and must not be imposed a priori on the Scripture. "Perhaps the best theory of inspiration is to have no theory," says Strong.

The Scriptures are the production equally of God and of man, he continues.

> Those whom God raised up and providentially qualified to do this work, spoke and wrote the words of God, when inspired, not as from without, but as from within, and that not passively, but in the most conscious possession and the most exalted exercise of their own powers of intellect, emotion, and will. . . .
>
> The inspiration of the Scripture writers . . . goes far beyond the illumination granted to the preacher, in that it qualifies them to put the truth, without error, into permanent and written form [p. 212].

Strong apparently used the term "imperfection" not as a synonym for actual error but simply as an acknowledgment of variations in accounts, for a lack of scientific precision in historical descriptions, or for the lack of total inclusiveness of all details in the modern absolute sense. The nineteenth-century emphasis upon scientific history as being that description which was most precise and most comprehensive surely influenced his thinking. Scripture is imperfect when judged by the standard of early-twentieth-century historiography. Strong writes, "Every imperfection not inconsistent with truth in a human composition may exist in inspired Scripture." He approvingly quotes Charles Hodge: "When God ordains praise out of the mouths of babes, they must speak as babes, or the whole power and beauty of the tribute will be lost."

God used all normal literary styles and a gradual process in communicating the successive steps toward a complete revelation, Strong says. There have been "divers portions" as well as "divers manners."

But inspiration did not involve personal infallibility or freedom from sin, says Strong. It only secured a trustworthy transmission of the truth the writers were commissioned to deliver. Strong clearly denies the verbal method of inspiration, because to him that method implied dictation.

> The Scripture writers appear to have been so influenced by the Holy Spirit that they perceived and felt even the new truths they were to publish, as discoveries of their own minds, and were left to the action of their own minds in the expression of these truths, with the single exception that they were supernaturally held back from the selection of wrong words, and when needful were provided with right ones. Inspiration is therefore not verbal, while yet we claim that no form of words which taken in its connections would teach essential error has been admitted into Scripture [p. 216].

The last sentence of the above quotation was changed for the 1907 edition. Earlier editions used a sentence that read: "Inspiration is therefore verbal as to its results, but not verbal as to its method." This earlier sentence is probably more helpful as a key for understanding how Strong was thinking.

Strong quotes Broadus from his commentary on Matthew 3:17 as agreeing that the verbal method of inspiration is a hypothesis that is not always warranted. Broadus had written:

> Of course, it cannot be that both of these [Matthew 3:17 and Luke 3:22] are the words actually spoken. As to the authenticity of the narrative, such slight and wholly unimportant variations ["This is" or "Thou art" my beloved Son, and so forth] really confirm it, being precisely such as always occur in the independent testimony of different witnesses. As to the complete inspiration of the Scriptures, we must accept it as one of the facts of the case that the inspired writers not unfrequently report merely the substance of what was said, without aiming to give the exact words. So, for example, at the institution of the Supper (26:26ff), in Gethsemane (26:39ff), in the inscription on the cross (27:27), etc. In some instances of such variation we may suppose that the exact expressions given by the different writers were all employed in the connection, but in other cases that hypothesis is unwarranted. While such facts as these should make us cautious in theorizing as to verbal inspiration, they do not require us to lay aside the belief that the inspiration of Scripture is complete, that the inspired writers have everywhere told us just what God would have us to know [Hovey, Broadus, p. 58].

Verbal inspiration is not possible, says Strong, in light of the fact that the gospel writers report the words of Jesus with variations from one writer to the next. In support of his position on errancy (as he uses the term) in unessential matters and thus not verbal inspiration, Strong names Luther, Calvin, Cocceius, Tholuck, Neander, Lange, Stier, Van Osterzee, John Howe, Richard Baxter, Conybeare, Alford, and Mead.

The fact that Strong refers to the Reformers as supporting his view makes it even more clear to those familiar with their views that Strong is not teaching errancy in the modern neoorthodox sense of the term. He is denying verbal dictation as being the method of inspiration, but he is not saying that Scripture actually teaches or affirms falsehood. The words are all true. Inspiration is verbal as to its result. The words do accurately reveal God's truth. They are to be believed without reservation.

> When the unity of the Scripture is fully recognized, the Bible, in spite of imperfections in matters non-essential to its religious purpose, furnishes a safe and sufficient guide to truth and to salvation [p. 218].

Though speaking of the "great imperfection" of Scripture in nonessential parts, Strong affirms that every part of Scripture is inspired and that there are degrees of value but not of inspiration (p. 220).

These "imperfections not essential to its religious purpose" are such things as the lack of modern technical precision in scientific descriptions or the lack of verbal exactness in the several gospel accounts of the same words of Jesus. Strong did not believe that Scripture was errant in any substantial sense of the word.

This semantic problem with the word "error" is a persistent one. Strong says that Scripture is not exempt from the possibility of error. He may mean only that there may be "legitimate" interpretations of a passage (that is, an interpretation based upon adequate exegetical and linguistic studies) that may turn out to be in some acceptable sense incorrect. He limits that possibility, however, to technical details that do not affect doctrine or ethics. Even here he does not admit that such "errors" actually exist, but only that they might. To paraphrase Strong's position, one could say, "I will not debate every conceivable point of controversy regarding the factual character of Scripture. I believe it to be totally true. If you are to challenge my faith, however, you must do more than prove that some verse can in some sense be interpreted to teach some minor factual discrepancy. You must treat the matter as it is. Scripture is overwhelmingly supported by the facts as we know them, and its truth makes claims upon your life and mine. Let's keep the discussion on the level of real issues."

But what about errors in matters of science? Strong says, "We do not admit the existence of scientific error in the Scripture."

> What is charged as such is simply truth presented in popular and impressive forms. . . . Would it be preferable, in the Old Testament, if we should read; "Where the revolution of the earth upon its axis caused the rays of the solar luminary to impinge horizontally upon the retina, Isaac went out to meditate (Gen. 24:63)? . . . It is not necessary to a proper view of inspiration to suppose that the human authors of Scripture had in mind the proper scientific interpretation of the natural events they recorded. It is enough that this was in the mind of the inspiring Spirit. . . . It may be safely said that science has not yet shown any fairly interpreted passage of Scripture to be untrue [pp. 223-24].

Strong closes his discussion on this matter with these comments:

> Even if error in matters of science were found in Scripture, it would not disprove inspiration, since inspiration concerns itself with science only so far as correct scentific views are necessary to morals and religion. . . . The Scripture writers seem to be preserved from incorporating into their productions much of the scientific error of their day. But entire freedom from such error must not be regarded as a necessary accompaniment of inspiration [p. 226].

That same approach is used regarding supposed historical errors. Some of them are called mistakes in transcription, others may be a permissible use of round numbers, or others may be due to the meagerness of the narrative. Strong does not admit major historical errors; he does say that Scripture seems not to be exempt from the possibility of such error.

Strong addresses and denies the suggestion that Scripture contains moral errors, but he admits possible errors in reasoning (although he believes their existence to be unlikely). Again he writes, "While we do not grant that the New Testament writers in any proper sense misquoted or misinterpreted the Old Testament, we do not regard absolute correctness in these respects as essential to their inspiration." Other objections to the doctrine of inspiration are raised, but for the most part Strong suggests that those objections come from improper interpretation, and thus that the objections are not valid.

Strong was a firm believer in inerrancy; that is, he did not believe that the Scripture contained any actual errors. He goes beyond "faith and practice" to deny the existence of scientific or historical errors in the autographs. But his post-Kantian theory of knowledge led him to deny the a priori doctrine of biblical infallibility. In other words, he believed that the human mind affected all ideas that passed through it. Thus, when God revealed truth to a man, that man necessarily modified that truth as it became a part of his thought and as he communicated it to others. Infallibility means not fallible, not capable of error. Strong does not view the Bible as infallible in that full sense of the word.

Under no conditions, however, does Strong allow the position that Scripture does actually include error except in the relatively minor sense of the so-called "imperfections" of the text. Even they are simply evidences of the work of God through real men who were eyewitnesses or faithful scholars committed to the Spirit's leadership in a unique, supernatural way. Inspiration for Strong is not verbal (in the sense of dictation or absolute literary harmony), but it is plenary and dynamic. Every part of Scripture is equally inspired, and it is all the product of the work of God's Spirit in God's men.

Alvah Hovey

Though born March 5, 1820, in Greene, New York, Alvah Hovey never remembered any other home than Thetford, Vermont, to which his parents moved in the autumn of 1820. They had lived there when first married, but had moved to New York in 1817. When Alvah (the second son) was born, he was weak and sickly. His life hung in the balance for several months. The move back to Thetford seemed to cure him, and he gained full health almost at once.

The greatest influence on young Alvah's life was his parents. Farm life dominated his summers, but the district school in winter gave him the beginning of his education. Although severe headaches caused him to miss a considerable amount of school time, he never fell behind academically.

One Sunday evening after Alvah was already in bed with his eldest brother, their father came in and sat in the darkness at the foot of the bed. He spoke very plainly to them about sin, God, judgment, and Christ.

> I did not probably make any reply to his words or manifest any feeling; but the arrow of conviction entered my soul; I felt that I was a sinner and I greatly feared that God would never forgive me [*Life and Letters,* p. 12].

A local revival touched two of his sisters and several other young people. Not long after that, Alvah experienced a change in his spirit. But it brought him no special joy. It simply made him more conscious of his sinfulness, gave him more reverence for God, and gave him more satisfaction in attending Christian meetings.

> Yet I had no settled hope that my own sins were forgiven, no clear impression that the change in my feelings were conversion. I did think of God as a holy and merciful Father, and I knew that his mercy was through Christ alone, but somehow I did not lay hold of Christ as my Saviour with a confiding faith. This was my secret state of mind for about three years [*Life and Letters,* pp. 12-13].

One beautiful summer morning the fifteen-year-old Hovey viewed the golden sunshine, the blue sky, the silver-grey clouds, the green fields, the thick forests, and the clear streams and had suddenly impressed upon him the power, the wisdom, and the goodness of God. He bowed his heart before God in humble devotion and grateful recognition. This new sense of God's presence remained with him, and his months of uncertainty slowly dissolved into a confidence in God the Creator.

At the age of seventeen he went to Brandon, Vermont, to begin preparing for college. After he had been there six months, he decided to profess his faith in Christ. The Rev. Elijah Hutchinson had come to preach for a small church at Union Village, about three miles south of Thetford. Hovey writes:

> After the morning service with trembling heart and stammering tongue I gave to the church a very broken account of the grace of God to my soul,

and to my surprise was followed by a young brother, William, who had also found peace in believing. We were accepted with some hesitation by the church, and the next day repaired to a quiet spot on the western bank of the river, and the minister, his face lighted with sacred joy, led the two lads, one by his right hand and the other by his left, down into the clear waters, and solemnly buried them, one after the other, in baptism [*Life and Letters,* p. 13].

That very summer Hovey's mother died; but he was at home very little after this, for his academic career was just beginning. He entered Dartmouth College (only nine miles from Thetford) in 1839 and graduated in 1844. While at Dartmouth, he served as the principal of Derby Academy for two years, and for one year following graduation he was principal of New London Academy in New Hampshire.

Hovey attended the Newton Theological Institution for three years and then pastored for one year in New Gloucester, Maine. Newton called Hovey back to the faculty in 1849 to serve as a tutor in Hebrew. He also served as librarian from 1849 to 1862 and from 1863 to 1866. He was Acting Professor of Biblical Literature and Interpretation from 1851 to 1852 and from 1858 to 1859.

During these years he began spending a great deal of time at the home of Marshall S. Rice. After three years of boarding in the Rice home, Hovey joined the family by marrying the eldest daughter, Augusta Maria Rice, on September 24, 1852. He was not yet at ease in such social gatherings, however. Dr. George Dana Boardman was fond of telling, in later years, how after the wedding Alvah had introduced him to "Miss Rice." For three years they lived in her parents' home, though out of conviction she left her Methodist church and followed her husband by being baptized into a Baptist congregation. In the years that followed, the Lord blessed the Hoveys with two daughters and two sons.

At Newton, Hovey served as Professor of Church History, 1853-54; Professor of Christian Theology, 1854-70; Professor of Theology and Christian Ethics, 1870-99; Acting Professor of New Testament Interpretation, 1892-94; President of Newton Theological Institution, 1868-98; Acting President, 1898-99; and then Professor of Introductions and Apologetics, 1899-1903. An editorial in *The Watchman* commented on his administration of Newton:

The personal impression he has made upon his students has been unique. Doctor Robinson was a more direct germinal force; Doctor Strong has been more distinctively a philosophical theologian; but as an expounder of a strictly Biblical theology Doctor Hovey has had no rival. . . . He is loved and trusted, intellectually and morally, as few men among us have been [*Life and Letters*, pp. 201-2].

In the early 1870s, H. G. Weston and John A. Broadus urged Hovey to edit a New Testament commentary to be prepared by Baptist scholars. On November 6, 1876, after considerable correspondence, Hovey entered into a contract with the American Baptist Publication Society to complete the series in five years. Fourteen years later the final volumes of *The American Commentary* were completed. Several original writers were unable to finish their work. C. H. Toy had done much of his work on Thessalonians and the pastoral epistles when in 1870 he reached the conclusion that Paul was not the author of the letters to Timothy. Being a man of integrity, Toy suggested that it might not be acceptable for him to contribute to the commentary series. Hovey agreed with Toy's suggestion and a new contributor was found. Basil Manly, Jr., was to write on Acts, but his other duties forced him to turn the project over to another man in May 1881. The first volume to be published was William Newton Clarke's commentary on Mark. The last volume appeared in 1890. Hovey himself contributed the volume—on John (1885).

The last years of his life were dominated by efforts to complete an Old Testament commentary set to complement the one on the New Testament. At the time of his death (September 6, 1903), eleven manuscripts had been completed and writers were at work on the other Old Testament books.

Eight months after his Golden Wedding anniversary, he suffered a slight paralytic stroke (May 29, 1903). On June 23 there came a more severe stroke. From that day he was confined to bed, though his mind was as clear as ever. He continued to work on his manuscript editing until a few hours before his death. The end came quietly at 6:45 on a Sunday evening following a third stroke.

Hovey's little book *The Bible* is a reprinting of the first part of the *Normal Class Manual*, published first in 1873. It contains an introductory section on the evidences of the divine origin of the Bible. Then the rules of interpretation are discussed. A third section provides general outlines of the Bible's contents; geographical information; explanations of manners, customs, and religious appointments; and a brief summary of Christian doctrines.

His opening proposition is that the Bible is from God.

This proposition does not mean that every sentence of the Bible expresses a thought of God; for a large part of the volume preserves the thoughts of men who were not inspired, perhaps not renewed, while a considerable part of it preserves the sentiments of evil men or of malignant spirits. Nor does it mean that God by his Spirit dictated to the sacred writers the very words which in all cases they used, so that children might have been employed as naturally as men in giving the Bible its actual form; for to this theory there are grave objections.

But the proposition means that in some way *God enabled the sacred writers to put on record just what he wished them, acting in his name, to say to men.* And surely he wished them to give truth, not falsehood, to mankind—a trustworthy account of his own acts and purposes, of the words and thoughts of men, whether good or bad, and of the character and conduct of created spirits, superior to man. Hence, by saying that the Bible is from God, it is affirmed that all its language, rightly interpreted, is strictly true and divinely important [*The Bible*, pp. 9-10].

In order to verify this proposition, Hovey first examines the accuracy of the Bible in statements not strictly religious—for example, geographical or historical statements. "When the vast number, the incidental character, and the wonderful accuracy of these allusions are considered," says Hovey, "it is natural to conclude that the writers of this remarkable book were kept from error by a wisdom higher than their own" (p. 12).

Thus the historical and geographical setting of religious doctrine in the Old Testament, as well as in the New, is above just suspicion. Any slight errors that may perchance now exist in the record should be ascribed to inaccuracy of transcription rather than to mistakes in the original documents. When now the improbability of this result, if the Bible were of merely human origin, is borne in mind, it will appear reasonable to concede that the sacred writers were not mistaken in professing to have had the assistance of the Spirit of God in their work [p. 14].

Hovey says that a second major evidence supporting the proposition that the Bible is from God is found in fulfilled prophecy (pp. 15-16). A third evidence is the remarkable originality and consistency of its religious teaching (pp. 17-23). This includes not only its doctrine of God but also its account of the moral state of man. A fourth evidence comes from the character of Christ as set forth in the New Testament (pp. 23-29). If the existence of Christ is the only adequate explanation for the existence of the New Testament accounts, then "these gospels must be pronounced veritable history instead of entrancing fiction," and "the inspiration of the apostles and the truth of the New Testament are established beyond a reasonable doubt" (p. 27).

Hence the divine origin of the Bible rests upon a sure foundation, and
may be taught without fear of error. . . . The Bible, rightly interpreted, is
the word of God to men, and not one jot or tittle of it will fail [*The Bible*,
p. 28].

Yet no one can deny the existence of difficulties that are not due to
textual corruption at the hands of a copyist or a scribe. Sometimes the
authentic text contains difficulties that appear to be in substance as well
as in form, that appear to mar the usefulness if not the authority of Scripture.

How, then, should an interpreter treat the difficulties which he meets
in the study of Scripture? No single method can be fairly applied to all
of them without distinction, but a few suggestions may be offered that will
be of service to the youthful teacher.

1. He should be careful to give them no undue prominence in his own
mind or teaching. For they are at most but tiny spots on the face of a sun,
but specks of cloud on a clear sky, not seriously affecting the brightness of
the air or the purity of the ether. It is folly to give them importance by
looking at them constantly, and magnifying them as by the use of a critical
microscope.

2. He should pass many of them by with the remark of Paul (1 Cor. xiii.
12): "Now we see through a glass darkly; but then face to face: now I
know in part; but then shall I know even as also I am known." (See also
1 John iii. 2). This rule is applicable to every case where the difficulty may
be owing to the necessary imperfection of his knowledge; and such cases
are, in fact, quite numerous. One of the best qualities of a teacher is the
moral courage, or humility which leads him to say, again and again, "I
don't know."

3. He should avail himself, if practicable, of the best modern helps, and
remove as many of the difficulties as possible. These helps are increasing
year by year, and in matters of history and topography are improving in
quality. . . . The use of such helps is important, not only because they serve
to assure one of the "intense exactness" of the word of God, but also because they add greatly to the vividness of its language and the interest
with which it is read [pp. 49-51].

Hovey provides an extensive discussion of the doctrine of the Bible as a
supernatural revelation from God in his well-known *Outlines of Christian
Theology: For the Use of Students in the Newton Theological Institution*
(1870) and in his *Manual of Systematic Theology and Christian Ethics*
(1877). The Scriptures, he says, "were written by men divinely inspired,
and have, therefore, the same authority which they would have if they had

been written by the finger of God" (*Outlines,* p. 32). "They are perfectly credible, as compared with the best works of history" (*Manual,* p. 45). This proposition is established, first, by explaining the nonbiblical evidence supporting the origin of Christianity in the first century of the Christian era. Then he shows that the New Testament books were written by apostles of Christ or by the associates of apostles. In conclusion, Hovey declares and gives supporting reasons for believing that the New Testament writers were "competent, upright, and perfectly trustworthy" (*Outlines,* p. 36).

The New Testament Scriptures, even considered merely as trustworthy historical records, provide moral evidence that Jesus claimed to be an infallible teacher. "By an 'infallible teacher' is meant one who teaches truth without any mixture of error; or one whose instruction, in whatever form it may be given, will prove, if rightly apprehended, to be wholly correct" (*Manual,* pp. 53-54). One can justify his assent to this claim through several evidences: (1) the disciples of Jesus were convinced that Jesus had perfect knowledge and that He was full of truth; (2) the moral perfection of Jesus supports His infallibility; (3) His doctrines were perfect; (4) many predictions made by Him have been fulfilled; and (5) great miracles were performed by Him. Hovey's conclusion is that Jesus is what He claimed to be, "a *humble, holy,* INFALLIBLE *Being*" (*Outlines,* pp. 39-48).

Hovey continues by pointing out that these historically reliable records testify that Christ promised the inspiration of the Holy Spirit to the apostles (*Outlines,* pp. 48-50). His next step is to show that the New Testament Scriptures were all either written or sanctioned by the apostles (*Outlines,* pp. 51-53). "It is, therefore, certain that they deserve our respect and confidence as a proper revelation from God. Nay, we may speak of them with propriety as the word of God" (*Manual,* p. 71).

In order to draw the argument out more fully, Hovey reminds his students that the Old Testament Scriptures were declared by Christ and His apostles to be the Word of God (*Outlines,* pp. 53-56). His conclusion is that the Holy Spirit moved and assisted the biblical writers to record everything that is in the authentic text of the Bible.

> The conclusion which has now been reached is this,—*that the sacred writers were moved and assisted by the Holy Spirit to put on record all which the Bible, apart from errors in the text, now contains* [Manual, p. 77].

Textual errors that have crept into the copies of the biblical manuscripts, of course, are not to be attributed to the influence of the Holy Spirit. That the Old Testament itself, however, as it was inspired by the Holy Spirit, is totally trustworthy (because it is God's Word) is the teaching of the Savior and His apostles.

The inspiration of the prophets and apostles is, moreover, different in kind from that of ordinary Christians (*Outlines*, p. 57). Hovey gives several reasons for asserting this, but he goes even further and declares that the inspiration of the prophets and apostles made them infallible teachers of truth (p. 58). By "infallible teachers" Hovey means "those who set forth by voice or pen the will of God in the best manner practicable, whose teaching the reason of man has no right to modify or reject, but only to ascertain and obey. Rightly interpreted," he says, "their teaching is correct so far as it goes" (p. 58).

With respect to the psychology, or the human side, of inspiration, Hovey has three comments:

> (a) The words which they were to employ appear to have been sometimes given to the sacred writers by inspiration. Prophets and seers of visions were addressed through their spiritual senses. (b) The mental powers of the sacred writers were raised and cleared and guided, but not suspended by inspiration. The action of their bodily senses may have been arrested in cases of ecstacy, but not the action of their mental or moral powers. (c) The apostles as well as the prophets received the truth by inspiration gradually and as they needed it for their work, and not all at once [*Outlines*, p. 58].
>
> These are the elements of our belief on the subject; and it will be seen that they point towards what is called *the theory of dynamical inspiration*. But no one of the prophets or sacred writers has attempted to describe the relation of his spirit to the Spirit of God in times of inspiration. Perhaps he could not [*Manual*, p. 81].

The sources of knowledge open to the minds of the inspired writers include revelation (for example, revelation of future events or doctrine), observation (for example, observation of historical events), experience (for example, the feelings expressed in the Psalms, Ecclesiastes, and Lamentations), and study (for example, the gospel of Luke).

Hovey then draws his final conclusions:

> In view of what has now been stated, we claim that our theory of inspiration accounts for all the phenomena of the Bible better than any other; for its varieties of style as well as numerous writers; for its verbal discrepancies, as well as essential harmony; for the personal feelings and tastes which are revealed by its writers; and for a thousand traces of high yet free spiritual action on their part. How any one can read the New

Testament, the Book of Revelation excepted, and doubt whether its writers speak with conscious freedom, and also with conscious authority, passes our comprehension. The letters of Paul are intensely natural, and equally supernatural: the Word was made flesh without losing its heavenly truth and power [*Outlines*, p. 59].

Of course there are many objections to this view. Hovey briefly treats twelve different objections (*Manual*, pp. 83-86). Some say that the Bible cannot be the infallible word of God:

I. *Because a belief in its infallibility leads to bibliolatry.* This is a mistake. The student of nature believes her testimony to be infallible, yet he is not led by this belief to pay religious homage to nature. And the same is true of those who accept the teaching of the Bible as infallible; they recognize the duty of worshipping God, and him only.

II. *Because this belief retards the progress of science.* Men, it is said, are rendered by it suspicious of the discoveries of science and slow to give it their support. This is also a mistake. Believers in the truth of the Scriptures believe in the truth of nature also, and encourage the highest schools of learning. They may be slow to receive scientific views which appear to be inconsistent with what they suppose the Bible teaches; but they have no fear of true science, no desire to prevent men from studying the works of God in nature.

III. *Because infallibility in the original Scriptures requires for its complement infallibility in all copies, translations, and, some would say, interpretations of them.* For otherwise, we are told, the benefit of infallibility is lost to all but the primitive readers. But this, again, is a mistake; for the errors from transcription, translation, &c., are such as can be detected, or at least estimated, and reduced to a minimum; while errors in the original revelation could not be measured [pp. 83-84].

Other objections include the problem of obscure language in the Bible, supposedly unsound arguments, supposedly false interpretations of Old Testament passages by New Testament writers, supposedly false prophecy, claims of bad theology, and claims of bad morality. Hovey also recognizes the objections against infallibility coming from apparent contradictions, scientific references, and historical problems.

VII. *Because it teaches scientific errors.* In reply to this charge, it may be remarked that all references to matters of science in the Bible are (1) Merely incidental and auxiliary; (2) Clothed in popular language, and (3) Confirmed by consciousness, so far as they relate to the mind. Remembering these facts, we say that the Bible has not been shown to contain scientific errors.—Astronomy, geology, ethnology.

VIII. *Because it teaches historical errors.* On the supposed historical errors of the Bible, we remark, (1) They relate, for the most part, to matters of chronology, genealogy, numbers, &c. (2) Transcribers are specially liable to mistakes in copying numbers, names, &c. (3) Different names for the same person, and different termini for the same period, are quite frequent. (4) Round numbers are often employed for specific. Making proper allowance for these facts, we deny that historical errors are found in the Bible.

IX. *Because it contains contradictory statements.* On this we remark, (1) That statements may be contradictory in words, but not in sense. "Answer not a fool," &c. (2) They may seem to be contradictory in sense, when they are not: for example, the unity of God and the Trinity; Paul and James on justification. (3) They may be contradictory in sense, but not in moral bearing; for example, rest on the Sabbath, yet extra work for priests; Moses and Christ on divorce. Bearing in mind these facts, it will be impossible for us to find in the Bible any contradictions which mar its excellence [*Manual*, p. 85].

"In establishing the divine authority and inspiration of the Scriptures," claims Hovey, "we have established the truth of the Christan religion" (*Manual*, p. 86)

Fig. 24. ALVAH HOVEY
From George Hovey's *His Life and Letters,* Judson, 1928.

BIBLIOGRAPHY

A. H. Strong

Hovey, Alvah, ed. *An American Commentary on the New Testament.* Philadelphia: The American Baptist Publication Society, 1881-90. *Commentary on the Gospel of Matthew,* by John A. Broadus, 1886.

Henry, Carl F. H. *Personal Idealism and Strong's Theology.* Wheaton: Van Kampen, 1951.

Robinson, Ezekiel Gilman. *Christian Theology.* Rochester, N.Y.: Press of E. R. Andrews, 1876.

Strong, A. H. *Christ in Creation and Ethical Monism.* Philadelphia: The Griffith & Roland Press, 1899.

———. *Lectures on Theology.* Rochester, N.Y.: Press of E. R. Andrews, 1876.

———. *One Hundred Chapel-Talks to Theological Students.* Philadelphia: The Griffith & Rowland Press, 1913.

———. *Philosophy and Religion.* New York: A. C. Armstrong & Son, 1888.

———. *Systematic Theology.* New York: A. C. Armstrong & Son, 1886.

———. *Systematic Theology.* Philadelphia: The Griffith & Roland Press, 1907. Currently kept in print by Judson Press.

———. *What Shall I Believe?* New York: Revell, 1922.

Alvah Hovey

Hovey, Alvah. *The Bible.* Philadelphia: Griffith & Rowland, 1873.

———. *Manual of Systematic Theology and Christian Ethics.* Philadelphia: American Baptist Publication Society, 1877.

———. *Outlines of Christian Theology: For the Use of Students in the Newton Theological Institution.* Providence, R.I.: The Providence Press Company, 1870.

Hovey, George R. *Alvah Hovey: His Life and Letters.* Philadelphia: Judson, 1928.

CHAPTER THIRTEEN

"Then Rose Up the Chief of the Fathers"

In the Summer of 1884, the property on the southeast corner of Fifth and Broadway in Louisville, Kentucky, was purchased in order to begin building permanent buildings for the Southern Baptist Theological Seminary. By March of 1888, New York Hall was erected as a result of the large gifts ($60,000) from friends of the seminary in New York. That same year Archibald Thomas Robertson began teaching.

J. P. Boyce died on December 28, 1888, having been named president of the seminary seven months earlier. (Technically he had served only as chairman of the faculty prior to that, for no office of president had been established during the early years of the school.) The 1888-89 session saw an enrollment of 164, making Southern the largest Baptist seminary in the land. John A. Broadus was elected president in May 1889, and by the year of his death (1895) the school's enrollment had reached 267.

William Whitsitt became president in 1895 and the enrollment immediately jumped to 316. Whitsitt's administration was marked by controversy over the origin of Baptists, including a question regarding the presence or absence of immersion as the proper mode of baptism in the centuries immediately prior to the seventeenth century. Enrollment declined to 262 in 1899.

Edgar Young Mullins was elected to succeed Whitsitt and again the enrollment soared above 300. Mullins wrote in 1913 that the seminary had grown to be "perhaps the largest protestant theological seminary in the world." In 1923 the campus was moved to "The Beeches," a fifty-three acre tract of beautiful wooded land on Lexington Road. By 1928, the last year of Mullins' administration, the total student body had reached 423. Those figures seem small compared to the current ones: Southern enrolled 2,542 during the 1977-78 year, surpassed in size only by Southwestern Baptist Seminary, with 4,136 for that same year. But the trend of growth and development was established during the Mullins years.

Mullins' administration saw its share of controversy, but he stood tall in the eyes of both the scholarly world and the common church-folk. These were the years of the Fundamentalist-Modernist controversies. Mullins served as a stabilizing influence on Southern Baptists during this time.

William R. Estep writes: "E. Y. Mullins and A. T. Robertson were both held in high esteem in leading Fundamentalist circles. Yet no prominent Southern Baptist [possibly excepting J. Frank Norris] played a leadership role in organized Fundamentalism" (Estep, p. 156). There is no doubt, however, that these two men have shaped the life and theology of Southern Baptists as much as any other academic leaders. Robertson was not a systematic theologian; he was, however, a world-renowned New Testament and Greek scholar. His "Big Grammar" is a heavyweight in every sense of the word. Mullins' writings in systematic theology literally replaced the manuals of J. L. Dagg and J. P. Boyce that were used previously. Truly these two men are the "chief of the fathers."

E. Y. MULLINS

Seth and Cornelia Mullins had eleven children. The fourth one, Edgar Young Mullins, was born on January 5, 1860, in Franklin County, Mississippi. When Edgar was eight years old, the Mullins family moved to Corsicana, Texas, where his father organized and became the pastor of the First Baptist Church of Corsicana.

Throughout his elementary and high school days, Edgar worked in a telegraph office. Skills gained there enabled him to put himself through Texas A&M University. After graduating he became a dispatcher for the Associated Press. His great desire, however, was to become a lawyer, and he began working toward that goal.

Major William Evander Penn, a former lawyer and the first full-time Southern Baptist evangelist, was preaching a revival at the First Baptist Church of Dallas, Texas, in the fall of 1880. Mullins went to hear him out of curiosity. The message made a powerful appeal to the young would-be lawyer, not by answering all his intellectual doubts but by challenging his will and changing his attitude toward those intellectual problems. Deeply moved by the message, Mullins publicly professed his faith in Jesus as Lord at the end of that evangelistic service. Then on November 7 of that year he was baptized by his father in Corsicana.

His conversion was so deeply meaningful for him that he immediately gave up the idea of a future law practice and turned to prepare for a full-time Christian ministry. In 1885 he graduated from Southern Baptist Theological Seminary, having majored in theology and philosophy.

On his doctor's advice, Mullins gave up a hoped-for career in foreign missions and turned to the pastorate. He married in 1886 and in the following years had two sons; one died in infancy and the other died at age

Fig. 25. E. Y. MULLINS

From *Baptist Principles Reset,* J. B. Jeter, ed. Edited by *The Religious Herald.*
New edition. (Richmond: The Religious Herald Co., 1902), opposite p. 158.

seven. He pastored churches in Kentucky and in Maryland (where he also attended Johns Hopkins University, 1891-92). Later he became an Associate Secretary of the Southern Baptist Foreign Mission Board. After a year with the Mission Board he went back to the pastorate in the First Baptist Church of Newton Center, Massachusetts. A. H. Strong's theological influence was dominant in this academic setting.

Southern Baptist Theological Seminary experienced several years of strife in the days that immediately followed the death of John A. Broadus. W. H. Whitsitt had been elected president of the school. He is remembered for his challenge to the idea that Baptists could trace an unbroken succession of Baptist churches all the way back to the days of the New Testament. Such a furious controversy arose over this matter that Whitsitt was forced to resign in 1899. The trustees immediately began the process of finding a new president.

During those days *The Baptist Argus*, a Louisville paper, sent Mullins a telegram asking for his picture. Naturally this aroused his curiosity. He went personally to the Newton Center telegraph office to send an inquiry regarding the matter. The regular telegrapher was not in when he got there, but Mullins' years of experience with the Associated Press came in handy. He was granted permission to send his own message. As he sat down and began to listen to the traffic on the wire, he heard a call from the Boston office with a message inviting him to accept the seminary presidency. Immediately he pounded out his acceptance on the telegraph key.

For twenty-eight years he served as president of Southern Seminary. From 1921 to 1924 he was also president of the Southern Baptist Convention. Controversies over the theory of evolution could well have led to a schism within the convention during those years. But Mullins' statements on the issue were so clearly consistent with biblical truth and Baptist theology that both sides accepted them.

In his opening address to the Southern Baptist Convention in Kansas City, May 16, 1923, Mullins spoke of "The Dangers and Duties of the Present Hour." The primary "danger," said Mullins, was the possibility of division over "secondary questions" such as the various millennial theories. He affirmed, however, that no division should ever come over the central doctrines of the faith.

> Again, there is no division among us on the question of the supernatural in the gospel of Jesus Christ. We believe in the Virgin birth of Christ, his deity, his substitutionary atonement, his resurrection from the dead, and his second coming. We believe in salvation by grace through faith. We believe in the coming of a divine power into human life to redeem man from guilt and the power of sin. We are against naturalism and any form of rationalistic philosophy which denies the supernatural. Here we must

plant our feet. On this we must insist for all teachers in our colleges and seminaries. This is the standard by which we must measure ourselves. We favor science, but we are against the anti-religious assumptions of so-called science. We are in favor of freedom of research, but not at the expense of the established facts of religion. In my view, the only requirement we can make of our teachers is that they be loyal to the above supernatural facts of the gospel. There may be variations in the way in which they state their positions on other matters. There is room for difference of opinion on many themes. There is no room for difference of opinion on the great fundamental verities. Let us make this the cardinal point—loyalty to the supernatural in the gospel of Christ. Let us not be divided on subordinate variations of opinion.

The "duties" of which Mullins spoke included a demonstration by Baptists that religious democracy could work and a renewed allegiance to the Great Commission. Southern Baptists must not fail, he said, to plan and accomplish a great missionary program.

Mullins also spoke directly to the question of science and religion. The statement, quoted below from Mullins' address, was adopted by the Convention as the "belief of that body" and is printed in the 1923 Convention *Annual.*

1. We recognize the greatness and value of the service which modern science is rendering to the cause of truth in uncovering the facts of the natural world. We believe that loyalty to fact is a common ground of genuine science and the Christian religion. We have no interest or desire in covering up any fact in any realm of research. But we do protest against certain unwarranted procedures on the part of some so-called scientists. First, in making discoveries or alleged discoveries in physical nature a convenient weapon of attack upon the facts of religion; second, using the particular sciences, such as psychology, biology, geology and various others, as if they necessarily contained knowledge pertaining to the realm of the Christian religion, setting aside the supernatural; third, teaching as facts what are merely hypotheses. The evolution doctrine has long been a working hypothesis of science, and will probably continue to be because of its apparent simplicity in explaining the universe. But its best exponents freely admit that the causes of the origin of species have not been traced, nor has any proof been forthcoming that man is not the direct creation of God as recorded in Genesis. We protest against the imposition of this theory upon the minds of our children in denominational or public schools as if it were a definite and established truth of science. We insist that this and all other theories be dealt with in a truly scientific way, that is, in careful conformity to established facts.

2. We record again our unwavering adherence to the supernatural elements in the Christian religion. The Bible is God's revelation of himself through man moved by the Holy Spirit, and is our sufficient, certain and

authoritative guide in religion. Jesus Christ was born of the Virgin Mary through the power of the Holy Spirit. He was the divine and eternal Son of God. He wrought miracles, healing the sick, casting out demons, raising the dead. He died as the vicarious atoning Savior of the world and was buried. He rose again from the dead. The tomb was emptied of its contents. In his risen body he appeared many times to his disciples. He ascended to the right hand of the Father. He will come again in person, the same Jesus who ascended from the Mount of Olives.

3. We believe that adherence to the above truths and facts is a necessary condition of service for teachers in our Baptist schools. These facts of Christianity in no way conflict with any fact in science. We do not sit in judgment upon the scientific views of teachers of science. We grant them the same freedom of research in their realm that we claim for ourselves in the religious realm. But we do insist upon a positive content of faith in accordance with the preceding statements as a qualification for acceptable service in Baptist schools. The supreme issue today is between naturalism and super-naturalism. We stand unalterably for the super-natural in Christianity. Teachers in our schools should be careful to free themselves from any suspicion of disloyalty on this point. In the present period of agitation and unrest they are obliged to make their positions clear. We pledge our support to all schools and teachers who are thus loyal to the facts of Christianity as revealed in the Scriptures.

From 1923 to 1928 Mullins served as president of the Baptist World Alliance. He was outspoken on the issue of religious freedom, and he gained the respect of Baptists around the world. A stroke led to his death on November 23, 1928. The *Louisville Times* used front-page, one-inch, red-ink headlines to announce his death. Few Baptists have been as widely known or as highly respected as E. Y. Mullins. His influence on contemporary Baptist theology has been enormous. Thus his views on the doctrine of Scripture take on a special significance.

One of his earliest explicit statements on the doctrine of inspiration is found in a 1913 publication, *Freedom and Authority in Religion.* Professor J. J. Reeve of Southwestern Baptist Theological Seminary wrote a major review of the book in the *Baptist Standard* (May 1, 1913; pp. 2-3, 10), in which he said:

> The present reviewer has only words of unqualified admiration for the book. Its positions meet with his entire approval. . . . Why could not this book like "The Fundamentals" be put in the hands of every preacher and teacher in the English speaking world?

The Bible is our authority in religion, writes Mullins, because it is "the outward literary expression of the truths acquired in man's interaction with the spiritual universe" (p. 342). Its authoritativeness comes from the fact that Scripture "preserves and brings to us in literary form the truths acquired by mankind in the free interaction of its individual units with God" (p. 343). All biblical revelation is rooted in life and history.

> God was in the history first; then in the writers and speakers who delivered his messages to his people. Criticism has done nothing more valuable than to emphasize this relation of the truth to the life of Israel. The literature arose then as the expression of the life-adjustments and life-experiences. These experiences cover many centuries. They all belong to a particular type. Jehovah and man's relations to him are conceived in a particular way. There is a progressive unfolding of truth. There is advance in ethical ideals and standards. But the literature is homogeneous; allowing for varieties and levels of experience, the unity of the parts of this literature is unquestionable [p. 345].

Jesus Christ is the center of unity for the Scriptures, says Mullins. God's activity of revelation gives us a life and a literature. The literature records, interprets, and explains the history of redemption. The life preceded the literature historically, but the literature is also indispensable to the life. As Mullins puts it, "Only a literature could give us the original form of the revelation in its purity and distinctness" (p. 349).

> Literature, or recorded thoughts, is the nearest approach to the nature of spirit which we possess which is at the same time reliable as a medium of transmission. Tradition is utterly unsafe [p. 349].

It is objected, however, that those holding to an authoritative Bible are in fact bibliolaters—that is, that they worship the Bible or that they interpose a book between the soul and God. Mullins replies by using an analogy:

> The telescope is interposed between the eye and the heavenly body. The astronomer is not accused of worshiping the telescope or advised to pursue the science of astronomy without its aid. The telescope tells him what he could never discover without it. He relies upon it as an "authority," and carries forward the discoveries of science. Thus it appears that the objector to an authoritative Bible is on the wrong scent altogether. He is unconvinced by arguments for an infallible or inerrant Bible, or he is unwilling to accept the decree of the early councils which may be supposed to have fixed the canon of Scripture. From these premises he proceeds to the attempt to convict the others of bibliolatry. But he has missed the point entirely. He has torn the Bible away from its true context in its own spiritual order and judged it thus.
>
> If, however, men look through this rent in the veil, that is, the biblical writings, and thus obtain the vision of God and find redemption through his power in their lives, they simply repeat the experiences of the men who first had the experience and were inspired to write the Bible. For them

the Bible is authoritative because it leads them to God and relates them to the redemptive forces. To argue against the authority of the Bible, therefore, to men who have had the life-adjustment and life-experience which it enshrines, is like arguing against the symmetry of the Venus de Milo or the beauty of the Sistine Madonna to the artistic soul, on the ground of some defect in the material or the mechanical execution [pp. 352-53].

In coming to speak specifically to the various theories of inspiration, Mullins contends that one's attitude toward Christ is the key issue that must be resolved.

Let us make this point perfectly clear that it is the question of the person and work of Christ which modern theories of inspiration either explicitly or implicitly assume as the starting point [p. 376].

Mullins classifies the various theories in a threefold way. First there is the radical view. This view "rejects the authority of Jesus in religion altogether and therewith the authority of the Bible" (p. 377).

There is also a compromise view of inspiration. One form of this is the attempt to divide the Scripture into Christian and non-Christian parts. (Although progressive revelation is a part of the true view, insists Mullins, it is a matter of interpretation and not of authority or inspiration.) This form of the compromise view "fails in consistency and convincing power" (p. 393). The other form of the compromise view is the attempt to combine some form of subjective authority with the authority of the Scriptures. However, Mullins does not approve of this method at all.

It is impossible to make the Christian consciousness final and then in turn subject it to the Scriptures. The true method leaves an authoritative Scripture which Christian experience does not and cannot transcend [p. 383].

This "true method" is the conservative view favored by Mullins. He speaks of two forms of the view, but he sees no substantial disagreement between these two forms.

This [conservative view] presents itself in two forms which proceed in very different ways, but which arrive at results which do not radically differ. These are what we shall describe with Professor Sanday in his work on "Inspiration" as the Inductive and the Traditional theories of inspiration. The traditional view is that built up by scholastic Protestantism. We outline it briefly in its extreme form in order to indicate its essential characteristics, as follows: It begins with an abstract principle not derived from Scripture, which conceives of the biblical writers as mere unintelligent instruments or pens used by the Holy Spirit to dictate the truths of revelation. The Bible speaks, according to this view, with equal authority on science and related subjects as upon religion. A single mistake in matters of science would invalidate the authority of the Bible. Even the He-brew vowel-points were inspired of God in the Old Testament equally with the consonants and the language generally. This will sufficiently characterize the view. There are, of course, various modifications of it as stated needless to mention here. Its laudable aim is to preserve and main-tain the authority of the Scripture as the word of God.

The Inductive view proceeds in another way, but arrives at a similar general result. It refuses to adopt any abstract or *a priori* starting-point, but rather goes directly to the Bible itself for the evidence of its own in-spiration. Its watchword is conformity to the testimony of Scripture as to the inspiration of Scripture. In other words, it gathers the data from the Bible and on them builds up its view of the authority of the Bible. This view recognizes that God was in the history as well as in the literature; that he spoke to Israel through the prophets; that Jesus Christ is the supreme and final revelation of God; that miracles and the supernatural must be admitted as a part of God's method of reve-lation; that the Scriptures are the final and sufficient and authoritative rec-ord of God's revelation; and that when we have correctly interpreted the Scriptures we have found God's truth for our religious life. This view emphasizes the fact, however, that the biblical writers employed the lan-guage and forms of speech in common use in their own age to convey their religious message from God; that primarily the Bible is a religious and not a scientific book; that we must not look for authoritative deliverances on questions about physical nature in the Bible; and, indeed, that premature revelations of science through prophets and apostles would not only have robbed man of his own proper task of investigation, but would have de-feated the ends of revelation by introducing a needless confusion of sci-ence and religion.

On the other hand this must not be taken to justify the sweeping asser-tations as to error and discrepancy so often made about the Scripture. As Dr. James Orr, who holds the inductive view, well says: "Ascribe it to 'superintendence,' to 'suggestion,' or what one will—and inspiration is probably more subtle and all-pervading than any of these things—it remains the fact that the Bible, impartially interpreted and judged, is free from demonstrable error in its statements, and harmonious in its teachings, to a degree that of itself creates an irresistible impression of a supernatural fac-tor in its origin." The inductive view of course takes account of the various literary forms and media, such as the parable and the allegory; it allows for the distinction between literal and figurative passages; and for the peda-gogic adaptation of the method and means of revelation to the state of mind and degree of religious maturity of hearer and reader. The advocates of the inductive view make Jesus Christ the core and center of the revela-tion; and while they allow for the instances in which Christ adopted the language of his contemporaries in order to instruct or refute them on the basis of their own assumptions, they hold him free from all error in his revelation to men of the mind and will of God. The inductive view holding, as it does, the higher view of the person of Christ, finds no difficulty in accepting the Old Testament revelation, since it was all preparatory to, and derives its chief significance from, its relations to Jesus. It also accepts the inspiration of the New Testament books other than the synoptic Gospels, since it comports with its general view of Christ that he should have given the promise of future guidance recorded in John 16:13, 14, and fulfilled the promise in the subsequent history.

It appears from the foregoing very condensed account of the two views, the traditional and the inductive, that they both stand for the authoritativeness of the Scriptures. As Professor Ramsay says in his closing chapter, his own view involves an inspiration quite as real and quite as fundamental as the traditional view. The differences between the two views refer to matters of detail, to the way in which God employs the human factors in revelation, and to similar points which do not touch the fundamental issue. One is rather rigid and mechanical in its view of how the Bible came into existence; the other regards it as a living thing, like an organism, full of life and power, instinct with the life of God in human experience. Between the two views there is no difference as to the reality of the supernatural revelation; as to its sufficiency for our religious needs; and as to the finality and authoritativeness of the Bible.

Now a great deal has been gained when we reach this point. For it shows clearly that the doctrine of the authority of Scripture is not at all bound up with the abstract theories and elaborate philosophic attempts to explain inspiration. Logic never did and never will succeed fully in expressing all the meaning of God's action in and upon the men who wrote the Bible. Men may vary as they will in these attempts, the main point has to do with the question, What function is assigned to the Bible in the religious life; is it authoritative or is it not? The simplest and most direct method for reaching a conclusion is the inductive, which takes into account all the facts of Scripture and all the facts of experience [pp. 378-82].

In 1917 Mullins published his major theological treatise, *The Christian Religion in Its Doctrinal Expression.* The work was dedicated to the memory of James Petigru Boyce. In his preface, Mullins speaks about the impact of the intellectual shifts that had occurred during the nineteenth century. Major changes can be detected, he says, in science, sociology, economics, psychology, and philosophy, to name only a few areas.

Schleiermacher, at the beginning of the century had already anticipated the need for a change in the method of dealing with religious truth. . . . We are at length coming to see all things in a new perspective. . . . Methods have changed. . . . New statements of truth are required. But Christ remains the same. . . . The gospel remains [p. viii].

The new method Mullins proposed to follow was one that "gives prominence to Christian experience" (p. 2). This emphasis has led many to criticize Mullins mistakenly for his supposed subjectivism. But Mullins himself did not teach a pure experientialism. "When we speak of making experience explicit in expounding the doctrines of Christianity, we are by no means adopting that as the sole criterion of truth," writes Mullins. "He would be a very unwise man who should attempt to deduce all Christian doctrine from his own subjective experience" (p. 3). "It is in the union and combination of the objective source and the subjective experience that certainty and assurance are found" (p. 11).

Again and again Mullins emphasizes that the ultimate basis for Christian doctrine is fact. "The basis on which the Christian doctrine of revelation rests is a basis of fact in all its aspects" (p. 21). Mullins has no hesitancy in affirming that Christian theology (which is simply the interpretation of Christian religion) is a real form of knowledge. Theology is itself a science and is closely related to other forms of scientific research, he says (p. 25). Religious truth does not express itself in mathematical formulae, Mullins says, but it is nevertheless a form of truth (pp. 24-26).

Mullins does introduce an element into the epistemology of religion that has led to several modern problems. He says that the supreme source of the knowledge of God is "the revelation of God in and through Jesus Christ" (p. 41).

> The Bible is indeed our supreme and authoritative literary source of the revelation of God which leads to salvation. But salvation is not conditioned upon our belief in, or acceptance of, a book. . . . God's revelation of himself to us comes through his direct action upon our spirits [p. 41].

Christ, of course, was a historic person. At some length Mullins treats the virgin birth, the sinless life of Jesus, and his work of revealing God to men. Surely, then, Mullins himself never intended to imply any actual separation between one's knowledge of Christ and one's knowledge of the written Scripture. But the formal distinction he made (valid in itself) may have led some people in later years to believe that they could use their concept of Jesus as a theological tool with which to criticize or find error in the Bible. Mullins does not do that. For him it is the New Testament Scriptures through which we "maintain connection with the historical facts on which Christianity rests" (p. 47).

Mullins may perhaps be legitimately criticized for his use of experience as a primary theological tool. In chapter three of *The Christian Religion in Its Doctrinal Expression*, Mullins lists six assumptions that he considers to be obvious and in need of no defense. Each one of those assumptions has been seriously challenged in some contemporary philosophical circles. The assumptions may be capable of adequate justification, but his emphasis on experience and naive realism led him to ignore the objections. Whether or not Mullins can be faulted as being the root source of the shallowness of experientialist theology among some Baptists, it is certainly not correct to read that modern approach back into Mullins himself. He clearly defends the idea of doctrine as being a real truth claim.

> Here again we remind ourselves that the objective facts of God's historic revelation in Christ, and the record of those facts in the New Testament under the guidance of God's Spirit, constitute the basis of all we know of God in experience [p. 56].

For Mullins, God's revelation was primarily a personal communication of God's own being, not simply a communication of truths about God.

> Truths there are of course. Doctrines inevitably shape themselves as the revelation proceeds. But the primal fact is God entering human experience, and man becoming conscious of his presence and power [p. 141].

Revelation is not mere illumination of the intellect, says Mullins; it is primarily a spiritual transaction (p. 141). Thus it is primarily related to salvation. "Revelation is 'acquaintance with' and not mere 'knowledge about' God" (p. 141). It sprang directly from the needs of the people and it evoked an active response from them. "God's revelation is designed to awaken and develop human personality" (p. 142).

> There is nothing in Scripture to warrant the idea of mechanically dictated truth to a merely passive intellect. . . . On the contrary, the human faculties were, as a rule, intensely alive and active. The truth disclosed was molded in the forms required by the personality, training, and circumstances of the human organ of revelation [p. 142].

Mullins says that there are two basic ways to approach the question of the authoritativeness of the Scriptures. One emphasizes the processes of inspiration and the other emphasizes the results. The first way is the psychological method. It seeks to distinguish between revelation, inspiration, and illumination.

> These distinctions, when properly understood, are justified. . . . It would be a mistake, however, to hold these distinctions in too radical a manner. They are useful for thought. But the elements separated in thought are not always separate in fact [p. 143].

According to Mullins, this psychological method has led to various theories of inspiration. Naturalistic theories or mere illumination theories leave room for varying degrees of truth and error in the Bible. Those theories are not consistent with the biblical doctrine of inspiration.

Another is called the plenary verbal theory of inspiration. It holds that every word of Scripture was selected by the Holy Spirit and dictated to the writer. One form of the theory of plenary inspiration is called the theory of dynamical inspiration. This maintains that the thought rather than the language was inspired, and that men were enabled to declare truth unmixed with error, but permitted to convey their ideas in forms of their own selection [pp. 143-44].

No theory explains everything, says Mullins. We cannot fully analyze the process by which God's Spirit works through a human mind to reveal God. Psychological theories are misguided in that they emphasize our best explanations of how God must have worked in order to reveal Himself to us.

The true method, on the contrary, is to study the Bible inductively in order to learn what its claims are and what success it has had in meeting those claims, in the experience of Christians of the past and present. This is the experiential and practical method of approaching the doctrine of inspiration. It is much more concerned with the result than it is with the process of inspiration [p. 144].

Just how influential Mullins has been in Baptist thought can be estimated by the number of times this mistaken identification of plenary verbal and mechanical dictation theories has been repeated. Many who support the plenary verbal theory understand it to be primarily descriptive of the result rather than the process of inspiration. Of course, Mullins was probably reacting to the powerful influence of J. R. Graves, who favored the verbal method of inspiration. For Mullins, however, the dynamic theory also led to a Bible that could be properly characterized as the declaration of truth unmixed with error. The practical and experiential method led Mullins to ignore or at least to consider as unimportant the theological issues relating to the manner of God's work of inspiration. He was satisfied to ask only how the Bible meets the religious needs of men today. Mullins gives more than three pages to the idea that revelation is progressive and two pages to the affirmation that biblical revelation is sufficient, certain, and authoritative for religious ends, but he gives only the few sentences quoted above to the explanation of theories of inspiration.

With the notable exception of W. T. Conner, Southern Baptists have not had many outstanding, writing systematic theologians since Mullins. Those few scholars who have written systematic theologies often show a heavy influence from Mullins. Emphasis on "practical result" rather than "precise theory" has (perhaps unintentionally on the part of Mullins) led in some instances to a pragmatism in Baptist theology.

Bernard Ramm has expressed sincere and justifiable praise for much of what Mullins did. He does, however, recognize that Mullins has not provided an adequate doctrine of authority. In "Baptists and Sources of Authority" Ramm wrote:

> Pragmatism has the theory in reverse. The truth is practicable; not the practical is true. Unfortunately E. Y. Mullins, when he wrote *Freedom and Authority,* was under the charm of pragmatism and pursued its faulty logic, but the point he made is not to be lost: genuine religion does have a remarkable and beneficial effect in the life of the believer. Truth does lead to practical results, and religious truth leads to veridical religious experiences. Religious experience may be appealed to in its role of mediator of the authority of revelation, and as confirmer of the truths of revelation; but *in itself* it cannot be *the* authority in religion [p. 10].

Though he effectively introduced a change in theological method, Mullins had no intention of weakening Baptist theological thinking. He by no means doubted the full truthfulness of the Scripture. For him the Bible was God's revealed truth unmixed with error. Its purpose was religious, and it must be so interpreted and understood. But it was factual and truthful in every instance.

In the days of the so-called Fundamentalist-Modernist controversy, Mullins wrote in defense of the historic faith of the Christian church. In 1924 the Sunday School Board of the Southern Baptist Convention published his *Christianity at the Cross Roads.* In an especially revealing passage, Mullins writes:

> There is scarcely any controversy now as to what the New Testament teaches about Jesus Christ. Scientific exegesis has settled these questions in favor of our evangelical faith. . . . The attack now is upon the foundations of the records themselves. . . . It is vain for mediators and neutrals to shut their eyes to this issue. It is proposed to destroy the foundations of the Christian religion by discrediting the historical records. . . . The books that teach it are legion [p. 27].

Every issue, he continues, turns upon that one question: "What think ye of Christ?" Was there anything supernatural about Christ or not?

> It is my view that ultimately we must accept the records of the supernatural in the New Testament substantially as it stands, or else reject it as a whole. Meantime if there are people who accept it in part, we can only hope that further reflection will lead them to the logical outcome. As a matter of fact men usually proceed to total rejection or practically full acceptance. One or the other of these results seems to be inevitable [p. 30].

Not everyone will agree with everything Mullins may have said or believed, but there is no doubt about where he stands in his published works. He is theologically within the Calvinistic Baptist tradition, but he saw that

Fig. 26. A. T. Robertson

From *Proceedings of the General Association of Baptists in Kentucky.* 1934
edition, opposite p. 80.

the most basic issues were not the distinctives of Calvinism or even of Baptist doctrines. Although J. Gresham Machen clearly saw the inherent weakness in Mullins' doctrine of religious authority, he did write in *The Princeton Theological Review:*

> It is not merely a matter of interpretation, but it is primarily a question of fact. It is not a question of what the New Testament means, but whether what the New Testament says is true or false. Dr. Mullins deserves the thanks of the Church for making the issue so clear [p. 44].

A. T. ROBERTSON

Archibald Thomas Robertson was born November 6, 1863, near Chatham, Virginia. His teenage years were spent in North Carolina and his college work was done at Wake Forest College, where he made A's in every course. Between 1885 and 1888 he attended the Southern Baptist Theological Seminary, where he studied under Basil Manly, Jr., John Albert Broadus, James Petigru Boyce, and William Heth Whitsitt. He received his degree in May 1888 and became an assistant to Broadus in October. Two years later he was made associate professor and then later succeeded Broadus as the Professor of New Testament Interpretation at Southern Baptist Seminary, Louisville, Kentucky. Robertson married Ella Broadus, the daughter of John A. Broadus. He had five children and wrote forty-five books before he died, September 24, 1934.

Robertson was not a theologian, and he did not write a formal book on doctrine. Yet it is abundantly clear that he stood in the same tradition as his former teacher and father-in-law. His famous *Harmony of the Gospels* was a revision of the "Standard Broadus Harmony" (the first harmony to break away from the traditional division of the life of Christ by Passovers). "The world has never seemed the same to me," said Robertson, "since Broadus passed on."

> No man has ever stirred my nature as Broadus did in the classroom and in the pulpit. It has been my fortune to hear Beecher and Phillips Brooks, Maclaren, Joseph Parker and Spurgeon, John Hall and Moody, John Clifford and David Lloyd George. At his best and in a congenial atmosphere Broadus was the equal of any man that I have ever heard.
>
> It may be that I am not a competent judge of Broadus's powers as a man and minister because he put the stamp of his personality upon my very soul. It is not easy for me to write in an objective way concerning my Master in Christ and in the New Testament. My heart insists on being heard with every criticism of the intellect on this subject [*The Minister and His Greek New Testament,* p. 118].

Robertson, of course, is a recognized scholar in his own right. His views on biblical authority are not so much formally stated as they are everywhere implied. Biblical criticism is a valid tool if properly used, he says, but infallibility resides in the theological teachings of Scripture, not in the various critical theories.

> The modern Christian wishes to know the full truth about the gospels. He desires to follow no "Mother Goose" legends as the basis of his knowledge of Jesus. Nothing is gained by obscurantism and credulity any more than by obdurate skepticism. . . . There is need, however, of the caveat that we do not put critical infallibility in the place of theological infallibility. The historical or scientific method of gospel criticism is the true one, but it is not axiomatic and not always certain. It is possible to develop and apply certain broad principles of study, if only we avoid the intolerant dogmatism of a too narrow specialization [*The Christ of the Logia*, p. 170].

One of Robertson's best known and most significant works other than his Greek studies is *Luke the Historian in the Light of Research.* The book is a careful evaluation of the critical challenges to the historical integrity of Luke's gospel and the Acts. He writes:

> The items in Luke's books that were attacked have been taken up one by one. The work has been slow and piecemeal, of necessity. But it is now possible to gather together into a fairly complete picture the results. It is a positively amazing vindication of Luke. The force of the argument is cumulative and tremendous. One needs to have patience to work through the details with candor and a willingness to see all the facts with no prejudice against Luke or against the supernatural origin of Christianity. It is not claimed that every difficulty in Luke's books has been solved, but so many have been triumphantly removed that Luke is entitled to the benefit of the doubt in the rest or at any rate to patience on our part till further research can make a report. Luke should at least be treated as fairly as Thucydides or Polybius when he makes a statement that as yet has no other support or seems in conflict with other writers. Modern scholars are no longer defensive about Luke. His books can be used with confidence. The work of research has thrown light in every direction and the story is fascinating to every lover of truth [*Luke the Historian*, p. vii].

His famous *Word Pictures in the New Testament* gives several hints concerning his view of biblical inspiration. Robertson interprets 2 Peter 1:19-21 to mean that the transfiguration was for Peter a confirmation of the Messianic prophecies. It made clear the deity of Jesus. "Some with less likelihood," he says, "take Peter to mean that the word of prophecy is a surer confirmation of Christ's deity than the Transfiguration." No prophet starts a prophecy all by himself. "He is not a self-starter," says Robertson. Prophecy has a divine origin. The prophets were moved "from time to time" by the Spirit.

Peter is not here warning against personal interpretation of prophecy as the Roman Catholic says, but against the folly of upstart prophets with no impulse from God.

On 2 Timothy 3:16, most of the discussion concerns the meaning of the first clause, for there is no article in the Greek. Does it mean "every writing" or "all scripture"? The copula is absent in the Greek and must be inserted by the translator. The more natural meaning, says Robertson, is "all scripture (or every scripture) is inspired of God and profitable." In this form, as Robertson points out, there is "a definite assertion of inspiration." Inspired in this case means "God-breathed" and is perhaps used in contrast to the commandments of men in Titus 1:14.

John 14:17 calls the Holy Spirit the Spirit of truth. Robertson interprets this to mean that the Spirit is "marked by it (genitive case), gives it, defends it (cf. 1:17), in contrast to the spirit of error (1 John 4:6)." Speaking of the teaching ministry of the Spirit (John 14:26), Robertson says:

> The Holy Spirit knows "the deep things of God" (1 Cor. 2:10) and he is our Teacher in the Dispensation of the Holy Spirit of both new truth (verse 25) and old. . . . After Pentecost the disciples will be able better to recall and to understand what Jesus had said (how dull they had been at times) and to be open to new revelations from God (cf. Peter at Joppa and Caesarea).

The crucial passage, however, seems to be 1 Corinthians 2:13. In the King James translation the verse reads:

> Which things also we speak, not in the words which man's wisdom teacheth, but which the Holy Ghost teacheth; comparing spiritual things with spiritual.

Robertson says that the word translated "we speak" (*laloumen*) is used by Paul here to refer to "the utterance of the revelation which he has understood."

> That is to say, there is revelation (verse 10), illumination (verse 12), and inspiration (verse 13). Paul claims therefore the help of the Holy Spirit for the reception of the revelation, for the understanding of it, for the expression of it. . . . The verbal adjective *didaktois* (from *didasko*, to teach) is here passive in idea and is followed by the ablative case of origin or source. . . . So then Paul claims the help of the Holy Spirit in the utterance . . . of the words "which the Spirit teacheth." . . . Clearly Paul means that the help of the Holy Spirit in the utterance of the revelation extends to the words. No theory of inspiration is here stated, but it is not mere human wisdom. Paul's own Epistles bear eloquent witness to the lofty claim here made. They remain today after nearly nineteen centuries throbbing with the power of the Spirit of God, dynamic with life for the problems of today as when Paul wrote them for the needs of the believers in

his time, the greatest epistles of all time, surcharged with the energy of God.

Neither Mullins nor Robertson gave himself to the polemical battles that raged between conservative Christians. Their arrows were swift and deadly, however, when pointed toward the naturalistic presuppositions of modern criticism. There is too much good news to be spoken to a lost world to spend time debating which of the two forms of the plenary theory of inspiration one should hold. Yet it is equally clear that both of these men believed that biblical authority was indispensible for the Christian's world view. The "facts" of modern criticism have supported biblical truth. True theology has nothing to fear from truth in other areas. This is the legacy of the chief of the fathers.

BIBLIOGRAPHY

Estep, William R. "Southern Baptists in Search of an Identity." In *The Lord's Free People in a Free Land: Essays in Baptist History in Honor of Robert A. Baker,* edited by William R. Estep, pp. 145-69. Fort Worth, Texas: Evans Press, 1976.

E. Y. Mullins

Machen, J. Gresham. "The Relation of Religion to Science and Philosophy." *The Princeton Theological Review* 24 (January 1926):38-66.

Mullins, E. Y. *Christianity at the Cross Roads.* Nashville: Sunday School Board of the Southern Baptist Convention, 1924.

———. *The Christian Religion in Its Doctrinal Expression.* Valley Forge, Pa.: Judson, 1917.

———. "The Dangers and Duties of the Present Hour." The Opening Address of President E. Y. Mullins, Southern Baptist Convention, Kansas City, Mo., May 16, 1923.

———. *Freedom and Authority in Religion.* Philadelphia: The Griffith & Rowland Press, 1913.

Ramm, Bernard. "Baptists and Sources of Authority." *Foundations* 1 (July 1958): 6-15.

The Southern Baptist Convention Annual, 1923.

A. T. Robertson

Robertson, A. T. *The Christ of the Logia.* Nashville: Sunday School Board of the Southern Baptist Convention, 1924.

———. *Luke the Historian in the Light of Research.* New York: Scribner's, 1920.

———. *The Minister and His Greek New Testament.* Nashville: Broadman, 1977.

———. *Word Pictures in the New Testament.* Nashville: Broadman, 1932.

CHAPTER FOURTEEN

"Now These Are Thy Servants"

"Southern Baptists have just one Seminary. They desire but one. They are agreed to have just one." So stated a pamphlet distributed at the Baptist General Convention of Texas in 1907. B. H. Carroll had other ideas. At the same convention, he spoke in favor of a new school he had founded:

> This seminary [Southwestern Baptist Theological Seminary] was not established as a rival of any other. Its title to confidence neither now nor hereafter should be sought in the real or supposed demerit of other seminaries. If it would be a mere negation, let it perish. If our Father wills it to stand, it must be because there is need for it and merit in it [BGCT *Annual* 1907, p. 54].

Such strong conviction had characterized Carroll's involvement with the new school from its inception in 1901 as the theological department of Baylor University. When the seminary separated from Baylor in 1905, Carroll spent the summer raising $30,000. That sum was to support the school for three years. It was at that time called the Texas Baptist Theological Seminary.

In fact, Carroll had begun his quest for endowment in 1902, the year after the theological department had become a separate entity at Baylor University. Apparently the doctrine of the divine inspiration of Scripture motivated Carroll in this endeavor from the beginning. His pledge to uphold the traditional orthodox view of Scripture was evidently a strong factor in his ability to gain the confidence of the people. The first endowment Carroll gained for "proper theological education" came from G. R. Freeman of Hamilton, Texas. In his report to the Texas Convention in 1902, Carroll reflected the theological concerns of Freeman:

> He saw and deplored the manifest effort to strip the Holy Scriptures of authenticity, historical verity, inspiration, and to set up an ever wavering human standard according to which this and that book, this or that chapter, this or that doctrine should be hawked at, pierced, dislocated, and torn from an authoritative position in the holy library. . . . Though a man of moderately small means, he determined, before he passed away, to start

a movement towards erecting a permanent breakwater against this invad-
ing tide of practical infidelity [BGCT *Annual* 1902, p. 35].

It requires little subtlety to find Carroll's own concerns writ large between
those lines.

In the spring of 1908, Walter Thomas Conner graduated from the new
institution, which was called Baylor Theological Seminary from 1906 to
1908. In 1910, Calvin Goodspeed, Conner's teacher in systematic theology,
resigned his teaching position due to ill health. At the Texas Convention
that year Carroll expressed deep regret at the loss of Goodspeed and stated:
"It is questionable if Systematic Theology and Apologetics ever had, anywhere, an abler and more judicious expounder." In the fall, the seminary
moved to Fort Worth, and Carroll chose W. T. Conner to teach systematic
theology. The imprint made in Southern Baptist life by this young successor
to Goodspeed went far deeper than that of Goodspeed himself.

The ministries of Carroll and Conner at Southwestern overlapped for
only four years. Carroll's work there began after he was sixty years old.
Conner started his teaching career when he was thirty-three. Their lives
spanned 109 years of Baptist history. The fights and fortunes which molded
Carroll were far different from those which shaped Conner. Their statements on biblical inspiration are couched in somewhat dissimilar outward
forms; yet the differences lie in the areas of emphasis and personal temperament rather than in essence. Both men did what they could "towards
erecting a permanent breakwater against . . . practical infidelity."

B. H. CARROLL

Benajah Harvey Carroll was born in Carroll County, Mississippi, on
December 27, 1843, but Texas felt the greatest impact of his ministry. He
was an amazing scholar, a self-taught theologian who could read up to
three hundred pages per day without neglecting his other duties, and then
years later recall the material—including the page references. He stood
six feet four inches tall and weighed two hundred pounds. He proudly
wore a long white beard that led many to imagine that he resembled
Moses.

Carroll enlisted in the Texas Rangers in 1861, and instead of carrying
food in his saddle bags he carried books. He fought with the Texas Infan-
try in the Civil War until he was seriously wounded and sent home. During this period of his life he was a fanatical infidel. He had vowed never to
enter a church again. Somewhat on a dare from his friends, in 1865 he
attended an old-fashioned camp meeting where he heard a challenge to
make a practical, experimental test of Christianity. Carroll took the challenge, and while riding home through the woods that evening he stopped
his horse, got down on his knees, and turned his life over to Christ. In

Fig. 27. B. H. Carroll

From picture on file in the Treasure Room, Fleming Library, Southwestern Baptist Theological Seminary, Fort Worth, Texas. Used by permission of Fleming Library.

November 1866 he was ordained to the gospel ministry. Four years later, Carroll went to the First Baptist Church of Waco, Texas, where he pastored for twenty-eight years. He was made the dean of the Bible department at Baylor, where he stayed until he founded Southwestern Baptist Theological Seminary in 1908 and became its first president. He died November 11, 1914, after an extended illness.

George W. Truett, the famed pastor of the First Baptist Church of Dallas, Texas, for forty-seven years and one of the greatest Baptist preachers of modern times, said of Carroll:

> I am more indebted to him for my reverence for God's Holy Word than I am to any other human being. His was the greatest personality I ever knew and, unlike some historic characters, he ever increasingly loomed largest to those nearest him. . . . The expression, "Mighty in the Scriptures," could be applied to Dr. Carroll as to few other men of his own or any other age.

This noteworthy compliment was included in a special introduction to Carroll's book entitled *Inspiration of the Bible.* J. B. Cranfill, who edited Carroll's works through the years, wrote a foreword to the volume in which he echoed Truett's praise:

> I join him in appraising the author of this volume as the most commanding figure that has ever marched through the history of American ecclesiasticism. . . . I published Carroll's first sermon in 1884. . . . I am now older than he was when he passed into rest, and I wonder, as these words are done, if my service in the editing and compilation of these works of B. H. Carroll is not my crowning contribution to the world.

If those words are not enough, L. R. Scarborough, the second president of Southwestern Baptist Theological Seminary, wrote in "A Further Introduction" to the same volume:

> He was the greatest preacher and the mightiest soul I ever knew. He made deep tracks in Christ's kingdom in Texas and the South—tracks that time cannot wear out.

Carroll's first chapter in this volume of his collected essays on Scripture deals with "Inspiration of the Scriptures as Believed by Baptists." The term "inspiration" speaks of a divine breath that conveys the Holy Spirit, he says, "in order that those inspired may speak or write what God would have spoken or written" (p. 15).

> Inspiration is that communication of supernatural power from God which invariably and adequately and even perfectly accomplishes the end designed by it, whatever that end may be, and which (and this is an important part of the definition) no inherent force that is resident in na-

ture, and no development of, or combination of inherent forces would in any length of time or under any environment bring about . . . and so that no human gift of mere genius could have brought it about [pp. 37, 42].

When God does the in-breathing it communicates super-natural spiritual power that in every case secures, with absolute certainty and infallibility, the result aimed at, without any error and in such a way that no mere genius . . . could have attained [p. 48].

Second Timothy 3:15-16 and 2 Peter 1:20 stand as affirmations of the inspiration of the Old Testament books, says Carroll. John 14:26 and 16: 12-13 give the promise that the New Testament would be inspired. What is to be communicated by inspiration is not human thoughts and ideas. It is not what the eye sees or the ear hears or what the heart conceives, but what the Spirit reveals.

It has always been a matter of profound surprise to me that anybody should ever question the verbal inspiration of the Bible. The whole thing had to be written in words. Words are signs of ideas, and if the words are not inspired, then there is no way of getting at anything in connection with inspiration. . . . What is the object of inspiration? It is to put accurately, in human words, ideas from God. . . . When you hear the silly talk that the Bible "contains" the word of God and is not the word of God, you hear a fool's talk. I don't care if he is a Doctor of Divinity, a President of a University covered with medals from universities of Europe and the United States, it is fool talk. There can be no inspiration of the book without the words of the book [p. 20].

When these inspired declarations were written, they were absolutely infallible. . . . That is one of the most important points in connection with inspiration, viz.: that the inspired word is irrefragable, infallible; that all the powers of the world cannot break one "thus saith the Lord" [p. 25].

Let me say further that only the original text of the books of the Bible is inspired, not the copy or the translation. Second, the inspiration of the Bible does not mean that God said and did all that is said and done in the Bible; some of it the devil did and said. . . . The inspiration means that the record of what is said and done is correct. It does not mean that everything that God did and said is recorded. It does not mean that everything recorded is of equal importance, but every part of it is necessary to the purpose of the record, and no part is unimportant. One part is no more inspired than any other part [p. 26].

Carroll's involvement in academic theological education led him to be deeply concerned with the growing influence of critical theories about the Bible. The question of inspiration "which had been settled eighteen hundred years" has been reopened by the higher critics, he says. The "disturber" is not science (How could the study of the natural ever bring the supernatural into question?), but speculative philosophy. Such philosophy has no legitimate claims to make against the supernatural either, Carroll continued. All of human philosophy "is not worth one sermon on religion by the Negro preacher, John Jasper, of Richmond."

Three facts, says Carroll, bear on the reopening of the inspiration question. First, in Athens, Paul opposed and buried the Greek theories of evolution and blind fate. Yet, second, Darwin reintroduced and through his coadjutors popularized the claim that man is derived from the lower forms of life. (Huxley and Paul are in perfect agreement, Carroll writes. Huxley describes himself by the term agnostic, one who claims not to be able to know whether God exists; and Paul says the things of God are foolishness to the natural man who cannot know them, because they are spiritually discerned.) Then the third fact is that some teachers in Christian schools began to apply evolutionary principles to biblical history.

> These so-called Christian expositors of the Darwinian theory of evolution are hard to describe. They are neither fish nor fowl, neither pig nor puppy.... They have done more to discount the value of Christian schools than all the other agencies in the world put together.... Whenever you sow a nation down with the heathen theory as applied to the Bible, you may look for a crop of anarchy.... When this trouble comes; when the practical men put into application what the schoolmen teach, the schoolmen will stand off and say, "We did not mean that; we didn't mean to be devilish like that." They did not ... but this crop came from the evolution-seed they sowed....
>
> I say that a breath of this modern theory is as cold as the last gasp of a dying man, and that what they teach is more fatal to the human race than any fire that fanaticism ever kindled, or any superstition that ever darkened the land....
>
> Now, that is what has re-opened this question of inspiration. That is where it came from, and wherever one of them enters a school as a teacher, I don't care who he may be nor what his qualities may be in other directions, as sure as rain will bring up Johnson grass, he will raise a crop of religious doubters in the school where he teaches [pp. 32-34].

Carroll's most famous work is his *Interpretation of the English Bible*, edited by J. B. Cranfill and originally published in 1913 by the Sunday School Board of the Southern Baptist Convention. In the pages of this interpretative commentary, Carroll analyzes and provides an alternative to the theories of higher criticism.

In his "Introduction to Genesis," Cranfill comments:

> For our own part, we are willing to let the book of Genesis tell its own story in its own simple way, and accept it just as simply and as truly as

we accept the statement that Jesus Christ came to John the Baptist when he was preaching near the Jordan and was immersed by John in the Jordan. The mission of the preacher of God's Word is to proclaim the Bible rather than to criticize the Bible, and that same statement applies to teachers in our theological seminaries everywhere. No man who doubts the authenticity and the inspiration of God's Word should be called to teach God's Word. The Bible is either true or it is false. There is no halfway ground. The Genesis story is either true or false. That it is true, Dr. B. H. Carroll's discussion eminently shows [pp. 4-5].

What Carroll's discussion shows is that the Genesis narrative, in his opinion, is fully historical. He calls the "alleged discrepancies" between Genesis 1 and 2 examples of "far reaching and destructive criticism" (p. 15). This conclusion comes from his conviction that truth is a unity. To give up the factual, historical basis is to lose the theology as well.

Carroll is impressed by the "marked difference in style" between the second chapter of Genesis and the first, but his way of accounting for this difference is simply to suggest that style depends upon the nature of the subject matter (p. 95). He points out the major stylistic differences just as C. H. Toy had done in his classes, but Carroll explains them as deliberate variations.

Genesis consistently follows a pattern of moving from the general to the particular, he says. For example, the history of all mankind and the origin of the nations is recounted in the early chapters, and then Genesis moves to the history of one particular family (Abraham's) which becomes one nation. In the same stylistic pattern the general account of creation in Genesis 1 is followed by a more detailed study of the man, who was last in creation yet first in dignity and importance.

Genesis 2, then, according to Carroll, was not intended to convey the chronological order of creation. Surely all true interpretation must attempt to reproduce the intent of the author. As for the historical-critical theory which concludes that these stylistic differences indicate different authors and different documents, Carroll replies:

> There is no convincing reason for accepting this explanation. The book of Genesis is not a patchwork of different documents by different authors crudely and artificially joined together; one purpose runs through the book. Whoever wrote one part of it wrote all parts of it, from whatever source his materials were derived [pp. 96-97].

Thus the integrity of the historical narrative is defended not by pure blind faith but by argument based, for one thing, on the literary structure of the book.

Carroll goes on to deal with Darwin's evolutionary theories. He attempts to show that the theory of biological evolution is "at war with revelation and common sense, and also with all of the clearly proved facts gathered by man's research" (p. 99). Among other things, Carroll pointed to a recently excavated phosphate bed in Ashley, South Carolina, that produced a collection of fossils. These fossils supposedly showed that animals and men who were theoretically separated by vast geological ages were in fact living at the same time.

To demand historical accuracy in the biblical account of creation is to come into inevitable conflict with naturalistic theories of biological evolution. Carroll frequently points out that one motivating factor behind the shift away from a theologically conservative interpretation and the shift toward the historical-critical approach has been this very issue of scientific conflict. If one is convinced scientifically that evolution is a proved fact ("the way God did it," as it is sometimes expressed), then one is forced to conclude that Genesis is not historically accurate. Therefore, one either gives up the theology of the passage and becomes liberal, or he accepts the dual theory of truth and maintains the claim of doctrinal infallibility in spite of scientific and historical error.

Carroll would not make such a shift in his thinking. He never considered giving up the theology of the passage, and he could not accept any dual theory of truth. Thus, he opposed evolution and documentary theories. For Carroll, God's Word spoke the truth, the whole truth, and nothing but the truth. The Bible abounds with figurative and symbolic language, but that is not the issue. The issue is truth. Can the theological implications of the passage be considered true if the framework in which they are cast is discovered to be out of touch with reality? For Carroll, truth is defined in terms of its correspondence with reality.

Carroll is careful to state that he does not think Genesis has as its primary purpose the instruction of believers in scientific disciplines. But he does believe that theological affirmations about God as the Creator have binding implications for scientific questions. For Carroll, theological truth and scientific or historical truth are not separate, autonomous realms of thought. They are all related, and this is just as true in Genesis 1 and 2 as it is in Matthew 3:13-17 (the account of the Lord's baptism by John in the Jordan). Either the Bible tells us what actually took place or it does not. There is no middle ground.

Of course, some people have objected at this very point. Carroll states the objection and his reply in *Inspiration of the Bible*:

> They say that if the Bible is inspired, and all of its records are accurate, and that there is no errancy in it, then it puts a man of science in the position that he must choose between science and the Bible, their teachings being diverse.

> To this man I would say that he is mistaken. . . . I challenge him to bring up a single contradiction between the teachings of Scripture and real science.
>
> I have seen that tested on the first chapter of Genesis. That gives an account of the creation of the universe, the formation of the earth, and the creation of man, and to this very day science—not science as represented by some men who try to set the teachings of science over against the Bible by butting their heads against the accounts in Genesis, Job, certain of the Psalms, and Paul's declarations at Athens—but true science is and has ever been in harmony with the Scriptures [pp. 116-17].

Carroll continues to apply his conservative grammatical-historical approach throughout the Bible. Though he does not mention the controversy directly, Carroll seems to be well aware of the interpretive issues developed by C. H. Toy in the 1870s. In *An Interpretation of the English Bible,* Genesis 49:10 is called a "remarkable Messianic prophecy" (p. 444), and nearly a full page of Carroll's commentary is devoted to an exposition of that text, showing how it was and could only be fulfilled in Christ. Carroll attributes Abraham's monotheism to a manifestation of the true God which must have been "in some visible form and deeply impressive" (p. 279). These views were in direct contrast with those of Toy just a few decades earlier.

In his commentary on Isaiah, Carroll devotes fully ten pages to the question of authorship. He analyzes every major objection to the traditional view and finds them highly speculative and unconvincing. Not only did Isaiah write all of his book, but Daniel surely wrote his as well, Carroll says. He speaks so directly to this whole issue of radical historical criticism in his commentary on Daniel that it seems appropriate to let him speak in his own words. The following is taken from pages 5-7 and 12 of the 1947 edition of Carroll's *An Interpretation of the English Bible,* volume 9: *Daniel and the Inter-biblical Period,* published by Broadman Press.

> Do not understand me to decry the value of textual criticism. Its achievements have been great, though its work is well nigh done. Nor do I deny an honorable place to historical criticism. Every good expounder employs it and every good commentator gives much valuable space to it. . . .
>
> The historical criticism that, in my judgment, is most poisonous is that which, in the name of Christianity, attempts to apply to biblical criticism the methods and conclusions of an unverified heathen hypothesis, or a merely speculative theory of philosophy. Though this hypothesis, or theory, of evolution is both atheistic and materialistic, and repugnant *per se* because unscientific, yet it is relatively harmless coming from avowed atheists and materialists. It genders poison when it comes in the name and guise of Christianity. In countries where church and state are united and religious officers are appointed by political power and supported by the state purse, we may not be surprised to find many church and theological

dignitaries utterly unregenerate. But yet their scepticism goes forth in the name of Christianity.

In this country they appear mostly as professors in so-called Christian schools that are not responsible to any organized religious bodies. Outside the Christian camp they are not formidable. But when atheists, deists, materialists, and pantheists pose as the only reliable expounders of Christianity, then the dishonesty of the masquerade smells unto heaven. The poison is most shrewdly diffused in mixed topical dictionaries, encyclopedias, and commentaries. As the article of a dictionary or encyclopedia or the comment on the several Bible books are assigned to different authors (as in the "Cambridge" and the "Expositor's" Bibles), there, side by side, appear rankest infidelity and soundest orthodoxy. The poor young preacher, unable to buy but one Bible dictionary, or religious encyclopedia, or set of commentaries, knows not what to do, and his safest friends know not how to advise him. If he buys the "Cambridge Bible" and the "Expositor's Bible," all the light he will have on Daniel must come from Driver and Farrar, and that light on vital points is darkness. When he turns to his Pentateuch he may find the Moses of his Genesis unlike the Moses of Deuteronomy, and the Moses of Leviticus no Moses at all. These observations are stressed here because the radicals claim their most assured result in treating the book of Daniel. And if we meet what they say against the book of Daniel we need not fear them on any other book. . . .

When we come to New Testament references to the book, one alone ought to satisfy every man who claims to be a Christian, and that is the reference of our Lord in his great discourse on Mount Olivet, to the book of Daniel, the prophet, and to a specific prophecy of Daniel that is yet to be fulfilled.

Thus, Carroll indicates the implications of his belief in full biblical authority. In the pages of his commentary he tackles all the major objections to Daniel's authenticity and finds them unconvincing, weak, and false.

But perhaps the clearest statement of Carroll's attitude toward doctrine comes from his discussion of Ephesians 4:1-16. He titles the section (pp. 139-50) "The Great Unities." One Lord, one baptism, and one system of faith were among the unities. "A church with a little creed is a church with a little life," he wrote. Cries for "less creed and more liberty," said Carroll are "a degeneration from the vertebrate to the jelly fish."

Very solemnly I would warn the reader against any teaching that decries doctrines, or which would reduce the creed of the church into two or three articles.

We are entitled to no liberty in these matters. It is a positive and very hurtful sin to magnify liberty at the expense of doctrine. A creed is what we believe. A confession of faith is a declaration of what we believe. The church must both believe and declare. The longest creed of history is more valuable and less hurtful than the shortest. . . .

The standard is the holy Scriptures. . . . Again I solemnly warn the reader against all who depreciate creeds, or who would reduce them to a minimum of entrance qualifications into the church (pp. 146-47, 150).

The impact of Carroll on the Baptists in Texas and the South was enormous. It was Carroll who helped to "discover" George W. Truett and get him established in the ministry. Truett lived in Carroll's home for several years. For four consecutive years Truett sat in Carroll's classes at Baylor to hear him expound the Scripture. L. R. Scarborough, at his father's request, for four and a half years went to hear Carroll preach in Waco on Sunday mornings and then in the afternoon wrote out a report of the message to send home. Scarborough unhesitantly writes in his introduction to Carroll's *Inspiration of the Bible:*

> My faith is the faith of a simple, plain Baptist. I accepted from my father and Dr. Carroll the verbal inspiration of the Bible, the deity of Jesus Christ, His perfect humanity, His atoning death, His bodily resurrection, His second coming. All my studies since have confirmed the simple faith I received from them.
>
> I greatly joy in the publication of this volume of Dr. Carroll's sermons on the inspiration of the Bible. His interpretative authority has great weight with me, but I have never had occasion to depart from his teachings on these great themes [pp. 11-12].

Probably Carroll's most famous passage concerning Scripture is the one reprinted below from his *Inspiration of the Bible.* It is characteristic not only of Carroll but of Baptists generally in his day. He has just spent several pages defending the proposition that "inspiration was an inspiration of the records, which made those records inerrable, not only in idea, but in word" (p. 113). This naturally raised the question of supposed contradictions in Scripture.

> I have seen these contradictions melt away until I have lost all confidence in them. Now, a boy is usually a great deal smarter than his father, and than he is when he gets to be a father. When I was a boy I thought I had found a thousand contradictions in the Bible. In the Old Bible of my young manhood I marked them.
>
> Well, I had then nearly a thousand more contradictions than I have now. I do not see them now; they are not there. There are perhaps a half dozen in the Bible that I cannot explain satisfactorily to myself. I don't say that my explanation of all the others would satisfy everybody. There are some that I cannot explain satisfactorily to myself; but since I have seen nine hundred and ninety-four out of the thousand coalesce and harmonize like two streams mingling, I am disposed to think that if I had more sense I could harmonize those other six; and even if I forever fail to harmonize them, God knows better than I know, and that when I know perfectly just

as I now know only in part, and only a very small part, I will be able to understand that; and so when I come to things of that kind and cannot master them, I put them in a parenthesis and say, "I will come back; God won't leave you penned forever; He will send somebody that can take away the difficulty and make it clear to me." I assume that it can be done. [121-22].

W. T. CONNER

Walter Thomas Conner was born (January 19, 1877) and raised in Center, Arkansas. When he was a teenager, his family moved to Texas. He was converted in 1894 and one year later preached his first sermon, using Luke 2:49 as a text. In 1899 he was ordained to the gospel ministry. He faced serious obstacles in his path toward a formal education, but he did complete the Th.B. degree at the Baylor Theological Seminary and spent two years in graduate study at Rochester Theological Seminary and the University of Chicago. B. H. Carroll then invited him to join the faculty at Southwestern Baptist Theological Seminary in Fort Worth, Texas. He taught there for thirty-nine years, retiring in 1949. His death in 1952 came after a teaching career in which he produced twelve books.

The publication of Conner's *Revelation and God: An Introduction to Christian Doctrine* (Broadman Press) came in 1936. This was an enlargement of portions of an earlier book, *A System of Christian Doctrine* (1924). The next year (1937) Conner printed a revised version of the 1924 work with the new title *Christian Doctrine*. That book was dedicated to the memory of Conner's three "teachers in theology," as he called them: Calvin Goodspeed, A. H. Strong, and E. Y. Mullins.

His major treatment of the doctrine of revelation is found in the first half of *Revelation and God*. Three chapters treat "general" revelation by discussing man's capacity to know God and the revelation of God in nature. Then two chapters treat topics of "special" revelation. One chapter focuses on the revelation of God in Christ, and the other treats biblical revelation.

Revelation, says Conner, is always an activity of God; therefore, it is always supernatural. Biblical revelation is built on the assumption of general revelation. It is written to men who are expected already to have a consciousness of God. Revelation preceded the Bible, but the Bible does have revelation value for us.

> It was not as if God came to these men and said: "I want to communicate to men of all future times a knowledge of myself. So I want you to take this revelation and write it down for them." It was rather that these men, as they lived their lives, wrestled with their problems, received in different ways thoughts of God, had experiences with God. These thoughts and experiences they wrote down. These records, in God's good providence, have been passed down to us. They are not messages sent first of all to us from God, using these writers as amanuenses or stenographers. The mes-

Fig. 28. W. T. Conner

From picture on file in the Treasure Room, Fleming Library, Southwestern Baptist Theological Seminary, Fort Worth, Texas. Used by permission of Fleming Library.

sages concerned, first of all, the biblical writers themselves. These records reflect their situation, oftentimes record their victories, deal with the problems, trials, struggles, even the religious doubts and perplexities of the biblical writers and their people. It is a revelation, then, not immediately to us, but mediately through the biblical writers and their situation. . . .

The record of the events can help us to find God because in the events the people back there found God. Only events that had revelation value for them can have revelation value for us. . . .

The Bible records events in which God was revealing himself to men. As the record of such events, it enables us also to know God. As we read about God's dealings with men, we too are enabled to come into fellowship with him. In that sense the Bible is God's revelation to us [pp. 78-80].

One crucial question, of course, is whether the significance of biblical revelation is in "the series of events recorded" or in "the interpretation placed upon the events." Conner makes a strong case for the importance of prophetic interpretation, but he goes on to say that the final differentiating factor is not simply the interpretation but is in fact the history itself. This is seen most clearly in the gospels, which record the life and work of Christ.

The Bible is not, then, simply the record of a segment of the history of the race religiously interpreted; it is rather the record of a series of unique events. . . . God was in the history in a peculiar way and not simply in its interpretation [p. 83].

For Conner, the primary issues are hermeneutical. Seventeen pages of the twenty-five-page chapter are devoted to interpretive issues. The Bible must always be interpreted in its environmental context, he says. Inspiration did not take place apart from historical and social situations. In fact, Conner so emphasizes this that he uses the terminology of God being "limited" by the medium through which He worked. Inspiration "acted not as an external clamp put on a man's mind"; rather, it "acted as a liberating and releasing power" causing each man to be "his best self" (p. 86). Here, as in other places, Conner shows the influence of A. H. Strong's views.

This concept of inspiration leads the interpreter to distinguish between form and substance in Scripture. We do not greet one another with a holy kiss, says Conner, because we distinguish the essential teaching from the social form of that day. This principle applies in scientific matters as well. The religious validity of the Bible is not affected by the fact that the biblical writers thought the earth was only recently created and that the earth was the center of the universe. Such scientific questions, says Conner, have nothing to do with the substance of biblical teaching. The permanent spiritual truth of Scripture will not change whatever changes may take place in scientific views.

Most of the difficulties that arise with regard to the Bible can be resolved, says Conner, if Christians will remember to distinguish between form and substance in the Scripture and if they will recognize the progressive nature of revelation. Jesus said that He had come to fulfill an incomplete revelation. Paul spoke of Christ coming in the fullness of time. Revelation must be progressive because it is morally and spiritually conditioned. Conner is quick to deny that there is any connection between his concept of progressive revelation and theories of naturalistic evolution. "God can give only as man receives; but man's receptivity is God's creation" (p. 89).

Conner uses the principle of progressive revelation to relieve so-called moral difficulties of Scripture. The psalmist who thought it was a pious thing to slaughter infant children was surely imperfect when judged by Christian standards. But he should be judged by the moral standards of his own day. The wholesale destruction of the Canaanites has always been an ethical problem for Christians to explain.

> But when we understand that the men God was using to carry out his purpose were men of very low moral ideals as compared with a later age, and when we remember that the nations to be destroyed were so morally and spiritually corrupt that their complete extermination was probably the best thing for the world, then the question is not so difficult [p. 89].

The central theme of the Bible, says Conner, is redemption. The "older view" is that the Bible is "a record of divine truth." But for Conner revelation is more "vital and personal." Revelation "is self-disclosure on the part of God" (p. 90). This comment in 1936 shows the clear influence of E. Y. Mullins and points up one instance among many in which Conner was on the cutting edge of a decidedly contemporary emphasis with regard to the doctrine of revelation. Man needs a "vital contact with God" far more than he needs a system of theology.

God is known by what He does, says Conner, and He has acted finally and supremely through Christ. The center and the unity of the Bible is found in Christ. Conner believed that "Jesus foresaw his death at least as early as his baptism" (p. 93). The gospel accounts reveal to us Christ's life, death, resurrection, and ascension. The rest of the New Testament speaks of His glorification, the extension of His Kingdom, and His final return to consummate His Kingdom.

The Bible is not "simply offering to man advice on spiritual matters"; rather, it is speaking authoritatively. "The authority of the Bible is the authority of Christ," says Conner. "We do not have two authorities" (p. 96).

> It is commonly said that, in the reformation of Luther, so far as authority

> is concerned, an infallible Bible was put in the place of an infallible pope;
> the authority of the church was displaced by the authority of the Bible. But
> this does not express the whole matter. The locus of authority was changed;
> but not only the locus but also the nature of that authority was changed.
> The authority of the church is repressive and oppressive in its nature. . . .
> Man's mind and conscience are enslaved. . . . All is decided for him. The
> Bible is not that kind of authority. . . . The Bible is sometimes represented
> as a book of statutes of that nature, but it is not. We must make our own
> moral decisions. We must seek to know the truth. . . . There is no authority
> for a rational being except one that is rationally followed. . . . The authority
> of the Bible does not suppress but stimulates and develops personality
> [p. 97].

Conner suggests that the purpose of the Bible is "to awaken faith in
man" (p. 99). Faith is necessary in order to understand the Bible. Faith
is not credulity. Certain questions of date, authorship, and historical reliability must be answered by historical and literary criticism. But Conner
says that the response of faith is as necessary to evaluate the Bible as are
eyes to evaluate the sun or ears to evaluate music. The world of spiritual
realities will be unintelligible to the man without faith. "Faith is the sympathetic response of the whole personality of man to God as revealed in
Jesus Christ" (pp. 99-100).

For Conner, the Bible is an inspired book. He is concerned for proper
interpretation and proper recognition of the nature of biblical authority.
He quotes Paul's words to Timothy: "All scripture is given by inspiration
of God" (2 Timothy 3:16). Then he writes:

> Doctor Warfield is probably correct when he says that this means that
> God produced or caused the Scriptures. New Testament writers (and
> speakers) regard God as the author of Old Testament sayings and teachings
> (Mark 12:36; John 10:35; Heb. 1:5, 3:7, *et al*). The Scriptures, then,
> are God's work. He produced the Scriptures. He was in the events of
> history and experience out of which the Scripture records grew and he
> was in the producing of the records. In a general way we might think of
> God's presence and activity in the former as revelation and in the latter
> as inspiration. But this distinction can be carried through only in a gen-
> eral way. To try to maintain a hard and fast distinction is sure to lead to
> confusion and error. The relation between the two is so close and vital
> that no absolute distinction can be maintained. It is evident that inspira-
> tion as above defined is dependent (as previously pointed out) on revela-
> tion, and on the other hand is a means to making the Scriptures a further
> revelation to the world. The Scriptures, then, are the product of revelation
> and inspiration, and they also become God's revelation to us [p. 84].

Conner was one of those rare men who seem to be greater rather than
weaker the better they are known. Few men become legends in their own

lifetimes, but W. T. Conner and B. H. Carroll did. Carroll was more of an apologist and was more gifted in expository skills than was Conner, yet Conner's systematic mind produced some of the most useful handbooks on theology ever published in Baptist life for the busy pastor or layman.

In the preface to his *Faith of the New Testament,* Conner wrote:

> I have not paid much attention to critical questions. . . . My purpose was to find out as nearly as I could what the books of the New Testament teach as they stand, not how they came to be what they are. I have assumed in general the reliability of the records. This I think the results of recent criticism will justify [p. 11].

Carroll's confidence in Conner was richly repaid. Biblical theology has remained at the center of Southwestern's curriculum through the years. Both men strongly supported theological views that assumed the reliability of the biblical content. Both men left an indelible mark on the lives of hundreds of men and women now serving Christ around the world.

BIBLIOGRAPHY

Baptist General Convention of Texas Annual. 1902, 1907.

B. H. Carroll

B. H. Carroll. *Inspiration of the Bible: A Discussion of the Origin, the Authenticity and the Sanity of the Oracles of God.* Compiled and edited by J. B. Cranfill. Introduction by George W. Truett and L. R. Scarborough. New York: Revell, 1930.

————. *An Interpretation of the English Bible.* This set was first published by Revell in 1913 under the title page imprint of the Sunday School Board of the Southern Baptist Convention. In 1942 Broadman bought the copyright from Revell. Those early volumes, edited by J. B. Cranfill assisted by J. W. Crowder, were incomplete. Crowder, Carroll's assistant, had the remaining material (mostly from the Old Testament poetical and prophetic sections), and in 1947 Broadman began copyrighting a "New and Complete" edition. In 1973 Baker Book House, of Grand Rapids, Michigan, reprinted Broadman's 1948 new and complete edition in six volumes, but the Baker reprint preserved the pagination and format of the earlier seventeen-volume set.

W. T. Conner

Conner, W. T. *The Faith of the New Testament.* Nashville: Broadman, 1940.

————. *Revelation and God: An Introduction to Christian Doctrine.* Nashville: Broadman, 1936.

CHAPTER FIFTEEN

"Do Men Gather Grapes of Thorns?"

Several of the leading American liberal theologians in the early decades of the twentieth century were Baptists. Sidney E. Ahlstrom correctly observes that "the Baptist's anticreedal congregationalism left the way more open to theological departures" (*Religious History,* p. 912). Northern Baptists were far more affected by these changes in theological patterns than were Southern Baptists. The influence of liberal thought was felt in the South, however. Nineteenth-century ideas were by no means confined to the North.

Romanticism's emphasis on emotion and experience together with the historicism growing out of evolutionary patterns of thinking led to several theological consequences. Baptists who were open to these new emphases found an interesting way to justify these changes. Because Baptists had traditionally emphasized the liberty of conscience and the right of every individual to interpret the Bible for himself, some Baptist scholars began claiming that these principles allowed them to give up all traditional doctrines and yet remain Baptist.

It was a new day when Baptists, in the name of religious freedom, allowed doctrinal diversity to become so widespread that they trivialized their identity. Doctrines were reduced to an ambiguous affirmation of the New Testament as "the rule of faith and practice." What Protestant denomination could not affirm such a statement? Thus distinctives were either lost or were at least in danger of being lost.

Several men represent this "liberal" element in Baptist life. Walter Rauschenbusch is probably the most theologically conservative of the ones being studied below, though he is definitely the most radical in his interpretation of the social implications of the gospel. Shailer Matthews was anxious to call himself a "Modernist." The critical approach to Scripture was the only proper approach, he said, and it was inevitable that one's theology must be adjusted to fit the modern view. William Newton Clarke was the most serious and respected theologian among the Baptist liberals. Experience became, for Clarke, the key to understanding theology, the mediator between doctrine and revelation. Scripture was a record of religious experience, and thus was no longer truly a norm for faith but merely an example of faith. Harry Emerson Fosdick took this theology along with an evolutionary optimism and became one of the most popular preachers in America.

Each of these men represents a stream within Baptist life that influenced many people. Some Baptist scholars, such as J. J. Reeve, reacted by pointing out the unbiblical nature of the assumptions that underlay this new theology. What implications these developments had in American Baptist life will be traced briefly in the following chapter.

The twentieth century has been truly a century of instability and change. Optimism turned to despair. Peace became almost continual war. And Baptist theology began to splinter and fragment.

WALTER RAUSCHENBUSCH

Most Baptists considered Walter Rauschenbusch to be theologically liberal because of his emphasis on the social implications of the gospel. However, Henlee H. Barnett has ranked Rauschenbusch along with Martin Luther, John Calvin, Roger Williams, Jonathan Edwards, and John Wesley as a deeply spiritual and intellectual Christian leader.

Rauschenbusch was born in Rochester, New York, on October 4, 1861. He died on July 25, 1918. In those nearly fifty-seven years he made a tremendous impact on the Baptist social conscience. He received the B.A. degree in 1884 from the University of Rochester and then graduated from Rochester Theological Seminary in 1886. He also studied in Berlin, Kiel, and Marburg in the years 1891-92 and 1907-8. Between 1886 and 1897 Rauschenbusch pastored the Second German Baptist Church of New York. He entered his ministry with pietistic ideals of winning individual souls to Christ and thus fulfilling the heavenly mandate. But the harsh realities of the slums, the poverty, and the poor housing aroused in him a strong social consciousness. He sincerely believed that the Kingdom of God could be brought in by a Christian effort for social change. Because of the events related to World War I, he had great disillusionment when he died. His optimism was shattered.

In 1897 Rauschenbusch became the Professor of New Testament at Rochester Seminary, and then in 1902 he shifted his teaching field to church history, where he remained until his death. In those last years he continued to speak to Baptists on a national level. One of his most straightforward comments about the Bible came in an article he wrote for the *Rochester Baptist Monthly* entitled "Why I Am a Baptist."

> Now we Baptists have no authoritative creed. Our ministers and professors are not required solemnly to declare that they adopt some obsolete statement as their belief and will always teach that. We have a couple of

Fig. 29. WALTER RAUSCHENBUSCH

From the American Baptist Historical Society, William H. Brackney, Director. Used by permission.

summaries, called the New Hampshire and the Philadelphia Confessions, which are often adopted by newly organized churches, but no one is compelled to use them. So far as I remember I never read either of them until I had been several years a Baptist minister, and when I did read them, I was not interested in them. This freedom from creeds has left Baptists free to grow without jars and struggles. We used to be strict Calvinists, just like our Presbyterian brethren, and we, too, have grown away from rigid Calvinism, but we have had no creed to tinker with and therefore no conflict about it. . . .

Baptists have always insisted that they recognize the Bible alone as their sufficient authority for faith and practice. There are indeed, many Baptists who have tried to use the Bible just as other denominations use their creeds. They have turned the Bible into one huge creed, and practically that meant: "You must believe everything which we think the Bible means and says." They have tried to impose on us their little interpretation of the great Book as the creed to which all good Baptists must cleave.

But fortunately the Bible is totally different from a creed. A creed contains sharply defined and abstract theology; the Bible contains a record of concrete and glowing religious life. A creed addresses itself to the intellect; the Bible appeals to the whole soul and edifies it. A creed tells you what you must believe; the Bible tells you what holy men have believed. A creed is religious philosophy, the Bible is religious history. A creed gives the truth as it looked to one set of clever men at one particular stage of human history; the Bible gives the truth as it looked to a great number of God-filled men running through many hundreds of years. The strength of a creed is in its uniformity and its tight fit; the beauty of the Bible is in its marvelous variety and richness. A creed imposes a law and binds thought; the Bible imparts a spirit and awakens thought. . . .

These books are the deposit of the purest and freshest form of Christianity. It is the mountain brook before it has grown muddy in the plain by the inflow of other waters. The New Testament has been the conscience in the heart of the church, always warning and recalling it from its sinful wanderings. It is still calling us up higher today, beyond traditional Christianity to the religion of Christ. In the New Testament lies the power of perpetual reformation for the Church. Baptists, in tying to the New Testament, have hitched their chariot to a star, and they will have to keep moving [p. 9].

Rauschenbusch did not so much deny any of the basic doctrines as much as he simply deemphasized them. His interest was in the moral implications of Christian faith. Thus, Rauschenbusch apparently was not really a liberal in the classic theological sense. He cried out like one of the Old Testament prophets for social justice. But instead of building his call on "Thus saith the Lord" or on "The word of the Lord came unto me saying," as did the ancient prophets, Rauschenbusch built upon a "freedom" from creeds and a view of the Bible that sees it only as a record of "religious history." This anticreedalism seems to be a Baptist tradition, but in the past this attitude had never been used to open the door for doctrinal diversity. Yet that seems to be exactly what Rauschenbusch had in mind, for he viewed Scripture itself as a book of diverse religious experiences that Baptists were to expand in ever new and changing ways. This view is typically romantic and evolutionary, and thus it is clearly influenced by nineteenth-century thought. To see the actual results of this new attitude toward Scripture it is necessary to study someone who made the application more specifically in the doctrinal realm. Such a man was Shailer Matthews.

SHAILER MATTHEWS

Born in Portland, Maine, in 1863, Shailer Matthews became one of the better known Baptist scholars of his day. He attended Colby College and after his graduation was employed there as a faculty member from 1887 to 1894. His fame, however, came after he moved to the faculty of the Divinity School at the University of Chicago. He began by teaching New Testament and then taught theology until 1933. During those years he also served as the dean of the Divinity School.

Probably his most famous book is *The Social Gospel* (1910), but one of his clearest statements on Scripture itself is in *The Faith of Modernism* (1924).

Matthews did not understand the term "Modernism" to be an equivalent of liberalism. Modernists are evangelical Christians, he says, although not dogmatic religionists.

> The position of Protestant dogmatists is to all intents and purposes the same as that of Pius X. All over the world they are asking ministers and teachers to answer "Yes" or "No" to questionnaires concerning belief in the literal inerrancy of the Scripture; the deity and virgin birth of Jesus; the substitutionary atonement offered by Christ to God; the biblical miracles; the physical resurrection, the ascension, and the physical return of Jesus from heaven. The acceptance of all these supernatural elements, they hold, is essential to real Christianity; they are the "fundamentals" without which religion is not Christianity [p. 21].

The Modernist position is a direct outgrowth of the use of historical-critical methodology. Matthews was persuaded that this "modern" method was not motivated by theological bias but was the natural, necessary, and scientific way to study Scripture.

> But no sooner do men thus study the Bible than facts appear which make belief in its verbal inerrancy untenable. As facts they naturally must be accounted for. In consequence there has grown up a general view of the

Fig. 30. Shailer Matthews

From the Department of Special Collections, the University of Chicago Library, Chicago, Illinois.

Bible which is the basis of the Modernist position. It was never voted upon or formally adopted by any group of scholars. Like views commonly held in biology or any other science, it is the result of investigators working without collusion, sometimes in rivalry, but without dogmatic assumptions, seeking to find and organize facts by scientific methods. Now that their work in the critical field is largely done, we find general agreement as to how the Bible originated, how it was composed, where it was written, why it was written. Differences as to details exist but the world of undogmatic biblical scholarship is certainly as much at one as to these matters as are the various theologies. How complete is the result of this study can be seen from the fact that there is no serious attempt to refute its conclusions by its own methods. There is plenty of anti-creedal literature, plenty of denunciation of higher critics as enemies of the faith, plenty of attempts to enforce the conformity in views of doctrines declared to be the teaching of the Bible; but there is little appeal to method and facts. It could not be otherwise. One cannot use the methods of critical scholarship without adopting them. Once adopted they can be trusted to give trustworthy results. . . . It is this method which the Modernist endeavors to shape and use [pp. 38-39, 43].

Matthews recognized that the ultimate question was whether one had a right to use the methods of literary criticism to interpret the Bible. He concluded, however, that the critical method was unavoidable by responsible scholars, and, beyond that, that the critical method was the most helpful approach to the Bible. Only the dogmatist expects the Bible to be historically true at every point.

It is urged that if one portion of the Bible is folk-tale and so cannot be given full historical weight, we cannot be sure that all of the Bible is not the same sort. The answer is simple: The dogmatic mind cannot be sure. It does not recognize or correctly use the facts of the Bible.

But there are methods by which we can tell whether the Bible is history or not. Such methods require intellectual attention and training as truly as any other scientific procedure. The inability of the uninstructed to understand Christianity has always been asserted by dogmatic authority. What the Modernist is doing is, therefore, nothing new. The Christian church in its study of the Scriptures has never delivered itself into the hands of the unintelligent leader. The work of men like Clement of Alexandria, Chrysostom, Ambrose, Augustine, Bernard, Francis, Thomas Aquinas, the Schoolmen, Luther, Melancthon, Calvin and Wesley, that is to say, of the very men who have shaped Western Christianity, makes it plain that their treatment of the Scriptures is not farther from that of the believer in literal inerrancy than from that of the Modernist's. They all insisted that revelation must conform to realities of the universe and in their interpretation they took pains to show that such agreement existed with the universe as they knew it. If ordinary grammatical interpretation left them in any uncertainty, they promptly found an allegorical meaning in the Scriptures which satisfied the demands of what they regarded as truth. The Modernist rather than the champion of verbal inerrancy is a true successor of such fathers of orthodoxy. His regard for the Bible is just as sincere, his use of the Bible for building up the spiritual life is no farther removed from an assumption of inerrancy, his attempt to understand the experiences of God in the Bible are no less intellectual than theirs. And he knows how to separate between the permanent and the temporary in its pages [pp. 46-47].

For Matthews, the difference between the Modernist and the conservative theologian was not in the degree of loyalty to the Bible but in the method used for studying it. The critical method has different presuppositions from the ones traditionally assumed.

There is no static religion or standardized formula in the Bible. In that fact is one of the most significant of the Modernist points of view, viz., that the true attitude toward God and the true experience of his presence are possible and discernible in the midst of imperfect and even mistaken scientific and other views. The author of Genesis may declare that the sun and stars were created after the creation of the earth and plant life, a conception which our knowledge of astronomy shows is incorrect. But this error does not prevent our sharing in the author's faith that in the shaping of the universe, God was present. So, too, it is only something to be expected when we find in the religious experiences of men who lived before the siege of Troy conceptions of God which to our Christian morality seem unworthy. Such conceptions are, however, no bar to the discovery that with all the human infirmities attributed to Him, the Yahweh of the Book of Judges possessed qualities which had only to be expanded as men's experience expanded, to give the righteous monotheism of the prophets. Belief in the providence of God can be expressed in poetry, folktale and legend just as truly as in literal statement.

In consequence, the Modernist enjoys the spiritual ministry of the Bible quite undisturbed by objections which the believer in the inerrancy of the scriptures has either to answer or to denounce. Poetical statements as to the sun standing still, the story of Jonah, miracles like those of Elijah and Elisha and some of those of the New Testament, can be used at their full religious value. Whether they are sober history or not they are current ways of expressing belief in God's care for men. They are material for understanding the developing consciousness of God and a growing religion. They were contemporary ways of expressing religious faith. In them the Bible is recording trust in a good God whose law is righteous and whose love and power are coextensive. From such a trust we gain help as we seek to have a kindred faith in our day. We face our different tasks and problems in accordance with their trust in God. Our knowledge has grown, but we are still "sons of the faithful Abraham."

Thus, although the historical and critical study of the scripture does not begin with a doctrine of inspiration, Modernists believe in inspiration rather than inerrancy. But in the inspiration of men, not of words. Men were inspired because they inspire. In this Modernists are one with writers of the Bible themselves, for inspiration within the Bible is always regarded as the experience of the Spirit of God on the part of some individual [pp. 51-52].

Thus Matthews denies the very concept of biblical authority except in the matter of experience. Religious experience was recorded in Scripture and is produced by Scripture, but the words are not binding in their authority beyond that.

Undoubtedly Matthews was the "leading voice" of the Modernist movement until his death, in 1941. He developed and guided the so-called "Chicago School of Theology." He championed the cause of Modernism against American Fundamentalism. He spoke with clarity and simplicity. But more important for this study, he clearly indicated the direction of a growing segment of Baptist theology in the early twentieth century. It took, however, an even greater theologian and scholar to provide a carefully constructed theological base upon which to build the new "liberal" structure. Such a man was William Newton Clarke.

WILLIAM NEWTON CLARKE

When James E. Tull wrote his significant study entitled *Shapers of Baptist Thought,* he chose William Newton Clarke as the Baptist representative of theological liberalism. Born in Cazenovia, New York, in 1841, Clarke grew up in a Baptist home that taught him to love Christ and the Bible. He attended the Oneida Conference Seminary in his home town and then attended Madison University and Madison Theological Seminary (graduating in 1863). Beginning in May 1869 he pastored the First Baptist Church of Newton Center, Massachusetts, for eleven years. Next he pastored in Montreal at the Olivet Baptist Church. Then in 1883 he became the Professor of New Testament Interpretation at the Baptist Theological School in Toronto. Four years later he went back into the pastorate in Hamilton, New York, and later began teaching theology at Colgate University. He resigned his professorship in 1908. Clarke's death was rather sudden, apparently caused by a fall in his winter home in De Laud, Florida (January 1912).

Widely known as a Baptist scholar, Clarke first published *An Outline of Christian Theology* in 1894. The book went through twenty editions by 1914 and became the most widely used textbook among liberal Baptists. In 1905 Clarke delivered the Nathaniel William Taylor Lectures at the Yale Divinity School on *The Use of the Scriptures in Theology.* The four-

Fig. 31. WILLIAM NEWTON CLARKE

From the frontispiece of his biography, published by Charles Scribner's Sons, New York, 1916.

teenth edition of his *Outline* was also printed in 1905. These two sources provide a clear picture of the liberal tendencies that had entered into Baptist life by this first decade of the twentieth century.

Clarke begins his *Outline* by distinguishing between religion and theology. "Religion is the reality of which theology is the study," he says (p. 1). Religion is a natural part of man and is thus universal among men. Christianity is a religion just as is Hinduism or Islam, but it has a unique fullness of truth and power.

> The great religions of the world are not false, in the sense of being the fruit of imposture, or of intending to deceive men. . . . All the great religions contain some truth concerning religion. But the various religions of the world have not attained to truth, that is, to accordance with reality, in their conceptions of God and the relations of men to him, and in this fundamental sense they are not true religions [p. 3].

Christianity, says Clarke, does claim to be a true religion. Theology is the science of religion. It does not treat matters that are not religious. The Christian conception of God is derived from a self-revelation of God that culminated in Jesus Christ. Christian theology is mainly concerned with presenting Christian doctrine in the light of its scriptural and historical development.

> Among the many views that may be taken of God and man, good and evil, duty, life, and destiny, there is a Christian view, obtained mainly by means of Christ; and Christian theology aims to present that view in systematic order and proportion. Its great themes are, God as Christ has made him known, and man, sin, salvation, duty, life, and destiny, in the light of Christ's revelation [p. 6].

Were one to suppose that Clarke here is attempting to distinguish between a revelation of God in Christ and a revelation of God in Scripture, one would suppose correctly. Revelation, for Clarke, is "not primarily the giving of information on the various themes of religion: the chief and central theme of revelation is God himself, and revelation is self-expression" (p. 9).

To study the Old Testament correctly, according to Clarke, is to read it as the gradual discovery of God on the part of men. The historical records are trustworthy, and thus one may come to see that Christ stood in a unique relationship to God. But Christ is not the only revelation of God. The universe (including man and nature) is also revelation. "Theology may find material for its use in the constitution, history, and religious experience of man, and in the creation of God as it is known through science and interpreted by philosophy" (p. 11). Christian revelation, however, is primarily through Christ.

Clarke was careful to emphasize the manner in which he understood Christian revelation to have come to man.

> It was not made in written history, or in writing at all, or primarily in speech, but in act and fact,—by doing. Not in writing, but in living history, in actual life, God showed himself to men. . . . "Thus saith the Lord" was one form of revelation; but "Thus hath the Lord done" was the form in which the richest expression of God was made [p. 13].

Of course, Clarke at this point is saying only that the events precede the recording of the events. What God did in the days of Moses was God's revelation to the Israelites, and those actions were revelation before they were recorded in the book of Exodus. But how has that revelation been preserved? Clarke answers that it has been preserved in the "religious life that sprang from" the revelation. Christ revealed God. That revelation was preserved in the lives of the disciples. "For years it was preserved in life alone, without aid from writings" (p. 17). Christian experience has always been the great preserver of Christian revelation, says Clarke.

> This experience is the actual life of Christianity itself; in it Christianity lives and has its being. The Bible itself is an expression of experience. . . . This experience . . . would have preserved Christ's gift to man if there had been no Bible [p. 18].

> Experience cannot be set aside as mediator between theology and its chief source, the Christian revelation [p. 19].

In fact, Clarke argues that Christianity is not a book-religion. Scripture is its servant, not its source. Revelation is the basis of the Scriptures. God revealed Himself in life, and Scripture tells us of that life. Critical inquiry has full rights when it comes to the questions of date and authorship of the various books.

Concerning the doctrine of inspiration, Clarke contends that there is no reason why theologians should use the word "inspiration" to refer to a quality of the Bible as a whole. The word is ambiguous and should no longer be used (pp. 37-38). Christianity is not affected one way or the other by the degree of veracity and correctness of the human documents that make up the scriptural record.

> We have no right to start with the assumption that Scriptures must be inspired after such or such a manner. . . . The Bible is inspired as it is inspired, not as we may think it should be [pp. 39-40].

> Primarily men are inspired not writings. . . . It is certain that divine influence did not enter the Scriptures by dictation to the writers. . . . Nor does any theory of verbal inspiration holding that God gave the writers the very words accord with the facts. It would be of no permanent use

for him to give the very words unless he afterward took care of them in his Providence. But the original manuscripts have been allowed to disappear, the text has been subject to the fortunes that befall written documents in general, and our present Scriptures differ (we know not just how widely) from the original Scriptures. For us, therefore, there are no verbally inspired Scriptures, and we have no evidence that there ever were any. Direct or virtual dictation of these writings is at once unprovable in history and impossible in fact [p. 40].

For Clarke, inspiration was that divine influence upon men that exalted them, quickened their ability, stimulated their spiritual power. "Inspiration inspires,—that is, it spiritualizes, exalts, suggests, empowers; it gives a man's powers to the divine Spirit for all high uses" (p. 41). This "high quality belongs to different parts of the Bible in different degrees" (p. 43). "The inspiration of the Bible does not prove its excellence, but its excellence proves its inspiration" (p. 44.).

> The Spirit who spake by the prophets and apostles dwells with the church to guide it into truth. We cannot write an eighth chapter of Romans, it is true; but we do not see the greatness of the chapter until we see it as something that we could equal if we had enough of the divine life that Christ imparts. The wonder of the New Testament is that the Spirit of God could bring it forth, in all its richness, from the Christian life of men. And if that Spirit should someday bring forth something more that was equal to the New Testament, all Christians ought to rejoice and be thankful [pp. 44-45].

Clarke believed that the long practice of using Scripture as the final and authoritative source for theology had brought about a whole group of injurious consequences. In *The Use of the Scriptures* he clearly and unambiguously denied that the Bible taught infallible truth even about God.

> If we are to receive our Scriptures as absolutely authoritative, we have first to assent to the ground on which their authority rests. The doctrine of an equal and final authority stands, historically, upon the foundation of an equal and infallible inspiration. On no other foundation has it ever been supposed to stand. Not because these writers had authority of their own, not because they knew the truth so perfectly as to be entitled to think for us, has the Bible been regarded as authoritative in theology, but solely because the eternal Spirit gave to these writers truth and thought and words, and thus imparted his own infallibility and authority to what they wrote. On no other foundation could such an authority stand. But when we open our Bible to-day we open a book that is undergoing examination on the inductive method. Our generation is learning to read the Bible in the historical light, and let the book itself show what it is. We seek to discover how these utterances came to be made, and what they meant to the men who made them. The result is that the better we know the Bible

in this manner, the less does it match the theory of an inspiration that imparts infallibility to all its statements, or even to all its utterances in the field of religion. There is no claim of such inspiration, and there is no proof of it. The high doctrine proves untenable, and consequently it is passing out of sight. Those who hold it modify it so as really to destroy it,—for such a doctrine is intolerant of modifications, since it is nothing if not perfect. The high qualities of the Bible are of another kind, and the doctrine of an inspiration that imparts infallibility and direct divine authority to the entire body of the Scriptures is no more.

But out of the history of the matter it has come to pass that theology is burdened in the name of reverence for God with the weight of an untenable doctrine. To this day Christian theology is supposed to be grounded in the doctrine of an infallible inspiration. The outside world may be excused for understanding it thus, in view of the long-asserted claim of theology itself: but now the outside world has heard on good evidence that a sound theology cannot be built on such a foundation, since the doctrine is not true. Nevertheless on that foundation a large part of the Christian world continues insisting that theology must be built. Christianity itself, they affirm, stands or falls with infallible inspiration. I once knew a minister of high genius who said to me, "If I had to give up verbal inspiration, I should have to give up Christ." One who had ever heard him pray knew better, for he had a spiritual foundation deeper and better than his theory; but except upon the most rigid theory of inspiration he supposed a Christian theology, and even a Christian faith, to be impossible. That belief is still abroad in power, and the hurtful reputation of it is abroad also. If we propose a Christian theology we shall be expected by a multitude of outsiders to ground it in infallible inspiration, on which they know that we cannot build a structure that will stand; and at the same time we shall be required by a multitude of Christians to ground it in the same, where we know that we cannot build safely. Not only so, but we shall be expected to prove the doctrine. Thus theology is burdened with a task that cannot be performed, and the ill name of a theory that cannot be defended, and unbelievers are encouraged in their impression that a valid Christian theology is impossible.

By the doctrine of a finally authoritative book another burden has been placed upon theology, of which the weight has not yet ceased to be felt, although it is beginning to pass away. That burden is the task of so interpreting the Bible that it shall agree with itself. Of course an authoritative book will agree with itself. Its statements, probably everywhere and certainly in the field of religion, will be free from contradictions. If they seem to differ, it must be assumed to be no more than seeming, and interpretation must be relied upon to reconcile the differences. This is a long-established view of the Bible. How many books have been written on biblical difficulties, to vindicate the Bible as divine by showing that it nowhere contradicts itself,—no, not even as to details of history or incidental statements of fact! Especially on the matters that enter into theology must the Bible speak in unison. Its voice is the voice of God, and its utterance must be one; and the interpreter must find the unity which certainly must be there. This reasoning is good. Absolute authority must be accompanied by unity of teaching. But what a work to lay upon an interpreter or a theologian,—to interpret so large and various a book as the Bible into unanimity! It is a very large undertaking. Perhaps it cannot be done by fair means, and yet it must be done. Any failure, leaving a discrepancy unreconciled, can only stand as a difficulty unremoved where difficulties may be fatal, a rock on which a whole system of theology may go to ruin. And as to the process itself: is it not a strange and anomalous thing that a theologian should be set to harmonize his authoritative material? Does it seem likely that a divine standard will need interpreting into unity? And is it really a high process, consistent with true reverence for a divine standard, to be interpreting it with the preconceived intention of bringing its statements into agreement? We do not so elsewhere. Honest interpretation of other writings they may say: indeed, honest interpretation may also be said to consist in doing this. But theology has long been expected to interpret its Scriptures into unanimity, and even into assertion of a scheme of thought accepted in advance as representative of their teachings. The process is not a high one, and theology stands at a serious moral disadvantage because of this legacy from the doctrine of an authoritative Bible. Somehow we must clear ourselves from this complication, and use our Scriptures for what they are and what they mean, free from the morally damaging assumption that they must always agree with themselves [pp. 24-29].

Undoubtedly Clarke remained somewhat conservative in many of his own personal doctrinal views. As a teacher his sweet temper and his apparent, deep, emotional commitment to Christian faith endeared him to most students. Harry Emerson Fosdick was one of his ablest students who went on to lead the liberal causes among Baptists. As Tull writes:

An estimate of Clarke's influence among the Baptists must take account of the fact that he spent his whole public career as a pastor of Baptist churches and as a teacher in Baptist institutions. The theological convictions which have been elaborated in the foregoing pages of this chapter were the convictions which Clarke taught to Baptist students and which he preached in Baptist pulpits, for a whole generation. These views were also widely disseminated among Baptists, as well as among others, through his books. He became a theological mentor to a host of Baptist ministers, as well as to many thoughtful laymen [*Shapers*, p. 179].

HARRY EMERSON FOSDICK

Harry Emerson Fosdick was born on May 24, 1878, in Buffalo, New York. One of his great-grandfathers is remembered as a Baptist preacher who was defrocked because he refused to believe in hell. Fosdick wrote that, among other things, the "hell fire preaching" that he heard as a child deeply disturbed him as well.

He attended Colgate University and then in 1900 entered Colgate Seminary. One year later he moved to Union Theological Seminary and Columbia University in New York. Doubts about biblical infallibility plagued him in those days. Finally he read Andrew D. White's *History of the Warfare of Science with Theology in Christendom,* and that settled the matter for him. He no longer simply doubted, he positively opposed any concept of biblical inerrancy. He has been quoted as saying that liberal theology was the only thing that kept him within the Christian faith at all. Had it not been for William Newton Clarke's influence, Fosdick may have never spent his life in Christian ministry (*Twenty Centuries,* pp. 5-6).

Though he suffered a severe nervous collapse while he was in seminary, he did serve as an associate minister of the Madison Avenue Baptist Church in 1903. In 1908 he began to teach at Union. He held several pastorates while serving as a professor, but he finally retired in 1946.

In 1925 Fosdick became pastor of the Park Avenue Baptist Church while continuing to teach at Union. John D. Rockefeller built the famous Riverside Church to be Fosdick's pulpit and the transition took place in 1926. There is no doubt that Fosdick became one of the most popular preachers the modern world has ever known. More than fifteen thousand people attended his memorial service in 1969.

As a popularizer of evangelical liberalism and biblical criticism, his influence on American preaching style has been enormous. He used a "problem-centered" homiletical approach that was psychologically oriented. In 1943 he published one of his best known works, *On Being a Real Person.* His autobiography, *The Living of These Days,* was published in 1956.

When Fosdick wrote *The Modern Use of the Bible* (1924) he was a professor of practical theology at Union Theological Seminary in New York. He noted in the preface:

> The position represented in this book will of course be distasteful to those bound by a theory of literal inerrancy in their approach to the Bible. I am hoping, however, that many not so bound but anxious, it may be, over the possible effects of modern scholarship, may be led to see how consonant with a reverent estimate of the Book and an inspiring use of it the new views are.

Fosdick was fully convinced that scientific study had finally made the Bible truly intelligible. "For the first time in the history of the church," he writes, "we of this generation are able to arrange the writings of the Bible in approximately chronological order" (p. 6).

Fig. 32. HARRY EMERSON FOSDICK

Property of *New York Times*. From picture on file in Fleming Library, Southwestern Baptist Theological Seminary, Fort Worth, Texas.

From the purely scientific point of view this is an absorbingly interesting matter, but even more from the standpoint of practical results its importance is difficult to exaggerate. It means that we can trace the great ideas of Scripture in their development from their simple and elementary forms, when they first appear in the earliest writings, until they came to their full maturity in the latest books. Indeed, the general soundness of the critical results is tested by this fact that as one moves up from the earlier writings toward the later he can observe the development of any idea he chooses to select, such as God, man, duty, sin, worship. Plainly we are dealing with ideas that enlarge their scope, deepen their meaning, are played upon by changing circumstance and maturing thought, so that from its lowliest beginning in the earliest writings of the Hebrews any religious or ethical idea of the Bible can now be traced, traveling an often uneven but ascending roadway to its climax in the teaching of Jesus.

That this involves a new approach to the Bible is plain. To be sure, our fathers were not blind to the fact that the New Testament overtops, fulfills, and in part supersedes the Old. They had the Sermon on the Mount and the opening verses of the Epistle to the Hebrews to assure them of that. But our fathers never possessed such concrete and detailed illustration of that idea as we have now. We shall have occasion later to applaud the school of interpretation made notable by Theodore of Mopsuestia and to appreciate great exegetes like Calvin, but even such interpreters never dreamed of arranging the documents of the Bible in chronological order and then tracing through them the development of those faiths and ethical ideals that come to their flower in the New Testament. Rather, they lacked both the historical apparatus that could have made this possible and the idea of development which interprets everything in terms of its early origin and gradual growth. In consequence, the older interpreters of the Bible consistently tended to read the meanings of the New Testament back into the Old, to level up the Old Testament toward the New, until there was nothing in the New Testament which could not by direct statement, by type, symbol, or allegory, be found in the Old [pp. 7-9].

Fosdick did not mean that one could get no benefit from studying these great expositors of the past, but he did think that they had missed the most basic historical insights into the nature of Scripture.

Fortunately for us, spiritual efficiency in the use of the Bible is not entirely dependent upon correctness of exegesis. These older interpreters who used the Book in ways now impossible for us did not on that account fail to find there the sustenance and inspiration which we may miss if we trust too much to our keener instruments and too little to spiritual insight. Just as men raised life-sustaining crops from the earth's soil long before they analyzed the earth's strata, so they got from Scripture the bread of life even if the chronological arrangement of the documents was yet undreamed. Nevertheless, it is of obvious importance that a new approach to the Bible has been forced upon us. No longer can we think of the Book as on a level, no longer read its maturer messages back into its earlier sources. We know now that every idea in the Bible started from primitive and childlike origins and, with however many setbacks and delays, grew in scope and height toward the culmination in Christ's Gospel [p. 11].

It is interesting to trace Fosdick's own theological development. He was obviously influenced by Clarke, but it is especially provocative to note that he recognized the first introduction of this modern critical methodology in Baptist life to have been the work of C. H. Toy.

> The first book of which I know that endeavored to take this general idea and fill in its outline with definite content by actually tracing through the Scripture the development of significant ideas was written by Professor Toy of Harvard, and was published thirty-four years ago. Since then the material has grown richer year by year [p. 12].

Probably no one has expressed the results of the critical method in a more positive light than has Fosdick. The evolutionary assumptions are obvious, but Fosdick makes it sound as if the evolutionary approach is in fact "God's best" for true believers. The rather lengthy quotation that follows is a good example not only of Fosdick's attitude toward the interpretation of Scripture but also of why Fosdick became so popular as a preacher.

> To start with God conceived like a man who walks in a garden in the cool of the day, or as one who comes down from the sky to confuse man's speech lest they should build their tower so high as to reach his home; to know the road that leads out from that beginning until in the New Testament God revealed in Christ is the spiritual Presence in whom we live, and move, and have our being, whose name is love, and whose temples are human hearts; and to be able in any book or passage to locate oneself with reference to this progressive revelation of the meaning of God—that is to know the Bible.
>
> To start with man whose only soul is his physical breath and who, lacking alike separate rights here and immortality hereafter, is identified with his body and lost in his social group; to see the individual shaken loose from the mass and lifted up into royal worthfulness, and within the individual the spiritual distinguished from the physical until in the New Testament man is spirit, inwardly renewed though the outward man perish; to know the details of the journey which men made from that starting point to that conclusion, with all its rough acclivities, its devious wanderings, its glorious vistas, its doubts and its victory—that is to know the Bible.
>
> To start with the demands of God on man interpreted in terms of tribal custom, with ethics and rubric jumbled together so that God equally hates David's sin with Bathsheba and David's taking of a census, or re-

quires alike freedom from murder and the refusal to seethe a kid in its mother's milk; to see the prophetic task so magnificently performed by which righteousness was made central in the character of God and in his requirements of mankind, until in the Gospel God's will, freed from clinging ceremonialism, is completely moralized and men to please him must be inwardly right in thought and outwardly merciful in life; and at any point in this development to know the men whose insight brought new light, and the books and passages which represent the crucial hours of choice—that is to know the Bible.

To start with man's suffering as a curse from God, with all trouble regarded as divine punishment, so that wherever there was misery at all there was the double misery of interpreting it as a sign of God's disfavor; to see wiser, truer ideas of God surely but hardly dislodging more ancient thoughts as the book of Job argued against the old theology, or Isaiah's 53rd chapter sounded a new note in the interpretation of suffering; to see suffering gradually redeemed from its old interpretation until, while some of it is still punishment, more of it is welcomed as spiritual discipline, and a part of it is lifted up into the glory of vicarious sacrifice; to see the process crowned in the Cross of Christ, where suffering becomes voluntary sacrifice as the means by which alone God can save the world; and at any point in this whole development to know the road by which the truth had traveled hitherto and where it is going next—that is to know the Bible.

From our youth up many of us have been familiar with the phrase "progressive revelation." It is a good phrase. But now the means are in our hands to fill it with rich, substantial content. Not only can we believe that the Bible does represent a progressive revelation, but we can clearly and in detail watch it progress. We can know where the Scripture's major ideas started; we can trace the routes they took; we can watch them in periods of rapid traveling and in days when the going was difficult and slow. We can enter into their defeats, their hair-breadth escapes, and costly victories; and we can see the way the Gospel of Jesus carried them up to a great height "not to destroy, but to fulfil."

That is the new approach to the Bible [pp. 22-24].

Fosdick found that this new approach relieved him of the necessity of seeking to harmonize the Bible with itself. One does not need "to resolve its conflicts and contradictions" (p. 24). This new approach has no need for harmonizing ethical conceptions in the Old Testament with the Sermon on the Mount. Nor should the modern approach ever lead one to apologize for the immature stages of the Bible.

Now, the older Hebrew and Christian interpreters, lacking the modern historic point of view and scientific apparatus, had one resource in their difficulties. They allegorized away the things they did not like. They read out the literal sense and read in the sense they wished to find. They ascribed to ancient writers a mystical knowledge of all later learning and made the early stories of a childlike age the parables and symbols of the Greek philosophy or of Christian theology. Such a resource is no longer possible to us. We know that the early writings of the Bible meant what they said. But we do not need to apologize for their crudities. They are early stages in a great development. Their lack is the lack of immaturity, not of perversion. They are as acorns to the oak, fountains to the river, and as such they require no defending as though they were impertinences in the revelation of God. They are the infancy of a progressive unfolding of the divine character and purpose, and they are to be judged, as all things are to be judged, by what they came to in the end. And what they came to in the end was Christ and his Gospel [p. 28].

The real problem, says Fosdick, is much deeper than just recognizing that revelation is progressive. In fact some Fundamentalists could affirm a progressive (though not an evolutionary) development of theological ideas. No, the real problem was the supernaturalistic world view of Scripture.

When one moves back to the Scripture with a mind accustomed to work in modern ways, he finds himself in a strange world. The people who walk through its pages often do not speak his language, nor use his intellectual viewpoints, nor explain occurrences by his categories. Knowing modern astronomy he turns to the Bible to find the sun and moon standing still or the shadow retreating on Ahaz' dial. Knowing modern biology he hears that when Elisha had been so long dead that only his bones were left, another dead body, thrown into the cave where he was buried, touched his skeleton and sprang to life again, or that after our Lord's resurrection many of the saints long deceased arose and appeared in Jerusalem. Knowing modern physics he turns to the Bible and reads that light was created three days before the sun and that an axe-head floated when Elisha threw a stick into the water. Knowing modern medicine he finds in the Scripture many familiar ailments, epilepsy, deafness, dumbness, blindness, insanity, ascribed to the visitation of demons. Knowing that the sky is blue because of the infinite number of dust-particles that catch and break up the light, he finds himself in the Bible living under a solid "firmament" "strong as a molten mirror," or a "paved work of sapphire stone" from which a fiery chariot came down to snatch a living man by literal levitation from the flat earth to his heavenly reward.

Here is the perplexity which more than any other afflicts the minds of educated men. They honor the Bible. They know that in it are the springs of the noblest elements in our civilization. They stand uncovered before Jesus Christ. But they are honestly bothered by many things in Scripture. They do not know what to make of them. They find it hard to use one set of mental presuppositions and categories in every other realm of life and another set in religion [pp. 34-35].

Fosdick lived in a "new world" that had outgrown these primitive beliefs. Modern man could not read the Bible and accept it as an ancient man would. Modern man simply knows better than to believe in these outdated scientific views. Apparently Fosdick assumed that ancient man had never understood the distinction between popular and technical language. Fosdick considered all biblical descriptions of nature to be culturally bound, literal cosmological affirmations rather than culturally transcendent phenomenological descriptions.

> On the one side is the Semitic world-view with its flat earth surrounded by the sea, and the solid firmament a little way above; on the other our modern universe of immeasurable distances. On the one side is a world where God's providence is specially revealed in miracle; on the other our world of law where God is seen, not in the irregular, but in the regular. On the one side we find a world thronged with demons who cause sickness, drive men mad, inspire sin, and enter into a universal conspiracy to overthrow God; on the other a world where the fear of demons is a superstition. On the one side are apocalyptic hopes where expectations of God's triumph center in a supernatural invasion of the world; on the other are our social hopes that foresee a prolonged fight ahead, with many a catastrophe, and many a long, hard pull. In the Bible immortality is associated with the resurrection of the body; among us immortality is conceived as escape from the body. There the person of our Lord is interpreted in terms of the Jewish Messiahship or of Alexandrian Platonism; here are philosophical methods and structural ideas that have no kinship with apocalypses or with Philo. There is an ethic developed in a theocracy under autocratic governments; here an ethic inevitably shaped by the new democracy and the new economic order.
>
> That is the problem which the modern man faces with his Bible, and to say that it is serious is to speak mildly [pp. 44-45].

Difficulties in the Bible, says Fosdick, have in the past been handled in a very simple way. Things which seemed offensive or irrelevant or scientifically wrong were just allegorized. But Jesus never resorted to allegory, Fosdick says; He simply opposed the binding literalism of the oral tradition and gave the people a new, free, and spiritual exposition of Scripture. According to Fosdick, Jesus recognized that there were "outgrown elements" in the Bible.

> Let us frankly take our stand with the Master on this basic matter! Of course there are outgrown elements in Scripture. How could it be otherwise in a changing world? [p. 94].

> Here, then, is the first essential of intelligent Biblical preaching in our day: a man must be able to recognize the abiding messages of the Book, and sometimes he must recognize them in a transient setting. No man will

ever do this well if he does not divest himself of vanity and pride and clothe himself with humility as with a garment. He must see that many of our ways of thinking are very new; that they, too, are transient, and that many of them will soon be as outmoded as our forefathers' categories are. He must see that just because our ways of thinking are new, the garnered riches of the world's thought have been stored up for us in other forms of thought than ours and in other ways of speaking. If he sees this clearly he will see also what a pitiable provincial life a man must live whose appreciations are shut up to that truth only which is expressed in modern terms [p. 95].

Fosdick closes his book with a chapter on Jesus as the Son of God. It is here that the full impact of his theology is seen.

Let us say it abruptly: *It is not so much the humanity of Jesus that makes him imitable as it is his divinity.* If he be only a good man, he is an isolated phenomenon, like Shakespeare or Napoleon in other realms. How can we, pulling on our own bootstraps, set out to lift ourselves by imitation to the likeness of such? But if Jesus is divine and if divinity hedges us all about like the vital forces which in winter wait underneath the frozen ground until the spring comes, that is a gospel! Then the incarnation in Christ is the prophecy and hope of God's indwelling in every one of us. . . . He is unique. . . . Yet the God who was in Jesus is the same God who is in us. You cannot have one God and two kinds of divinity. While like drops of water we are very small beside his sea, yet it was one of the supreme days in man's spiritual history when the New Testament started men singing that they were "children of God: and if children, then heirs; heirs of God, and joint-heirs with Christ" [pp. 270-72].

Let me bear a personal testimony as my closing word. From naive acceptance of the Bible as of equal credibility in all its parts because mechanically inerrant, I passed years ago to the shocking conviction that such traditional bibliolatry is false in fact and perilous in result. I saw with growing clearness that the Bible must be allowed to say in terms of the generations when its books were written what its words in their historic sense actually meant, and I saw that often this historic sense was not modern sense at all and never could be. There, like others, I have stood bewildered at the new and unaccustomed aspect of the Book. But that valley of confusion soon was passed. I saw that the new methods of study were giving far more than they were taking away. They have restored to us the historic Christ. They have led us to abiding, reproducible experiences of the soul revealed through him. They have given us his imperishable Gospel freed from its entanglements, the Shekinah distinguished from the shrine, to be preached with a liberty, a reasonableness, and immediate application to our own age such as no generation of preachers in the church's history ever had the privilege of knowing before. Have no fear of the new truth! Let us fear only our own lack of wisdom, insight, cour-

Fig. 33. J. J. Reeve
From *Baptist Standard* (Dallas, Texas) June 3, 1904, p. 15.

age, and spiritual power in using it for the redemption of the souls and societies of men [p. 273].

JAMES JOSIAH REEVE

The so-called Fundamentalist reaction to the growing influence of liberal theology among Northern Baptists and among several Protestant denominations presented a united front about 1910 with the publication of *The Fundamentals: A Testimony to the Truth* in twelve volumes. Actually these volumes were made up of a series of short essays, each one treating one of the basic doctrines of conservative biblical theology or treating some related topic. The publication was financed by two Christian laymen, and these volumes were sent free to three hundred thousand preachers, missionaries, Sunday school leaders, and others throughout the English-speaking world. Several Southern Baptists contributed to the series, including E. Y. Mullins, who wrote on the apologetic value of Christian experience. Two professors at Southwestern Baptist Theological Seminary in Fort Worth, Texas, also wrote for *The Fundamentals.* James Josiah Reeve testified to "My Personal Experience with the Higher Criticism" and C. B. Williams added an essay on "Paul's Testimony to the Doctrine of Sin."

J. J. Reeve had graduated from Southern Baptist Theological Seminary in Louisville, Kentucky, in 1905. His doctoral dissertation was *Calvinism: A Brief Historical Sketch and Estimate.* He began teaching at the Kansas City Theological Seminary, but in June 1908 he was invited to join the first faculty of the new Southwestern Baptist Theological Seminary in Fort Worth, Texas. B. H. Carroll was the founder and first president.

From 1909 to 1913 he served as the Professor of Hebrew, Cognate Languages, and Biblical Theology of the Old Testament. During those years he taught a special graduate level course called "Pentateuchal Criticism." For one of his textbooks he used S. R. Driver's *Introduction to the Literature of the Old Testament,* a standard presentation of the higher critical theories, and he used James Orr's *The Problem of the Old Testament* as his basic source for an alternative to Driver. Then through the years his third textbook varied from Goodspeed's *Introduction to the American Commentary on Genesis* to Wiener's *Essays in Pentateuchal Criticism.*

The Baptist Standard, the Texas Baptist newspaper, published a special seminary issue dated June 3, 1909. In that issue Reeve published an article on the value for a preacher of the study of the biblical languages. Among other things, he wrote:

> A knowledge of Greek and Hebrew is valuable to the modern preacher to help fortify him against error. Say what we will there are many "isms" in the land that would not be if our ministers knew their Bibles better. Besides this the rationalistic movement of the Higher Criticism is slowly

but surely filtering into the pulpit and pews of our Baptist ranks. These movements are the greatest menace of the church today [p. 15].

Reeve believed that the real heart of the issue concerned the methodology employed by modern critical scholarship within the theological world. In his essay in *The Fundamentals* he says:

It is their philosophy or world-view that is responsible for all their speculations and theories. Their mental attitude towards the world and its phenomena is the same as their attitude toward the Bible and the religion therein revealed. These presuppositions appealed to me very strongly [p. 348].

Reeve describes his own pilgrimage at this point. He had studied the modern theories and had been greatly impressed by them. At first he thought that the new method was surely the true method.

The results at which they had arrived seemed inevitable. But upon closer thinking I saw that the whole movement with its conclusions was the result of the adoption of the hypothesis of evolution. . . . That this theory of evolution underlies and is the inspiration of the Higher Criticism goes without saying or not, as we see fit, but the whole question is, what kind of evolution is it that has given rise to this criticism [p. 349].

On examining the evolution of the leaders of the Critical School I found that it was of a naturalistic or practically deistic kind. All natural and mental phenomena are in a closed system of cause and effect, and the hypothesis applies universally, to religion and revelation, as well as to mechanisms.

This type of evolution may not be accepted by all adherents of the Critical School, but it is substantially the view of the leaders, Reuss, Graf, Vatke, Kuenen and Wellhausen. To them all nature and history are a product of forces within and in process of development. There has not been and could not be any direct action of God upon man, there could be no break in the chain of cause and effect, of antecedent and consequent. Hence there can be no miracle or anything of what is known as the supernatural [p. 350].

For Reeve, the Bible makes obvious claims to be a divine revelation. It claims to be a supernaturally produced record of God's miraculous activity in human history.

Are the writers of the Bible correct, or are the critics? It is impossible that both should be right.

Reasoning thus, it became perfectly clear to me that the presuppositions and beliefs of the Bible writers and of the critics were absolutely contradictory. To maintain that the modern view is a development and advance upon the Biblical view is absurd. No presupposition can develop a presupposition which contradicts and nullifies it. To say the critical position and the Biblical position, or the traditional evangelical view which is the same as the Biblical, are reconcilable, is the most fatuous folly and delusion. Kuenen and others have recognized this contradiction and have acknowledged it, not hesitating to set aside the Biblical view. Many of their disciples have failed to see as clearly as their masters. They think the two can be combined. I was of the same opinion myself, but further reflection showed this to be an impossibility. I thought it possible to accept the results of the Higher Criticism without accepting its presuppositions. This is saying that one can accept as valid and true the results of a process and at the same time deny the validity of the process itself. But does not this involve an inner contradiction and absurdity? If I accept the results of the Kuenen-Wellhausen hypothesis as correct, then I accept as correct the methods and processes which led to these results, and if I accept these methods, I also accept the presuppositions which give rise to these methods. If the "assured results" of which the critics are so fond of boasting are true, then the naturalistic evolution hypothesis which produced these results is correct. Then it is impossible to accept the miraculous or supernatural, the Bible as the authoritative record of supernatural revelation is completely upset and its claims regarding itself are false and misleading. I can see no way of escaping these conclusions. There is no possible middle ground as I once fondly imagined there was. Thus I was compelled to conclude that although there is some truth in the evolutionary view of the world, yet as an explanation of history and revelation it is utterly inadequate, so inadequate as to be erroneous and false. A worldview must be broad enough to admit of all the facts of history and experience. Even then it is only a human point of view and necessarily imperfect. Will any one dare to say that the evolutionary hypothesis is divine? Then we would have a Bible and a philosophy both claiming to be divine and absolutely contradicting each other. To attempt to eliminate the miraculous and supernatural from the Bible and accept the remainder as divine is impossible, for they are all one and inextricably woven together. In either case the Book is robbed of its claims to authority [pp. 351-52].

There is no doubt that the historical-critical method is persuasive. It is a consistent application of the evolutionary theories that have captured the scientific world. Yet the value of this careful historical analysis is destroyed by the philosophical attitudes of the theologians who use this new methodology.

At first I was enthusiastic over the method. Now at last we have the correct method that will in time solve all difficulties. Let it be readily granted that the historical method has settled many difficulties and will continue to do so, yet the whole question lies in the attitude of mind a man brings to the task. Among the critics their hypothesis is absolute and dominates every attempt to understand the record, shapes every conclusion, arranges and rearranges the facts in its own order, discards what does not fit or reshapes to fit. The critics may deny this but their treatment of the Old Testament is too well known to need any proof of it. The use of the Redactor is a case in point. This purely imaginary being, unhistorical and unscientific, is brought into requisition at almost every difficulty. It is acknowledged that at times he acts in a manner wholly inexplicable. To assume such a person interpolating names of God, changing names and making explanations to suit the purposes of their hypothesis and imagination is the very negation of science, notwithstanding their boast of a scientific method. Their minds seem to be in abject slavery to their theory. No reason is more impervious to facts than one preoccupied with a theory which does not agree with these facts. Their mental attitude being biased and partial, their methods are partial and the results very onesided and untrustworthy. They give more credence to the guesses of some so-called scholar, a clay tablet, a heathen king's boast, or a rude drawing in stone, than to the Scripture record. They feel instinctively that to accept the Bible statements would be the ruin of their hypothesis, and what they call their hard-won historical method. In this their instinct is true. The Bible and their hypothesis are irreconcilable. As their theory must not be interfered with, since it is identical with the truth itself, the Bible must stand aside in the interests of truth.

For this reason they deny all historicity to Genesis 1-11, the stories of Creation, the Fall, the Flood, etc. No theory of naturalistic evolution can possibly admit the truth of these chapters [pp. 354-55].

By its arbitrary methods, Modern Criticism does wholesale violence to the record of the discovery of the Law Book as recorded in 1 Kings 22:8-20. It denies any real discovery, distinctly implies fraud upon the part of the writers, assumes a far too easy deception of the king, the prophetess, the king's counsellors, Jeremiah and the people. It implies a marvelous success in perpetrating this forged document on the people. The writers did evil that good might come, and God seems to have been behind it all and endorsed it. Such a transaction is utterly incredible. . . . According to the critics also, Ezra perpetrated a tremendous fraud when he palmed off his completed Code as of Mosaic origin. That the people should accept it as genuinely Mosaic, although it increased their burdens and contradicted many laws previously known as Mosaic, is incredible. That such a people at such a time and under such circumstances could be so easily imposed upon and deceived, and that such a man as Ezra could perform such a colossal fraud and have it all succeed so well, seems inconceivable except by a person whose moral consciousness is dulled or benumbed by some philosophical theory. According to the critics, the authors of Deuteronomy and the Levitical Code not only produced such intensely religious books and laws, but were at the same time deliberate inventors and falsifiers of history as well as deceivers of the people [pp. 357-58].

Thus the real question becomes one of the authority, viz.: shall the scientific hypothesis be supreme in my thinking, or the presuppositions of the Christian faith? If I make my philosophical viewpoint supreme, then I am compelled to construe the Bible and Christianity through my theory and everything which may not fit into that theory must be rejected. This is the actual standpoint of the critic. His is a philosophical rather than a religious spirit. Such was Gnosticism in the early centuries. It construed Christ and Christianity through the categories of a Graeco-Oriental philosophy and thus was compelled to reject some of the essentials of Christianity. Such was the Scholasticism of the Middle Ages, which construed Christianity through the categories of the Aristotelian Logic and the Neoplatonic Philosophy. Such is the Higher Criticism which construes everything through the hypothesis of evolution [p. 360].

Reeve came to realize not only that the whole critical movement was contrary to the traditional Christian approach but also that it was a purely intellectual approach that had a strong bias against the fundamental tenets of biblical Christianity. It leads not to humility but to pride and snobbery. Liberal scholars consider themselves to be intellectually superior to all who still maintain traditional views of Scripture.

Under the spell of this sublime contempt they think they can ignore anything that does not square with their evolutionary hypothesis. The center of gravity of their thinking is in the theoretical not in the religious, in reason, not in faith. Supremely satisfied with its self-constituted authority, the mind thinks itself competent to criticise the Bible, the thinking of all the centuries, and even Jesus Christ Himself. The followers of this cult have their full share of the frailties of human nature. Rarely, if ever, can a thoroughgoing critic be an evangelist, or even evangelistic; he is educational. How is it possible for a preacher to be a power for God, whose source of authority is his own reason and convictions? The Bible can scarcely contain more than good advice for such a man [p. 361].

Probably Reeve had his own Baptist seminary in mind as well as other Baptist schools and newly established evangelical schools in other denominations when he went on to write of the growing strength of true biblical theology.

Conservative scholarship is rapidly awakening, and, while it will retain the legitimate use of the invaluable historical method, it will sweep from the field most of the speculations of the critics. A striking characteristic of these [critics] is a persistent ignoring of what is written on the other side. They think to kill their antagonist by either ignoring or despising him. They treat their opponents something as Goliath treated David, and in the end the result will be similar. They have made no attempt to answer Robertson's "The Early Religion of Israel;" Orr's "The Problem of the Old Testament;" Wiener's "Studies in Biblical Law" and "Studies in Pentateuchal Criticism," etc. They still treat these books which have undermined the very foundations of their theories with the same magnificent scorn. There is a nemesis in such an attitude.

But the spirit of the critical movement manifests some very doubtful aspects in its practical working out among the pastors and churches which hold fast to the Biblical view of the Bible, while they know that their own views will undermine many of the most cherished beliefs of the churches. Many try to be critics and conservative at the same time. They would "run with the hare and hunt with the hounds," professing to be in full sympathy with evangelical Christianity while abiding their opportunity to inculcate their own views, which as we have seen, is really to forsake the Christian standpoint. The morality of such conduct is, to say the least, very doubtful. It has led to much mischief among the churches and injury to the work. A preacher who has thoroughly imbibed these beliefs has no proper place in an evangelical Christian pulpit. Such a spirit is not according to the spirit of the religion they profess to believe [p. 362].

Not only does Reeve believe that the critics are mistaken in their theories, he considers this critical methodology to be positively harmful. In fact it is the first step toward theological disaster.

When one makes his philosophy his authority, it is not a long step until he makes himself his own god. His own reason becomes supreme in his thinking and this reason becomes his lord. This is the inevitable logic of the hypothesis mentioned, and some adherents of the school have taken this step. They recognize no authority but their own moral instincts and philosophical reason. Now, as the evolution theory makes all things exist only in a state of change, of flux, or of becoming, God is therefore changing and developing, the Bible and Christ will be outgrown, Christianity itself will be left behind. Hence, there is no absolute truth, nothing in the moral religious world is fixed or certain. All truth is in solution; there is no precipitate upon which we can rely. There is no *absolute* standard of Ethics, no *authority* in religion, every one is practically his own god [p. 363].

I am far from saying that all adherents of this school go to such lengths, but why do they not? Most of them had an early training under the best conservative influences which inculcated a wholesome reverence for the Bible as an authority in religion and morals. This training they can never fully outgrow. Many·of them are of a good, sturdy religious ancestry of rigid, conservative training and genuine religious experience. Under these influences they have acquired a strong hold upon Christianity and can never be removed from it. They hold a theoretical standpoint and a religious experience together, failing, as I believe, to see the fundamental contradiction between them. . . . Churches are none too soon or too seriously alarmed [p. 364].

For Reeve, the basic question is very simple. Even the untrained layman can see the logic of this question, and the layman is likely to wonder how an educated theologian could ever answer it in the affirmative.

Can a God who is absolutely just and holy teach men truths about Himself by means of that which is false? Men may have taught truth by means of falsehoods and other instruments and perhaps succeeded, but God can hardly be legitimately conceived of as using any such means. Jesus Christ taught the greatest of truths by means of parables, illustrations, etc., but every one was true to life or nature or history. The Christian consciousness, which is the highest expression of the religious life of mankind, can never conceive of Jesus as using that which was in itself untrue, as a vehicle to convey that which is true. In like manner if God had anything to do with the Old Testament, would He make use of mere myths, legends, sagas, invented and falsified history, which have no foundation in fact and are neither true to nature, history nor life? Will God seek to uplift mankind by means of falsehood? Will He sanction the use of such dishonest means and pious frauds, such as a large part of the Pentateuch is, if the critics are right? Could He make use of such means for such a holy purpose and let His people feed on falsehood for centuries and centuries and deceive them into righteousness? Falsehood will not do God's will; only truth can do that [p. 365].

Shailer Matthews, Harry Emerson Fosdick, and others believed that the modern theories would inevitably win the day. All reasonable men would finally be forced to give up the older views that affirmed biblical infallibility. Reeve, however, took strong exception to that claim.

All critics believe that traditional Christianity will largely, if not altogether, give place to the modern view, as it is called. But we maintain that traditional Christianity has the right of way. It must and will be somewhat modified by the conception of a developing revelation and the application of the historical method, but must prevail in all its essential features. It has a noble ancestry and a glorious history. The Bible writers are all on its side; the bulk of Jewish scholars of the past are in the procession; it has Jesus, the Son of God, in its ranks, with the apostles, prophets, the martyrs, the reformers, the theologians, the missionaries and the great preachers and evangelists. The great mass of God's people are with it. I prefer to belong to that goodly company rather than with the heathen Porphyry, the pantheistic Spinoza, the immoral Astruc, the rationalistic Reuss, Vatke, Graf, Kuenen and Wellhausen, with a multitude of their disciples of all grades. Theirs is a new traditionalism begun by those men and handed down to others in England and America. Most of these disciples owe their religious life and training almost entirely to the traditional view. The movement has quickened study of the Old Testament, has given a valuable method, a great many facts, a fresh point of view, but its extravagancies, its vagaries, its false assumptions and immoralities will in time be sloughed by the Christian consciousness as in the past it has sloughed off Gnosticism, Pantheism, Scholasticism and a host of other philosophical or scientific fads and fancies [pp. 367-68].

A large group of Northern Baptists and almost all of the Southern Baptists were in agreement with the scholarly presentation of conservative theology that characterized these original "Fundamentalists." Some of the other men who wrote in this series of essays were men of high caliber, such as: G. Campbell Morgan, H. C. G. Moule, Thomas Spurgeon, Sir Robert Anderson, R. A. Torrey, F. Bettex, James Orr, W. H. Griffith Thomas, Charles R. Erdman, A. C. Dixon, Arthur T. Pierson, Benjamin B. Warfield, Arno C. Gaebelein, and James M. Gray. But as so often happens, the high ideals of the original leaders did not successfully survive the "friends" who supported the movement, and increasingly Fundamentalism became characterized by rigid legalism. Many Baptists could not support a movement that so often expressed itself in bitter polemics. Some Baptists, of course, did participate in the continuing movement, and they frequently proved to be as rigid as the next fellow.

BIBLIOGRAPHY

Ahlstrom, Sydney E. *A Religious History of the American People.* New Haven: Yale U. Press, 1972.

Clarke, William Newton. *An Outline of Christian Theology.* 14th ed. New York: Scribner's, 1905.

———. *The Use of the Scriptures in Theology.* New York: Scribner's, 1905.

Fant, Clyde E., Jr., and Pinson, William M., Jr. *20 Centuries of Great Preaching.* Vol. 9. Waco: Word, 1971.

Fosdick, Harry Emerson. *The Modern Use of the Bible.* New York: Macmillan, 1924.

Matthews, Shailer. *The Faith of Modernism.* New York: Macmillan, 1924.

Rauschenbusch, Walter. "Why I Am a Baptist." *Rochester Baptist Monthly* 20 (1905-6). Reprinted in booklet form with an introduction by Henlee H. Barnett from a reprinting in *Baptist Leader,* January 1958, pp. 1-10.

Reeve, James Josiah. "The Value of Greek and Hebrew in a Preacher's Education." *The Baptist Standard,* 3 June, 1909, p. 15.

———. "My Personal Experience with the Higher Criticism." In *The Fundamentals: A Testimony to the Truth,* edited by R. A. Torrey and A. C. Dixon, 1:348-68. 4 vol. ed. Los Angeles: Bible Institute of Los Angeles, 1917.

Tull, James E. *Shapers of Baptist Thought.* Valley Forge, Pa.: Judson, 1972.

CHAPTER SIXTEEN

"The Beginning of Sorrows"

Northern Baptists were drawn into a serious continuing controversy over the supposed movement toward theological liberalism that had begun to characterize their Convention in the first half of the twentieth century. Southern Baptists, on the other hand, were far more harmonious in their theological convictions. That can be illustrated in various ways. For example, J. Frank Norris, a Fundamentalist leader from Texas, was never able to mount a successful attack against Southern Baptist leadership. He was so extreme in his views during one period of his life that he even accused George W. Truett (pastor of the First Baptist Church of Dallas) of compromising the biblical faith. Theologically the Southern Baptist people were almost all conservatives; most of them believed the same doctrines Norris believed; however, they would not give themselves to the bitter polemical style of the Fundamentalists such as Norris. Southern Baptists voted to approve a major confession of faith in 1925. This confession clearly sets forth a conservative system of theology although it has been criticized for its ambiguity at some points. Nevertheless, the Southern Baptists did not experience the clear division in their ranks between conservatives and liberals that Northern Baptists did.

Northern Baptists

The Northern Convention faced liberalism not only in its schools but also on the mission field and in the churches. So serious did the problems with liberalism become that J. C. Massee, Curtis Lee Laws, Joel B. Slocum, Tillman B. Johnson, John Roach Straton, John Donaldson, and Warren Steeves, along with nearly one hundred fifty others, issued a call for a general conference on Baptist fundamentals. This conference met in the Delaware Avenue Baptist Church in Buffalo, New York, just prior to the National Convention of Northern Baptists in 1920. Some of those who signed the statement that called for the conference were Russell H. Conwell, J. E. Conant, A. C. Dixon, Clarence Larkin, W. B. Riley, W. H. Rogers, and D. F. Rittenhouse.

Rationalism was working havoc in the churches, they said, and the teaching in many of the schools was considered to be a hindrance rather than a help to students.

We believe that there rests upon us as Baptists an immediate and urgent
duty to restate, reaffirm, and re-emphasize the fundamentals of our New
Testament faith. Beyond all doubt the vast majority of our Baptist people
are as loyal as were our fathers to our Baptist principles and our Baptist
policy, but this loyalty will not long continue unless something is done to
stay the rising tide of liberalism and rationalism and to preserve our principles in their simplicity and purity [*Baptist Fundamentals*, p. ix].

J. C. Massee served as the president of the Buffalo Conference. All the
messages delivered there were published in a volume entitled *Baptist
Fundamentals*. In his opening address, Massee told of standing one day
in a tropical garden in Tampa, Florida. Some joker had thrown a cat into
a cage of monkeys. The poor cat was anxious to get out, but each time
he made an attempt to escape, one of those monkeys, hanging by his
"caudal appendage," would reach down and catch the cat by his tail and
throw him back across the cage. That incident was an illustration of the
trend in Baptist life, he said.

Our educational cages contain many scholastic monkeys, who with Darwinian complacency confess their parentage. A student in such an institution is like the cat in the Tampa Bay cage, with the ridiculous hand of
some evolutionist upon the tail of his religious beliefs. It seems to me high
time for us to take the hands of our theological, philosophic, and scientific
monkeys off the tail of our denominational conviction [*Baptist Fundamentals*, p. 9].

Frederick L. Anderson, speaking on "Historic Baptist Principles," said:

We have always believed in the Word. This spiritual religion of ours is
not unintelligent. It does not propagate itself by magic or mere enthusi-
asm. It depends upon truth. Its method is preaching—the appeal of the
reasonable spirit of man. The gospel, which is the very essence of the Holy
Bible, is fundamental, and the great principles of Scripture the authoritative court of appeal, which will save the church from vagaries and fanati-
cism [p. 24].

Frank M. Goodchild, pastor of the Central Baptist Church in New York
City, brought a message to the conference on "The Divine Unity of Holy
Scripture." Among other things, he said:

I have no use for a superstitious credulity that is determined to believe the
Book, no matter what its contents. And I have no use, on the other hand
for the critic, who is determined not to believe the Book, no matter what
its contents. The blind believer and the blind disbeliever are equally fools
—both of them having cast reason to the winds. And I do not know but
the man who professes to believe in the Bible, but denounces those who
undertake to examine its contents and manifests fear for the results of an

examination, does the Bible more harm than the worst critic of the Word can do. It is another case of our needing to have the Lord take care of our friends, while we ourselves are quite able to take care of our enemies. He does not believe in the Bible who hugs it to his bosom and runs off with it into the darkness of superstition and traditionalism, fearing to bring it to the light, lest its statements be disproved. But he believes the Bible who confidently seeks to have all light possible shed upon it; who says, "The more light, the better," and who feels that the more we study the Bible, the more we shall see what an infinite treasure we have in this Book of God.

Now, while I have not shut my ears against anything that scholarship has had to say about the Bible, and while I have done all that a busy pastor could do to keep up with the work of Biblical students at home and abroad, yet I am obliged to say, and I say it without any sense of shame whatever, that I have today pretty much the same Bible that my godly father gave me so many years ago. There are just as many books in my Bible as there were in his. The parables are all there; the miracles are unshattered; the history remains trustworthy; the requirements are just as high; the assurances are just as comforting; the promises are just as reliable. I find myself preaching from the Book pretty much as he did. And I make the bold claim today, that, in spite of the supposedly superior light of the present, he was as expert a student of the Word as are we. Not with grammar and lexicon. He did not know much about variant readings, or interpolations, or clay tablets, or the results of excavation. But he knew GOD as the men who walk the halls of Scripture knew him, and he knew how to make others acquainted with God. . . . He did not know anything about the "Joseph-traditions" that modern scholars have guessed about, and when he told me the story of Joseph as I stood by his armchair one Sunday afternoon, he spoke as though it was all true. He did not know that Abraham was simply "a typical example of unworldly goodness elaborated by several schools of writers," as Cheyne says. He thought Abraham was a real man, faithful enough to be called "the friend of God," and when he told me the story of Abraham offering his son Isaac as a sacrifice, I could fairly see the angel swoop down and arrest the uplifted hand. Of course he did not know anything about the story of the deluge being a myth which the Hebrews had borrowed from the Babylonians, and that it is "fundamentally a myth of Winter and the Sun-god." He thought it was a true record of God's wrath against the world that had given itself up to sin. And so one Sunday afternoon after a shower, when we took a walk together, he told me that there was once a terrific and prolonged downpour of rain, and that the waters prevailed over the earth and God's enemies were destroyed, and only through the handful of people that were saved in an ark did humanity have another chance. And I remember walking by his side that afternoon, full of awe, as one who had seen the judgments of the Lord. And when every day that dear father of mine used to read from that Book and then fall on his knees and talk with God, every one of his children felt that God was a reality and that he was in that room with us. You will understand then, brethren, that having spent my childhood under the tuition of a man who knew God face to face, I feel much more obligation to him for showing me the Bible as a *living* book than to these scholars who, taking what Astruc called his "Conjectures," have extended them and have acted as though they were certainties, and have merely shown how skilfully the wonderful Book can be *dissected* [pp. 57-58].

A. C. Dixon delivered a message on "The Bible at the Center of the Modern University." It was mostly an analysis of the philosophical and moral implications of evolutionary thought. But he included a ringing affirmation of his belief in the Bible:

One of the great needs of the Christian Church today is a university with the Bible at its center as the standard of all truth, religious, moral, historic, and scientific, and the Lord Jesus Christ preeminent in the realm of knowledge as in all other realms [p. 138].

William Bell Riley, pastor of the First Baptist Church of Minneapolis, Minnesota, shifted the emphasis of the meeting when he began aggressively to attack "Modernism in Baptist Schools." The three pillars of Baptist doctrine that Riley saw being threatened by Modernism were (1) the inerrancy of Scripture, (2) the deity and thus the infallibility of Christ, and (3) the absolute necessity of the new birth, regeneration. The first point is no more important than the second or the third, for no tripod can stand on any two legs alone. But the first one is crucial:

Baptists believe the Bible to be an inspired Book, and hence inerrant! The editor may tell us that "from the beginning Baptists have boasted that they have no creed," but in the next sentence he will be compelled to concede the first article of our faith, namely, that "The Bible is the only rule of faith and practice"; and, if, instead of a mere reference to that article, he rehearsed it in full it would read after this manner:

We believe that the Holy Bible was written by men divinely inspired, and is a perfect treasure of heavenly instruction; that it has God for its author, salvation for its end, and truth without any mixture of error, for its matter; that it reveals the principles by which God will judge us; and therefore is, and shall remain to the end of the world, the true center of Christian union, and the supreme standard by which all human conduct, creeds, and opinions should be tried.

And if he consulted the proof-texts printed after this article he would immediately discover that there is no difference between the Baptist creed and the Bible; that the first is the succinct statement of the elaborate teachings of the second; and that instead of men entering this denomination having to make a choice between a human statement and Divine Scripture, the second is absolutely included in the first and demanded by it!

If Baptists have never had any Confession of Faith, what does Thomas Armitage mean when he says of the Swiss people, "It was customary for the ancient Baptists to use private declarations of their principles, drawn up by some member of their communion"? Why did they take such pains "to conceal these Confessions" lest the State lay hands upon them and charge them with treason against the State religion? If they never had any "Confession of Faith," what was the significance of "the seven articles" drawn in the year 1527? And did Zwingli lie when he declared that he had "two copies" of that Confession in his pocket; and charged every Baptist with having a concealed copy somewhere about his person? If Baptists have never had any "Confession of Faith" what was that instrument drawn up by John Bunyan, and forty elders, deacons, and brethren, and approved by more than twenty thousand Baptists, and presented to King Charles II in London in 1660; and concerning which they declared, "We are not only resolved to suffer persecution to the loss of our goods, but also life itself, rather than decline from the same." If Baptists have never had a "Confession of Faith," what was the origin of the phrases, "The New Hampshire Confession" and "The Philadelphia Confession"?

We would not at all be willing to have Baptist churches replace the Bible with a creed, but we did suppose when we united with this denomination (and we imagine that other people proposing to unite with it, still suppose) that there is a certain set of beliefs concerning God, Christ, the Scripture, and the Ordinances, etc., to which Baptists universally subscribe.

Our problem is not, as stated by the editor, "Where shall we find our infallible interpreters of this inspired volume?" The question is an altogether different one—have we an inspired and an infallible volume to interpret? If not, the first leg is gone from beneath the Baptist vase; and the denomination that was steady on its tripod will be found tottering on two remaining legs. The attitude, therefore, of professors, schools, and preachers toward the first fundamental of our holy faith will determine the whole question as to whether the denomination is being menaced by Modernism [pp. 169-71].

At the conclusion of Riley's message the conference voted to request that the Convention investigate the attitudes of professors and trustees regarding the traditional Baptist doctrines. The conservatives did force an investigation, but this move drove the Convention into a state of wild disorder. The controversy produced bitterness and tension that began to carry over from one year to the next.

The next year the committee appointed to investigate the schools made its report. The committee recognized some problems, but in essence the report supported the Baptist institutions. The attempts by conservatives to get the convention to adopt a confession of faith failed time after time.

The liberal-conservative controversy of the twenties spilled over into the thirties and the forties.

In 1932 the General Association of Regular Baptists was formed when a group of ministers withdrew from the Convention over doctrinal matters. The Convention leadership consistently refused to deal decisively with theological tensions within the denomination. The leadership did not wish to label Modernism as heresy. Even the emphasis on evangelism seemed to some to be at the expense of theology and doctrinal distinctives.

Carl F. H. Henry described the continuing controversy and the unfortunate results:

> In 1946 this smoldering resentment burst into open conflagration in the fundamentalist-modernist test of strength at the Grand Rapids convention. The plotted political maneuvering, both of the Roger Williams Fellowship and of the Fundamentalist Fellowship, as well as of forces seeking to moderate between them, was a disheartening spectacle and debacle to younger ministers who had come in search of Christian unity in uniqueness. Under conviction to oppose recognition of modernism as authentic Christianity, I permitted my name on the fundamentalist ballot. The fundamentalist ticket was defeated 2,483 to 605, with 236 split ballots. Thereafter no substantial Christian minority was either so repeatedly ignored or so tirelessly pressured for conformity. This harassment led finally to a costly outcome, namely, withdrawal of about 300 churches under the banner of the Conservative Baptist Association, and increasing support of the Conservative Baptist Foreign Mission Society, which had been formed in 1943.
>
> While the theological issue is frequently represented as the only issue at stake in Grand Rapids, that was not the case. The test of strength did not show that there were 2,483 liberal delegates. Membership in Northern Baptist churches at that time was about 85% evangelical; so it is likely that most delegates who voted antifundamentalist were actually disposed to various shades of conservative theology. Many resented the pugnacious features of fundamentalism, and feared the consequences of Convention control by a power bloc. Even if lacking in courage to register their theological convictions, many evangelicals who voted against the fundamentalists were motivated by a sense of Baptist concern. These delegates may not have realized to what extent the official life of the Convention was already at that time being maneuvered by leaders who ignored Baptistic answerability to the local churches. But while denominational executives were often culpable of a questionable political shrewdness, the fundamentalist revolt was infected with an equally serious characteristic, that of a vitriolic spirit ["Twenty Years," pp. 50-51].

Not all conservatives left the Convention. Carl Henry and J. C. Massee were notable examples of those who remained. Massee apparently believed that this latest withdrawal from the Convention was more over millennialism and creedalism than over the belief in the authenticity and authority of the Bible. Whatever the case, division within the Convention had the net effect of weakening the Baptist witness in the North.

Southern Baptists

Southern Baptists had responded to the evolutionary and Modernistic theories in 1925 by drafting and passing a confession known as the *Baptist Faith and Message*. This act demonstrated the doctrinal unity of the Southern Convention. Though some ambiguity existed in the article on Scripture, no real challenge to the conservative interpretation of that statement surfaced until 1961, when Ralph H. Elliott, a professor of Old Testament at Midwestern Baptist Theological Seminary in Kansas City, published with Broadman Press a commentary entitled *The Message of Genesis*.

Elliott took essentially the same position C. H. Toy had taken almost eighty years before. Because Elliott refused to comply with a request from the trustees that he not republish the book, he was dismissed from the faculty in October of 1962. He was quoted as saying that to withdraw the book from publication voluntarily "would have the overtones of repudiating my work and suggesting that I did not now share the same perspective."

This controversy had been building up for several years. As early as 1959 some students had begun to speak out openly against certain teachers at Midwestern who were using critical methodology in biblical studies. In 1960 some of the trustees met with the criticized professors, and that meeting seemed to resolve the problems. The publication of Elliott's book, however, resulted in severe criticism not only of Elliott but also of theological education as a whole.

On Wednesday afternoon, June 6, 1962, K. Owen White from Texas presented a motion to the Southern Baptist Convention messengers. The Convention president, Herschel Hobbs, ruled that White had in fact presented two motions. So on Thursday, June 7, they were both considered during the regular business sessions.

First, the Convention heard and unanimously adopted this motion:

> That the messengers to this convention, by standing vote, reaffirm their faith in the entire Bible as the authoritative, authentic infallible Word of God.

The second motion, after some discussion, was also adopted by the convention messengers:

> That we express our abiding and unchanging objection to the dissemination of theological views in any of our seminaries which would undermine such faith in the historical accuracy and doctrinal integrity of the Bible, and

that we courteously request the trustees and administrative officers of our institutions and other agencies to take such steps as shall be necessary to remedy at once those situations where such views now threaten our historic position.

During the fall of that year, the state conventions spoke out on this issue as well. State conventions in Michigan, New Mexico, and Oklahoma asserted their conviction that the Bible is "the immutable, eternal and infallible Word of God." Arizona Baptists declared "our belief that the Genesis account is the true and accurate Word of God." Tennessee Baptists adopted a resolution asserting "faith in the historical accuracy and doctrinal integrity of the Bible." In Texas, K. Owen White was elected as President of the Baptist General Convention.

In many ways, of course, Elliott was not a radical theologian. He affirmed a personal belief in biblical inspiration. He specifically agreed to a statement presented by the trustees of Midwestern Baptist Theological Seminary which said: "We reject any theory that the Bible is a book of folklore and mythology." Yet obviously he was out of step with what most Southern Baptists understood those words to mean. The trustees also stated that they did not oppose the historical-critical method of interpreting the Scripture. The theological issues involved were, therefore, somewhat confusing, because the use of the historical-critical method is what made Elliott's book controversial.

Elliott's first sentence in *The Message of Genesis* begins to raise a question about the Mosaic authorship of the book. On page two he suggests that the presence of "duplicate" accounts indicates a multiple authorship. However, the real controversy about the book seems to have centered on his method of dealing with the historical accuracy of the creation account and the Garden of Eden narrative. This not only raised questions of literary genre or historical evidence, but it also involved the philosophical question about the nature of truth.

Elliott, following the lead of S. H. Hooke, tried to make a distinction between the level of historical event and the level of interpretation *The Message of Genesis*, p. 12). There is, of course, a complicated philosophical question about the relationship between event and interpretation. Elliott's solution to the problem was to take the position that there is no necessary unity between them. The early chapters of Genesis, as well as some other parts of the Old Testament, are to be taken as composed of symbolic parables including historical and nonhistorical elements, he said.

> Suppose that a biblical writer should now or then use poor grammar, poor science, or even poor history in reporting God's act. The important thing is the fact that the divinely inspired writer presents the act itself with

clarity and truth. Error in literary vehicle does not necessarily mean error in message or in the essential purpose of God [p. 14].

In discussing the world-picture of Genesis 1, Elliott says: "The compiler used the concept of the world prevalent in his day as a vehicle for showing the proper concept of God" (p. 26). He means that the writer simply adopted Babylonian or other ancient mythologies and modified their theological content while continuing to use their mythological forms. Genesis 1:26 is speaking of man in the collective sense, claimed Elliott, with the context arguing against the creation of a single man and a single woman (pp. 39-40). The "insight" of the "Priestly" writer is that woman was created *along with* man *not after* him (p. 40). Such a conclusion seems to be directly contradicted by 1 Timothy 2:13, but Elliott refers only to Galatians 3:28. Throughout the book, Elliott is very consistent in his application of modern critical theories. He had just graduated from Southern Seminary with a Th.D. in Old Testament in 1956. Other than his dissertation, this was his first major writing project. He was apparently surprised at the reaction the book caused.

For the first time in several decades Southern Baptists faced a theological crisis. Many within the Convention rallied to support Elliott. Essentially their argument was that the 1925 *Baptist Faith and Message* was broad enough to allow these views. Liberty of conscience was emphasized. Baptist doctrine did not dictate critical methods or conclusions, they said. But the controversy was not settled until Elliott had resigned from his teaching post.

H. H. McGinty, editor (1947-67) of *The Word and Way* (the official journal of the Missouri Baptist Convention), stated in an editorial dated September 6, 1962:

> The real issue in this consideration is the question: Do Southern Baptists who build these seminaries, maintain them and pay the salaries of those who administer them and teach therein, have the right to stipulate what may or may not be taught, in these institutions? When a teacher is elected to the faculty in one of these seminaries, is he free to teach without restriction? Do Southern Baptists have the prerogative of prescribing some limitations beyond which, if one goes, he will be considered out of bounds?

No one suggested that Elliott did not have the freedom of conscience to hold whatever views he pleased. Nor did the school (or any church) charge him with heresy. He had not technically violated the letter of the 1925 *Baptist Faith and Message* or of the trustees' guidelines. But many Southern Baptists felt and continue to feel that such teaching from the historical-critical perspective creates tensions and raises doubts about the full inspiration of Scripture. The 1963 *Baptist Faith and Message* statement was produced in direct response to this theological controversy.

In January of 1962 the Southern Baptist Sunday School Board tried to defend itself from criticism for publishing the book by appealing to what they called the "historic Baptist principle" of the individual's freedom to interpret the Bible for himself. Baptists, they claimed, had historically affirmed the right of any Baptist "to hold a particular theory of inspiration of the Bible which seems most reasonable to him, and to develop his beliefs in accordance with his theory" (*Encyclopedia*, 3:1842).

This declaration is especially interesting in light of another 1962 decision by the governing board of Broadman Press to authorize the publication of a multivolume commentary to be known as *The Broadman Bible Commentary*. Broadman had been doing preliminary studies since 1958, but the selection of a general editor and an advisory board was not finalized until 1966. Volume one, *Genesis–Exodus*, was published in 1969.

Clifton J. Allen, for many years the Editorial Secretary of the Southern Baptist Sunday School Board, was chosen as the General Editor. He wrote the introductory article on "The Book of the Christian Faith." The initial sentence reads: "We begin with the affirmation—the Bible is the Word of God." Almost eleven columns of type are given to the discussion of revelation and inspiration.

Verbal inspiration, says Allen, "obviously reduces the writer almost to the equivalent of a tool in the hands of God and makes him virtually the completely controlled agent of God" (p. 6). The context implies that Allen sees this as an inadequate view. He distinguishes the "verbal" theory from the "plenary" theory by saying that the plenary theory led to "practical inerrancy" of the whole and of the part without committing itself to the extreme literalism of the verbal theory. The "dynamic" theory lacks preciseness, says Allen, but means that inspiration refers to the "completeness and adequacy" of Scripture as a guide for faith and practice rather than to its "inerrancy in wording and analogy and certain details about persons and events."

Allen makes it clear that this dynamic view is to him the most adequate one. The dynamic view is not "dependent on a mystical, inexplicable, and unverifiable inerrancy in every word of Scripture or on the concept that inspiration can allow no error of fact or substance" (p. 7). Scripture is "inerrant as the only completely authentic witness to God's self-revelation in Christ." Its truth is a "perfect instrument" to bring men to faith. Scripture inerrantly teaches us how to live and what to believe.

Allen writes that there are at least seven problems with verbal inspiration theories. Problem two is that a careful reading of the Bible "discloses some obvious contradictions or discrepancies" which do not involve major doctrinal points. Problem five is that Scripture seems to attribute to God actions that are "out of harmony with his nature as holy love." Problem seven is that the modern historical-critical method has given evidence of a multiple authorship for the Pentateuch and has shown that the Bible was produced through collation and editing, thus ruling out verbal inspiration.

Dynamic theories have problems, too, such as explaining scriptural claims for plenary inspiration and the tendency to minimize the divine element. But for Allen the problems "do not invalidate this view" (p. 8). "The fact of divine revelation and inspiration is in no sense dependent on a particular view of inspiration and is in no jeopardy from critical research and scholarly study" (p. 9).

> Let this principle of revelation be stressed. The treasure of inspired revelation, the truth of the biblical revelation, has come to us in "earthen vessels." The writers were men. They were finite and fallible. They were human, and hence subject to limitations of knowledge and understanding. But they were persons through whom the transcendent power of God operated—quickening, illuminating, guiding, and enabling them to be the media of the saving message of God in Christ. The Holy Scriptures have their essential character in their nature as the inspired revelation of God. Pointing to Christ and finding their meaning and unity in Christ, they are the Word of God [p. 9].

Thus, the General Editor of *The Broadman Bible Commentary* openly states that his guiding assumptions are the same as those that had directed C. H. Toy and Ralph H. Elliott. Allen clearly has gone beyond the concept of "dynamic" inspiration that A. H. Strong had used. Strong never affirmed actual errors in the Bible. In fact, he clearly denied that Scripture taught "obvious contradictions" or that Scripture affirmed God's immorality at any point. Allen has also failed to see the point that E. Y. Mullins had made that the inductive-dynamic theory is actually a form of the plenary theory and that results (the complete truthfulness of the text) are the point at issue rather than theories about supposed methods of inspiration.

It should be recognized, however, that all the contributors to *The Broadman Bible Commentary* spoke for themselves, and it is obvious that many of them did not necessarily agree with Allen. Most of the exegetical work reflects the highest quality of conservative scholarship. The commentary on Genesis, however, was written by G. Henton Davies, a British Baptist scholar from Oxford. Almost at once that volume began to create controversy within the churches. On June 3, 1970, at the Southern Baptist Convention meeting in Denver, Colorado, Gwin Turner, pastor of the First Baptist Church at Mar Vista in Los Angeles, California, introduced the following motion:

That because volume one of the new Broadman Bible Commentary is out of harmony with the beliefs of the vast majority of Southern Baptist pastors and people, this convention requests the Sunday School Board to withdraw volume one from further distribution and that it be rewritten with due consideration of the conservative viewpoint.

Speaking on behalf of his motion, Turner read a prepared statement:

I have written my discussion of this motion so as to be as careful, as precise and as Christian as I know how to be.

My motion is a result of my own personal study of this commentary over the past six weeks, reading the passages in question two, three and four times.

I ask, please, that in all of the discussion that follows from anyone, we all avoid vindictive, harsh or unchristianlike remarks of any sort, and that we be very prayerful in attitude.

I appeal for unity, and one of my main interests in making the motion that volume one of the Broadman Bible Commentary be recalled and rewritten is in the interest of unity, because in its present form it is very hurtful to our unity.

I shall mention only two examples from the commentary that I consider to be extremely out of character with the historic Baptist position on the Bible and in glaring conflict with the beliefs of the vast majority of the people in our convention.

First, the commentator on Genesis in outright contradiction of the direct statement of the Bible declares that God did not command Abraham to offer Isaac. He writes, "Indeed what Christian or humane conscience would regard such a command as coming from God? How then did this conviction arise in the mind of Abraham, since we believe that God did not put it there?" He then goes on to answer that it was simply the climax of certain psychological developments in Abraham's life that caused him to be obsessed with the idea of "what if I should lose him?," and then moved on to the mistaken notion that God wanted him to sacrifice Isaac.

Now if we permit this type of exposition of Holy Scripture to remain in print as representative of the scholarship of the Southern Baptist Convention, we greatly endanger ourselves as a people committed to the Bible.

If this writer is allowed with our approval, under our sponsorship, to directly contradict the Word of God because an idea offends his intellectual presuppositions, then we are approving the idea that anyone can explain away any passage that he finds offensive or repulsive to this thought pattern.

It is one thing to interpret the Bible. It is something else to directly contradict its clear statements. This kind of approach to the Bible is completely out of character with this convention's statement of faith.

Second, volume one espouses the documentary hypothesis which makes the Bible a patchwork of conflicting records, written by many different authors who had conflicting theological ideas and differing religious purposes.

I know of not one great evangelistic pastor who accepts this philosophy of the Word of God. We are already in trouble in our convention with reference to reaching people for Christ. You can be assured that this commentary will place before us an additional stumbling block to hinder us in effecting a spiritually dynamic outreach ministry.

There are other statements in this volume that I believe are very objectionable, but these are all that I shall mention.

If this commentary in its present form continues to be distributed as representing the scholarship of Southern Baptists, and is not immediately rejected as not representative of us, like some others, we shall be one of the "has been" denominations.

However, I have great confidence in this convention. I believe that the vast majority of you with me believe in the accuracy of the Bible not only in salvation and doctrine but also in what it says about persons and events, and wish to see the hurtful ideas expressed in this commentary recalled and removed. I therefore urge you to vote for this motion.

The motion passed by a vote of 5,394 to 2,170. The discussion raged for months, but the volume was withdrawn and rewritten. Not all theological questions were resolved even in the revision. Tensions still exist, and only the future will know their final resolution.

Historically, Baptists have not hesitated to affirm clearly their belief in biblical authority. Since the advent of modern critical theories of the Bible, however, a whole new set of issues has appeared. Pastors and laymen, almost without exception, claim to be Bible believers. But the words no longer seem to have clear definitions. Harry Emerson Fosdick and J. J. Reeve both claimed to be "Bible-believers."

Critical theories do alter the meaning of Scripture. Can a biblical affirmation be both true and false? Can a single scriptural passage teach two different things? Can the traditional interpretation and the modern "critical" interpretation both be correct? Does Scripture in fact contain intentional affirmations of truth that even when properly interpreted remain absolutely false? Do obvious contradictions exist in Scripture even from God's viewpoint? Does Scripture actually teach that God has acted in ways that because of His nature He could not so have acted? Does Scripture at some points affirm false ideas about God Himself? Baptists cannot leave these and other similar related questions unresolved.

BIBLIOGRAPHY

Allen, Clifton J., general editor. *The Broadman Bible Commentary.* Nashville: Broadman, 1969-72. Vol. 1, *Genesis–Exodus,* 1969.
Baptist Fundamentals. Philadelphia: Judson, 1920.

Elliott, Ralph H. *The Message of Genesis*. Nashville: Broadman, 1961.

Encyclopedia of Southern Baptists. 3 vols. Nashville: Broadman, 1958; *Supplement*, 1971.

Henry, Carl F. H. "Twenty Years a Baptist." *Foundations* 1 (January 1958): 46-54.

McGinty, H. H. "Editorially Speaking: What Is the Real Issue?" *The Word and Way*, September 6, 1962, p. 2.

Southern Baptist Convention Annual, 1962; 1970.

Turner, Gwin. *A Positive Declaration of the Intent of the Denver SBC Action on the Broadman Bible Commentary*. Published privately, 1970.

Part Three

"WHOM SAY YE THAT I AM?"

CHAPTER SEVENTEEN

"Things Which Are Most Surely Believed Among Us"

Confessions of faith have been used in various ways in Baptist life. In recent decades some groups have used confessions (in the words of the 1952 confession of the Minnesota Baptist Convention) "to distinguish between Baptists within Baptist ranks." Although the earliest confessions of Smyth and Helwys and the *Orthodox Creed,* a 1678 General Baptist confession, tended toward a similar purpose, the major emphasis of most Baptist confessional statements has been expression rather than repression. Instead of attempting to set Baptists apart from other Christians (or from themselves), several early confessions sought to demonstrate Baptist agreement with mainline Protestant theology. The 1644 *First London Confession* was for "the vindication of the truth of Christ." That is not a purpose unique to Baptists.

The confessions do, of course, defend Baptist views on the church and on the ordinances. However, the ruling principles in these statements are *sola scriptura* (Scripture alone) and *sola fide* (faith alone), points that the writers expected would appeal to other Protestant Christians. Early Baptists did not think exclusively in terms of Baptist distinctives. They affirmed Christian doctrines. They believed that they were being true to Scripture in their view of the ordinances, their view of God, and so forth, and they called other Christians to join them in their faithfulness.

Scriptural authority is normally acknowledged near the beginning of each of these confessions. No Baptist considers a confession to be a deposit of final or infallible truth. Instead, confessions are just what their names state—"confessions." They express faith through relating doctrinal ideas to one another in a systematic and comprehensive fashion. This makes it possible to compare the beliefs of various denominations or groups directly. Baptists frequently publish confessions as a way of communicating what they believe to be pure New Testament truth.

Charles R. Andrews writes:

372   *Baptists and the Bible*

It is not denied to us by the nature of our faith to formulate Confessions.
When Fenwick T. Fowler in the March 1958 Crusader, for example, remarks that "since one of our distinctives is our belief in the liberty of conscience, obviously no creedal statement can be presented," he certainly
reflects the attitude of our Baptist forefathers in the sense that they would
not by "creedalism" repress liberty of conscience where such liberty is
obedient to Scripture. But, as we have seen, they would have other, and
more valid, uses for Confessions. Baptists do not *have* to be speechless.
We are free to express our faith jointly if it is desirable to do so. We are
not a people so disagreeable as to make it somehow impossible in principle
to point together to Jesus Christ. Nor is it distinctively Baptistic to disagree ["The Maine Wheele," p. 37].

Thus, the confessional statements examined below must be studied in
context. Admittedly the contextual setting given in this chapter is a bare
minimum. The affirmations of biblical authority in each confession, however, must be taken seriously. To formulate a confession is not to reject the
final or unique authority of the Bible. In fact in most cases it is obviously
the very opposite. Baptists confessions do not have as their primary purpose the setting forth of "Baptist" distinctives; their primary purpose is the
setting forth of true doctrine. If that results in some distinctiveness, then so
be it. Baptists have nothing to be proud of if they cannot show that their
beliefs are true to the biblical teaching on every Christian doctrine.

For Baptists, confessions are not immutable documents. They are not
static, absolute, complete, exhaustive, or final summaries of all that Baptists
believe. They are expressions, declarations, or affirmations of the Christian
faith as Baptists understand it.

The Charlestown Confession of 1665

Perhaps the earliest Baptist confession of faith in America came from a
small group of persecuted church members in Charlestown, Massachusetts.
Thomas Goold, a freeman, refused to have his newborn infant baptized
and was suspended from his Congregational church in 1656. Though it was
illegal to do so, Goold began to hold private meetings of Baptist believers
in his home. The group formed a Baptist church in 1665 by joining with
some who had been immersed in England in Baptist churches. The local
constable set out to break up their meetings and to require them to attend
the established public worship. The Baptists refused to obey the legal demands and were brought before the local Court of Assistants. In order to
defend themselves in court, the little congregation produced a written confession of faith "to let the world know there [sic] faith & order proved from
the word of god." The entire confession is reprinted below. The use of
several Scriptural references to support each point is typical of many Bap-

tist Confessions. This in itself shows the practical or functional application of the doctrine of biblical infallibility in Baptist life. But it is also to be noted that this confession makes specific references to the Scripture in sections (e), (i), and (y). In fact, the language of those three sections is almost a duplication of the seventh, fifteen, and fifty-second articles of the *1644 Confession.* This confession is preserved in volume one of *American Christianity* by Smith, Handy, and Loetscher, pages 171-72.

> Wee believe with the heart & Confess with the mouth that there is but (a) one god (b) Creator & governor of all things (c) distinguished into father, son, & holy Spirit (d) & that this is life eternall to know the only true god & Jesus Christ whom hee hath sent (a) deut: 6: 4 1 tim 2: 5: eph: 4: 6: (b) gen: 1: 1: hebr: 11: 3: (c) matt 3: 16 1 john 5: 7: (d) john 17: 3: hebr: 5: 9: (e) & that the rule of this knowlidge faith & obedience Concerning the worship & service of god & all other Christian duties is the written word of god Contained in the bookes of the old & new testaments (e) john 5: 39: 2 tim 3: 15: 16: 17: deut: 4: 2: 5: 6: gen: 6: 22: exod: 20: 4: 5: 6: & 39: 42: 43: 1 Cron: 28: 19: psal: 119: esea: 8: 19: 20: & 29: 13: gall: 1: 8: Rev: 22: 18: 19: (f) wee believe Christ is the foundation laid by the father (g) of whom Moses and the prophets wrote & the Apostles preached (h) who is that prophet whom wee are to hear in all things (i) who hath perfectly revealed out of the bosom of his father the whole word and will of god which his servants are to know believe and obey (f) gen: 3: 15: & 22: 18: (g) deut 18: 15: psal: 22: 6: 7: 12: & 17: (h) deut 18: 15: acts 3: 22: 23: (i) john 1: 18: & 12: 29: & 15: 15: & 17: 18: matt: 17: 5: 2 tim: 3: 15: 16: 17: (k) Christ his Commission to his desciples is to teach & baptise (1) And those that gladly received the word & are baptized are saints by Calling & fitt matter for a vissible Church (m) And a competent number of such joyned together in Covenant & fellowship of the gosple are a Church of Christ (k) matt 28: 19: acts 9: 10: 18: & 10: 28: (1) acts 2: 24: (m) 1 Cor 1: 1: 2: 4: 5: jer: 50: 4: 5: psal: 50: 5: micha 4: 5: matt: 18: 15: 20 (o) wee believe that a Church thus Constituted are to walk in all the appointments of Christ (p) And have power from him to Chuse from amoung themselves there owne officers whom the gosple allowes to administer in the ordinances of Christ amoung them whom they may depute or ordaine to this end (o) matt 28: 20: (p) acts 14: 23: & 6: 3: 5: 6: Rom: 12: 4: 8: acts 9: 10: 18: & 10: 47: 48: (q) And this Church hath power to receive into there fellowship vissible believers (r) & if any prove scandelouse obstenate & wicked to put forth such from amoungst them (s) when the Church is mett to gather they may all propesie one by one that all may learne & all may be Comforted (t) & they ought to meete togather the first day of the weeke to attend upon the Lord in all his holy ordinances Continuing in the Apostles doctrine & fellowship &

breaking bread & praise (q) [acts] 2: 47: rom: 14: 1: & 16: 2: (r) matt
18: 7: 1 Cor: 4: 5: (s) 1 Cor: 14: 23: 24: 25: 31: (t) acts 20: 7:
1 Cor: 16: 2: acts 2: 42: (v) wee acknowlidge Majestracy to bee an ordinance of god & to submit our selves to them in the lord not becawse of
wrath only but also for Conscience sake rom: 13: 1: 1 pet: 2: 13: 14:
(w) thus wee desire to give unto god that which is gods & unto Ceasere
that which is Ceaseres & to every man that which belongeth to them (x)
endeavoring alwaise to have a Cleare Conscience voide of offence to
wards god & to wards men having hope in god that the Resurection of
the dead bee of the just unto life & of the unjust unto Condemnation everlasting (y) if any take this to bee heresie then doe wee with the Apostles
Confess that after the way which they Call heresie wee worship the father
of our Lord Jesus Christ believing all things that are written in the law &
in the prophets & in the psalms (w) matt 22: 21: (x) acts 24: 14: 15:
16: john 5: 28 . . . 3: (y) 2 tim 1: 13: & 3: 14: 15: 16: 17: matt
10: 32. This was delivered to A Court of Assistants on the . . . of the
seventh month 1665.

THE PHILADELPHIA CONFESSION OF 1742

The earliest Calvinistic Baptists in America generally did not have written confessions. Especially was this true in New England. The Middle
Colony Baptists, however, were more closely related to English Baptists,
and they did begin to make common use of confessions during the eighteenth century.

Elias Keach, the son of Benjamin Keach, became the pastor of the
famous Pennepack Baptist Church of Philadelphia in 1688. The church
membership became so large and was so widely scattered that several
churches were started from within the membership. Various doctrinal
controversies arose and these churches met together to discuss them. In
1707 they formed the Philadelphia Baptist Association.

In 1692 Elias Keach had returned to London to pastor the Tallon Chand-
ler's Hall Church there. In 1697 he worked with his father to publish a
confession of faith that was almost a duplication of the *1689 London Confession.* This new confession included an article on hymn-singing and the
laying on of hands, and was commonly called "Keach's Confession." In
1712 one church in New Jersey that was having doctrinal difficulties was
counseled by neighboring churches that the members should subscribe to
Keach's Confession, and the members who did so subscribe became the
reconstituted church.

The Philadelphia Association made it clear in 1724 that it subscribed to
the *1689 London Confession.* Some question had arisen concerning the
Sabbath, and the Association referred to that confession in its statement of
reply. It is not clear whether the Association had formally adopted the

A CONFESSION OF FAITH,

Put forth by the
Elders and *Brethren*
Of many

CONGREGATIONS OF

CHRISTIANS

(Baptized upon Profeſſion of their Faith)
In *London* and the *Country.*

Adopted by the Baptiſt ASSOCIATION
met at Philadelphia, Sept. 25. 1742.

The SIXTH EDITION.

To which are added,
Two Articles *viz.* Of Impoſition of Hands,
and Singing of Pſalms in Publick Worſhip.

ALSO

A Short Treatiſe of Church Diſcipline.

*With the Heart Man believeth unto Righteouſneſs, and with the
Mouth Confeſſion is made unto Salvation,* Rom. 10. 20.
Search the Scriptures, John 5. 39.

PHILADELPHIA : Printed by B. FRANKLIN.
M,DCC,XLIII.

Fig. 34. *Philadelphia Confession of Faith*

From Lumpkin's *Baptist Confessions of Faith,* Judson, 1969. Facsimile of 1743
title page.

confession in 1724, but a formal adoption must have taken place by 1742 when the Association commissioned a new printing of the *1689 Confession* (the *Second London Confession*). Benjamin Franklin did the printing in 1743. Several small changes were made in what now was called the *Philadelphia Confession* and two articles were added, but the view of Scripture upon which the *1689 Confession* rests remained the same. (A discussion of that article on Scripture is included in chapter 3 of this book.)

Over the years, several editions of this confession were published by the Philadelphia Association. Other churches and associations also adopted it. W. L. Lumpkin names these associations in his *Baptist Confessions of Faith* (pp. 352-53). Referring to the *Philadelphia Confession*, Lumpkin writes:

> A fourth edition appeared in 1850 and is an indication of the continued use of the Confession in the South. Indeed in this region it influenced Baptist thought generally and has been perhaps the most influential of all confessions. Local church covenants still reflect its outlook and summarize its doctrines [p. 352].

In 1783 even the Separate General Association of Virginia agreed to adopt the *Philadelphia Confession*. Separate Baptists had opposed written confessions, but they did accept this one along with an additional statement that such formal acceptance did not bind every Baptist to strict observance of every detail, nor should anyone ever think that the confession stood above or even equal to Scripture itself. They did say, however, that they agreed that this confession was "the best composition of the kind now extant" (Lumpkin, p. 353).

Articles of Faith of the Kehukee Association of 1777

Probably the first Baptist associational confession of faith that was written in America is the *Articles of Faith of the Kehukee Association* (1777) of North Carolina. A serious controversy had arisen—partly over the practice of retaining members who admitted that they had not been converted prior to their baptism. This confession was a declaration against Arminianism and was an attempt to restore harmony in the churches. It is still maintained by the Kehukee Primitive Baptist Association. There are seventeen articles. The first two read:

> 1. We believe in the being of God as almighty, eternal, unchangeable, of infinite wisdom, power, justice, holiness, goodness, mercy, and truth; and that this God has revealed Himself in His word under the characteristics of Father, Son and Holy Ghost.

> 2. We believe that Almighty God has made known His mind and will to the children of men in His word which word we believe to be of divine

authority, and contains all things necessary to be made known for the salvation of men and women. The same is comprehended or contained in the Books of the Old and New Testaments as are commonly received.

PRINCIPLES OF FAITH OF THE SANDY CREEK ASSOCIATION OF 1816

The Separate Baptist movement grew out of the Great Awakening in New England. Members of Congregational churches began to insist on a more revivalistic or experiential emphasis in worship. Many of them formed "separate" churches. Some of these groups soon began to preach the necessity of having a personal conversion to faith in Christ before baptism and thus became "Separate Baptists." Shubael Stearns and Daniel Marshall led some of these Baptists to establish a church at Sandy Creek, North Carolina. This church was intensely evangelistic and mission minded, and the association organized in that area became one of the most influential Baptist associations in the South throughout the eighteenth century.

As noted earlier, Separate Baptists generally opposed written confessions of faith. However, in 1816 Luther Rice (representing the Board of Foreign Missions) met with the Sandy Creek Association and helped them write the *Articles of Faith* for the Association. Article two reads:

> That the Scriptures of the Old and New Testaments are the word of God, and only rule of faith and practice.

TERMS OF UNION BETWEEN THE ELKHORN AND SOUTH KENTUCKY ASSOCIATIONS OF 1801

Separate Baptists did not unite with the Regular Baptists easily or readily for several reasons. However, in Kentucky during the great Frontier Revival there was a union between the (Regular) Elkhorn Association and the (Separate) South Kentucky Association. The Separates could not agree to accept the Philadelphia Confession, thus a document setting forth the *"Terms of Union"* was produced. After these two associations agreed to unite, a general union of Kentucky Baptist churches took place based on this same set of terms drawn up in 1801. The very first article of this document for union reads:

> We, the committees of Elkhorn and South Kentucky Associations, do agree to unite on the following plan:
>
> 1st. That the Scriptures of the Old and New Testament are the infallible word of God, and the only rule of faith and practice.

THE NEW HAMPSHIRE CONFESSION OF 1833

The strictly Calvinistic views of many Baptists in New Hampshire (and throughout New England) were somewhat modified by the rise of the so-called Free Will Baptists. In 1830, the Baptist Convention of New Hampshire appointed a committee to write a new declaration of faith that would generally reflect the theological views of all the Baptist churches in the state. That first year, N. W. Williams, William Taylor, and I. Person worked on a draft of this new confession. For a second year Person continued work on it alone. Then when the draft was submitted to the Convention in 1832 it was referred to another committee composed of Baron Stow, John Newton Brown, Jonathan Going, and I. Person for final editing. They recommended adoption of the articles of faith. However, it was after another year, some further editing, and some minor alterations that the board of the Convention approved the confession and recommended it to the churches.

John Newton Brown published the confession (along with two additional articles that he had written) in his *Baptist Church Manual* (1853). Other church manuals adopted it, and it soon became the most widely distributed statement of doctrine among Baptists in America. J. M. Pendleton, the famous "Landmark" Baptist leader, published the confession in his *Church Manual* (1867). Landmark Baptists particularly emphasized the local, visible congregation as being the church in its true form, and they opposed the idea of an actual universal church. The *New Hampshire Confession* does not mention the doctrine of a universal church.

The General Association of Baptist Churches, a Landmark group formed in 1902, adopted the *New Hampshire Confession* along with some supplementary articles. The General Association of Regular Baptist Churches (a group of conservative churches who were protesting theological liberalism in the Northern Convention) organized in 1933 and adopted the *New Hampshire Confession* with only slight changes to clarify their views on eschatology. As will be noted below, in 1925 the Southern Baptist Convention adopted a statement of faith that was essentially the *New Hampshire Confession*. The first article of the *New Hampshire Confession* concerns the Scriptures and reads:

> We believe that the Holy Bible was written by men divinely inspired, and is a perfect treasure of heavenly instruction; that it has God for its author, salvation for its end, and truth, without any mixture of error, for its matter; that it reveals the principles by which God will judge us; and therefore is, and shall remain to the end of the world, the true centre of Christian union, and the supreme standard by which all human conduct, creeds, and opinions should be tried.

A TREATISE ON THE FAITH OF THE FREE WILL BAPTISTS
(1834 AND 1948)

Free Will (Arminian) Baptists began to grow in strength as a result of the preaching of Benjamin Randall. He was converted in 1770 and at first joined a Congregational church. After a careful study of his New Testament, however, he came to believe in the doctrine of believer's baptism, and in 1776 he was baptized into a Baptist church in Berwick, Maine. His preaching was opposed by Calvinistic Baptists, and eventually he founded a Free Will church in New Hampshire and began a strong evangelistic and missionary ministry.

When Randall died in 1808, New England had at least 130 Free Will churches. They opposed written confessions at first, but by 1832 the General Conference (as the group was now designated) agreed that a treatise on doctrine was needed. In April 1834 they adopted a carefully prepared doctrinal statement.

Several editions were published, and through the years revisions were made. In 1911 the Free Will Baptists merged with the Northern Baptist Convention. This union was made possible by the theological shifts within both groups. In the South, the Original Free Will Baptists did not seek to join the more Calvinistic Southern Baptist Convention. They formed a General Conference of churches that covered a six-state area. In 1916 they formed the Cooperative General Association of Free Will Baptists, which split in 1921 over the practice of footwashing. In 1935, however, the two groups merged and took the name National Association of Free Will Baptists. At the organizational meeting, they drew up a treatise on doctrine for Free Will churches. This treatise was based upon Benjamin Randall's original confession and was modified in light of later statements of doctrine for Free Will Baptists. In 1938 a revision was adopted which is still in use. The first chapter of this treatise is entitled "The Holy Scriptures."

> These are the Old and New Testaments; they were written by holy men, inspired by the Holy Spirit, and are God's revealed word to man. They are a sufficient and infallible rule and guide to Salvation and all Christian worship and service.

LANDMARK BAPTIST CONFESSIONS (1905 AND 1950)

J. R. Graves led a movement in the South that is now called the Landmark Controversy. Graves called for a renewal in the churches based upon a return to the "Old Landmarks." Those distinguishing marks by which Graves sought to identify the true church included an emphasis on the local congregation (with a corresponding denial of the current existence of a universal church) and the necessity of a properly authorized administrator of the ordinances before they could be considered validly performed. Graves also emphasized his belief that the Great Commission promised that there would be a succession of true churches from Christ to the present day. The name may have varied through the years, but Graves identified these churches as Baptist churches. No baptism could be accepted if it was not performed by an authorized Baptist preacher, and the Lord's Supper was to be taken only by the members of the local Baptist church where it was served.

Because Landmark theologians and other Baptist theologians had such a broad area of common belief, and because some of the tenets of Landmarkism grew logically out of legitimate Baptist doctrinal positions, elements of Graves' particular ecclesiological emphases were accepted by many as normative Southern Baptist theology. However, ecclesiology was not the only doctrinal area in which J. R. Graves found an audience with ears to hear. His views on the inspiration of the Scriptures were also popularized, and they became perhaps the most widely accepted views of the origin of the Bible among the Southern Baptist laity. Using the broad circulation of his newspaper *The Tennessee Baptist* as a platform, J. R. Graves became the doctrinal instructor for many Baptists in the Deep South. Largely because of his influence, the plenary verbal theory of inspiration became widely accepted as a true description of the process of inspiration itself, not simply a description of the resulting product.

Graves' treatment of inspiration is an expansion, and to an extent an amendment, of the statement made by his good friend J. M. Pendleton in *Christian Doctrines* published in 1878. Pendleton devotes only two pages to the subject and does not attempt to name his theory. Rather, he claims "Inspiration is a mystery." He does not claim to know how men spoke and wrote the words given by the Holy Spirit (1 Corinthians 2:13) and yet retained their "individuality of style" (p. 39). However, Pendleton is firm in his conviction that the Spirit's governance of inspiration extended to the very words of the text.

> That is to say, God by his Spirit influenced the sacred penmen to write just what they did write, no more, no less; so that the Bible is as much the book of God as if he, without the intervention of men had written it himself [p. 40].

Pendleton's statement, therefore, while compatible with plenary verbal inspiration, does not employ that nomenclature. Instead, the statement relates more directly to the resultant text than to the precise method God used in producing His written word.

Graves desired more. Therefore, he presented a short but systematic statement of his views on inspiration in his book entitled *The Work of*

Christ in the Covenant of Redemption Developed in Seven Dispensations.
His discussion of inspiration, which covers only five full pages, establishes
unequivocally two major points in Graves' view of Scripture: Scripture is
without error, and Scripture is the result of the plenary verbal inspiration
of the Spirit of God.

Because the whole of the Bible is God's word, the whole of the Bible is
unadulterated truth. "To intimate that the least sentence or allusion of the
Scriptures is inaccurate or false, is to make God a liar?" (p. 24). Graves
decidedly rejects a partial inerrancy. As far as he is concerned, a person
who affirms infallibility of the religious portion of Scripture, and leaves
the other portions open to the possibility of error, is no friend to Christianity. Graves indicates both his tenacity and his theology in his reply
to such a position.

> I can not accept this proposed betrayal of the Word of God. I accept no
> compromise. It is all God's Word, or none of it is God's Word. Can all
> Scripture be indeed inspired of God and yet abound with manifest and
> manifold errors touching secular things? Is not God as regardful of his
> veracity in small things as well as in the greatest—concerning Science,
> Geography and History as [well as] purely "religious matters?" When one
> falsehood can be undoubtedly fixed upon any part of the Sacred Book,
> then its claims upon any credence are forever forfeited. If one statement
> is found to be false, I know not which ones are true [p. 24].

Graves is not claiming this inerrancy for any particular translation or for
any single copy of one of the original manuscripts. He is aware of the
problems of the text's transmission and candidly recognizes that there
were "errors in the transcription . . . errors in translation, and errors many
in interpretation." His claims relate only to the genuine text of Scripture.
As he puts it, "The original Scriptures are the words of the living God"
(p. 24).

In addition to his affirmation of the absolute truthfulness of Scripture,
Graves adamantly insists that plenary verbal inspiration is the only acceptable view of the divine process by which the inerrant text was produced.
His foundation for such an affirmation is Scripture itself. Luke 1:70 ("as
he spake by the mouth of his holy prophets"); Hebrews 1:1 ("God . . .
spake in time past . . . by the prophets"); and 1 Corinthians 2:13 ("Which
things also we speak, not in the words which man's wisdom teacheth, but
which the Holy Ghost teacheth") are cited in support of this view. Second
Timothy 3:16 provides the strongest statement as far as Graves is concerned. "All scripture" means the whole of Scripture, and the whole is no
greater than the sum of all its parts. Therefore, all parts of all the canoni-

cal books are equally inspired, according to Graves. This is plenary. Furthermore, the parts, the thoughts, are made up of words, and "we can not certainly know that we have the inspired thoughts without knowing the inspired words, for how else can thought be known except by the words that convey them?" (p. 25). This is verbal. He also cites several examples of the Holy Spirit's having given words to the apostles and prophets to illustrate that direct verbal inspiration in no way destroyed the uniqueness of the person who wrote the words (pp. 26-27).

Graves specifically rejects what some have described as "plenary or dynamic inspiration," in which only a thought, accompanied by a general superintendence to keep him from error in recording the thought, was given to a biblical writer. He recognizes and admits that this view might well be acceptable "since the result was always truth unmixed with error, and the message would be authoritative, as though every word was God-given" (p. 25). However, in spite of those strengths, Graves could not accept that view because, in his opinion, "to grant this would be to deny God's Word. It would be man's production, assisted by God. . . . If this is the correct theory of inspiration, then the Bible is a partnership work— neither God's nor man's, but partly both. And this is the popular theory." Graves believed that this theory did not give sufficient weight to the biblical claims that the words of Scripture were "inbreathed by God."

Graves' treatment of inspiration highlights two significant factors. One, he recognized that the dynamic or plenary view of the mid-nineteenth-century Baptist theologians affirmed an inerrant text of Scripture. Two, this peculiar emphasis on the plenary verbal theory as being a necessary description of the method of inspiration, rather than as a description primarily of the product of inspiration (an inerrant Bible) led various Landmark factions to emphasize that same idea in their confessions.

The United States General Association of Landmark Baptists organized in 1905 as a result of the members' distrust of centralizing tendencies in Southern Baptist denomination life. Work began at once to produce a statement of doctrine. A *Statement of Principles* was agreed upon in November of 1905. Later the group took its present name, American Baptist Association. There are twelve articles in the *Statement of Principles*. The introduction and the first article are printed below:

> We, your committee on the statement of our doctrinal belief, would respectfully submit the following and recommend:
>   That this body reaffirm its acceptance of the New Hampshire confession of faith; so long held by our American Baptist people, and that it be printed in full in the minutes of this session.

And that we would further recommend that in explanation of said Articles of Faith and in view of the attacks being made by the advocates of modern science, falsely so-called, on certain fundamentals of the revealed truth, do most positively emphasize our adherence to the following:

1. We believe in the infallible verbal inspiration of the whole Bible. II Tim. 3:16.

In 1950 several churches broke away from the American Baptist Association to form the North American Baptist Association. The split was not essentially doctrinal. The group's *Doctrinal Statement* contains twenty-five articles The introduction and the first two articles read:

The churches of this Association heartily subscribe to and agree to defend and promulgate the historic Missionary Baptist Faith and Practice, the interpretation of which is tersely stated as follows:

1. The Trinity of God.
2. The infallibility and plenary verbal inspiration of the Scriptures.

FUNDAMENTALIST BAPTIST CONFESSIONS (1921 AND 1923)

Many denominations were affected by the Fundamentalist-Modernist controversy that raged throughout the twenties. Several of these twentieth-century Baptist confessions of faith came directly from demands by conservatives for clear doctrinal stands by the denominational agencies and leaders. The first one was written in 1921 by conservatives from the Northern Baptist Convention. Most Baptist liberals were associated with the Northern Convention. For several years the conservatives tried to turn the Convention back to a more orthodox stance on Scripture. So serious did the issues become that a Conference on the Fundamentals of the Baptist Faith was called, and conservatives gathered in large numbers at Buffalo, New York, just prior to the national convention in 1920.

The result of this meeting was the formation of the Fundamental Fellowship of the Northern Baptist Convention. Later they named the group the National Federation of Fundamentalists of the Northern Baptists. Frank M. Goodchild presented a brief confessional statement to the preconvention meeting of this group in 1921. Apparently the statement was drafted by Goodchild and Curtis Lee Laws in consultation with J. C. Massee and Floyd Adams. This *Goodchild Confession* was almost unanimously adopted, and for several years the Fundamentalist leaders tried to get the Northern Convention to adopt the same or some similar confession. The Convention consistently voted against the use of a confession to attain doctrinal agreement. It even voted against W. B. Riley's motion in 1922 that the *New Hampshire Confession* be recommended to the churches. Cornelius Woelfkin, a liberal leader from New York, offered a substitute motion that prevailed. Woelfkin suggested the doctrinally ambiguous wording that "the New Testament is the all-sufficient ground of our faith and practice, and we need no other statement." After three hours of debate, Woelfkin's motion passed 1,264 to 634. Northern Baptists never officially went beyond this broad posture.

After 1925 the *Goodchild Confession* was deemphasized in favor of the *New Hampshire Confession,* and it was the *New Hampshire Confession* that formed the basis of the 1933 split. Several Fundamentalist churches withdrew from the Northern Baptist Convention to form the General Association of Regular Baptist Churches.

Those conservatives who remained in the Convention did eventually organize the Conservative Baptist Foreign Mission Society in December of 1943. This Society adopted the *Goodchild Confession* as its formal (and nonamendable) doctrinal statement. All employees of the Society had to sign the statement every year.

In May 1947 the conservatives met prior to the Northern Convention in Atlantic City, New Jersey, and formed the Conservative Baptist Association of America. Their constitution was similar to the one used by the Conservative Baptist Foreign Mission Society. Thus their doctrinal platform is (with only minor changes) the *Goodchild Confession.* This confession has seven articles plus an introductory paragraph. The introduction and the first article read as follows:

> The adoption of a creed to which allegiance is demanded would be contrary to our historic Baptist principles and repugnant to our deepest spiritual instincts. On the other hand, the adoption of a confession of faith, as a standard about which our Baptist people may rally, is consistent with the practice of our fathers from the earliest days of our denominational history. Living in a day of doubt, unbelief, and irreligion, we feel that the time has come for Baptists publicly to reaffirm their faith in the great fundamentals. As Baptists and members of churches connected with the Northern Baptist Convention, we desire to restate the foundation doctrines of our faith in the following brief and simple confession which is but a re-affirmation of the substance of the historic Philadelphia and New Hampshire confessions of faith:
>
> > 1. We believe that the Bible is God's word, that it was written by men divinely inspired, and that it has supreme authority in all matters of faith and conduct.

In 1921, 130 conservatives in the Northern Convention issued a *Call and*

Manifesto that called upon Baptists to oppose all doctrinal disloyalty among the Convention agencies. A plea was made asking for doctrinally sound literature, and support was expressed for doctrinally sound schools. These conservatives, believing that the Fundamentalist Federation was more concerned with avoiding schism than they were in standing for truth, began to organize under the name Baptist Bible Union (1923). One of those proverbial last straws that brought about this new Fundamentalist organization was Harry Emerson Fosdick's sermon "Shall the Fundamentalists Win?" The Convention refused to recall certain missionaries accused of heresy in 1925, and the Union promptly withdrew support from the Convention agencies and set up its own mission departments.

The controversy continued to escalate, with the Union reaching a peak of its influence in 1928. It had set up a publication society and had taken over Des Moines University. But the leadership of the Union was not strong enough to produce a lasting organization, and it soon disappeared after 1928. In fact, the Baptist Bible Union seems to have spent as much time fighting the less extreme Fundamentalists as it did in fighting Modernism.

T. T. Shields was the most outstanding leader of the Baptist Bible Union, and apparently he is responsible for writing its *Articles of Faith*. There were eighteen articles plus the full quotation of all Scripture passages that accompanied each article. The first article reads:

> We believe that the Holy Bible was (a) written by men supernaturally inspired; (b) that it has truth without an admixture of error for its matter; and (c) therefore is, and shall remain to the end of the age, the only complete and final revelation of the will of God to man; the true center of Christian union and the supreme standard by which all human conduct, creeds and opinions should be tried.

(Explanatory)

1. By "THE HOLY BIBLE" we mean that collection of sixty-six books, from Genesis to Revelation, which, as originally written, does not contain and convey the word of God, but IS the very Word of God.

2. By "INSPIRATION" we mean that the books of the Bible were written by holy men of old, as they were moved by the Holy Spirit, in such a definite way that their writings were supernaturally inspired and free from error, as no other writings have ever or ever will be inspired.

Northern Baptists as a whole were both unwilling to publish a general confession and unable to agree on any single doctrinal confession. In the South, however, the situation was quite different. There was a general doctrinal uniformity within the Southern Baptist Convention, and the Fundamentalist-Modernist controversy did not affect Southern Baptists in the way it did Northern Baptists. Southern Baptists had no problem in producing a generally acceptable statement of faith. In fact, the Convention leadership wrote and recomended the statement to the churches.

THE BAPTIST FAITH AND MESSAGE: THE MEMPHIS ARTICLES OF 1925

When the World's Christian Fundamentals Association was formed in 1919, J. Frank Norris, a Fundamentalist leader from Fort Worth, Texas, participated in the initial conference. He also helped create the Baptist Bible Union of America. He was expelled from the Tarrant County Baptist Association in 1922 and 1924 and by the Baptist General Convention of Texas in 1923 and 1924.

Norris found only scant grounds for doctrinal charges against the Convention, but he apparently used Fundamentalism to provide a platform for personal controversies. He frequently wrote and spoke about the theories of biological evolution that he believed were creeping into the colleges, seminaries, and churches of the Convention.

When Tennessee passed a law forbidding the teaching of any "theory that denies the story of the divine creation of man as taught in the Bible," the smoldering controversy broke out into the open. John T. Scopes agreed to admit that he had taught evolution after the law was passed (though the fact of the matter was that he did not actually teach it at all). This test case turned into a highly publicized trial in Dayton, Tennessee, during July 1925. It was the first court trial ever broadcast on radio, and it has been reported that more words were cabled overseas about this trial than about any previous news event in America.

All this excitement heightened the controversy within the Southern Baptist Convention. As early as 1919 the Convention had appointed E. Y. Mullins, L. R. Scarborough, J. B. Gambrell, Z. T. Cody, and William Ellyson to prepare a letter of greetings to be sent to other Baptist fellowships as a way of restoring communications after World War I. Mullins did most of the composing, and the greetings took the form of a simple and basic statement of faith. In 1920 the Convention asked Mullins and Gambrell to circulate these "greetings" as broadly as possible.

By 1923, however the evolutionary conflict had begun. Mullins, who was

Convention President that year, delivered the Presidential address on the subject "Present Dangers and Duties." E. D. Cameron, from Oklahoma, made a motion that the Convention adopt that part of the address referring to "Science and Religion" as the "belief of this body." That motion passed, but the controversy remained. So in 1924 a committee was appointed to consider the advisability of producing a full confessional statement.

Mullins and Scarborough were named to the committee along with C. P. Stealey, W. J. McGlothlin, S. M. Brown, E. C. Dargan, and R. H. Pitt. They enlarged the 1919 statement by using the *New Hampshire Confession* as a model. Stealey tried to include a strong pro-creation statement in the article on "The Fall of Man" that would affirm man's origin as "by direct creation of God, and not by evolution." Having failed in the committee, he went to the Convention floor, but again the statement failed. The article reads: "Man was created by the special act of God as recorded in Scripture." Stealey wanted to add:

> This creative act was separate and distinct from any other work of God and was not conditioned upon antecedent changes in previously created forms of life.

The 1925 confession did reproduce the statement on "Science and Religion" that had been adopted in 1923. Also added to the statement was a lengthy preface, in which the noncreedal status of the confession was clearly expressed. One of the introductory statements that were adopted as a part of the total confession reads:

> (4) That the sole authority for faith and practice among Baptists is the Scriptures of the Old and New Testaments. Confessions are only guides in interpretation, having no authority over the conscience.

The first article is on the doctrine of Scripture. It reads as follows:

> We believe that the Holy Bible was written by men divinely inspired, and is a perfect treasure of heavenly instruction; that it has God for its author, salvation for its end, and truth, without mixture of error, for its matter; that it reveals the principles by which God will judge us; and therefore is, and will remain to the end of the world, the true center of Christian union, and the supreme standard by which all human conduct, creeds and religious opinions should be tried.

This confession served to stabilize the Convention. In 1926 President George MacDaniel said as he closed his major address:

> This Convention accepts Genesis as teaching that man was the special crea-

tion of God, and rejects every theory, evolution or other, which teaches that man originated in, or came by way of, a lower animal ancestry.

M. E. Dodd of Louisiana moved that MacDaniel's statement be adopted as the sentiment of the Convention and that the issue be dropped from further formal Convention consideration. The motion passed unanimously.

THE BAPTIST FAITH AND MESSAGE: THE KANSAS CITY CONFESSION OF 1963

For several decades following the adoption of the *1925 Baptist Faith and Message* Southern Baptists continued to grow as a strong, theologically conservative group of Christians. But in the late 1950s a growing concern developed over a rather nebulous and undefined feeling that perhaps the denominational agencies and schools had moved in the direction of liberalism. When Ralph H. Elliott published *The Message of Genesis* (1961), the controversy broke out into the open. Elliott was a professor of Old Testament at the newly formed Midwestern Baptist Theological Seminary, and the book was published by Broadman Press, the denominational publisher. Some people predicted that the 1962 Convention would be so theologically divided that a major split would occur among Southern Baptists.

The crisis appeared to be so serious that the two men in the top places of denominational leadership, Porter Routh and Albert McClellan, met with Convention President Hershel H. Hobbs in Oklahoma City to discuss ways to preserve the unity of the Convention. In the *Review and Expositor* Hobbs describes the meeting.

> Porter Routh spoke of the widespread concern that Southern Baptists were becoming more liberal doctrinally. He added that if this were true we should know it. The best way to determine this would be for a representative committee to make a study of the 1925 statement of the Baptist Faith and Message [p. 58].

An agreement was reached to call the elected presidents of the State Conventions to serve on the committee with Hobbs as the chairman. Those on the committee included: Howard M. Reaves, Edward J. Packwood, C. Z. Holland, W. B. Timberlake, C. V. Koons, Malcom B. Knight, Dick H. Hall, Jr., Charles R. Walker, Walter R. Davis, Garth Pybas, V. C. Kruschwitz, Luther B. Hall, Robert Woodward, W. Douglas Hudgins, Paul Weber, Jr., R. A. Long, Nane Starnes, C. Hoge Hockensmith, Hugh R. Bumpas, David G. Anderson, E. Warren Rust, James H. Landes, and

R. P. Downey. Six of these men had academic doctorates from Southern Baptist Theological Seminary, and all but four (two were laymen) had the basic theological degree from a Convention-supported seminary.

According to Hobbs's account, the 1925 statement was studied word by word and thus revised. The committee consciously tried to write a statement broad enough to represent all Southern Baptists, not any regional group. Hobbs says that "every single item in the proposed statement was adopted by a unanimous vote!" (p. 60).

The draft copy was widely distributed and comments were solicited from seminary professors, Sunday School Board personnel, and others. The denominational press was furnished copies and full discussion was allowed. Hobbs says that to his knowledge "all written reactions at this point were favorable" (p. 61).

Thus, the *1963 Baptist Faith and Message* claims to be a broad based, carefully worded statement. The preface to these articles contains several significant paragraphs that were added to those included in the 1925 confession. The added words are an essential part of the new confession itself.

> Baptists are a people who profess a living faith. This faith is rooted and grounded in Jesus Christ who is "the same yesterday, and to-day, and for ever." Therefore, the sole authority for faith and practice among Baptists is Jesus Christ whose will is revealed in the Holy Scriptures.
>
> A living faith must experience a growing understanding of truth and must be continually interpreted and related to the needs of each new generation. Throughout their history Baptist bodies, both large and small, have issued statements of faith which comprise a consensus of their beliefs. Such statements have never been regarded as complete, infallible statements of faith, nor as official creeds carrying mandatory authority. Thus this generation of Southern Baptists is in historic succession of intent and purpose as it endeavors to state for its time and theological climate those articles of the Christian faith which are most surely held among us.
>
> Baptists emphasize the soul's competency before God, freedom of religion, and the priesthood of the believer. However, this emphasis should not be interpreted to mean that there is an absence of certain definite doctrines that Baptists believe, cherish, and with which they have been and are now closely identified.
>
> It is the purpose of this statement of faith and message to set forth certain teachings which we believe.

When presented to the Convention meeting in Kansas City, there was almost no debate about the seventeen articles. Some people questioned an affirmation in article six that the New Testament word for "church"

can properly be applied to the body of Christ which includes all the redeemed of all the ages. However, this affirmation was adopted along with
the total confessional statement by an overwhelming majority.

The doctrinal unrest that produced this document subsided but did not
disappear. At least three times in subsequent years the Convention has
reaffirmed its acceptance of this confession. In 1978 and 1979, the Convention adopted resolutions that again reaffirmed its confidence in article one,
"The Scriptures."

> The Holy Bible was written by men divinely inspired and is the record
> of God's revelation of Himself to man. It is a perfect treasure of divine
> instruction. It has God for its author, salvation for its end, and truth,
> without any mixture of error, for its matter. It reveals the principles by
> which God judges us; and therefore is, and will remain to the end of the
> world, the true center of Christian union, and the supreme standard by
> which all human conduct, creeds, and religious opinions should be tried.
> The criterion by which the Bible is to be interpreted is Jesus Christ.
>   Ex. 24:4; Deut. 4:1-2; 17:19; Josh. 8:34; Psalm 19:7-10; 119:11, 89,
> 105, 140; Isa. 34:16; 40:8; Jer. 15:16; 36; Matt. 5:17-18, 22:29; Luke
> 21:33; 24:44-46; John 5:39; 16:13-15; 17:17; Acts 2:16ff.; 17:11; Rom.
> 15:4; 16:25-26; 2 Tim. 3:15-17; Heb. 1:1-2; 4:12; 1 Peter 1:25; 2 Peter
> 1:19-21

In the first sentence a phrase was added that describes the Bible as being
"the record of God's revelation of Himself to man." For most Baptists this
simply affirms the obvious fact that the Bible tells of God's revelatory activity as such activity was historically manifested. In other words, to take
one example, God actually spoke to Moses in a burning bush. The historical event was the moment of direct revelation. The Bible, then, is the
record of that historical event. Some scholars, however, have suggested
that a human "record" is one step removed from the divine revelation itself;
and thus, they suggest, the Bible is likely to be characterized by human
error just so long as it provides a generally trustworthy account of the theological "matter" that was revealed. This subtle distinction did introduce
an element of ambiguity into the statement, which was welcomed by some.
The next two sentences were seen by other Baptists as being an adequate
safeguard against this more liberal interpretation. However, if one takes
the word "matter" to be a reference only to the theological content (as
opposed, for example, to all historical affirmations), then this article makes
no claim at all for biblical infallibility in its traditional sense. The claim
is only for "religious truthfulness," not total truthfulness. If, on the other
hand, one understands the term "matter" to mean the properly interpreted

meaning of the text (including facts and explanations), then the confessional statement clearly does affirm the traditional position on biblical infallibility. The article, worded in this way, does not exclude either group of interpreters from affirming the confessional statement.

Another significant change in this article from the 1925 statement is the last sentence, which reads: "The criterion by which the Bible is to be interpreted is Jesus Christ." For most Convention messengers this simply focused attention on Jesus Christ as the supreme and final revelation of God in line with the affirmations in Hebrews 1:1-2. For others this was a move toward a less conservative view of Scripture. As Clifton Allen writes in volume one of *The Broadman Bible Commentary:* "The wording of various passages, directly or indirectly, seems to attribute to God acts and attitudes out of harmony with his nature as holy love and clearly in conflict with the example and teaching of Jesus" (p. 7). Allen is saying that some parts of the Scripture are out of harmony with the teachings of Jesus, and thus are not properly described as "truth, without mixture of error."

Historically, Baptists had affirmed that Scripture was to be interpreted by Scripture. That is, obscure passages need to be interpreted by clearer passages, and the progressive and cumulative nature of biblical revelation must be recognized. But to affirm that all Scripture is true and authoritative when understood properly within the total context of "all Scripture" is quite different from saying that all Scripture is true if it is in harmony with only some specific portions of the gospels. For Allen, not all Scripture is true, or at least it is not all authoritative. Some of it is out of harmony with the teachings of Christ, he says. As an example of these "out of harmony" passages, Allen mentions Deuteronomy 17:2-7, which describes execution by stoning for the sin of idolatry. Again he mentions 2 Samuel 21:1-9, which describes David allowing the Gibeonites to avenge themselves by killing seven of Saul's sons. Because these passages, according to Allen, do not agree with other biblical teachings concerning God's nature as holy love, the writers must have been mistaken about God's revelation at this point. We can recognize the "errors" or "falsehoods," however, by comparing them to the clear teachings of Jesus, he says.

Hershel Hobbs, in *Review and Expositor* says that this sentence added to the 1925 statement came about because of the controversy over Ralph Elliott's book *The Message of Genesis.* Some question had been raised about Melchizedek that seemed to reflect upon the priesthood of Jesus Christ. Thus, the committee, says Hobbs, added the sentence describing Christ as the criterion of interpretation in order to clarify that issue. "Of course," he adds, "the purpose of this 'criterion' extends far beyond the above instance" (p. 62).

Baptists surely agree with Hobbs that Jesus Christ is "the full and final revelation of God to man." That is the most common interpretation of the final sentence added to the 1963 confession. What implications this Christological interpretive principle might have for the integrity of the confessional statement on Scripture remain to be seen.

SCRIPTURE IN BAPTIST CONFESSIONS OF FAITH

It is obvious from the preceding survey that Baptist confessions of faith have a common characteristic, that of pointing to the Bible as a higher authority than any confessional statement. Sometimes the various articles are supported by numerous citations of biblical passages. Baptist confessions often contain specific articles on Scripture, usually declaring them to be the Word of God and, thus, to be worthy of full trust and belief.

James Leo Garrett, Jr., in *Review and Expositor*, has given a comprehensive summary of those confessions that do and do not use biblical citations, and of those that do or do not contain a separate and distinct article on Scripture. Due to the brief length of his article, he does not attempt to treat the context of each statement, nor does he investigate the theology of the writers as a means of interpreting the language of the confessional statements. However, he does recognize the crucial element that must be taken into account by all who interpret confessions.

> The question of biblical infallibility and/or inerrancy, which has evoked controversy among Baptists during the twentieth century, was not mentioned in the ancient creeds of Christianity, with their focus on the Trinity and Christology, [or] in the major sixteenth-century Reformation confessions of faith, because the issue had not yet arisen [p. 45].

When Garrett goes on to include early English Baptist confessions as among those without reference to infallibility, he means they do not use the term as such, not that they in any way lend support to the idea of the errancy of Scripture. Again the theological context of the confession must be the guide for interpreting confessional statements. For example, the noncreedal stance of Baptists and their radical commitment to the normative truth of Scripture led writers of the *Second London Confession* (1677) to designate Scripture as "the only sufficient, certain, and infallible rule of all saving Knowledge." The *Westminster Confession* does not include those words. When the *Westminster Confession* describes the whole counsel of God, it describes it as that which is "either expressly set down in Scripture, or by good and necessary consequence may be deduced from Scripture." The Baptist *Second London Confession* speaks of the whole counsel of God as that which is "either expressly set down or necessarily contained in the Holy Scripture." Whereas infant baptism might be deduced from the biblical teachings about circumcision and the covenant, Baptists would say that the command to Israel to circumcise infants is not a command to the church to baptize infants. Infant baptism is not "necessarily contained" in Scripture and, thus, is to be rejected. The New Testament teaching about the necessity of repentance and faith, moreover, seems to rule out infant baptism altogether. Thus, Baptists consciously limit themselves to the sole authority of Scripture. This limitation is reflected in the wording of their confessional statements. Baptists do not locate religious authority in creeds.

The 1978 *Chicago Statement on Biblical Inerrancy* in part reads:

Article II

We affirm that the Scriptures are the supreme written norm by which God binds the conscience, and that the authority of the Church is subordinate to that of Scripture.

We deny that Church creeds, councils, or declarations have authority greater than or equal to the authority of the Bible.

A study of Baptist confessions leads to the conclusion that Baptists would agree with this affirmation and denial. In an article entitled "Sources of Authority in Baptist Thought" which appeared in the July 1978 issue of *Baptist History and Heritage,* Garrett has demonstrated that considerable support for the idea of the Bible as the "supreme authority" can be found in the popular monographs on Baptist doctrine. However, Baptist theology would be more consistently expressed by the word "only" instead of "supreme," and Baptists would be more likely to deny that creeds, councils, or declarations have any authority at all apart from their affirmation of scriptural truths.

All Baptist confessions must be interpreted from within the historical and theological context out of which they were written. For example, the omission of the word "infallible" in the 1858 *Abstract of Principles* of the Southern Baptist Theological Seminary should not be interpreted simply by comparing it to the *Philadelphia Confession.* One should also study the other writings of Basil Manly, Jr., who wrote the *Abstract of Principles.* Surely the *New Hampshire Confession* is not to be considered seriously weakened in its view of Scripture when it uses the phrase "truth, without any mixture of error" instead of "infallible."

It is to be noted that the application of the word "infallible" to the method of the inspiration of the Bible ("the infallible verbal inspiration," and so forth) is found only in Landmark and Fundamentalist confessions. The historic Baptist affirmation is not a description of the method but is a statement about the results of inspiration. Traditionally the confessions have declared that the Scriptures, which resulted from the process of inspiration, are infallible, certain, true, without error, and so forth. In fact, it may be argued that most of the people who have defended a "plenary verbal" theory of inspiration were not primarily describing or thinking of any sort of rigid, dictational method; rather, they were referring to the results (that "all the words" are true because they were written down by men who were influenced and directed by the Holy Spirit, not necessarily mechanically controlled by Him). Many scholars mistakenly identify all "verbal" theories of inspiration with "dictation" theories of inspiration. However, the distinction between the two must be maintained. The process of inspiration is mysterious, complex, and difficult to understand. But Baptists have always clearly believed and faithfully affirmed that Scripture alone is the true and authoritative Word of God.

Garrett makes a distinction between a "functional" infallibility (the Bible as the norm for faith and practice) and a "modal" infallibility (that the method of inspiration is akin to dictation). Functional infallibility would include the hermeneutical principle that clear passages must govern the interpretation of obscure passages. Functional infallibility would not automatically resist all literary criticism. Functional infallibility could be reinterpreted today, he says, "in terms of the supremacy or finality of special revelation as climaxed in Jesus Christ in the face of rival claims of non-Christian religions and ideologies." Infallibility would then become a "synonym for the unique authority of the message of the Bible" (Sources of Authority," p. 48).

While few Baptists would not agree that Scripture has this unique authority, it should not be argued that Baptists historically intended only to affirm the Bible as superior to the rival scriptures of other religions. They clearly intended to affirm that it was also the direct revelation of the true and only God, and that man could and should trust it and obey it as it was interpreted correctly. The other articles of the confessions were to be used as guides for correct interpretations, not as final, exhaustive, and absolute creedal affirmations.

Baptists are free to hear the Word of God, and they are free to confess their faith. Other Baptists are not to be intimidated by these confessions. They are to be guided by their Christian brothers toward an ever greater unity based upon the truth as it is revealed in Scripture.

BIBLIOGRAPHY

Allen, Clifton J. "The Book of the Christian Faith." In *The Broadman Bible Commentary*, 1:1-14. 12 vols. Nashville: Broadman, 1969.

Andrews, Charles R. "The Maine Wheele That Sets Us Aworke: Examining Certain Purposes of Early Baptist Confessions of Faith." *Foundations* 1 (July 1958): 28-40.

Garrett, James Leo, Jr. "Biblical Authority According to Baptist Confessions of Faith." *Review and Expositor* 76 (winter 1979): 43-54.

———. "Sources of Authority in Baptist Thought." *Baptist History and Heritage,* July 1978, pp. 41-49.

Graves, J. R. *The Work of Christ in the Covenant of Redemption Developed in Seven Dispensations.* Memphis: Baptist Book House, 1883.

Hobbs, Hershel H. "Southern Baptists and Confessionalism: A Comparison of the Origins and Contents of the 1925 and 1963 Confession." *Review and Expositor* 76 (winter 1979): 55-68.

Lumpkin, W. L. *Baptist Confessions of Faith.* Rev. ed. Valley Forge, Pa.: Judson, 1969.

Pendleton, James Madison. *Christian Doctrines: A Compendium of Theology.* Philadelphia: American Baptist Publication Society, 1878.

Smith, H. Shelton; Handy, Robert T.; and Loetscher, Lefforts A. *American Christianity: An Historical Interpretation with Representative Documents.* New York: Scribner's, 1960. Vol. 1. *1607-1820.*

CHAPTER EIGHTEEN

"Of Them Which Keep the Sayings of This Book"

Baptists, not unlike many other Christian groups, are often not fully aware of their theological heritage. The Baptist emphasis upon direct New Testament authority has sometimes had the side effect of producing a historical vacuum in the churches. An investigation such as the one presented in this book, however, depends upon the assumption that the study of history is a valid enterprise. The Christian should pursue the study of history with a unique motivation. The Christian faith is intimately historical. The apostle John expresses his convictions at this point quite clearly when he affirms the historicity of the incarnation and when he indicates the unique apostolic obligation flowing from that event. "The Word became flesh, and dwelt among us, and we beheld His glory. . . . What we have seen and heard we proclaim to you" (John 1:14; 1 John 1:3, NASB).

Luke indicates that Theophilus' establishment in the "exact truth" of the gospel message was possible because of the integrity of Luke's historical methodology (Luke 1:4, NASB). In the first chapter of Galatians, Paul defends his divine appointment as an apostle and, thus, his doctrine of justification by faith, with a detailed historical argument explaining that he had no opportunity to receive his appointment or his message from men. Christian believers have consistently asserted that God's truth can undergo the most rigorous historical scrutiny.

Furthermore, by extension, the Christian concept of fellowship and community leads the believer to consider the saints of years-gone-by also as a part of the body of Christ. Even though they have departed from this present world, they are children of God, and the present Christian generation must consider them as brothers. They are, therefore, objects of the admonition: "The one who loves God should love his brother also" (cf. 1 John 4:7-21, NASB). Any effort to become acquainted with those in the body of Christ living or dead is in obedience to the expectations of the Savior.

In addition, the Christian responsibility to be truthful and not bear false witness requires an adequate understanding of the past as well as the present. A Christian should neither purposefully nor ignorantly misrepresent the actions or beliefs of another person. Two factors compound the complexity and soberness of such responsibility when dealing with the theological beliefs of past leaders. First, moral and ideological issues teem with delicacies that require determined integrity in order to understand them and explain them to others. Second, dead men cannot respond to modern criticism; therefore, every effort to understand rightly and communicate truthfully the ideological position of personalities in the past requires and deserves the highest intellectual and spiritual energies of today's Christian. The study of history is an indispensable part of basic Christian honesty.

This particular doctrine, the inspiration of Scripture, deserves special historical attention because of its inherent importance. Moreover, present-day Baptists have inherited the churches, associations, societies, agencies, and boards that were founded by men who held a particular, definitive view of Scripture. Present-day Baptists, if only for the sake of tradition and historical identity, are under obligation to understand the view of Scripture that bolstered the founding of their vigorous and active institutional life. What did the Baptist forefathers mean by "the sole authority of Scripture?" Once that is determined, extreme caution should characterize any movement away from the position that has produced the basic and successful institutions of Baptist life.

However, Christian honesty places a second demand on contemporary believers: they must act on the basis of truth, not tradition. Often, men of the past established patterns of life that the conscientious Christian today should reject. Many Baptists have stood resolutely in positions that were wrong. Smyth, Helwys, Gill, Fuller, Carey, Keach, Williams, Wayland, and others rejected elements within the Christian community (even within Baptist life) that they considered fallacious, harmful to pure Christian faith, and alien to the will of God. Their example is worthy of emulation, for a Christian's commitment to truth should supersede all vested interests in historical and pragmatic concerns.

Therefore, the Christian's obligation goes beyond simple descriptive historical investigation that limits itself to an accurate restatement of someone else's thought and life. He must also commit himself to determine, as far as possible, whether or not that person's ideas were true and what kind of demands that truth makes on the Christian's own contemporary thought and life. When ideas about God and His revelation to man are under consideration, the obligation to discern truth becomes significant indeed.

Up to this point, the present study has sought to answer two questions. First, what have Baptist leaders believed about biblical inspiration and religious authority? Second, why have they believed those things? Having faithfully and with integrity determined the answer to those questions, one cannot ignore a more important question: Were they right? This question is not only more important, it is also more difficult to answer. Since the end of the nineteenth century, Baptist thinking on this issue has not reflected the unity of earlier days. Some of the modifications to the traditional theories have been because of the implications and presuppositions of the historical-critical method of study. Determining whether modern biblical criticism, including the various individual elements of that discipline, is right or wrong is a task beyond the scope of this present study, though not unrelated to it.

What can be done, however, is to summarize the findings of this study, restate the historic Baptist view, and then consider various issues surrounding the more obvious implications of this view. These things will be taken up in that order in the following pages. The discussion is, of course, contemporary. However, the lines of thought used have been consciously drawn from precedents in Baptist life. Finally, the study will be concluded with an affirmation of the practical strength of the traditional Baptist position. If a view is empirically adequate, rationally coherent, and experientially justifiable, then its truth claims are not to be lightly discounted. Baptists rightly believe that their historical position regarding the truthfulness and the authoritativeness of Holy Scripture is in fact the correct position. It is the position held by Jesus Himself. It is the view taught by the apostles. It is the view that most adequately affirms God's own absolute authority. It is the majority view among true believers through the centuries. If anything, Baptists have been more consistent in their insistence upon the sole authority of Scripture than have many other Christian groups.

THE SAYINGS OF THIS BOOK

The most prominent and most general term Baptists have employed to describe the biblical text is the Pauline phrase "inspired by God" (2 Timothy 3:16, NASB) or its equivalent. Without exception and with virtually no variation in understanding for the first two and one-half centuries of their modern existence, Baptists joyfully and confidently affirmed: "All scripture is given by inspiration of God." Quite often Baptists have written polemical literature defending divine inspiration against the denials of Deists and Socinians. In this literature they developed certain words and phrases to explicate more fully the intention of such an affirmation. Baptists found themselves speaking with one voice against those who questioned the divine origin of Scripture.

The first major intradenominational disagreement over the meaning of inspiration occurred in America among Southern Baptists in 1879. C. H. Toy's views were the subject of controversy at Southern Baptist Theological Seminary. Though his personal attractiveness, his scholarly image, and his evident piety won him some supporters among Baptists, the details of his position and the implications of his views apparently lay outside the conscious awareness of most Baptists at that time. One must not forget that his resignation was asked for and accepted by those who knew him best and loved him most. As in most controversies, there were many factors that complicated attempts to act on principle alone. It would be a gross injustice to Boyce and Broadus, however, to suggest that they simply yielded to political or financial pressure. Theological issues are often costly. Boyce and Broadus believed that Toy's shift in viewpoint was a serious theological matter. As the implications became clear to them, they acted as they knew they must to preserve the theological integrity of the school.

The same controversial issues created an actual division among English Baptists within a decade of the Toy controversy. The number of those willing to follow the intellectual trend of the times into what Spurgeon characterized as the "downgrade" was much larger in England than in America. However, in these late nineteenth-century conflicts, none of the Baptists involved actually denied the "inspiration" of the Scripture, though they sometimes did reinterpret the meaning and implications of inspiration.

Whenever controversy arose, whether in the seventeenth, eighteenth, or nineteenth centuries, Baptists were forced to direct their attention toward the issues involved in the definition of biblical inspiration. In these historical conflicts—first with those outside the faith and then among those within—several consistent streams of thought can be isolated. Those streams of thought serve to express what Baptists have meant when they say: "The Bible is inspired by God."

"Infallible" is a time-honored expression used by Baptists to describe the result of inspiration. At least as early as 1651, Particular Baptists described the Bible as infallible. Williams, Bunyan, and Keach all used the word, as did the *Second London Confession* and several subsequent individuals. Later adherents to infallibility include Boyce, Broadus, Manly, Spurgeon, Carroll, and others. They used "infallible" as a word that made a theoretical claim about the nature of Scripture as an inspired volume—it is inherently truthful in facts and ideas and is, therefore, incapable of misleading the careful interpreter in what it affirms or denies. Two major reasons have traditionally bolstered this viewpoint. First, a divinely inspired volume would reflect God's character. God is truthful and is incapable of lying. Second, Jesus believed and taught that the Scripture was an infallible revelation of God's truth. Jesus promised guidance from the Holy Spirit to the apostles as they completed the written revelation in the New Testament. A third supporting argument, though used less frequently, has been called the assumptive argument. This argument seeks to determine, before any inductive investigation, the standards to which a special revelation must conform. Wayland, Dagg, Boyce, and Manly employed this argument in support of infallibility. Basically it states that if special revelation, identified with Scripture, is to meet man's moral and epistemological needs and be superior to natural revelation or natural religion, it must be secured from all liability to factual or theological errors.

"Inerrant," or "without error," expresses a second descriptive qualification Baptists have attributed to the result of inspiration. This word is merely a nuance of "infallible" and is implied by that term. Although the word has recently taken on an inflammatory character, it has significant historical precedent among Baptists. From John Smyth's characterization of Scripture as being "without error in the first donation" to the 1963 Southern Baptist Convention's *Baptist Faith and Message* phrase "truth, without mixture of error, for its matter," some concept equivalent to inerrancy has been judged by most Baptists to express accurately their understanding of the nature of Scripture. Whereas "infallible" in a general sense has referred primarily to the doctrinal content of Scripture, "without error" has been more directly applied to the factual character of Scripture. Matters of apparent contradiction; alleged inaccuracies in history, in geography, and in references to nature; and acts supposedly antithetical to the revealed nature of God are problems within the area that Baptists have traditionally described as being without error. As a result of their commitment to an interpretation of the Bible as being without error, Baptists in the past have engaged in numerous projects to explain and harmonize the apparent discrepancies and have judged themselves highly successful in those attempts. In the end, they have felt even greater justification in their assertion of biblical authority, because apparent contradictions that can be shown to be in actual harmony when properly interpreted serve to show that the different authors did not contrive with each other in their accounts. The credibility of the text is thereby increased. Broadus states the historical conviction succinctly: "They were preserved by the Holy Spirit from error. . . . There is no proof that the inspired writers made any mistake of any kind" (*Catechism*, section 3, part 2: c,f).

Another concept characteristically Baptist is the conviction of the "sole authority" of Scripture. A document might be without error and yet hold no unique authority over the consciences of men. However, Baptists have not conceived of God as dealing in trivialities by inspiring messages that were never intended as authoritative. Because God has inspired the Bible, its precepts are binding on the conscience and its teachings are designed for molding the human mind. In addition to affirming the Bible's authority, Baptists have been virtually unique in claiming that it is the "sole" authority. Wherever the Bible speaks, it is binding. Areas where it is silent must be considered areas of freedom. While creeds, councils, and tradition may serve as enlightening factors in the process of interpretation, in the last analysis the only authority is Scripture itself. Binding and authoritative doctrinal truth is either expressly stated or necessarily contained in Scripture. Through application of this principle, Adoniram Judson was forced to reject infant baptism and seek believer's baptism. In his book on Christian baptism he writes:

> Notwithstanding the obvious import of the law of baptism, the greater part of the Christian world baptize the children of believers, on the faith of their parents, or the profession of their sponsors, and refuse baptism to believers, if they have been baptized in infancy. Does their practice appear consistent with the command of Christ? Christ commands those who believe to be baptized. Pedobaptists adopt a system which tends to preclude the baptism of believers. They baptize the involuntary infant, and deprive him of the privilege of ever professing his faith in the appointed way. If his system were universally adopted, it would banish believers' baptism out of the world. But leaving the evident discordance between the system of Pedobaptists, and the command of Christ, let us inquire whether infant baptism has any just support, either direct or inferential.

> When any practice is proposed and enforced as a binding duty, we have a right to examine the grounds of the alleged obligation. It is not sufficient for the proposer to show, that the practice is innocent, and even compatible with every other duty: it is requisite, that he prove it binding. If one should enforce the ancient custom of dressing in white, for several days after baptism, as the duty of every Christian, it would not be necessary for us to urge one argument against it; nor would it be sufficient for him to prove it innocent, and even compatible with every other duty. We might reasonably refuse compliance, until he should prove, that we are bound to comply. So, in the case of infant baptism, it is not necessary for us to urge one argument against it; nor is it sufficient for the proposer to prove, that every objection is groundless. It is requisite for him to prove, that it is obligatory. The question with every parent ought to be, Am I under obligation to have my children baptized? Now, on what grounds, is this obligation predicated?

> We should naturally expect, that the baptism of infants, if enjoined at all, would have been enjoined in the law, which instituted the ordinance of this Christian baptism. But this law is silent on the subject of infants. Has

not Christ, however, left some other command, enjoining infant baptism? Not one. Have not the apostles, who were intrusted with farther communications of the will of Christ, left some command on this subject? Not one. Have they not left us some example of infant baptism? Not one. Have they not spoken of baptized infants, and thus given undeniable intimation of this practice? No, in no instance. On the contrary, whenever they have spoken of baptism, or of those to whom it was administered, their language implies, that baptism was a voluntary act of worship, and the baptized, professing believers [*Christian Baptism*, pp. 33-34].

Baptists have used these descriptive terms—infallible, without error, sole authority—to relate specifically to the Scripture in its original languages. Therefore, historically one of the main principles of interpretation has been the linguistic principle. The truest interpretation of a passage is that which most accurately reflects the meaning of the original words. Therefore, the study of Greek and Hebrew and the practice of textual criticism has generally found abundant endorsement on the part of Baptists. A. T. Robertson's name is almost synonymous with Koine-Greek scholarship. Even Roger Williams could say that he knew Baptists who gave themselves up to a serious study of the Hebrew language.

Accompanying the linguistic principle as a canon of interpretation has been the analogy of faith, or the principle that Scripture interprets Scripture. Assuming the absolute consistency of Scripture's witness to truth, Baptists have traditionally sought to bring the light from clear passages of Scripture into the shadows of a difficult passage to gain clues and set parameters for the meaning of the difficult passage. Passages that fail to yield their meaning after a proper attempt at interpretation have not been considered, in the past, as evidence of error or even lack of clarity on the part of Scripture, but as evidence of the dullness of the fallen human intellect.

Given the basic doctrine of the perspicuity, or clarity, of Scripture, and the fact that Christian truth is not mysteriously tied to the supposed sacred sounds and letters of an ancient language, Baptists have consistently asserted the validity and integrity of translations. Thomas Grantham and John Bunyan were early defenders of the idea that God's truth could be effectively translated into the languages of the heathen, and, while not technically identified with the Sacred Oracles, these translations could communicate Christian truth. Even John Smyth, although he did not allow the reading of a translation in worship, recognized its necessity for personal study. Baptists historically have confidently declared that God's Word can certainly be in English, as well as Greek, as long as the translation accurately reflects the meaning of the original words.

The next section of this chapter will attempt to restate, in contemporary terms, this positive historical view of Scripture. What is offered here is a suggested reconstruction of the view of Scripture as found within Baptist confessional life throughout the last three hundred fifty years and in the writings of many of the individuals examined in this study. The remaining parts of the chapter engage in an application of this historical-contemporary restatement to various historical and contemporary objections to the view here expressed. Each section is intended to present a discussion of the issues by employing the same kinds of responses Baptists have previously presented to such objections. Historically, Baptists have considered their answers adequate replies to the objections raised.

From the beginning, God has continually existed as a communicating Being. He is worthy of all honor, praise, and glory because He has created and does sustain all things that have been made. God is the source of all truth. God is one, and, thus, truth is a unity. Truth is defined and described by His character and His nature. His will and His actions, His attitudes, and His relationships are unknown and unknowable apart from His self-revelation. God has revealed Himself to mankind in both a general and a special way. He is known by the natural things He has made, and He is known through His written Word, which is centered upon the Incarnate Word, Jesus Christ.

Mankind is a race of conscious, intelligent beings; but mankind is severely limited in many ways. Humans are self-conscious, rational, personal agents, but unaided, they are seemingly unable to achieve substantial unity among themselves regarding the meaning of life or the nature and content of ultimate truth. God's gracious activity of revelation is the only adequate point of contact that mankind has with the source of truth.

God's activity of special revelation has taken many forms. God has revealed Himself supremely and fully through the Lord Jesus Christ in the days of His historical incarnation. He has at times spoken to His prophets and apostles in an audible voice, in a vision, or in a dream. On still other occasions, He has revealed His character and His will through miraculous events. He has sometimes used yet other means, some of which remain a mystery to Christians today. Nevertheless, throughout history God has truly communicated with the biblical writers, directing them in their understanding, teaching them His thoughts, leading them in acceptable praise and worship, helping them to discern the true meaning of history, explaining to them the truth about man's origin and destiny, revealing to them the true framework for decision-making and for interpreting all knowledge, and guiding them to preserve His revelation accurately in human language. God's revelation is summed up in Jesus Christ.

The Bible is God's special written revelation of truth. Each human writer of the various biblical books was motivated, informed, and guided by a specific and a unique activity of God's Holy Spirit. The divine choice of human writers was not arbitrary or capricious. God's choice did not violate human responsibility, nor did it destroy the contextual relationships of each writer. Each biblical book is written in the language, in the style, and from the cultural perspective of the human writers. However, the words used, the truths taught, the interpretations given, the facts presented, and the affirmations made have God as their original source and are rightly acknowledged as God's truthful Word to mankind. The Bible, properly interpreted, is to be believed and not doubted, obeyed and not ignored.

The correct interpretation of the authentic text of Scripture is the final, authoritative word on the matter intentionally being discussed; and the actual teaching of any biblical passage is to be interpreted in harmony with the actual teaching of other parts of Scripture and with the actual facts of the created order. All truth is from God and finds its unity in Him. Scripture itself reveals the norms for interpreting all other facts. Scripture is properly interpreted only when it is assumed to be fully truthful and not deceptive. An impartial inductive or historical study of the text of Scripture will demonstrate that it meets all the necessary criteria for affirming its truthfulness in the whole and in the part. It is to be accepted, however, upon God's authority as expressed through Jesus Christ and not upon the agreement or lack of agreement expressed by human wisdom. The Scriptures testify truthfully about Christ. Everyone who submits to the authority of God will listen to His written Word of Scripture and learn from Him and will, thus, come to Christ. All who volitionally acknowledge, obediently trust, and commit themselves, as a result of God's elective grace, to the Lordship of the Messiah, Jesus, will receive the grace-gift of eternal life.

God is not limited in His ability to reveal truth by the nature of human language. He has used the various literary genre to their best advantage. The complexity of language is a divine gift designed for the very purpose of communicating truth.

Scripture teaches only that which is actually the case. Historical narratives in Scripture are to be taken as fully factual. Literary genre other than narrative are to be believed and accepted in keeping with the nature of the genre and the conscious intention of the writer.

The Bible is the ultimate arbiter of theological controversies. Scripture is the unique and only authoritative source of religious doctrines. The biblical world view is to be accepted as the correct framework for evaluating and directing the philosophical enterprise, for interpreting history, for understanding the natural universe, and for establishing a valid decision-making process regarding ethical issues. Human reason and human opinion must submit to biblical authority because Scripture, all Scripture, and Scripture only mediates the divine mind to modern man.

The word and the message of Scripture is the word and the message of God. The Bible is the only basis for Christian unity in this age, and it will not be superseded until Christ Jesus returns personally in glory to consummate the Kingdom of God.

He That Keepeth the Sayings

Several corollaries follow from this view of Scripture. First, there must be an authoritative text. If Baptists are going to claim that Scripture is the supreme standard by which theological disputes are to be settled, Scripture must exist in a definable form. There must be an authoritative answer to the questions: What is Scripture? and What does Scripture say?

Second, there must be an authentic interpretation of the text. If Baptists are going to claim that Scripture is the supreme standard by which theological disputes are to be settled, Scripture must be capable of yielding a definitive meaning. There must be an authentic answer to the questions: What does Scripture teach? and What does Scripture mean?

Third, there must be a philosophical agreement about the nature of knowledge and truth. If Baptists are going to claim that Scripture is the supreme standard by which theological disputes are to be settled, Baptists must justify their assumption that definite truth can be known. There must be an agreed-upon answer to the questions: What is the nature of scriptural authority? and What are the limits of scriptural authority?

Each of these corollaries has a colorful and a controversial history both inside and outside Baptist life. What follows is not intended to be anything more than a suggestive analysis of the ideas involved. It is hoped that several of the misunderstandings can be cleared up so that in whatever future discussions there may be in Baptist denominational life the substantial issues, not the semantic complexities, might be the focus.

Practical considerations

The issue concerning an authoritative text has several practical aspects. Despite the abundance of modern translations, or perhaps because of them, the King James Version of the Bible is still by far the best-selling book in the English-speaking world. Most English-speaking Baptist families have three or more copies of that one translation—in addition to whatever copies of other versions they may have. Most Baptist preachers still preach from the King James Version. The literary beauty and the dramatic impact of the rhythm, the vocabulary, and the style are perhaps unsurpassed by any of the newer versions. In some cases it is more faithful to the meaning of the Greek and Hebrew syntax than even some of the most scholarly revisions. Yet almost all Bible scholars prefer the American Standard Version or some other major, modern translation to the King James Version. It is false to attribute this to liberal theological bias. Even the most conservative scholars often turn to a modern translation as their favorite. Apparently, the traditional acceptance of the KJV among preachers and laymen led the Baptist compilers and editors of the recently published *Criswell Study Bible* to use the King James translation as their basic text.

A modern translation is nevertheless preferred for teaching purposes by most scholars because modern versions are more accurate translations overall, and particularly because the translations are thought to be based upon better manuscript evidence. Modern translations vary in quality, but their common purpose is to communicate the original intent of the writers to twentieth-century readers.

There are, however, some theological issues involved. Not all of the translations render the same meanings for every verse. Which translation should be used to settle theological disputes? The Baptist view of Scripture implies that some standard must exist. Theologians need to know exactly what Scripture says.

Some Baptist pastors and laymen may turn to a favorite translation, such as the King James, to solve their disputes. But it is generally recognized among Baptist scholars that the final appeal must be to the Greek or Hebrew text. In most cases, a study of the Scripture in its original languages serves to settle the question. A translation can serve as a final authority, a confidence expressed boldly by Bunyan and Grantham, if it is an accurate translation from the original languages. Most theological disputes are capable of being settled by the text of any good translation (King James, NASB, NIV, and so forth). When the issue is more complicated, the final authority must be in the Greek and Hebrew manuscripts. Technically, this has been the final authority all along, as explained succinctly by men such as John Smyth, John Gill, John Broadus, and others. If that affirmation was not always clearly specified, it was simply assumed. One accepts the word of Scripture. Where translations differ, one goes to the manuscripts behind the translations.

Seldom is there any theological issue of merit that cannot be settled on the basis of a good translation or from a study of the Greek and Hebrew manuscripts underlying those translations. However, in rare cases some issue may hang on a point in the manuscripts where variant readings exist. There are well over fifty-two hundred copies of Greek manuscripts of the New Testament. Some variations exist between these several manuscripts. Where is the final authority? Where can one find the answer to the question, What exactly did Paul or John say? The only absolutely authoritative source by which that question could be answered is the original copy, that is, the manuscript John wrote or that Paul's amanuensis wrote. Thus, only the "autograph" (the original self-writing of the biblical writer) can be that final authority by which all theological controversy can be judged.

This seems to be a logical, even an obvious, conclusion. Absolute and final authority can reside only in the autographs. Only what Matthew or Mark actually wrote could be defended as being what the Scripture says. Other studies must be consulted if doubt persists as to whether the book of Mark or Luke, for example, should even be called Scripture. That issue, however, has been settled among Christians for at least sixteen hundred years. Technically speaking, only the autographs could serve as the final, authoritative standard for settling a dispute over what Scripture says.

Thus rises the most obvious practical objection to this entire view of Scripture. The autographs apparently no longer exist. They seemingly have been lost or destroyed through the years. How could affirmations of truth be founded upon nonexistent manuscripts? How could anyone ever settle a theological controversy if the basis for settling it is restricted to a manuscript that does not exist?

Such a formidable-sounding objection, however, misses the point of the argument almost entirely. The important question is not whether the autographs do now exist but whether they ever existed. Is there a fully authoritative Word of God that stands behind the translations and manuscripts that are presently in existence? If so, then it is not impossible to discover that Word. Just as any accurate meter stick can measure distance because it is based on the official National Bureau of Standards meter, so any accurate copy can function as if it were the autograph. Any accurate translation functions as if it were the original writing. Whether or not accurate copies exist is a matter of evidence. In the case of the biblical writings, the evidence is overwhelmingly in favor of the most positive conclusion.

Where some doubt remains about the exact wording of a verse, any good biblical commentary will point out all the details. However, the amazing and miraculous providence of God has preserved His Word so completely that no aspect of the original text that has any significant bearing on possible doctrinal considerations has been lost. Current critical texts of the Hebrew and Greek Scriptures are virtually identical to the autographs, according to an abundant and fully adequate amount of trustworthy evidence. Accurate translations can be made and, thus, can be fully trusted.

Baptists have not usually claimed that the current translations needed to be doubted. For all practical purposes, even less than perfect translations function as the Word of God. Many are saved by reading the beloved King James Version. Except where one must speak with technical, philosophical precision, or where controversy might exist over the accuracy of the translation, the English translation serves well as it conveys God's revelation to English-speaking mankind. If translations cannot settle a doctrinal or factual question about the meaning of Scripture, one should turn to the best reconstructions of the underlying Greek and Hebrew texts. Textual criticism may not have yet absolutely settled every detail, but it has adequate evidence with which to work and its results are eminently trustworthy. In that rare case in which significant doubt about some reading may remain, the consistent Baptist response would be to state no doctrinal conclusions from that passage.

If one is to affirm the authority and the truthfulness of Scripture, as Baptists consistently have done, that affirmation of authority and truth logically could apply only directly to the autographs. Their loss is of no significance, however, if good and accurate copies exist, which they do by the thousands. The conclusion is that objections to the Baptist view of Scripture based upon the lack of the actual autographs is not a valid objection. Surely one could not affirm the falsity or the fallibility of the currently nonexistent autographs and then make any greater claims for the truthfulness of the existing copies. It is definitely possible, on the other hand, to admit the presence of transcriptional errors in many manuscripts while affirming the full truthfulness of the original words. This is exactly what Baptists have historically done.

Perhaps the objection has been underrated, however. The objection to an autograph theory of biblical authority is not at root a claim that autographs never existed, nor is it a claim that everything in them is false. The real, practical objection is found in this question: What possible use would infallible original manuscripts be unless there were also infallible interpreters? No one claims to be an infallible interpreter. If someone did, he would soon be challenged. Such a claim would be foolish. Does not the lack of infallible interpreters nullify any value that could come from an infallible text?

Again the argument sounds persuasive, but again it misses the point of the issue. To the extent that one misinterprets the text of Scripture, to that extent he misunderstands God's Word. The relevant question, however, is whether one would correctly hear and understand God's revealed truth if one did interpret correctly? If one misunderstands doctrinal truth, if he misunderstands the basis for ethical decision, if he misunderstands the true nature of reality; is that God's fault for not providing an accurate source of that knowledge? Would men still be in error even if they did interpret the Scripture correctly? Baptists, for the largest part of their history, have answered this question with the assurance that Scripture can serve as the arbiter of theological disputes and as the basis for Christian unity. Proper interpretation does yield divinely authoritative truth.

What could a claim for religious authority possibly mean if even the correct interpretation of the authentic inspired text only led to a reaffirmation of original error? This part of the autograph problem served as John

Clifford's main objection to the inerrancy of the autographs. Clifford found several elements of the undisputed text unacceptable; he therefore refused to believe them, removing any real external authority for Christian faith and practice. If there is no final authoritative source of truth in religion, the question of proper interpretation becomes irrelevant. Some modern religious experience might be considered as equally authoritative as some religious experience in A.D. 30. Thus Scripture becomes just one witness to religious truth among many. Baptists depart from their heritage if they treat Scripture only as a firsthand, eyewitness, primary source but not as a uniquely inspired, divinely authoritative, normative standard of revealed truth.

No claim has been made by Baptists that infallible interpreters exist. However, on basic doctrinal and ethical matters, a consensus of Baptist interpretations has been offered in confessional forms. These interpretations are believed to be true because they are believed to be accurate interpretations of God's revealed truth. Should further study reveal the erroneous character of traditional interpretations, Baptists' noncreedalistic structure and emphasis on liberty of conscience would make it not only possible but probable that renewed study and meaningful change would occur. The acknowledgment that infallible interpreters do not exist is, in fact, at the very heart of Baptist confessionalism. Scripture and only Scripture is the basis for religious authority. No creed is ever properly used as if it were a final, summarized, compendium of all scriptural teaching. Scripture itself is the only normative authority. Scripture stands above every creed or confession. Proper interpretation is possible; therefore, truth may be known. Human weakness in interpretation is no excuse for denying God's successful work of revelation.

One must keep in mind the legitimate and necessary distinction between hermeneutics and authority. Hermeneutics, the science of interpretation, is based on the study of grammatical principles discovered by an inductive study of the language. Interpretation depends upon one's ability to recognize verb tenses and noun cases. Interpretation is a skill requiring an intimate acquaintance with the subtle nuances of a language.

Interpretation involves and requires insight into vocabulary meanings. This comes only through historical studies. One must know as much as possible about the author, his background, his cultural and geographical context, his educational and social relationships, his motivations, his values, his goals, and his interests. If the writing is to be correctly interpreted, the interpreter must also have a similarly comprehensive knowledge about the intended audience. In the case of Scripture, this attention to proper interpretation is especially crucial. A high view of biblical inspiration ought to motivate one toward a strict view of proper interpretation. This concern for proper interpretation moved Boyce, Carroll, and others to found theological seminaries that would strive to produce men who were "Mighty in the Scripture." Proper interpretation prompted Francis Wayland to his deep concern for true biblical preaching. Out of conviction that Scripture was inspired of God, A. T. Robertson produced his scholarly works on Greek grammar and nuances of meaning in Greek words. These Baptists believed that man's understanding of God's truth depended on proper interpretation.

The easy way out of a difficult interpretive problem is to allegorize or spiritualize the passage. Misinterpretation of Scripture, however, is not the special province of any particular theological persuasion. Conservatives, who ought to know better, are sometimes among the worst offenders. Somehow the idea has arisen that divine inspiration must result in a text that contains a sermon in every verse and a direct contemporary application of every thought. Nevertheless, affirmations of full biblical truthfulness do not necessarily predetermine the content of that truthfulness. One must interpret a divinely inspired text correctly if the conclusions are to be affirmed as having divine authority. A command or a promise to Abraham or Moses or David is not necessarily directed also toward Ishmael, Aaron, or Solomon unless God intends the broader application. So it is with supposed contemporary applications of biblical teachings. Full authority resides only in that which Scripture actually teaches intentionally.

Language is inherently capable of multiple meanings. In some cases it may be that ambiguity is deliberately used by a biblical writer in order to convey the complexity of several meanings at once. As a general principle of interpretation, however, it should be recognized that the intended meaning is the true meaning, and that other meanings are simply applications of the true meaning. Divine authority should be affirmed only for the true meaning.

The practical objections to the historical Baptist view of Scripture are seen, thus, to be based on either a misunderstanding concerning the substance of the real issues involved or a confusion between authority and interpretation. Yet many sincere Christian people today still find the necessity for locating religious authority in the biblical autographs to be less than a compelling view. After all, they say, if belief in infallible autographs were a necessary part of theological orthodoxy, God would have delivered His Word to men on golden tablets, or at least He would have led men to preserve the inspired originals. Such reasoning carries great practical weight. The Baptist view is often said to be unnecessary, unduly restrictive, even deceptive (because claims are made about that which is not directly available).

Answers to these objections are not hard to come by, however. In a sense these objections are like those explaining that airplanes are unnecessary: God must not intend that people should fly, for He did not give them wings. A better analogy might suggest the proper approach to the objections. Thirst is an evidence that water does exist and that dehydration is not inevitable. The imperative need for an absolute authority is evidence (though not proof) that one is available. No significant loss occurs because of the absence of the actual autographs. The need for a normative standard is not lessened simply because the autographs are not directly available. However, Baptists have never intended to argue for a normative source of revealed truth that is not available at all. The original writings were never available in one sense of the word. Only Rome, for example, ever had the original of the letter from Paul to the Romans. All other churches that have ever had a copy had exactly that, a copy.

Christian claims about the authority of Scripture have never been made on the basis of anything more than copies. Baptists do not worship the Bible. Paper and ink are not worthy of adoration. What Scripture teaches is the basis for knowing what God has revealed. God and His Word are the final authority. That teaching of Scripture has not been lost; rather, it has been marvelously preserved in the unsurpassed quality and quantity of the copies and translations that are available.

The loss of the originals was no accident; it was providential. Thomas Grantham's argument concerning the absence of the autographs is adequate and convincing at this point. Errors that may creep into the text of various copies either intentionally or unintentionally can be detected by comparing the different manuscript copies. What if the originals had been preserved and were somewhere deceptively modified even by well-meaning scholars? Heresy might be mixed in with truth. One could never with certainty detect even substantial error. Scripture would lose its authority for teaching, rebuking, correcting, and training in righteousness. Human reason, personal opinion, and the consensus of scholarship would replace Scripture as the word of truth.

God is all-wise. His method of giving men His truth is realistic. He did not enclose the first copies in science-fiction "force-fields," nor did he make them physically indestructible. Yet they are indestructible in substance, and they are thereby enabled to serve His purpose. God has marvelously guaranteed the preservation of His revelation, while at the same time He has prevented the misuse of the documents used to make that revelation available to all people.

Superstitious adoration of the handwriting of John, for example, has been avoided by preserving the true content of his writings without preserving his actual manuscript drafts. God has graciously not subjected the theologians to the vagaries of graphology. Claims of miracles associated with the presence of an inspired original have not been allowed to degrade the character of Christian theology. Attempts to commercialize precious documents have characterized even the discovery of the ancient copies; what would the case be if the original biblical writings were still in existence? What if early Gnostic heretics had perpetrated a religious fraud based upon their surreptitious acquisition of the autographs? Would there ever have been a successful Protestant Reformation if the Pope had possessed the autographs? How many other theological pitfalls would lie in the path of the Christian churches if God had allowed the autographs to be perpetually preserved like golden tablets? God did not even preserve the tablets of stone on which the Ten Commandments were written except for a few hundred years. What God has done is best. His Word is available and is to be believed on His authority.

In brief, it is true that absolute biblical authority strictly applies only to the autographs, which no longer seem to be in existence. Full truthfulness may, however, be affirmed of any copy or translation to the extent that it is an accurate copy or translation. This method of preserving the divine revelation demonstrates God's wisdom. He has acted in the best way to convey His truth to mankind through the authority of His Word. Pious frauds have been prevented from the beginning as a result of the immediate and widespread circulation of copies that were accurate and adequate for the purpose of revealing truth and not error.

TECHNICAL CONSIDERATIONS

The second corollary of the Baptist view of Scripture relates directly to the matter of interpretation of the authentic text of Scripture. This point has implications that go beyond the practical considerations discussed above. The present translations, or at least the critical texts of the Hebrew and Greek Scriptures, have been described as being virtually identical with the original manuscripts. That in essence settles the question: What does the Scripture say? Yet here lies the very heart of the problem that some modern Baptists have with the view of Scripture that historically has characterized Baptist thinking in this area. The present text of the Bible seems to contain contradictions and errors and misstatements of fact, not all of which can be attributed to variant readings in the manuscripts.

An easy way, supposedly, to solve all such difficulties is to claim that the original manuscripts do not contain them. Matthew speaks of the thirty pieces of silver offered for Christ and says that this is a fulfillment of the words of the prophet Jeremiah (Matthew 27:9-10). However, it was not Jeremiah but Zechariah who spoke of thirty pieces of silver (Zechariah 11:12-13). The quotation is not even an accurate verbal quotation from Zechariah. Some people who naively hold to the theory of full biblical inspiration and authority might be tempted to dismiss this problem by saying that the original manuscripts do not contain this "erroneous" report. In the original, Matthew got it right. The problem is said to be a copyist error. Though this may be a common "solution" to the problem, it is totally uncharacteristic of scholarly Baptist thinking, and it is not the response required by the Baptist view of Scripture.

Jesus compares the Kingdom of God to a mustard seed, which he says is the smallest of all seeds (Matthew 13:31-32). Some people say that this is a botanical error, pure and simple. But does anyone actually think that in the original copy of Matthew's gospel Jesus was quoted as saying that the mustard seed is a very small but not the very smallest seed? Did God incite David (2 Samuel 24:1-2) or did Satan (1 Chronicles 21:1-2)? Must Baptists resort to the autograph theory of biblical inspiration to solve such problems?

The answer to this last question is so obvious that it is surprising to discover how prominent a place this kind of objection to full biblical authority has had in recent years. Apparently this kind of phenomenon (imprecision of expression or verbal variations) in the text of Scripture disturbs many people. Several misunderstandings have arisen concerning the nature of biblical authority in the last several decades because of the special attention some scholars have given these dissimilarities with no accompanying explanations. A few of those misunderstandings will be treated below. The Baptist view is not incapable of defense.

First, where variant readings exist among the manuscripts there may be some grounds for suggesting that a majority reading may be the wrong reading. However, only a few of the apparent discrepancies are solved by variant readings. Where the discrepancy is in the numbers used, or if there are unusual circumstances, an appeal to the autographs might be legitimate. In the biblical languages, alphabetic characters are used for the number system. Some of these letters (especially in Hebrew) are very similar and are easily confused in the transmission process. Sometimes the evidence may clearly point to transcriptional error even if there are no variant readings. Nevertheless, this possibility for copyist errors is seldom legitimate as a hermeneutical conclusion. The manuscripts available to modern scholars are readily able to substantiate the authenticity of all but a minute fraction of the words used in the autographs. The phenomena of apparent discrepancies, verbal differences, seeming contradictions, and so forth are real. Those things exist in the autographs. Matthew actually said "Jeremiah" and the reference to God and Satan in the same context actually exists in the autographs of Kings and Chronicles. If Scripture is to be believed as being totally true, that claim must be made with full recognition of these so-called phenomena. A simple comparative study of the synoptic gospels or of Kings and Chronicles will produce a deep awareness of the fact that biblical authority could not be maintained in its traditional sense if it depended upon some limp appeal to the "nonexistent" autographs to save the day over and over throughout the Bible. Baptists have not affirmed full biblical truthfulness out of ignorance. The traditional claims have not been made superficially. This is the point of so much of the current misunderstanding. Those who challenge the historic Baptist view often assume that those who maintain it do so purely out of ignorance and naivety. That may be true of some, but it is not necessarily true of all. What Baptists have argued historically is that these phenomena are not incompatible with authentic truth claims. Baptists have maintained that these phenomena are not properly described as errors mixed in with the truth.

Second, grammatical irregularities do not invalidate truth claims. Grammatical rules are, for the most part, descriptive, not prescriptive. Oughtness in grammar comes from a concern for clear communication. The fact that Peter may use participles in a different way from Luke has no substantial bearing on the truth of what he says. It may affect the manner in which an interpreter would handle the writings of each man, but it would not necessarily affect the believability of the ideas drawn from a correct interpretation. One writer may use the Greek verb tenses to their limits to describe clearly the various kinds of action that each tense can convey. Another biblical author may write without making use of the range of descriptive nuances available through the language. One author may generalize, use round numbers, or speak with grammatical peculiarities; another may specialize, use exact figures, or speak with classical form; but what is communicated by these various forms is not less true because of these grammatical differences. This is not to say that grammar is unimportant. But it is to say that when truth is the issue, communication is that which is important. It is foolish to try to separate the thoughts from the words as if one could be inspired and the other not. However, there are credible theories of verbal inspiration that do not entail dictation.

Third, as a continuation of the same line of thought, differences in style or literary genre are not the points at issue for the doctrine of religious authority. Amos speaks like a farmer, Isaiah like a statesman. Moses was highly educated, Peter was a fisherman. Luke is a sophisticated medical doctor, Daniel a government leader, Ezekiel a visionary. God created mankind with the potential for all these differences and more. All men are not alike. Why should anyone be surprised to find that God would use different kinds of people to speak His Word to the rest? The extension of inspiration to the very words of Scripture is not affected by the discovery of different styles. God is the creator of all things. He is the author of all styles. The thunderous warnings of judgment flow naturally in the earthy language of Amos. The glorious prophecies of Messiah, the pathos of profound sorrow and the intellectual challenge to unbelief comes best from an Isaiah. The mysterious prophecy of the kingdoms of this world being replaced by the Kingdom of Christ seems to be the message a believing representative of an unbelieving government, such as Daniel, would be most suited to convey. God chose each writer exactly because his style was His style. The background, vocabulary, and thought patterns of each writer were those God saw fit to use to convey His message.

Literary genre may be discussed the same way. No rule can be applied to God that would limit His revelation to narrative or didactic passages. Inspiration is not dictation; but even if it were, God would not be limited to only certain genres. Who cannot "feel" the differences between Exodus 20 and Psalm 23 and Daniel 9? God may didactically reveal His moral commands, or He may elicit the appropriate poetic response to His intimate care for His people, or He may astound men with intricate, symbolic visions of human destiny. Inspiration is not dictation; it is a work of God's Holy Spirit in guiding, teaching, and preserving the revelation of God's truth. The words used by each writer were not arbitrarily or randomly chosen. Each writer had flexibility in writing the truth, but the Spirit was not frustrated in His ministry of inspiring these men to write the truth. One should not forget that the biblical writers were "called" men. Their response to their call was one of commitment and dedication to their ministry of writing. Poetry, history, prophecy, gospel, epistle: all those genres have special features that suit them for certain tasks of communication.

Baptists have not leveled all parts of Scripture by their strong stand for biblical truth. Progressive revelation need not imply error or falsehood in early passages. Biblical criticism is not an inherently inappropriate hermeneutical task. Proper interpretation is not ignored by Baptist theologians. Just the opposite is the demonstrable conclusion of this study. But treating Scripture as anything less than God's truth is uncharacteristic of Baptists historically.

Thus, the discussion winds back to the phenomena themselves. Did not Matthew just have a lapse in memory and, thus, make an error? Did not Jesus simply accommodate Himself to the times and, thus, speak erroneously from His limited knowledge? Did not the Chronicler simply have a theological problem with the writer of Kings and, thus, try to correct the previous error concerning God's incitement of David to number the people? Do not these phenomena and others like them show that infallibility (if it is to be affirmed at all) must be directly applied only to the overall, general message of redemption and not to the actual text as it stands?

This formidable and persuasive argument leads to several other minor considerations as well. Would it not be the case that a proponent of full biblical truthfulness would be forced into a constant defense of trivial details and, thus, fail in the larger interpretive task? Does not this affirmation of full truthfulness put one on a limb that has already been sawed off? Does it not raise unnecessary problems for evangelism? Does it not result in reactionary attitudes toward modern achievements in biblical scholarship?

Let no one ignore the force of these questions. Ignorance and reactionary attitudes are a weak defense of truth. Baptists must not "blindly blunder on" in their view of the Bible by ignoring these issues.

Semantic issues have surfaced in greater numbers here than anywhere else. Proponents of full biblical truthfulness are sometimes forced into a defensive stance, but that is not because of the logic of their position so much as it is because of the methodology of their critics. It is the "wooden literalism" of the radical biblical critic that has become the straw man in this matter. Baptist scholars such as Bernard Ramm have used the term "literal" to designate the "basic, customary, socially designated meaning" of a word or a sentence.

> To interpret Scripture literally . . . is to commit oneself to a starting point and that starting point is to understand a document the best one can in the context of the normal, usual, customary, traditional range of designation which includes "tacit" understanding [*Protestant Biblical Interpretation*, p. 121].

Literal interpretation is the opposite of allegorical or spiritualizing methods of interpretation. Literal interpretation does not deny figurative and symbolic elements of speech; rather, it includes them. Berkeley Mickelsen, in *Interpreting the Bible*, devotes 160 pages to "Special Hermeneutics." He includes such topics as short figures of speech, opaque figures of speech, extended figures of speech, typology, symbols and symbolic actions, poetry, and other special literary devices. Mickelsen states, "Special hermeneutics needs particular attention and must be mastered in order to insure sound biblical interpretation" (*Interpreting the Bible*, p. 178). The Bible means what it means, not what some cunning mind can derive from the denial of linguistic complexity.

Individual Baptists may have failed in their interpretive task, but the Baptist view of Scripture does not demand an emphasis upon trivia. However, Baptists generally have believed that truth was important enough to be worth the demands of apologetic studies. It is precisely their point to affirm that the "limb has not been sawed off." Admission of biblical error has far more drastic consequences for evangelism than does affirmation of biblical truthfulness. To accuse the conservative of having "reactionary attitudes" is to express a prejudice. Opposition to some of the conclusions of modern biblical scholarship may arise from the recognition that those conclusions imply factual, ethical, or even theological error in God's Revelation.

But do not the actual phenomena in the text of Scripture invalidate all a priori deductive conclusions about how truthful Scripture ought to be? Is it not more appropriate simply to look and see how God inspired the Bible rather than set up rules ahead of time about how He should have done it? The answer here is both yes and no, because the question is not precisely formulated. Writing in defense of biblical inerrancy, Ramm states:

> In judging the inerrancy of the Scriptures we must judge them according to the customs, rules, and standards of the times the various books were written, and not in terms of some abstract or artificial notion of inerrancy [*Protestant Biblical Interpretation*, p. 203].

To argue that Jesus erred by accommodating Himself linguistically to Jewish usage is the same type of argument as one which says that He was necessarily sinful since He accommodated Himself to human flesh. It is a modern notion of precision, along with an often hostile wooden literalism, that presses Jesus into error in his mustard-seed analogy. In the Greek, Jesus uses a comparative form, but it need not be questioned that He intended to convey the superlative meaning. He is not making a botanical statement for all times and places. He is making an agricultural analogy in Palestine. His comparison of the smallest seed that made the largest garden plant is an accurate measurement of relative size and growth patterns among the seeds farmers actually used in Palestine. "So small a seed results in so large a plant."

This is not a strained interpretation arrived at only by skillful hermeneutical maneuvering. It is in fact the more obvious, normal interpretation of the passage if it is studied in context. To press Jesus beyond this simple, accurate analogy would be to ignore His normal manner of teaching in figures of speech and in parables. He is the Door, the Light, the Bread. The Kingdom is like a treasure hidden, like a fine pearl, like a fishing net, like a mustard seed. Another Baptist might interpret the reference to the mustard seed in some other way; each Baptist has the liberty to read and interpret for himself. But one departs from the historic Baptist view of Scripture if his interpretation attributes error or false teaching to Christ in this passage.

Several considerations are applicable to the God-or-Satan controversy in 2 Samuel 24:1-2 and 1 Chronicles 21:1-2. Would it not seem most unlikely that a dedicated, believing prophet would deliberately change the name from God to Satan? Why is there no apparent effort by some equally concerned scribe to emend the text in 2 Samuel? At the same time, a copyist error is unlikely here. Would a simple blunder or even a deliberate change of this magnitude go undetected by the other scribes and, thus, continue to be copied into the succeeding manuscripts? These suggestions are far more removed from reality than the several suggested interpretations that accept this as a variation existing in the authentic text of Scripture.

To read the passage closely, it is not an absolute, grammatical certainty that the pronoun "he" ("he moved David against them") refers to the Lord (Jehovah). It was the "anger of the LORD" that was kindled. Perhaps anger is personified in 2 Samuel and perhaps 1 Chronicles gives a more precise statement. Or it may be worthy of note that the Hebrew word *satan* has no definite article here and, thus, may legitimately be translated "an adversary." Because of David's sin, God had become David's adversary. First Kings 11:14-25 seems to use the word *satan* in this general descriptive sense without in any direct way implicating the Satan who is the personal source of temptation and evil.

Someone else might interpret the two passages as teaching two aspects of the same thing. Satan, himself, was the immediate, direct source of temptation, but Satan cannot tempt beyond what God will allow (see the book of Job). Thus, God may be legitimately thought of as the ultimate cause. In His anger (righteous anger over David's previous sin), He allowed Satan to tempt David and, thus, both passages are true. Job remained faithful while David did not.

There may be even more possibilities for interpretation here. Baptist views of biblical authority do not force anyone to hold only one particular interpretation. Upholding the assumption of full truthfulness, however, does force the interpreter to interpret. Concentrated study of one of these so-called difficulties is likely to make the student aware of the deep, complex, and profound nature of reality. To attribute a single event to Satan and to the anger of the Lord may reveal an aspect of the fathomless subtlety of theological knowledge and insight. Men have hardly begun to understand how abysmal is their ignorance and their depravity. Only God's revealed Word can lead men to a knowledge of the truth.

Matthew's reference to Jeremiah calls the interpreter again into a careful study of the text. Ramm points out that according to Jewish tradition "the spirit of Jeremiah was in Zechariah and such a method of citation would not offend their historical sense" [p. 203]. It is not impossible, however, to see a reason other than tradition for this reference. In Zechariah the money is symbolically thrown to the very person (a "shaper," literally) who had been previously used by Jeremiah as a representative of God's sovereignty (Jeremiah 18:1-17). Even though the reference to the specific detail of the thirty pieces of silver is found only in Zechariah, Matthew may be trying to emphasize the deeper theological significance of these things, and, therefore, he intentionally makes his primary reference to Jeremiah. The rejection of the Messiah is the clear basis for divine judgment.

One does not learn theology by giving up on difficult passages. The Baptist people may not be known for their profound theology as much as for their practical obedience and growth, but what holds them back is not their lack of an adequate view of Scripture. If one commits himself to finding God's truth, he has a base from which to build when he accepts full biblical authority.

But what if one apparent discrepancy remains unsolved, or what if some error appears indisputable? Would not that problem destroy the whole structure of a theology built upon full biblical truthfulness? No. Why should a humanly-supposed "error" be thought of as correcting God's revealed description of the character of His Word? The Baptist view of Scripture is an attempt to be faithful to the teachings of Scripture about itself. Baptists simply try to approach the Scriptures the same way Jesus approached them, with full confidence in their trustworthiness. Baptists try to imitate Paul's constant and conscious commitment to biblical authority. Baptists recognize the universal witness of the apostolic writers to the Bible's worthiness for belief.

Above the cross a sign was placed. Each gospel writer describes the wording of that sign with slightly differing vocabulary. Yet they all reveal the same affirmation that this man Jesus is the King of the Jews. Inspiration by dictation might have produced verbal identity among the gospels, but they are readily harmonizable as they stand. The words used convey the unintentional, ironic truth of Pilate's charge against Jesus. He was not found to have broken any law. He was crucified only because He was in fact the King of the Jews. Perhaps the sign could have had each of the various words; it was written in three languages. Yet even if that is not so, even if the variations are purely results of human memory or stylistic phrasing, the issue of truth is not in jeopardy because of these variations. The assertion that actual "error" was made in such cases is an example of a semantic argument. Verbal variation is not an example of error. Destructive criticism is characterized by an initial emphasis upon inconsequential variations. This is done in order to build a case for biblical errancy in spite of biblical claims to the contrary. Believing critics interpret upon the assumption of truthfulness.

Baptists have not been unaware of these textual phenomena when they have defined their view of biblical inspiration and authority. How precise the truth must be is not properly the decision of the modern scholar. God's character and His nature are the basis for defining truth. If God allows imprecision on some matters, it is not the task of the contemporary critic to decide a priori that God has failed to communicate truth. God defines truth.

B. H. Carroll spoke of seeing these contradictions and discrepancies melt away before the intensive study of a believing mind. Out of an original thousand, about half a dozen problems remained, he said, for him. His obligation was to continue to study and to learn. Perhaps God still has more in His Word to teach men. In humility, Baptists still seek God's truth in His Word.

THEOLOGICAL CONSIDERATIONS

Although discussions concerning theories of biblical authority are most often centered on either practical or technical matters, the "hidden agenda" more likely relates to philosophical assumptions. Epistemology, the philosophical study of knowledge, is at the heart of theological controversy. How does one come to know truth? Can one gain theological assurance from sources that are susceptible to factual errors? Are reason and revelation sisters, enemies, friends, or oil and water? If sisters, who is their father? If enemies, who made them so? If friends, how do they express their support for each other? If oil and water, which one rises to the top?

One important philosophical issue has been the unity of truth. That is, can a factually fallible document convey theologically infallible doctrine? The answer, of course, is yes. A. H. Strong wrote three massive volumes on systematic theology. It is not necessary to claim infallibility for his materials in all factual details in order to conclude that he presents God's revealed truth about the doctrine of sin, for example. However, such a conclusion is drawn legitimately only where there is some criterion by which doctrine and factual truth can be judged. Reason, in its broadest possible sense, is the means by which such judgments are made. An account of factual matters is compared to reality as it is rationally perceived. Men detect historical errors by an indirect form of rational perception; secondary accounts are compared to the firsthand testimony and to the artifacts left by others. Scientific errors are detected by comparing scientific propositions to the natural world as it is rationally perceived. But how does one judge the validity of rational perception?

Doctrinal truth, such as the origin, the result, and the implications of sin, does not involve factual matters obvious to anyone who looks. Heaven and hell are no less factual, however, because of their inaccessibility to scientific investigation in this life. A criterion for discovering, recognizing, and judging truths of this kind and a normative criterion for establishing the validity of reason itself are needed and are available. Holy Scripture is God's gracious gift to men to teach them, to correct them, to convey truth to them. Scripture is the truthful norm by which human thought is to be tested.

The Lord is one Lord. He made all things. All things are reconciled by Christ's blood. God's set purpose is to unify all things under one head, even Jesus. The unity of truth and the validity of reason follow directly from the unity and the necessity of God's being. Reason is no less contingent upon the rational nature of God than is any other created reality. All things are contingent upon God's existence. All things were made by Him. Where is the sacred-secular dichotomy in God's Word? All truth is God's truth, and all facts are God's facts. In reading A. H. Strong or any other theologian, men may discern truth mixed with error. That is possible because some normative, external standard for truth exists. Only God could stand as an authority over Scripture, but in this unique case it is Scripture itself that mediates God's mind to men. According to 1 Corinthians 2:9-13 the Spirit of God taught Paul the thoughts of God, and Paul delivered them to other men. God created man's mind. Reason is a part of the divine image. Reason is valid when it is properly related to the divine standard of truth. God reveals the truth; men must conform their thinking to that revelation. It is not the prerogative of men to sit in judgment upon Scripture. Lack of understanding is no license to accuse God's Word of being less than He intends it to be: fully truthful and authoritative.

Reason and revelation are sisters; the one God is their father. They have become enemies since reason attempted to move out and live alone. They can only fulfill their destiny as friends, yet revelation must have the priority regarding the content of truth. Oil and water is not the proper analogy, though, for reason and revelation by nature will mix. They are unified through the one Lord over all. Biblical facts, whether historical, natural, or theological, are truthful and trustworthy. To affirm the fallibility of the revelation of God as originally given is to assert the supremacy of human reason over the Spirit's work of inspiration. Traditionally, Baptists have denied that this was the appropriate intellectual response to the Word of Scripture.

In theological matters, critics of the traditional Baptist position have selected elements from the doctrine of man, the nature of God, and the work of the Spirit to discredit Baptist views. Baptists, however, have not generally been persuaded by these arguments.

For example, John Clifford and William Newton Clarke are two who especially emphasized the work of the Spirit as they opposed strict biblical authority. Jesus had promised that the Spirit would guide the apostles into all truth. Thus, they reasoned, the Spirit must continue to guide the church into new truth through the centuries. This theory provided a convenient theological justification for accepting the radically new ideas of the nineteenth-century German higher critics. Evolutionary development in theology became the unquestioned (and the unquestionable) assumption. To suggest that theological truths were fixed and settled by the text of ancient Scripture was to become an example of abysmal naivety. The psychological intimidation of this "progressive scholarship" created an impenetrable wall that excluded the traditional theologians from the so-called mainstream. Yet more of the pastors and lay people remained outside this mainstream than moved inside.

Baptists have traditionally contended that Jesus had promised the Spirit in a special guiding ministry to secure the integrity of the New Testament autographs. The Spirit's primary ministry is to convince men of sin, righteousness, and judgment and to witness to Christ. Scripture is the written source of all knowledge concerning sin, righteousness, judgment, and Jesus Christ. New Testament Scripture is a product of the Spirit's influence on the apostles and on their ministry of proclamation and interpretation. The apostles claimed unique authority, the early church leaders recognized that authority, the Christian community canonized the apostolic writings, the Reformers reaffirmed *sola scriptura,* and Baptists have built their theology upon the integrity and the purity of the doctrinal content of these New Testament writings.

A more serious step in the reaction against traditional views comes from the following apparently logical argument:

> Scripture is written by men.
> Men are fallible (i.e., men make mistakes).
> Therefore, Scripture is fallible (i.e., Scripture contains error).

Supposedly, this syllogism counteracts the following argument:

> God is perfect (i.e., God does not lie or make mistakes).
> God inspired the Scripture.
> Therefore, Scripture is perfect (i.e., Scripture is true and errorless).

True premises properly related should lead to deductive certainty. All four of the premises seem to be true, yet they seem to lead to contradictory conclusions.

The logic is deceptive, however, and the apparent contradiction does not exist. Restating the arguments may clarify the situation.

> **God is one.**
> His actions are consistent with His character.

God acted to inspire Scripture.
   Inspiration is consistent with God's character.
God's character is truthful and not deceptive.
   That which is inspired is truthful and not deceptive.
Therefore, Scripture is truthful and not deceptive.

God made man in His image.
   Man reflects God's character.
   Man's nature is such that he may be influenced by the God in whose
      image he is made.
Man has sinfully rebelled.
   Man's character has become error prone.
   Man's purely self-directed activity is liable to error.

Men wrote Scripture.
   Man's activity of writing Scripture was not purely self-directed.
God's Spirit influenced the men writing Scripture to such an extent as to
   make the result of the process consistent with God's purpose of
   revelation.

God is one.
   God's purpose of revelation is consistent with His character.
   God's character is truthful and not deceptive.
   The purpose and the result of the Scripture-writing process is consistent
      with God's character.
   Therefore, in the case of men writing Scripture, the result was truthful and
      not deceptive.

Notice that these arguments contain clarifications of the syllogistic premises used earlier. Scripture is perfect in the sense that it is truthful and not intrinsically deceptive. Men are fallible in their self-directed activity. That men can write a nondeceptive, truthful account of God's revelation is completely consistent with the idea of divine inspiration.

Some may suggest that sanctification is also a work of the Spirit, but it does not produce sinless men. Why should inspiration produce an errorless document? J. L. Dagg anticipated this argument and countered it by drawing a distinction between the work of the Spirit in sanctification and in inspiration.

Sanctification is a work of the Spirit that moves men toward moral conformity to God's will for their lives. This is a fallen world and sin has affected man's nature to such an extent that the Spirit never ceases His sanctifying work. The Spirit provides the Christian with spiritual weapons for the warfare with sin (Ephesians 6:10-18), one of which is the sword, the Word of God. The Spirit leads the Christian toward a deeper trust in Christ and His righteousness. However, the Spirit's purpose in sanctification is fundamentally different from his purpose in inspiration.

Inspiration is claimed only for a man's Scripture-writing activity. Moses is not less sinful or less fallible in his self-directed activity just because some of his activity is also divinely directed. The purpose of inspiration is to secure the truthfulness of what the inspired writer actually records. Moses' accurate communication of the commandment "Thou shalt not covet" was in no way dependent on his being free of all covetousness. Nor should the vocabulary "self-directed" and "inspired" be taken to demand no "self-direction" in the process of "inspiration." Mechanical dictation is not necessarily the alternative to pure self-direction. Inspiration does, however, involve enough influence by God's Spirit to produce God's intended result: a fully truthful and nondeceptive account of divine revelation.

Thus, man's admitted fallibility by no means rules out biblical infallibility, nor does biblical infallibility demand divine dictation in order to secure it. An unrepentant man can think and say: "Jesus demands repentance from sin" (see Luke 13:3, 5). This is true and it may be properly interpreted by any adult with normal intelligence. Inspiration secures the accurate recording of this true proposition. Sanctification begins by the act of repentance itself. Inspiration is not dependent upon completed sanctification.

The most profound and penetrating attack on the conclusions of Baptists about Scripture, however, comes from the most unexpected place, Scripture itself. There are two aspects of this theological consideration: the transcendence of God and the teachings of Jesus Himself. The first part is the easier to answer. It is said that God is too great to be captured in words. God transcends human language. By nature, words are limited, yet God is illimitable. Must men force God into thinkable thoughts and propositions? Surely knowledge of God must always be approached dialectically. No single verse, even of inspired Scripture, could possibly contain truth as such, for truth is larger than language, they say.

In reply, Baptists do not deny God's greatness, His limitless essence, or His inconceivable transcendence. Baptists need not reduce God's being in order to affirm God's revelational activity. Men did not call God down. God's initiative, God's volitional choice, God's planned action resulted in a written revelation through and to men. Baptists have not taught historically that God could be known apart from His revelation through nature and Scripture. But Baptists have also not denied that God could be known clearly and accurately by His revelation.

Exhaustive knowledge of God is not available to man in his present finite state. Man can know only what God reveals about Himself, but he can know all of that. Man does not choose to believe only that which seems reasonable, nor does man properly deny those paradoxical elements that are present in Scripture. Socratic or Platonic dialectical philosophy, however, is not the equivalent of belief and acceptance, the response God expects; and a Hegelian dialectic is an outright denial of the biblical concept of revelation as truth that corresponds to reality.

Baptists make only a modest claim: that they are theologically and ecclesiastically consistent with biblical teaching. They say the same for their ethical theory, though none of them claims to meet those standards perfectly. They claim no final Hegelian absolutes. They do not claim to know more of God than that which God has revealed. They do not even claim that they have perfect understanding of that which has been revealed. Nevertheless, they do claim that men are capable of understanding, that revelation may be described as both adequate and fully truthful, and that God's intended purpose for His revelation is not beyond man's grasp intellectually, or practically.

The second aspect of this problem comes from the teachings of Jesus. Simply put: "Love your enemies" is apparently in direct contradiction to "slaughter the Canaanites." The conclusion of so many has been: "Therefore, all other reasoning notwithstanding, God's truthful and noncontradictory revelation must not be identified with Scripture as such."

Some scholars have suggested that Scripture is to be theologically evaluated according to the idea that Jesus Himself is the great corrective norm for biblical revelation. Once that idea is accepted, the traditional view of biblical authority is dislodged, and it seldom regains its position. This concept cannot be harmonized with the historic stance of Baptists. Here discussion ends. Either Jesus teaches and accepts biblical revelation as the fully authoritative Word of God or else He corrects it, changes it, and challenges its authority. Surely "destroy the Canaanites" is no more difficult to believe than "Depart from me, ye cursed, into everlasting fire."

Jesus either stands under the authority of the Word or He stands above it and free from it. Either Jesus teaches men how to distinguish truth from error in Scripture or else He teaches them to submit to its authority. To be a Christian is to be a disciple (a learner) of Christ; thus, this issue is the crucial issue. What is the truth? Who can convince another on this point?

Someone honestly seeking answers might begin with the gospel of John or with any gospel. Key passages would include John 3:12; 5:39-40, 46-47; 7:16-17; 17:14-17; 20:31; Matthew 22:29; Mark 4:14-20; Luke 6:39-40; 16:29-31. Directly or indirectly, the attitude of Jesus is always the same. Scripture cannot be broken. It is all to be accepted, not rejected; believed, not doubted; obeyed, not ignored.

These questions are, thus, truly significant. Is Jesus the incarnation of the God revealed in the Old Testament? Is Jesus the promised Messiah of the Old Testament God? Does Jesus speak only truth? Or is the Old Testament a purely human record of the Jews' best efforts to figure out what God was trying to say to them through the ambiguities of human history? Is it only Abraham's opinion that God commanded the sacrifice of Isaac? Do men have the right to choose to believe only those parts of Scripture that express ideas similar to those of secular humanism?

There may be some doubt among a few, but Baptists generally believe that Jesus' view of Scripture is precisely that upon which Baptists have built their traditional viewpoint. It is on His authority that Baptists accept even those things they may not yet fully understand. Baptists do not claim that no problems remain or that no difficulties exist, but they consider their total trust in the Bible to be justified whether or not every aspect has been verified.

William Cathcart, the editor of the monumental *Baptist Encyclopedia*, gives voice to the historic Baptist position on inspiration at the close of the nineteenth century. In volume two of the *Encyclopedia*, in an article entitled "Inspiration of the Sacred Scriptures," he writes:

> The question is not, How did the sacred writers obtain the truths they record? but, How did they transmit that truth to their fellowmen?
>
> We hold that the Scriptures are divinely inspired,—that is, that in writing them the sacred penmen enjoyed the supernatural influence and guidance of the divine Spirit in a measure sufficient to secure its end,—the infallible communication of divine truth. This is what we mean by inspiration. . . .
>
> The very idea of inspiration involves divine assistance and guidance. A divine influence which does not extend to the language is not sufficient to secure its end,—the perfect infallibility of the Scriptures. If the writers had been left to themselves in the choice of words, it does not appear how they could have been preserved from error. Without a special divine protection the sacred writers were liable, as other writers are, to employ inadequate and erroneous expressions. Nothing short of a special divine interposition was sufficient to preserve them from all such errors in language. . . .
>
> Accepting, then, heartily, the fact that the Scriptures do not only contain a divine revelation, but that they are the infallible record of that revelation; that both as to thought and expression they were penned under the guidance, influence, and protection from error of the Holy Spirit; that they reveal to us God's thoughts in the words he has chosen to convey them; that though the Bible is given through man it is not to be taken as the word of men, but, as it is in truth, the word of God; . . . we believe that we have in these Scriptures the sole and sufficient divine authority and rule regard-

ing the way of salvation, and regarding every Christian doctrine, duty, and hope. Christians ask no other standard. No human authority can for a moment take its place. What it teaches they feel bound to believe; what it commands they feel bound to practice, and that only.

God blesses the preacher who preaches and the teacher who teaches the Bible as God's Word. The lay people who fully trust the Bible are those who find themselves uniquely related to Jesus Christ, their Lord. His Spirit testifies with their spirit that herein is truth.

HISTORICAL CONSIDERATIONS

No study such as this can conclude without a final look at history. Has the Baptist view been portrayed correctly? Is there not a basic misunderstanding in all of this? Modern controversies over the terms "infallible" and "inerrant" seem to carry highly charged yet often hidden implications that go beyond their older definitions. Would it not be more responsible historically to distinguish between the ideas and concepts standing behind early Baptist vocabulary and the ideas and concepts standing behind the modern usage of the same terms? Although the word "infallible" has been prominent and the concept "without error" has comprehensive historic precedence, is it not true that early Baptists used them in prescientific days and only intended to affirm a unique reliability in matters of religion? Are not these words now used in a sense totally out of harmony with their earlier use? If early Baptists were totally unaware of the complex issues that today's Baptists face, how could it be argued that they would continue to use those terms if they lived and wrote today?

After all, suggest some, an overriding emphasis that has characterized Baptist life and theology is the liberty of conscience. Baptists are free to interpret as they wish. Are they not also free to accept or reject any view of biblical authority that they find to be current in religious circles? Would not Roger Williams or John Bunyan stand against those who insist upon a strict view of biblical authority with the same intensity that characterized their resistance to the establishment churches of their day?

Finally, is it not a misreading of the Baptist position from the very outset to claim that "without any mixture of error" means "inerrant" in the contemporary sense? (Upon rare occasions some have read this confessional phrase as a tautology, saying that it is the "truth" that is "without error," not the content of Scripture itself. Such an interpretation is historically impossible, however.)

Several confessions read "truth for its matter, without any mixture of error." What is the "matter" of Scripture? Were not Baptists trying to shy away from public commitments to factual inerrancy by using this term? The "matter" is limited to the basic theological substance, so the argument goes. All that is being affirmed is that biblical truth is not misleading or erroneous in the sense that it adequately conveys true theology. No claims are made beyond that, if this interpretation is correct. Thus, the Baptist confession on Scripture requires no more than a "faith and practice" authority. Those people today affirming more than that are the innovators, so some suggest.

These suggested reinterpretations of the confessional phrases are not to be ignored, but they are not as likely as they may seem at first. The vocabulary problem concerning the definition of "matter" is most often raised by nonhistorians. An ideological study of the post-Reformation centuries is quite instructive for understanding the definition of "matter" in this context.

Some have pointed out that Peter Ramus (1515-72), a French Aristotelian philosopher who had a great influence on Calvinistic theology especially among the Puritans, made a clear distinction between "form" and "matter." This distinction is said to be the source of the phrase "truth, without any mixture of error, for its matter" in the *New Hampshire Confession*. Those who see this as the true context of the confessional affirmation contend that the "matter" of Scripture is its character as "a perfect treasure of heavenly instruction," a revelation of "the principles by which God will judge us," and "the supreme standard" in religion. All of this is distinguished from the "form"—that is, the actual words of Scripture. Thus, plenary verbal theories of inspiration are denied by the confessional statement itself if this interpretation is correct. The religious content (the matter) is true even though error may exist in the form (the words used). But this interpretation is not historically or philosophically accurate.

Ramist influence is surely pervasive among sixteenth- and seventeenth-century Calvinistic schoolmen. But the distinction between form and matter is slightly more complex than it appears to be above. The distinction is Aristotelian, not Platonic. It is rather like the distinction between propositions and sentences. Extensive philosophical controversy has surrounded this distinction, but for practical purposes it can be said that propositions are the meanings of sentences. "Matter," in the *New Hampshire Confession*, refers to the actual meaning of the words and sentences of Scripture. Styles and vocabularies (forms) may differ among various biblical writers. The degree of technical preciseness in chronology or in the description of events or in factual accounts may vary from writer to writer. But the actual meaning of the biblical passage (its matter) is true, and it is without error, according to the Baptist *New Hampshire Confession of Faith*. These Baptists were intentionally denying simple dictation as the method of inspiration; they were recognizing the existence and the nature of the phenomena in the authentic text; they were carefully placing the emphasis upon the doctrinal and ethical content of Scripture; but they were not using this language as a subtle cover for a denial of the full truthfulness of the Bible. They surely never intended for this terminology to be used to justify affirmations of biblical errancy in any sense. God's revelation might be expressed in Greek or Hebrew, English or Bengali (the form), but the essential meaning (the matter) is without error.

The arguments of the Deists and Socinians in the eighteenth and early nineteenth centuries were tacked upon the same framework as the one that was utilized by late nineteenth- and twentieth-century critics. The same phenomena of Scripture reputed to be biblical inaccuracies by modern critics were used in earlier days by Deists as evidence that the Bible could not be divinely inspired. Deists were quite vocal about identifying the verbal variations and supposed inconsistencies in Scripture as errror. Even so, it was the emphasis placed upon these phenomena, not the existence of the phenomena, that was new to the theological scene. Since the days of the Patristic writers, Christian theologians have examined and discussed the meaning and the purpose of these aspects of the biblical text. The consistent approach of Christian scholars has been to seek the interpretation that promotes harmony among the various ideas. Baptists have continued to follow that interpretive practice.

Baptist forefathers were undoubtedly cognizant of the full range of supposed problems with the biblical texts. Andrew Fuller, Benjamin Keach, and John L. Dagg are merely representative of a host of Baptists who glued their minds to the sticky problems of biblical phenomena and sought to interpret these passages in accordance with the analogy of faith. They also managed to give credible answers to those objections and emerged from the conflicts with unshaken confidence in their confessional statements about the nature of Scripture. No Baptist should defend "inerrancy" if "error" is defined by nonbiblical criteria. Baptists are not unaware of the substantial issues, but neither are they simply "playing to the gallery" in their positive affirmations.

Furthermore, the technical aspects of modern biblical criticism were not unknown to leading Baptist scholars in the past. Modern critics see themselves as rescuing the church from a creedal Fundamentalism. The assumption from which they work is that the Bible both in form and content is essentially and intrinsically a human work. Scripture must be treated exactly as one would treat secular literature. The Bible is thought to be man's statement of his beliefs. The movement is not thought to be from God to man at all. Rather than speak of Scripture as the Word of God, they would view it only as a history of Israel or a history of early Christian ideas. The Bible is a source book, even a primary source, but not a final or ultimately authoritative source that must be believed.

Broadus, Boyce, Manly, Reeve, and Robertson (among others) indicated a full grasp of the theories and the details of those critical methods. Yet, being fully aware of the claims of "assured results," they chose scriptural infallibility over critical infallibility and set forth good and sound reasons for their choice.

Some who have departed from the historic Baptist position, characterized by acceptance of the full truthfulness of the biblical text, have done so by appealing to another Baptist affirmation: religious liberty. The most cherished principle of Baptist life, they say, is liberty of conscience. This principle is then extended into the area of religious authority. The "historic Baptist principle" suddenly becomes the Baptist's right to hold any view of inspiration that seems most reasonable to him and to develop his theology in relation to that view. No Baptist should want to restrain anyone's freedom in religious matters, but only a most severe misreading of history can justify the conclusion that "any view of inspiration" is part of the essence of being a Baptist.

Religious liberty historically refers to the right of any individual to live in civil society and remain free from governmental or eccesiastical coercion in matters of religion. The doctrine of religious liberty is a nonformative teaching. It merely exempts a person from forced submission to existing structures, but it has no power (nor has it ever intended) to create a structure. A citizen may voluntarily unite with a religion, or he may abstain from uniting. As far as Baptists have been concerned, the nature of the gospel demands an uncoerced response. In no other way can a regenerate church membership be maintained.

However, when a person chooses Baptist life as his personal expression of faith, he voluntarily submits to basic formative principles. That which is by nature nonformative (religious liberty) cannot become the primary formative principle. To assert freedom from doctrine as the basic doctrinal norm would be to engage in an exercise of purposeful contradiction. Such an effort is in itself ludicrous and is tantamount to making Baptist church life coterminous with society in general, a result directly inconsistent with the implications of the doctrine of religious liberty.

BLESSED ARE THEY THAT DO HIS COMMANDMENTS

A belief in the absolute truthfulness and essential clarity of Scripture carries with it no magical potions that liberate one from intellectual, moral, and spiritual demands. Rather, for the one who takes seriously this commitment, the demands are compounded. If Scripture is God's Word, the interpreter labors under the awesome obligation of "rightly dividing the Word of truth." Once that truth is determined, one must make personal application of the moral demands of Scripture and labor earnestly for the propagation of that faith by which all men will be judged. Personal scholarship, Christian education, biblical preaching, social ministry, fine arts, and evangelism and missions have a greater and more solemn appeal to the one who feels bound by "Thus saith the Lord."

Personal scholarship in Baptist life is epitomized in the ministries of John Gill, John Broadus, A. T. Robertson, and C. H. Toy. Toy's early commitment to biblical infallibility led him into an academically rigorous course of personal study. His change of commitment issued from a gradual shift toward naturalism rather than supernaturalism as a governing philosophic principle. While this philosophical assumption destroyed his belief in biblical infallibility, it did not destroy, but rather redirected, his scholarship.

The argument, therefore, is not that commitment to the "sole authority" of Scripture will either automatically or exclusively lead to personal academic greatness. However, the natural and moral implication of such a persuasion is that the Christian should be "mighty in the Scriptures." His mind must be captive to the Word of God, and he must be willing to explore fully every opportunity bestowed by providence to enhance his knowledge of the language, culture, and people of the Bible. None is excluded from this stewardship of mind. "Butchers, bakers, candlestickmakers, doctors, lawyers, and Indian chiefs" must take personal responsibility in this quest for understanding the mind of God.

The concern for personal scholarship broadens into a concern for Christian education. Commitment to biblical authority is also a commitment to the unity of truth and an affirmation of God's sovereignty over all creation and all areas of knowledge. B. H. Carroll stated his concern for an educated ministry in his inimitable, picturesque style:

> We respectfully submit with both humor and solemnity, that it is not violative of Divine prerogative, nor wrong per se, to teach a God-called man how to spell association, or how to make his verbs agree with their nominatives, or how to preserve and promote his health, or how to train his voice or mind, or how to study the Bible and oversee the Church. And since God himself has embodied the subject matter of preaching in at least two earth languages it can not be against his duty of exegesis to know somewhat of the laws of the language whose words he undertakes to interpret. But we are not left to an argument on history, axioms and analogies. The Book itself speaks with no uncertain sound. The schools of the prophets established by Samuel, rendered illustrious under Elijah and Elisha, is a case in point. From these schools came the historians, prophets, poets and orators who gave us the greater part of the Book itself. These trained men were the conservators of their age and the benefactors of all subsequent time. Our Lord's school of the prophets is a brighter example. Long were

they called before they served and long were they trained before they preached. If a college assumes to call preachers, or to put education in the place of the Spirit, or to usurp the ordaining prerogative of the Churches, it is both rebellion and blasphemy, but for a God-called, Spirit-endued and Church-ordained preacher to fail in all necessary preparation possible to him is downright sin [BGCT, *Annual*, pp. 39-40].

However, ministerial education is not the only kind of Christian education. True Christian education will employ Christian educational theory in the classroom and teach all subjects from a Christian philosophical basis. Science, literature, psychology, history, philosophy, and all other disciplines can be taught from a Christian world view. Commitment to Christian education is no shallow or flippant decision; it is a solemn lifetime calling. This has been clearly seen by Baptists in the past. Carey, Wayland, Dagg, Boyce, Broadus, Carroll, Spurgeon, and others invested a significant amount of energy, money, and time into the establishment of schools for various phases of Christian ministry and other callings consistent with Christian character. Baptists who accept the full authority of Scripture cannot conscientiously refuse to do less.

The historical Baptist view of Scripture also makes demands on preaching. Nothing is quite so distressing as to hear a preacher, who supposedly is convinced that the Bible is God's Word, consistently depart from the plain meaning of a text. Broadus's opinion at this point should be instructive:

It is manifest that to take a text gives a tone of sacredness to the discourse. But more than this is true. The primary idea is that the discourse is a development of the text, an explanation, illustration, application of its teachings. Our business is to teach God's Word. And although we may often discuss subjects, and aspects of subjects, which are not presented in precisely that form by any passage of Scripture, yet the fundamental conception should be habitually retained, that we are about to set forth what the text contains [Broadus, *Preparation and Delivery*, p. 21].

The purposeful and knowledgeable misrepresentation of a text of Scripture is not only misleading, it is immoral. When a man with a calling to communicate God's truth neglects the discipline of proper interpretation and clear explication, he commits what Roger Williams called "the crime of proud laziness." Dullness and monotony characterize the pulpits of many Bible-believing Baptists because they have failed to grasp the incalculable variety of themes available to the preacher simply through developing the true meaning of a text. Left to his own ingenuity, or lack thereof, a speaker will inevitably fall into a discourse on some theme familiar to him and will seldom depart from the circle of his personal illustrations and his traditional thought patterns. Biblical exposition will rescue the preacher and the pew from such a fate and will restore freshness and appeal to the weekly sermons. Bible believers should feel a keen sense of obligation to be preachers of Bible content.

Another practical implication of this view of Scripture relates to social ministries. Baptists cannot escape the explicit scriptural admonition to love one's neighbor as oneself. Neither can they escape the duties implied by the parable of the good Samaritan. James's definition of pure religion must be taken seriously by those who feel that their consciences are bound by the word of Scripture.

> This is pure and undefiled religion in the sight of our God and Father, to visit orphans and widows in their distress, and to keep oneself unstained by the world [James 1:27, NASB].

Obedience to this biblical statement, and others like it, produced Spurgeon's orphanages, Wayland's opposition to slavery, Williams's advocacy of the rights of the Indians, and multitudinous hospitals, nursing homes, rescue missions, and emergency-relief funds. Though not often recognized for such action, Baptists have been in the forefront of active social ministry. Obedience to the divine Word demands it.

The historical Baptist view of Scripture assumes the unity of all truth and a coherent view of reality. One of the most powerful and persuasive methods of presenting a particular world view is through the medium of the fine arts. While Bunyan is recognized as one of the creative, literary geniuses of modern history, generally, Baptist contributions to the fine arts have been sparse. Early Baptists even argued over the viability of hymn-singing in worship. Even today, only one in ten among Southern Baptists is involved in a church music program. Commitment to full biblical authority, however, should enlarge the imagination, broaden the spirit, and tantalize the mind with the myriads of possibilities for interacting with a created universe alive with the marvelous works of a self-revealing God.

Every encouragement should be given to those who indicate interest and aptitude for involvement in the fine arts. Not only does theological truth justify, and even demand, creativity on the part of believers, the different genres of literature found within Holy Scripture show that it is impossible to comprehend the tri-unity of God in one literary form. If more than one literary form is needed and justified, then certainly more than one art form may be used to reflect the vibrancy and beauty of the present created order. Since Scripture also talks about a time when this world was unfallen, a future time of a new heaven and new earth, and an unseen world alive with principalities, powers, thrones, dominions, angels, and demons, the subject matter for artistic expression is limitless. One committed to biblical infallibility in all areas sees reality as extremely complex and exciting. Fine arts is the most versatile medium through which the creature can seek to emulate the art of the Creator.

Evangelism and missions, an obvious result of the Baptist view of Scripture, has enjoyed a place of prominence in Baptist practice. Obedience to the Great Commission, the doctrine of regenerate church membership, the lostness of man, the necessity of repentance and faith, the redemptive work of Christ, and other doctrines all point to the Christian's obligation to evangelize in the neighborhood and in the world. A man who has no doubt about the veracity of the biblical teaching in these areas must find avenues through which he can engage in the propagation of the gospel.

Long before Carey, personal evangelism and the founding of churches characterized Baptist life in England and America. Individuals, churches, and associations engaged in significant missionary activity and searched for ways of expanding and enlarging their witness. Baptist soldiers in Oliver Cromwell's army took advantage of their mobility by founding Baptist churches in Wales, Ireland, and England. In America, the Philadelphia Association sent preachers into the back country to evangelize the settlers and assist churches in preaching to people moving to the frontier. The Sandy Creek Baptist Church, founded in 1755, grew from one church with sixteen members to three churches with over nine hundred members within a three-year period. Within seventeen years it had spawned forty-two churches from which God had called 125 men to the gospel ministry.

Since Carey's day the lifeblood of Baptists has coursed through the channels of organized mission activity. The men who organized the missions and evangelism agencies and the missionary personnel connected with those organizations were adherents of biblical infallibility. Adoniram Judson, representing the Baptists of America in a time before the various schisms occurred, epitomizes the characteristic Baptist passion for missions in concert with the commitment to the all-embracing authority of God's Holy Word. May all Baptists join Judson in his missionary spirit, his submission to the Bible, and his prayer for the coming of the Kingdom:

> Our hearts bleed when we think of Kyouk Phyoo, and the poor inquirers that one of our number lately left there, ready to embrace the Christian religion, if he would only promise to remain or send a successor. From Kyouk Phyoo, the way is open into the four provinces of Arracan, namely, Rek-keing, Chedubah, Ramree, and Sandoway; and what a grand field for our tracts, and the New Testament, now in press! Of all the places that now cry around us, we think that Kyouk Phyoo cries the loudest. No, we listen again, and the shrill cry of golden Ava rises above them all. O Ava!

Ava! with thy metropolitan walls and gilded turrets, thou sittest a lady among these eastern nations; but our hearts bleed for thee! In thee is no Christian church, no missionary of the cross. . . . O God of mercy, have mercy on Ava, and Chageing, and A-ma-ra-poo-ra. . . . Have mercy on our mission stations at Tavoy, Maulmain, and Rangoon, and our sub-stations at Mergui, Chummerah, and Newville. . . . Aid us in the solemn and laborious work of translating and printing thine holy, inspired word in the language of these heathen. O, keep our faith from failing, our spirits from sinking, and our influence of the climate and the pressure of our labors. Have mercy on the board of missions; and grant that our beloved and respected fathers and brethren may be aroused to greater effort, and go forth personally into all parts of the land, and put in requisition all the energies of thy people. Have mercy on the churches in the United States; hold back the curse of Meroz; continue and perpetuate the heavenly revivals of religion which they have begun to enjoy; and may the time soon come when no church shall dare to sit under Sabbath and sanctuary privileges without having one of their number to represent them on heathen ground. Have mercy on the theological seminaries, and hasten the time when one half of all who yearly enter the ministry shall be taken by thine Holy Spirit, and driven into the wilderness, feeling a sweet necessity laid on them, and the precious love of Christ and of souls constraining them. Hear, O Lord, all the prayers which are this day presented in all the monthly concerts throughout the habitable globe, and hasten the millennial glory, for which we are all longing, and praying, and laboring. Adorn thy beloved one in her bridal vestments, that she may shine forth in immaculate beauty and celestial splendor. Come, O our Bridegroom; come, Lord Jesus; come quickly. Amen and Amen [*Memoir of Judson*, pp. 52-54].

BIBLIOGRAPHY

Baptist General Convention of Texas, *Annual*, 1904.

Broadus, John. *A Catechism of Bible Teaching*. Philadelphia: American Baptist Publication Society, 1892.

Broadus, John. *A Treatise on the Preparation and Delivery of Sermons*. Edited by E. C. Dargan. New York: Hodder & Stoughton, 1898.

Cathcart, William, ed. *The Baptist Encyclopedia*. Rev. ed. 2 vols. Philadelphia: Louis H. Everts, 1883.

Judson, Adoniram. *A Sermon on Christian Baptism*. Boston: Gould, Kendall, & Lincoln, 1846.

Mickelsen, A. Berkeley. *Interpreting the Bible*. Grand Rapids: Eerdmans, 1963.

Ramm, Bernard. *Protestant Biblical Interpretation*. 3rd rev. ed. Grand Rapids: Baker, 1970.

Wayland, Francis. *A Memoir of the Life and Labors of the Rev. Adoniram Judson*. 2 vols. Boston: Phillips, Sampson, and Co., 1853.

ACKNOWLEDGMENTS. The authors wish to express their appreciation to Mary Anne Barroz, Ron Wilson, Bill Sumruld, Mark Matheson, Chad Brand, David Dockery, David Stubblefield, and Sheri Kuenzle for their help in the preparation of these four indexes.

Index of Persons

439

Index of Subjects

Index on the Doctrine of Scripture

451

Index of Scripture